T0320344

Smart Technologies in Healthcare Management

Offering a holistic view of the pioneering trends and innovations in smart healthcare management, this book focuses on the methodologies, frameworks, design issues, tools, architectures, and technologies necessary to develop and understand intelligent healthcare systems and emerging applications in the present era.

Smart Technologies in Healthcare Management: Pioneering Trends and Applications provides an overview of various technical and innovative aspects, challenges, and issues in smart healthcare, along with recent and novel findings. It highlights the latest advancements and applications in the field of intelligent systems and explores the importance of cloud computing and the designing of sensors in an IoT system. The book offers algorithms and a framework with models in machine learning and AI for smart healthcare management. A detailed flow chart and innovative and modified methodologies related to intelligent computing in healthcare are discussed, as well as real-world-based examples so that readers can compare technical concepts with daily life concepts.

This book will be a useful reference for academicians and the healthcare industry, along with professionals interested in exploring innovations in varied applicational areas of AI, IoT, and machine learning. Researchers, startup companies, and entrepreneurs will also find this book of interest.

Artificial Intelligence in Smart Healthcare Systems

Series Editors: Vishal Jain and Jyotir Moy Chatterjee

The progress of the healthcare sector is incremental as it learns from associations between data over time through the application of suitable big data and IoT frameworks and patterns. Many healthcare service providers are employing IoT-enabled devices for monitoring patient health care, but their diagnosis and prescriptions are instance-specific only. However, these IoT-enabled healthcare devices are generating volumes of data (Big-IoT Data), that can be analyzed for more accurate diagnosis and prescriptions. A major challenge in the above realm is the effective and accurate learning of unstructured clinical data through the application of precise algorithms. Incorrect input data leading to erroneous outputs with false positives shall be intolerable in healthcare as patient's lives are at stake. This new book series addresses various aspects of how smart healthcare can be used to detect and analyze diseases, the underlying methodologies, and related security concerns. Healthcare is a multidisciplinary field that involves a range of factors like the financial system, social factors, health technologies, and organizational structures that affect the healthcare provided to individuals, families, institutions, organizations, and populations. The goals of healthcare services include patient safety, timeliness, effectiveness, efficiency, and equity. Smart healthcare consists of m-health, e-health, electronic resource management, smart and intelligent home services, and medical devices. The Internet of Things (IoT) is a system comprising real-world things that interact and communicate with each other via networking technologies. The wide range of potential applications of IoT includes healthcare services. IoT-enabled healthcare technologies are suitable for remote health monitoring, including rehabilitation, assisted ambient living, etc. In turn, healthcare analytics can be applied to the data gathered from different areas to improve healthcare at a minimum expense.

This new book series is designed to be a first choice reference at university libraries, academic institutions, research and development centres, information technology centres, and any institutions interested in using, design, modelling, and analysing intelligent healthcare services. Successful application of deep learning frameworks to enable meaningful, cost-effective personalized healthcare services is the primary aim of the healthcare industry in the present scenario. However, realizing this goal requires effective understanding, application, and amalgamation of IoT, Big Data, and several other computing technologies to deploy such systems in an effective manner. This series shall help clarify the understanding of certain key mechanisms and technologies helpful in realizing such systems.

Next Generation Healthcare Systems Using Soft Computing Techniques
D. Rekh Ram Janghel, Rohit Raja, and Korhan Cengiz

Immersive Virtual and Augmented Reality in Healthcare: An IoT and Blockchain Perspective
Rajendra Kumar, Vishal Jain, Garry Han, and Abderezak Touzene

Handbook on Augmenting Telehealth Services: Using Artificial Intelligence
Edited by Sonali Vyas, Sunil Gupta, Monit Kapoor, and Samiya Khan

Machine Learning in Healthcare and Security: Advances, Obstacles, and Solutions
Edited by Prashant Pranav, Archana Patel, and Sarika Jain

Smart Technologies in Healthcare Management: Pioneering Trends and Applications
Edited by Nidhi Sindhwani, Sarvesh Tanwar, Ajay Rana, and Ramani Kannan

Smart Technologies in Healthcare Management
Pioneering Trends and Applications

Edited by
Nidhi Sindhwani
Sarvesh Tanwar
Ajay Rana
Ramani Kannan

CRC Press
Taylor & Francis Group
Boca Raton London New York

CRC Press is an imprint of the
Taylor & Francis Group, an **informa** business

Designed cover image: iStock - ipopba

First edition published 2024
by CRC Press
2385 NW Executive Center Drive, Suite 320, Boca Raton FL 33431

and by CRC Press
4 Park Square, Milton Park, Abingdon, Oxon, OX14 4RN

CRC Press is an imprint of Taylor & Francis Group, LLC

Library of Congress Cataloging-in-Publication Data
Names: Sindhwani, Nidhi, editor. I Tanwar, Sarvesh, editor. I Rana, Ajay, editor. I Kannan, Ramani, editor.
Title: Smart technologies in healthcare management : pioneering trends and applications / edited by Nidhi Sindhwani, Sarvesh Tanwar, Ajay Rana, and Ramani Kannan.
Description: First edition. I Boca Raton, FL : CRC Press, 2024. I Includes bibliographical references and index.
Identifiers: LCCN 2023054012 (print) I LCCN 2023054013 (ebook) I ISBN 9781032356914 (hardback) I ISBN 9781032361611 (paperback) I ISBN 9781003330523 (ebook)
Subjects: MESH: Health Information Systems I Health Information Management--methods I Medical Informatics I Artificial Intelligence
Classification: LCC R859.7.A78 (print) I LCC R859.7.A78 (ebook) I NLM W 26.55.I4 I DDC 362.10285--dc23/eng/20240228
LC record available at https://lccn.loc.gov/2023054012
LC ebook record available at https://lccn.loc.gov/2023054013
ISBN: 978-1-032-35691-4 (hbk)
ISBN: 978-1-032-36161-1 (pbk)
ISBN: 978-1-003-33052-3 (ebk)

DOI: 10.1201/9781003330523

Typeset in Times
by MPS Limited, Dehradun

Contents

Chapter 13 Empowering Harvest – Unlocking the Secrets to
Optimal Health 182

Parth Seth and Monika Sharma

Chapter 14 Violence-Based Object Detection in Streets for Effective
Monitoring of Safe Environments 195

Navneet Vishnoi, Thirukumaran Subbiramani,
Mohit Kumar Sharma, Sukhvinder Singh Dari,
Vikas Sagar, and Nitendra Kumar

            *Navneet Vishnoi, Aarushi Thusu, Harshita Kaushik, G.
            Ezhilarasan, Adapa Gopi, and Aarti Kalnawat*

            *Yaduvir Singh, Nupur Tripathi, Surendra Yadav, Namit Gupta,
            A. Uthama Kumar, and Janjhyam Venkata Naga Ramesh*

Preface

Smart health is an increasingly popular approach to disease treatment and prevention that takes account of an individual's genes, environment, and lifestyle. It allows doctors and medical practitioners to more accurately predict appropriate medical strategies and treatments for an individual. Precision health involves approaches that everyone can do on their own to protect their health as well as steps that public health can take. Precision health focuses on preventing disease before it starts, using the latest technological advances to develop the tools to do so. In the current scenario, ad-hoc and wireless networks have played an important role in allowing the unprecedented transition of work from physical offices to digital platforms. The detection competence of today's smartphones is being used to enable mobile epidemic detection, data sharing, and analysis during an epidemic. New applications are evolving and rapidly deploying, from symptomatic self-report to coordination and monitoring of essential personnel, volunteers or patients. Detection potential are also being used for contact tracing and early isolation of infected people or zone. A series of educational and social apps are being launched to address mental and physical health related issues under lockdown

The objective of this book is intended to provide academic and business researchers with a platform to introduce their new ideas on how smart and current technologies can quickly address the present epidemic situation toward wellbeing management sector caused by COVID-19 can solve to get better. Basically, this book caters to the better understanding of topics related to the development of smart health care system. This book will enable the researchers to use their knowledge of Artificial Intelligence, IoT, Sensors, machine learning, and electric circuits in order to develop projects towards building smart health infrastructure. It covers challenges and issues related to different fields as per the requirement of different key components of smart health. This book will bring the researchers and technocrats from different parts of our country to a common gathering for exchanging and sharing knowledge about the recent developments in this area. This book will elaborate the concept of various thrust technologies as the pivotal component of diverse industrial applications and academic research, varying from health care to social networking and many more. The book focuses on developing the understanding of the current and pioneer innovations in intelligent healthcare system. Such methodologies are crucial for implementation of the intelligent systems advocating real time communication and data analysis for enhanced decision making.

About the Editors

Dr. Nidhi Sindhwani works as an assistant professor at Amity School of Engineering and Technology Delhi, Amity University, Noida, India. She earned her Ph.D. (ECE) from Punjabi University, Patiala, Punjab, India. She has 15-plus years of teaching experience and is a life member of the Indian Society for Technical Education (ISTE) and a member of IEEE. She has published three chapters in reputable books, ten papers in Scopus/SCIE Indexed Journals, and has four patents to her credit. Dr. Sindhwani has presented various research papers at national and international conferences and was asked to chair a session at two conferences. Her research areas include wireless communication, image processing, optimization, machine learning, and IoT.

Dr. Sarvesh Tanwar is an associate professor at Amity Institute of Information Technology (AIIT), Amity University, Noida. She is the head of the AUN Blockchain and Data Security Research Lab. She completed her M. Tech (CSE) degree from MMU, Mullana, and her Ph.D. in (CSE) from Mody University, Laxmangarh (Raj.), and has more than 14 years of teaching and research experience to her credit. Her areas of research include public key infrastructure (PKI), cryptography, blockchain, and cyber security. She has published more than 50 research papers in international journals and conferences and has filed 17 patents. Dr. Tanwar is a journal reviewer and a member of the board of IJISP, IGI Global, USA.

Dr. Ajay Rana has demonstrated his intellectual, interpersonal, and managerial skills through his teaching experience in academics and industry, with roles ranging from lecturer to professor to director to Dean over 20-plus years. He is an educator, a teacher, an innovator, a strategist, and a committed philanthropist. Dr. Rana's core life philosophy includes deep organizational ethics, equality, and a desire to help every individual who wishes to succeed in life. Dr. Rana's areas of interest include machine learning, the internet of things, augmented reality, software engineering, and soft computing. He has 60-plus patents under his name in the field of IoT, Networks, and Sensors. He has published more than 271 research papers in reputed journals and presented at international and national conferences. He has co-authored eight books and co-edited 36 conference proceedings. Dr. Rana is chairman of AUN Research Labs, an executive committee member of IEEE, and a life member of the Computer Society of India/ISTE. He is also a member of the editorial board and review committee of several journals.

Dr. Ramani Kannan is currently working as a senior lecturer at the Center for Smart Grid Energy Research, Institute of Autonomous Systems at the University Teknologi PETRONAS (UTP), Malaysia. Dr. Kanan completed his Ph.D. (Power Electronics and Drives) from Anna University, in India, in 2012, his M.E. (Power Electronics and Drives) from Anna University, in India, in 2006, and his B.E. (Electronics and Communication) from Bharathiyar University, in India, in 2004. He has more than 15 years of experience in prestigious educational institutes and has published more than 130 papers in various national and international journals and conferences. He has been the editor, co-editor, guest editor, and reviewer of various books and received the award for best presenter at the CENCON 2019, IEEE Conference on Energy Conversion (CENCON 2019) Indonesia.

Contributors

Laxmi Ahuja
Amity University
Noida, Uttar Pradesh, India

Rohit Anand
Department of ECE
G. B. Pant DSEU Okhla-I Campus
(Formerly G. B. Pant Engineering
College)
New Delhi, India

Ahateshaam Ansari
Department of Physiotherapy
IIMT College of Medical Sciences
(Allied)
IIMT University
Meerut, Uttar Pradesh, India

Sumaiya Ansari
Department of Physiotherapy
IIMT College of Medical Sciences
(Allied)
IIMT University
Meerut, Uttar Pradesh, India

N. Beemkumar
Department of Mechanical Engineering
JAIN (Deemed-to-be University)
Bangalore, India

Vimal Bibhu
Amity University
Greater Noida, Uttar Pradesh, India

Priyanka Chandani
Noida Institute of Engineering &
Technology
Greater Noida, Uttar Pradesh, India

L. Chandrashekhar
Department of Mechatronics
Engineering
Acharya Institute of Technology
Bengaluru, Karnataka, India

Khushi Dadhich
Amity University
Greater Noida, Uttar Pradesh, India

Sukhvinder Singh Dari
Symbiosis Law School Nagpur
Symbiosis International (Deemed
University)
Pune, India

Lipsa Das
Amity University
Greater Noida, Uttar Pradesh, India

Dharmesh Dhabliya
Department of IQAC
Symbiosis Law School
Pune, Maharashtra, India

R. Dilip
Department of Electronics and
Communication Engineering
Dayananda Sagar Academy of
Technology & Management
Udayapura, Bengaluru, India

Shalini Dixit
Department of Allied Healthcare &
Sciences
Vivekananda Global University
Jaipur, India

G. Ezhilarasan
JAIN (Deemed-to-be University)
Karnataka, India

Adapa Gopi
Department of Computer Science and
   Engineering
Koneru Lakshmaiah Education
   Foundation
Vaddeswaram, Guntur, Andhra Pradesh,
   India

Bhupesh Goyal
Department of Allied Healthcare &
   Sciences
Vivekananda Global University
Jaipur, India

Ankur Gupta
Department of Computer Science and
   Engineering
Vaish College of Engineering
Rohtak, Haryana, India

K Gurnadha Gupta
Department of CSE-HONERS
KL Deemed to be University
Green Fields, Vwdeswaram
Guntur, Andhra Pradesh, India

Namit Gupta
College of Computing Science and
   Information Technology
Teerthanker Mahaveer University
Moradabad, Uttar Pradesh, India

Rupal Gupta
College of Computing Science and
   Information Technology
Teerthanker Mahaveer University
Moradabad, Uttar Pradesh, India

Himangi
Department of Computer
   Science and Engineering
Baba Mastnath University
Rohtak, Haryana, India

Aryan Jain
Amity University
Noida, UP, India

Aarti Kalnawat
Symbiosis Law School Nagpur
Symbiosis International (Deemed
   University)
Pune, India

Harshita Kaushik
Vivekananda Global University
Jaipur, India

Gulista Khan
College of Computing Science and
   Information Technology
Teerthanker Mahaveer University
Moradabad, Uttar Pradesh, India

Jayasri Kotti
Department of Computer Science
   and Engineering
GMR Institute of Technology
Rajam, Vizianagaram, Andhra Pradesh,
India

A. Uthama Kumar
Department of Data Science &
   Analytics
Data Science & Analytics School of
   Sciences
Jain (Deemed-to- be University)
Bangalore, India

Mukesh Kumar
IIMT College of Medical Sciences
   (Allied)
IIMT University
Meerut, Uttar Pradesh, India

Nitendra Kumar
Accurate Institute of Management
   and Technology
Greater Noida, Uttar Pradesh, India

G. Sindhu Madhuri
Department of Computer Science and
   Engineering
JAIN (Deemed-to-be University)
Bangalore, India

T.R. Mahesh
Department of Computer Science
and Engineering
JAIN (Deemed-to-be University)
Bangalore, India

M.G. Manasa
Department of Electronics and
Communication Engineering
Maharaja Institute of Technology
Mysore, Karnataka, India

Reshmi Mishra
Department of Biotechnology
Noida Institute of Engineering &
Technology
Greater Noida, Uttar Pradesh, India

Janjhyam Venkata Naga Ramesh
Department of Computer Science and
Engineering
Koneru Lakshmaiah Education
Foundation
Vaddeswaram, Guntur, Andhra Pradesh,
India

Vikas Sagar
Department of Artificial Intelligence(AI)
Noida Institute of Engineering and
Technology
Greater Noida, Uttar Pradesh, India

Abhilash Kumar Saxena
College of Computing Science and
Information Technology
Teerthanker Mahaveer University
Moradabad, Uttar Pradesh, India

Ashendra Kumar Saxena
College of Computing
Science and Information Technology
Teerthanker Mahaveer University
Moradabad, Uttar Pradesh, India

Kumud Saxena
Department of (CSE, IT, M.Tech
Integrated)
Noida Institute of Engineering &
Technology
Greater Noida, Uttar Pradesh, India

Parth Seth
Amity University
Noida, Uttar Pradesh, India

M.G. Shalini
Department of Electronics and
Communication Engineering
Dayananda Sagar Academy of
Technology & Management
Udayapura, Bengaluru, India

Bhuvi Sharma
Amity University
Greater Noida, Uttar Pradesh, India

Mohit Kumar Sharma
Department of Electrical Engineering
Vivekananda Global University
Jaipur, India

Monika Sharma
Amity University
Noida, Uttar Pradesh, India

Raj Sharma
Department of Physiotherapy
IIMT College of Medical Sciences
(Allied)
IIMT University
Meerut, Uttar Pradesh, India

Rajbala Simon
Amity University
Noida, Uttar Pradesh, India

Nidhi Sindhwani
Amity University
Noida, Uttar Pradesh, India

Akanksha Singh
Amity University
Greater Noida, Uttar Pradesh, India

Ashutosh Kr. Singh
Department of Electronics and
 Communication Engineering
Noida Institute of Engineering &
 Technology
Greater Noida, Uttar Pradesh, India

Yaduvir Singh
Noida Institute of Engineering and
 Technology
Greater Noida, Uttar Pradesh, India

Priyank Singhal
College of Computing Science and
 Information Technology
Teerthanker Mahaveer University
Moradabad, Uttar Pradesh, India

M.S. Sowmya
Department of Information Science
 and Engineering
JAIN (Deemed-to-be University)
Bangalore, India

Thirukumaran Subbiramani
Department of Data Science & Analytics
Data Science & Analytics
School of Sciences
Jain(Deemed-to-be University)
Bangalore, India

N. Tejashwini
Department of Computer Science
 and Engineering
Sai Vidya Institute of Technology
Yelahanka, Bengaluru, India

Ayush Thakur
Amity University
Noida, Uttar Pradesh, India

Aarushi Thusu
Noida Institute of Engineering and
 Technology
Greater Noida, Uttar Pradesh, India

Nupur Tripathi
Symbiosis Law School Nagpur
Symbiosis International (Deemed
 University)
Pune, India

Bhagirathi Bai V.
Department of Mechatronics
 Engineering
Acharya Institute of Technology
Bengaluru, Karnataka, India

Rashmi Vashisth
Amity University
Noida, Uttar Pradesh, India

Vivek Veeraiah
Department of R & D Computer
 Science
Adichunchanagiri University
Mandya, Karnataka, India

Navneet Vishnoi
College of Computing Science and
 Information Technology
Teerthanker Mahaveer University
Moradabad, Uttar Pradesh, India

Madhu Yadav
Department of Physiotherapy
IIMT College of Medical Sciences
 (Allied)
IIMT University
Meerut, Uttar Pradesh, India

Surendra Yadav
Department of Computer Science and
  Engineering
Vivekananda Global University
Jaipur, India

Mohammed Zabeeulla
Department of Computer Science and
  Engineering
JAIN (Deemed-to-be University)
Bangalore, India

1 Role of Big Data Analysis for Smart Healthcare in Large Cities

Janjhyam Venkata Naga Ramesh,
Nidhi Sindhwani, Asha Yadav,
Shambhu Bhardwaj, Jayanthi Kannan,
Rohit Anand, and Ankur Gupta

1.1 INTRODUCTION

1.1.1 HEALTHCARE SYSTEMS

Healthcare systems around the world are confronting various obstacles in providing effective care to patients, particularly in metropolitan cities with fast growing populations. Population growth has led to a rise in demand for healthcare services, resulting in resource limitations, time constraints, and difficulty maintaining patient data [1–3]. However, technological advancements in recent years have made large amounts of healthcare data available for analysis in order to improve healthcare delivery. This data contains patient records, medical histories, and demographic information, all of which can provide significant insights into patient health and the effectiveness of healthcare systems.

Big data analysis has emerged as a helpful technique for analyzing and interpreting enormous datasets in healthcare. It allows for the finding of hidden patterns and insights that can assist healthcare providers in making educated decisions and improving the quality of treatment provided to patients. Big data analysis has the potential to transform healthcare by providing patients with personalized and efficient care while lowering expenses [4,5].

The use of this study is to look into the function of analysis of big data in smart healthcare systems in large cities. We concentrate on the use of Birch clustering, a prominent clustering method, to analyze healthcare data. We use a public dataset published by the Centres for Medicare & Medicaid Services [6] that summarizes Medicare beneficiaries' utilization and payments for surgeries, services, and prescription medications given by individual hospitals, physicians, and other suppliers. The study's goal is to demonstrate the Birch clustering algorithm's usefulness in analyzing healthcare data and its potential application in establishing smart healthcare systems in major cities.

1.1.2 APPLICATIONS OF BIG DATA AND HEALTHCARE SYSTEMS

Numerous disciplines have seen the dominance of AI, including but not limited to:

DOI: 10.1201/9781003330523-1

- Creating prediction models for healthcare resource allocation in major cities based on patient demands and demographic trends.
- Identifying high-risk patients and developing disease-prevention strategies.
- Evaluating the success of various healthcare delivery models in large cities, such as telemedicine and home-based treatment.
- Improving patient outcomes in major cities by detecting and correcting gaps in healthcare access and quality.
- Improving patient engagement and satisfaction in major cities by providing personalized care based on individual health data.
- Recognizing trends and patterns in disease outbreaks or epidemics to allow for rapid reaction and mitigation in major cities.
- Improving the availability and affordability of pharmaceuticals and medical supplies in large cities through optimizing healthcare supply chains.
- Creating automated systems for disease detection and diagnosis in large cities.
- Improving hospital efficiency through detecting bottlenecks and reducing wait times in large cities.
- Improving medical research by discovering new study fields based on patterns and trends in large-scale healthcare data.

This data gives a large opportunity to improve healthcare delivery and patient outcomes, especially in large cities where healthcare systems are frequently overworked. As a result, having sophisticated analytical tools and algorithms that can process and extract important insights from these huge and complicated datasets is critical. The Birch clustering method is a promising technique for analyzing healthcare data in large cities due to its scalability and efficiency. We investigate the possibility of Birch clustering for analyzing healthcare data in large cities and its application in the development of smart healthcare systems in this study and as shown as an example in Figures 1.1 and 1.2.

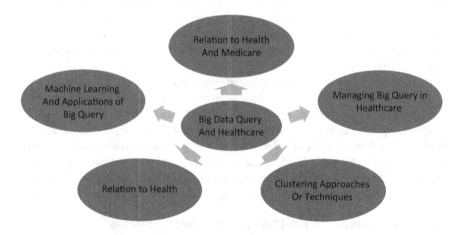

FIGURE 1.1   Applying of big data query systems and healthcare.

FIGURE 1.2 Average total stays in medicare vs length of stays in US states.

1.1.3 Clustering Algorithms

Clustering algorithms are critical in the analysis of healthcare data in large cities. They are capable of detecting patterns and similarities in huge and complicated datasets, allowing healthcare providers to make more informed decisions and enhance patient outcomes. Clustering algorithms are critical tools for establishing personalized and efficient healthcare systems that can address the different demands of patients in large cities in the context of smart healthcare [7]. The capacity of clustering algorithms to locate groupings of similar data points, often known as clusters, is one of their key advantages. Clustering algorithms put data points together based on their similarity, helping healthcare providers to spot patterns and trends in vast datasets. This feature is especially valuable in healthcare, as patient data might vary greatly depending on factors such as age, gender, medical history, and lifestyle. Clustering algorithms, which aggregate comparable data points into clusters, can assist healthcare practitioners in identifying patients with similar health profiles and providing personalized therapy customized to their unique needs.

Furthermore, clustering algorithms can help to develop predictive models for healthcare resource allocation. Healthcare practitioners in major cities can estimate future healthcare requirements by clustering individuals based on demographic features. This data can be used to develop targeted interventions for disease prevention or management of chronic conditions. Clustering algorithms can also assist healthcare practitioners in evaluating the success of various healthcare delivery models in major cities, such as telemedicine and home-based treatment. Healthcare providers can identify which delivery models are best suited for distinct groups of patients by clustering people based on their healthcare requirements and preferences. Scalability is another key feature of clustering methods [7]. With the exponential growth of healthcare data, having algorithms that can handle huge and complicated datasets is critical. Birch clustering techniques, for example, are very scalable and can handle huge amounts of data. This scalability is critical for creating smart healthcare systems capable of handling massive amounts of data.

Clustering algorithms can assist healthcare practitioners in identifying patterns and similarities in vast datasets, creating personalized and efficient healthcare systems, and developing tailored therapies to prevent disease and manage chronic disorders. Clustering algorithms, such as Birch clustering, are vital for designing smart healthcare systems that can fulfill the different demands of patients in large cities because of their scalability and efficiency.

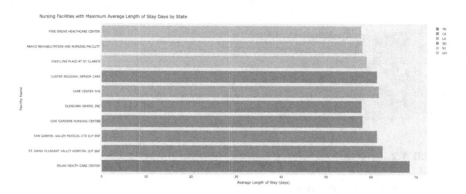

FIGURE 1.3 Average length of stays in days for different facilities in the US states.

To improve healthcare delivery in major cities, the length of stay in facilities is an important measure that may be analyzed using clustering algorithms. By examining this, healthcare providers can uncover patterns and trends that will assist them in making educated decisions and improving patient outcomes. In Figure 1.3, we use a bar chart to illustrate the top ten nursing facilities with the longest average length of stay by state. This visualization can provide significant insights into the performance of nursing facilities in various states, which can drive resource allocation and patient care decisions. States with longer average lengths of stay, for example, may require more resources and manpower to successfully manage patient care. Furthermore, by grouping nursing homes based on average length of stay, healthcare providers can identify similarities and differences in their performance and develop targeted interventions to improve patient outcomes. Other metrics connected to nursing facilities, such as readmission rates, prescription mistakes, and patient satisfaction scores, can also be analyzed using clustering methods such as Birch clustering. Healthcare providers can find best practices and areas for improvement by grouping nursing facilities based on these parameters.

Figure 1.4 depicts the link between total day supply, total drug cost, and total claim count for each state using a scatter plot visualization. The size of each point shows the overall claim count in millions, while the hue uses a cool color palette to symbolize the total claim count in millions. This visualization can provide valuable insights about prescription drug utilization trends and costs in various states, which can drive resource allocation, cost control, and patient care decisions. Healthcare providers can detect patterns and trends in prescription medicine utilization and expenditures in different states by analyzing the scatter plot. States with greater total medication expenditures, for example, may require additional resources to successfully control drug expenses. Furthermore, by grouping states based on prescription drug utilization and costs, healthcare providers can identify similarities and differences and develop targeted interventions to improve patient outcomes.

1.3.1.1 Working of the Birch Algorithm

Birch (Balanced Iterative Reducing and Clustering Using Hierarchies), similar to algorithm given by [6] is an unsupervised learning clustering algorithm.

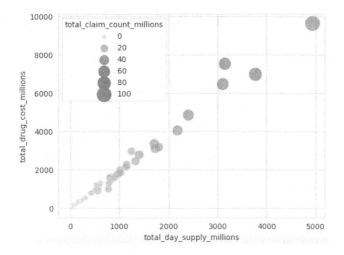

FIGURE 1.4 Scatter plot showing relationship between total day supply in millions and the cost of the drugs for each state with point size representing total claim count.

It is a hierarchical clustering algorithm that can analyze large datasets with a large number of features efficiently. The Birch algorithm constructs a tree structure of subclusters, with each node representing a subcluster of the data. The technique begins by establishing a root node and sequentially reading in the data points. The method evaluates each data point read in to see if it is close enough to an existing subcluster to be added to that subcluster. If not, the algorithm forms a new subcluster and adds the data point to it. A set of centroids and a count of data points in the subcluster are used to represent the subclusters. The branching factor and the threshold distance are both maintained by the algorithm. The branching factor specifies the maximum number of subclusters that can be merged into a single subcluster, whereas the threshold distance specifies the maximum distance between a data point and a subcluster's centroid that permits the data point to be added to the subcluster. The method merges subclusters that are near together as it constructs the tree structure of subclusters until the branching factor is reached or the distance threshold is exceeded.

After constructing the subcluster tree structure, the method can perform cluster analysis by traversing the tree and aggregating the subclusters. The Elbow approach entails charting the sum of squared distances of data points and centroid against the number of clusters and locating the elbow point, which is the point at which the rate of change in the sum of squared distances begins to level off. The Birch method is well-known for its scalability and efficiency in processing huge datasets with many attributes. It is a common clustering technique in the field of healthcare because it can handle noisy data and is resistant to outliers. The Birch algorithm can help healthcare providers make better-informed decisions and improve patient outcomes by discovering patterns and similarities in massive healthcare datasets.

1.1.4 Big Data Processing in Healthcare Query Processing

The Birch algorithm is an effective method for analyzing huge healthcare datasets such as those from the CMS. The dataset contains a large amount of data that can be difficult to analyze using typical approaches. Because it is designed to handle large datasets with high dimensionality, the Birch algorithm is well-suited to analyzing CMS data on BigQuery. The method is scalable, efficient, and capable of processing massive amounts of data in a short period of time, making it an ideal tool for healthcare practitioners to analyze CMS data on BigQuery. Healthcare providers can analyze CMS data in real-time using BigQuery and the Birch algorithm, gaining insights into patient health outcomes, healthcare facility performance, and prescription drug utilization and costs.

1.2 LITERATURE REVIEW

Thayyib et al. [8] summarize 711 bibliometric publications published in diverse fields on AI and big data to identify disciplines with substantial research. The paper highlights five main research clusters of discipline that conduct considerable AI and BDA research and offers many research possibilities.

Rodgers et al. [9] use a dataset of approximately 64% of orthopedic doctors serving Medicare patients; the article explores gender representation among practicing surgeons in the US. The findings show that women are significantly underrepresented in this speciality, and the study emphasizes the necessity of mentoring programmes as well as gender-based equity and diversity measures to overcome these discrepancies.

Khanna et al. [10] present an overview of big data in healthcare, highlighting its potential and market challenges. It summarizes several research tools and techniques for managing big data in healthcare that are currently available, with the goal of benefiting the research community.

Diez et al. [11] uses artificial intelligence and statistical methodologies to suggest a new strategy for predicting on the kidney transplant waiting list. The method incorporates clustering approaches for identifying risk profiles and a new way for determining the least number of people to research, allowing for high-accuracy predictions of a new patient's survival time.

Wang et al. [12] offers a multi-stage network-based feature learning strategy for high-dimensional electronic data in adverse event prediction, with a focus on concurrent medical use. In risk prediction, the method improves accuracy by 5–10% and lowers false alarms by 3–5%, benefiting clinical research and the optimization of multidimensional time series.

Zeng et al. [13] looks at how machine learning approaches can be used to detect Medicare fraud and abuse in the US healthcare business. It makes recommendations for practitioners, such as the necessity for the government to develop machine learning models for healthcare providers, introduce different machine learning methods for fraud prevention, and implement machine learning techniques for financial fraud detection in healthcare systems.

Simbert et al. [14] offer a four-factor approach for tackling security and privacy problems in commercial information systems' big data applications. The framework involves gathering the proper data, safeguarding the data correctly, and using the data correctly, and it provides methodologies and models for each component to improve big data security and privacy.

Zuo et al. [15] explores the impact of big data on perioperative medicine and how developments in electronic health records and other analytic tools will open up new avenues.

Chen et al. [16] uses a Hadoop framework to give a distributed storage technique for huge data in healthcare systems. In the storage process, the suggested algorithm has been empirically validated to have high distribution balance.

To secure the privacy and security of sensitive health data, Bansal et al. [17] suggest a big data architecture for network security.

Gupta et al. [18] use IoT data to create a ML model for breast cancer prediction, showcasing the power of big data and machine learning to improve healthcare outcomes.

Talukdar et al. [19] employ a machine learning approach to detect and classify suspicious behavior in IoT environments, emphasizing the necessity of data analytics in the maintenance of safe healthcare systems.

Veeraiah et al. [20] integrate IoT data to improve the metaverse's capabilities, demonstrating the potential for big data and IoT to revolutionize healthcare delivery.

Gupta et al. [21] investigate the use of wearable sensors for health monitoring in a smart home context, highlighting the potential for machine learning to enhance health outcomes in cities.

Keserwani et al. [22] employ machine learning to detect and prevent assaults in 5 G networks, emphasizing the significance of secure and dependable healthcare data systems in urban contexts.

Olson et al. [23] examines ethical challenges in healthcare analytics and provides a summary of the usage of categorization models in various healthcare applications.

The researchers investigate the application of various criteria for evaluating classification performance in highly imbalanced big datasets, notably in the context of detecting Medicare fraud [24] and big data [25]. Researchers also look at how machine learning and prediction methods based on massive datasets are used in clinical decision-making, emphasizing the significance of having adequate clinical knowledge and minimizing bias.

Bansal et al. [26] address how these technologies discussed in this paper could be used to improve digital health literacy among large metropolis populations.

Jain et al. [27] present a blockchain-based transaction classification technique for major cities that could be utilized to increase the accuracy of machine learning models in healthcare analytics.

Kaushik et al. [28] investigate the cybersecurity potential of machine learning and deep learning, which is critical for protecting sensitive healthcare data in major cities.

Gupta et al. [29] provide the proceedings of an international symposium on medical data artificial intelligence, which is relevant for establishing effective and accurate prediction models in smart healthcare systems in major cities.

Onggirawan et al. [30] perform a literature review on the use of distance learning in the COVID-19 using virtual education in the metaverse, which can be used to support telemedicine and remote health services in major cities.

Athar et al. [31] study the uses and problems of the healthcare metaverse, which has the potential to provide immersive and personalized healthcare experiences for city dwellers.

Awasthy and Valivarthi [32] address the evolution of Hadoop and big data trends in smart cities while Hichri et al. [33] investigate the notion of data-driven smart areas and their impact on innovation and sustainability, while. Ali et al. [34] propose a general IoT middleware for smart city applications, whereas Rane et al. [35] examine the roles and future of IoT-based smart healthcare models. Nair et al. [36] describe a privacy-preserving federated learning framework for IoMT-based big data analysis, whereas Vasa et al. [37] offer a technical perspective on smart city architecture, applications, and data analytics tools. Finally, Kang and Zhang [38] discuss their experiences with COVID-19 and big data technologies in China, emphasizing big data's potential in pandemic management.

1.3 PROBLEM STATEMENTS

Every day, the healthcare industry creates huge amounts of data, and as the volume of data grows, so does the demand for effective analysis and interpretation. One of the most serious difficulties confronting large cities is the provision of smart healthcare, which can be accomplished through big data analysis. A public dataset that can be used for big data research is the Centres for Medicare & Medicaid Services (CMS) dataset.

1.4 PROPOSED WORK

Our suggested approach makes use of big data analysis to provide smart healthcare in huge cities. We use the Birch clustering algorithm to discover patterns in Medicare beneficiaries' healthcare utilization and payments. First, we preprocess the dataset by removing irrelevant columns and using the median to fill in missing values. The features are then scaled using sklearn's Standard Scaler. We apply the elbow approach and plot the within-cluster sum of squares for several values of k to discover the best number of clusters. We select k = 4 and use Birch clustering on the scaled data. We use a scatter plot to visualize the clusters after running PCA on the data and plotting the first two main components. We also create a dendrogram to demonstrate the clusters' hierarchical nature. Finally, we scale the data and use Birch clustering to display the algorithm's results in a scatter plot with cluster labels. The proposed work intends to provide insights about Medicare beneficiaries' healthcare utilization and payments in large cities, which may be used to improve healthcare provision and cut costs.

1.5 RESULTS AND DISCUSSION

We used the Birch clustering algorithm to analyze a public dataset published by the Centres for Medicare & Medicaid Services in our proposed work. We used the

Elbow approach to estimate the best number of clusters after preprocessing and scaling the data. The Birch clustering technique was then applied to 6 clusters, and the clusters were visualized using a scatter plot and PCA. The generated clusters indicated distinct groupings within the nursing facility data, each with its own distinguishing features. Some clusters, for example, had a higher number of beneficiaries and stayed longer, whereas others had fewer beneficiaries and stayed shorter. The clusters differed in terms of total charges and Medicare payments as well. Visualizing data is given in Figures 1.5–1.7.

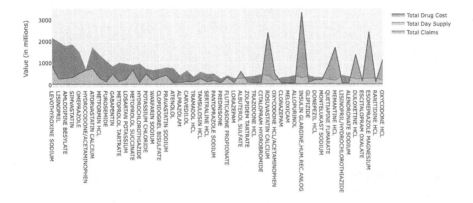

FIGURE 1.5 Total claims, supply, and drug cost by drug name in Medicare data.

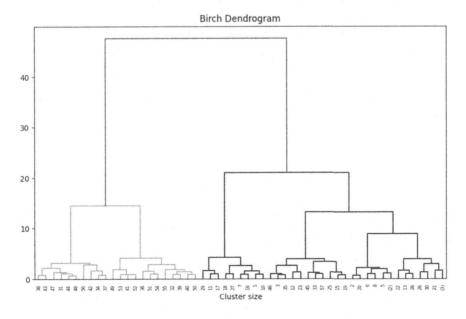

FIGURE 1.6 Clustering dendrogram of Birch.

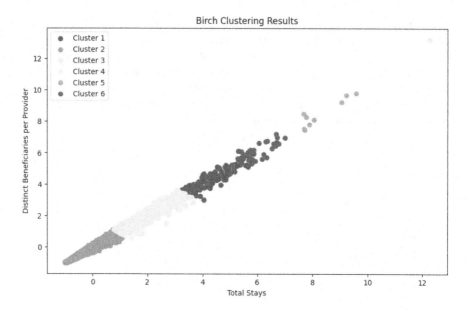

FIGURE 1.7   Clustering results for the Birch algorithm.

1.6   CONCLUSIONS

The proposed study sought to investigate the role of big data analysis in smart healthcare in large cities. We were able to identify six distinct clusters of nursing facilities based on their utilization and payments for procedures, services, and prescription drugs provided to Medicare beneficiaries by using Birch clustering on a publicly available dataset from the Centres for Medicare & Medicaid Services. Our findings indicate that big data analysis utilizing Birch clustering can be a valuable tool for healthcare practitioners in discovering patterns and trends in healthcare utilization and payments. Healthcare practitioners can optimize care, save costs, and enhance patient outcomes by better understanding these trends [39–42].

1.7   FUTURE SCOPE

This study can be expanded in the future by including other data sources and extending the investigation to a greater geographical area. Additional clustering techniques, such as density-based clustering, hierarchical clustering, and spectral clustering, can also be investigated [43–46]. Furthermore, the analysis can be enhanced by incorporating external data sources, such as census data or hospital quality data. Finally, the findings of this study can be used to inform policy decisions and resource allocation in order to improve the quality of care in nursing homes [47].

REFERENCES

1. Sansanwal, K., Shrivastava, G., Anand, R., & Sharma, K. (2019). Big data analysis and compression for indoor air quality. In K. Sansanwal, G. Shrivastava, R. Anand, & K. Sharma (Eds.), Handbook of IoT and Big Data, 1. CRC Press.
2. Gupta, A., Anand, R., Pandey, D., Sindhwani, N., Wairya, S., Pandey, B. K., & Sharma, M. (2021). Prediction of breast cancer using extremely randomized clustering forests (ERCF) technique: Prediction of breast cancer. International Journal of Distributed Systems and Technologies (IJDST), 12(4), 1–15.
3. Anand, R., Daniel, A. V., Fred, A. L., Jaiswal, T., Juneja, S., Juneja, A., & Gupta, A. (2023). Building integrated systems for healthcare considering mobile computing and IoT. In Integration of IoT with Cloud Computing for Smart Applications (pp. 203–225). Chapman and Hall/CRC Press.
4. Sindhwani, N., Sasi, G., & Meivel, S. (2022, October). Fuzzy acceptance analysis of impact of glaucoma and diabetic retinopathy using confusion matrix. In 2022 10th International Conference on Reliability, Infocom Technologies and Optimization (Trends and Future Directions) (ICRITO) (pp. 1–5). IEEE.
5. Sharma, G., Nehra, N., Dahiya, A., Sindhwani, N., & Singh, P. (2022). Automatic heart-rate measurement using facial video. In Networking Technologies in Smart Healthcare (pp. 289–307). CRC Press.
6. Zhang, T., Ramakrishnan, R., & Livny, M. (1997). BIRCH: A new data clustering algorithm and its applications. Data Mining and Knowledge Discovery, 1, 141–182.
7. Anand, R., Jain, V., Singh, A., Rahal, D., Rastogi, P., Rajkumar, A., & Gupta, A. (2023). Clustering of big data in cloud environments for smart applications. In Integration of IoT with Cloud Computing for Smart Applications (pp. 227–247). Chapman and Hall/CRC Press.
8. Thayyib, P. V., Mamilla, R., Khan, M., Fatima, H., Asim, M., Anwar, I., ... & Khan, M. A. (2023). State-of-the-Art of artificial intelligence and big data analytics reviews in five different domains: A bibliometric summary. Sustainability, 15(5), 4026.
9. Rodgers, B. M., Moore, M. L., Mead-Harvey, C., Pollock, J. R., Thomas, O. J., Beauchamp, C. P., & Goulding, K. A. (2023). How does orthopedic surgeon gender representation vary by career stage, regional distribution, and practice size? A large-database medicare study. Clinical Orthopaedics and Related Research, 481(2), 359–366.
10. Khanna, D., Jindal, N., Singh, H., & Rana, P. S. (2023). Applications and challenges in healthcare big data: A strategic review. Current Medical Imaging, 19(1), 27–36.
11. Díez-Sanmartín, C., Cabezuelo, A. S., & Belmonte, A. A. (2023). A new approach to predicting mortality in dialysis patients using sociodemographic features based on artificial intelligence. Artificial Intelligence in Medicine, 136, 102478.
12. Wang, T., Wang, N., Cui, Y., & Liu, J. (2023). The application mode of multi-dimensional time series data based on a multi-stage neural network. Electronics, 12(3), 578.
13. Zeng, L., Li, Y., & Li, Z. (2023, January). Research hotspots, emerging trend and front of fraud detection research: A scientometric analysis (1984–2021). In Data Mining and Big Data: 7th International Conference, DMBD 2022, Beijing, China, November 21–24, 2022, Proceedings, Part II (pp. 91–102). Singapore: Springer Nature Singapore.
14. Simbert, A. (2023). Machine Learning Methods to Detect Medicare Fraud and Abuse in US Healthcare (Doctoral dissertation, University of Maryland University College).

15. Zuo, Y. (2023). Big data and big risk: A four-factor framework for big data security and privacy. International Journal of Business Information Systems, 42(2), 224–242.
16. Chen, H., Song, Z., & Yang, F. (2023). Storage method for medical and health big data based on distributed sensor network. Journal of Sensors, 2023. https://doi.org/10.1155/2023/8506485
17. Bansal, B., Jenipher, V. N., Jain, R., Dilip, R., Kumbhkar, M., Pramanik, S., Roy, S., & Gupta, A. (2022). Big data architecture for network security. In Cyber Security and Network Security (eds S. Pramanik, D. Samanta, M. Vinay and A. Guha). US: Wiley.
18. Gupta, A., Kaushik, D., Garg, M., & Verma, A. (2020). Machine learning model for breast cancer prediction. In Fourth International Conference on I-SMAC (IoT in Social, Mobile, Analytics and Cloud) (I-SMAC), Palladam, India, (pp. 472–477).
19. Talukdar, V., Dhabliya, D., Kumar, B., Talukdar, S. B., Ahamad, S., & Gupta, A. (2022, November). Suspicious activity detection and classification in IoT environment using machine learning approach. In 2022 Seventh International Conference on Parallel, Distributed and Grid Computing (PDGC) (pp. 531–535). IEEE.
20. Veeraiah, V., Gangavathi, P., Ahamad, S., Talukdar, S. B., Gupta, A., & Talukdar, V. (2022, April). Enhancement of meta verse capabilities by IoT integration. In 2022 2nd International Conference on Advance Computing and Innovative Technologies in Engineering (ICACITE) (pp. 1493–1498). IEEE.
21. Gupta, N., Janani, S., Dilip, R., Hosur, R., Chaturvedi, A., & Gupta, A. (2022). Wearable sensors for evaluation over smart home using sequential minimization optimization-based random forest. International Journal of Communication Networks and Information Security, 14(2), 179–188.
22. Keserwani, H., Rastogi, H., Kurniullah, A. Z., Janardan, S. K., Raman, R., Rathod, V. M., & Gupta, A. (2022). Security enhancement by identifying attacks using machine learning for 5G network. International Journal of Communication Networks and Information Security, 14(2), 124–141.
23. Olson, D. L., & Araz, Ö. M. (2023). Applications of predictive data mining in healthcare. In Data Mining and Analytics in Healthcare Management: Applications and Tools (pp. 105–116). Cham: Springer Nature Switzerland.
24. Hancock, J. T., Khoshgoftaar, T. M., & Johnson, J. M. (2023). Evaluating classifier performance with highly imbalanced big data. Journal of Big Data, 10(1), 1–31.
25. Scali, S. T., & Stone, D. H. (2023, March). The role of big data, risk prediction, simulation, and centralization for emergency vascular problems: Lessons learned and future directions. In Seminars in Vascular Surgery. Pennsylvania, USA: WB Saunders.
26. Bansal, R., Gupta, A., Singh, R., & Nassa, V. K. (2021, July). Role and impact of digital technologies in E-learning amidst COVID-19 pandemic. In 2021 Fourth International Conference on Computational Intelligence and Communication Technologies (CCICT) (pp. 194–202). IEEE.
27. Jain, V., Beram, S. M., Talukdar, V., Patil, T., Dhabliya, D., & Gupta, A. (2022, November). Accuracy enhancement in machine learning during blockchain based transaction classification. In 2022 Seventh International Conference on Parallel, Distributed and Grid Computing (PDGC) (pp. 536–540). IEEE.
28. Kaushik, D., Garg, M., Annu, Gupta, A., & Pramanik, S. (2022). Utilizing Machine Learning and Deep Learning in Cybersecurity: An Innovative Approach. Cyber Security and Digital Forensics: Challenges and Future Trends (pp. 271–293). USA: Wiley.

29. Gupta, M., Ghatak, S., Gupta, A., & Mukherjee, A. L. (Eds.). (2022). Artificial Intelligence on Medical Data: Proceedings of International Symposium, ISCMM 2021 (Vol. 37). Singapore: Springer Nature.
30. Onggirawan, C. A., Kho, J. M., Kartiwa, A. P., & Gunawan, A. A. (2023). Systematic literature review: The adaptation of distance learning process during the COVID-19 pandemic using virtual educational spaces in metaverse. Procedia Computer Science, 216, 274–283.
31. Athar, A., Ali, S. M., Mozumder, M. A. I., Ali, S., & Kim, H. C. (2023, February). Applications and possible challenges of healthcare metaverse. In 2023 25th International Conference on Advanced Communication Technology (ICACT) (pp. 328–332). IEEE.
32. Awasthy, N., & Valivarthi, N. (2023). Evolution of hadoop and big data trends in smart world. In Sustainable Computing: Transforming Industry 4.0 to Society 5.0 (pp. 99–127). Cham: Springer International Publishing.
33. Hichri, S. M., Jamoussi, H. B. O., & Keraani, W. (2023). The data–driven smart region, innovation and sustainability. In Knowledge Management for Regional Policymaking (pp. 191–221). Cham: Springer International Publishing.
34. Ali, Z., Mahmood, A., Khatoon, S., Alhakami, W., Ullah, S. S., Iqbal, J., & Hussain, S. (2023). A generic Internet of Things (IoT) middleware for smart city applications. Sustainability, 15(1), 743.
35. Rane, D., Penchala, S., Jain, R., & Chourey, V. (2023). Roles and future of the Internet of Things-based smart health care models. In Punit Gupta, Dinesh Kumar Saini, Pradeep Rawat, & Kashif Zia (Eds.), Bio-Inspired Optimization in Fog and Edge Computing Environments (pp. 223–248). Auerbach.
36. Nair, A. K., Sahoo, J., & Raj, E. D. (2023). Privacy preserving federated learning framework for IoMT based big data analysis using edge computing. Computer Standards & Interfaces, 86, 103720.
37. Vasa, J., Yadav, H., Patel, B., & Patel, R. (2023). Architecture, applications and data analytics tools for smart cities: A technical perspective. In Sentiment Analysis and Deep Learning: Proceedings of ICSADL 2022 (pp. 859–873). Singapore: Springer Nature Singapore.
38. Kang, J., & Zhang, J. (2023). COVID-19 and big data technologies: Experience in China. In Transportation Amid Pandemics (pp. 359–370). Netherlands: Elsevier.
39. Sindhwani, N., Rana, A., & Chaudhary, A. (2021, September). Breast cancer detection using machine learning algorithms. In 2021 9th International Conference on Reliability, Infocom Technologies and Optimization (Trends and Future Directions) (ICRITO) (pp. 1–5). IEEE.
40. Anand, R., Sindhwani, N., & Juneja, S. (2022). Cognitive Internet of Things, its applications, and its challenges: A survey. In Harnessing the Internet of Things (IoT) for a Hyper-Connected Smart World (pp. 91–113). US: Apple Academic Press.
41. Anand, R., & Chawla, P. (2016, March). A review on the optimization techniques for bio-inspired antenna design. In 2016 3rd International Conference on Computing for Sustainable Global Development (INDIACom) (pp. 2228–2233). IEEE.
42. Jain, N., Chaudhary, A., Sindhwani, N., & Rana, A. (2021, September). Applications of wearable devices in IoT. In 2021 9th International Conference on Reliability, Infocom Technologies and Optimization (Trends and Future Directions) (ICRITO) (pp. 1–4). IEEE.
43. Saini, P., & Anand, M. R. (2014). Identification of defects in plastic gears using image processing and computer vision: A review. International Journal of Engineering Research, 3(2), 94–99.

44. Anand, R., Singh, B., & Sindhwani, N. (2009). Speech perception & analysis of fluent digits' strings using level-by-level time alignment. International Journal of Information Technology and Knowledge Management, 2(1), 65–68.
45. Anand, R., Sindhwani, N., & Dahiya, A. (2022, March). Design of a high directivity slotted fractal antenna for C-band, X-band and Ku-band applications. In 2022 9th International Conference on Computing for Sustainable Global Development (INDIACom) (pp. 727–730). IEEE.
46. Anand, R., Arora, S., & Sindhwani, N. (2022, January). A miniaturized UWB antenna for high speed applications. In 2022 International Conference on Computing, Communication and Power Technology (IC3P) (pp. 264–267). IEEE.
47. Sindhwani, N., Anand, R., Niranjanamurthy, M., Verma, D. C., & Valentina, E. B. (2022). IoT based smart applications. Springer International Publishing AG. https://doi.org/10.1007/978-3-031-04524-0.

2 Machine Learning-Based Inconsistency Detection in Medical Data

*Janjhyam Venkata Naga Ramesh, Jayasri Kotti,
Priyanka Chandani, Rupal Gupta,
Ahateshaam Ansari, T.R. Mahesh, and
Dharmesh Dhabliya*

2.1 INTRODUCTION

2.1.1 MEDICAL DATA AND ANOMALY DETECTION

The use of data analytics and machine learning techniques to detect abnormalities or irregularities in medical claims data is one method of combating healthcare fraud [1–4]. Anomaly detection is a useful method for spotting trends or outliers in a dataset that differs from the norm. Anomaly detection can be used in the context of medical claims data to identify claims that are likely to be fraudulent or suspicious. We investigate the application of unsupervised anomaly detection algorithms on medical claims data to uncover probable fraud or abnormalities in the claims in this study. We specifically assess and compare the efficacy of three unsupervised anomaly detection methods in detecting anomalies in data.

We use the Medicare Claims Synthetic Public Use Files (SynPUFs) dataset to perform our research, which includes information on beneficiaries, their medical problems, and the claims filed for healthcare services. The SynPUFs dataset was established to enable data analysts and software developers to create programmes and products that use the same formats and variable names as those found in CMS data files while maintaining beneficiary privacy.

The findings of our study have significance for healthcare systems and governments interested in reducing healthcare fraud and enhancing healthcare system efficiency and accuracy. Unsupervised anomaly detection can assist healthcare organisations cut costs, enhance quality of care, and ultimately benefit patients by recognising potential fraud or abnormalities in medical claims data [5,6].

2.1.2 INCONSISTENCY OR OUTLIER DETECTION IN MEDICAL DATA

Numerous disciplines have seen the dominance of AI, including but not limited to:

- Outlier detection can be used to detect fraudulent behaviors such as false claims, upcoding, and charging for services that were not rendered. This

DOI: 10.1201/9781003330523-2

can assist healthcare systems in saving money while also preventing unethical behavior.

- Outlier identification can assist in identifying odd trends in patient data that may suggest the presence of a rare or atypical disease. This can assist doctors in more correctly and effectively diagnosing and treating patients.
- Outlier detection can be used in patient monitoring to discover when a patient's condition deviates from the norm. This can assist doctors in identifying potential health issues and taking appropriate action.
- Outlier detection can be used in quality control to uncover errors or discrepancies in medical data, such as inaccurate diagnoses or medication errors.
- Outlier detection in clinical trials can be used to find odd or unexpected responses to treatments. This can assist researchers in developing novel medicines or improving existing ones.
- Patient deterioration early warning system: Outlier detection can be used to monitor vital signs and other patient data to find early warning indicators of patient deterioration. This allows doctors to intervene earlier and avoid consequences.
- Outlier detection can be used to discover high utilisation or resource consumption regions, such as pricey medications or procedures. This can aid healthcare systems in allocating resources more effectively and efficiently.
- Outlier identification can be used to identify patients who are at high risk of problems or readmissions. This can assist clinicians in prioritising care.
- Outlier detection can be used to find flaws or discrepancies in electronic health record (EHR) data, such as missing or erroneous information. This can aid in the improvement of the accuracy and completeness of patient records.
- Outlier detection can be used in public health surveillance to monitor population health data and discover odd or unexpected patterns that may suggest an epidemic or other public health emergency. This can aid public health professionals in responding fast and preventing illness transmission.

2.1.3 Use of Inconsistency or Outlier Detection in Medical Data Using the Dataset

In the medical field, detecting fraud is crucial to ensuring that healthcare resources are spent properly and effectively. Using outlier or inconsistency detection tools on medical claims data is one way to detect probable fraud. The Medicare Claims Synthetic Public Use Files (SynPUFs) collection, which contains information on beneficiaries, their medical issues, and the claims filed for their healthcare services, is an excellent resource for medical fraud detection research. Unsupervised anomaly detection algorithms can be useful in identifying probable fraudulent claims in this setting. An investigation is required to confirm or refute the suspicion of fraud.

Nonetheless, the application of unsupervised anomaly detection algorithms can be a valuable tool in detecting potential fraudulent activity in medical claims data, ultimately assisting in cost reduction and improving patient care quality. The application of unsupervised anomaly detection algorithms in claims data can be a powerful tool for detecting suspected medical fraud [7–9]. The SynPUFs dataset is a significant resource for investigating medical fraud detection, and the findings of this work can benefit healthcare systems and policymakers interested in increasing healthcare system efficiency and accuracy. Additional visualizations are shown in Figures 2.1–2.3.

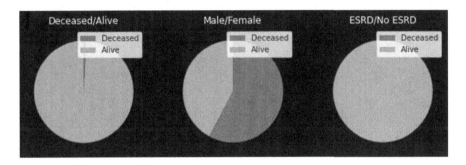

FIGURE 2.1   Pie chart showing important categorical features.

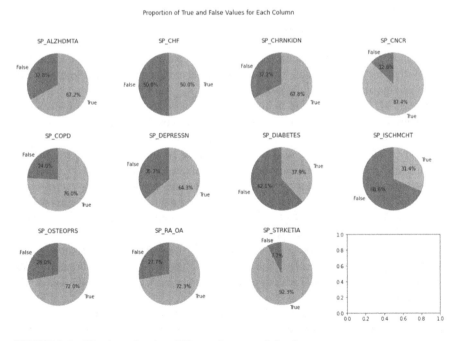

FIGURE 2.2   Pie chart showing different features of the dataset.

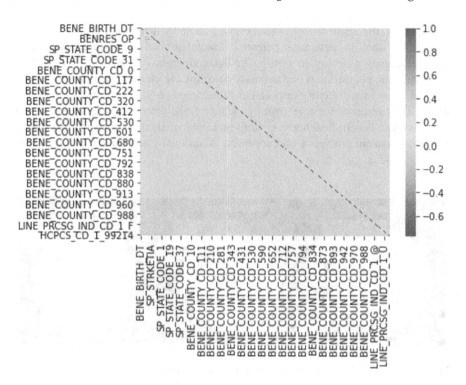

FIGURE 2.3   A heatmap showing correlation matrixes.

2.2   LITERATURE SURVEY

Cai et al. [10] suggested a dual-distribution discrepancy-based anomaly identification system for medical pictures based on one-class semi-supervised learning that be novel algorithms on benchmarks.

Pan et al. [11] suggested a transfer learning-based approach for detecting anomalies in civil infrastructure structural health monitoring data, demonstrating good accuracy even with sparse labeled training data.

Zhou et al. [12] suggested a semi-supervised anomaly detection framework that incorporates neural process models to evaluate uncertainty and increase the system's flexibility and robustness when labeled data is scarce.

Ahmed [13] demonstrated a deep learning-based method for detecting anomalies in industrial machinery through vibrational signal analysis, attaining an overall accuracy of 91% on the gearbox fault-diagnosis dataset.

Lei et al. [14] suggested a residual attention network based on mutual information correlation analysis for detecting anomalies in bridge measurement data, achieving outstanding classification and generalisation performance across several bridge datasets.

N. Sridhar et al. [15] suggested a k-nearest neighbor (KNN) machine learning approach with random forest (RF) algorithm for detecting anomalies in IoT networks.

Srivastava et al. [16] suggested a Hybrid Model SVM and Isolation forest (HMOI). On the Intel Berkeley Research Lab (IBRL) dataset, the model outperforms existing approaches.

Kumar et al. [17] conduct a thorough examination of IoT network security using quality-of-service measures and present a deep learning-based intrusion detection system (IDS) based on fuzzy CNN. The suggested IDS improves detection accuracy, detects DoS attacks correctly, and reduces false positive rates.

Jain et al. [18] suggested a machine learning strategy for accurate transaction classification in blockchain-based systems, which might potentially be used for anomaly identification in transactions with questionable behavior.

The use of ML and cybersecurity, including detecting anomalies and threats, was described by Kaushik et al. [19]. The proposed method could be beneficial in recognising and highlighting harmful behavior patterns.

Gupta et al. [20] provided a collection of research papers on the use of artificial intelligence in medical data analysis, including disease diagnosis and prediction using machine learning. This could be useful for detecting anomalies in healthcare, as odd patterns in medical data could indicate significant health problems.

During the COVID-19 epidemic, Onggirawan et al. [21] did a systematic literature study on the adaption of remote learning utilising virtual educational spaces. While not directly connected to anomaly detection, machine learning techniques could possibly be utilised to discover and flag anomalous trends in online learning behaviors.

Athar et al. [22] highlighted the possible applications and limitations of the healthcare metaverse, which uses virtual reality and other immersive technology in healthcare. Machine learning could be used to analyse data from the healthcare metaverse to find anomalies or abnormalities in patient behavior or treatment outcomes.

Tao Yi et al. [23] examines and analyses studies aimed at addressing issues in attack detection in networks using deep learning, such as in distribution of network attack samples.

Gómez et al. [24] suggest SUSAN outperforms comparable work on the SWaT testbed, with 0.910 recall rate, 0.633 precision, and 0.747 F1-score, detecting all cyberattacks that threaten the system's sustainability.

Talukdar et al. [25] propose a machine learning-based approach for detecting and classifying suspicious behavior in IoT environments, which can be used to detect anomalies in IoT devices.

Veeraiah et al. [26] propose connecting IoT devices with metaverse capabilities to improve the overall system, which may include anomaly detection using machine learning approaches.

Gupta et al. [27] propose employing sequential minimization optimization-based random forests to evaluate wearable sensor data over a smart house, which can be effective for anomaly identification in the context of smart homes.

Keserwani et al. [28] propose utilising machine learning to detect assaults in 5 G networks, which can aid in the detection of anomalies and potential security breaches.

2.3   PROBLEM STATEMENTS

The healthcare business is dealing with an increase in false claims, which can result in financial losses, resource waste, and impaired patient care. To fight this issue, effective methods for detecting and preventing fraud in medical claims data are required. While there are numerous fraud detection strategies, the use of unsupervised anomaly detection algorithms has shown promise in detecting potential fraudulent activities in medical claims data. However, research on the application of such algorithms in detecting medical fraud in huge datasets such as the Medicare Claims Synthetic Public application Files (SynPUFs) is lacking.

2.4   PROPOSED WORK

The proposed study will assess the performance of unsupervised anomaly detection algorithms in detecting potentially fraudulent activities in the Medicare Claims Synthetic Public Use Files (SynPUFs) dataset. To do so, we first generated a table with 1 million entries by connecting the SynPUFs dataset's claims and beneficiary's tables. The table contains 42 columns of data, including beneficiary demographics, medical conditions, and reimbursement information. Then, to identify probable fraudulent claims, we used anomaly detection techniques.

2.5   RESULTS AND DISCUSSION

We were able to visualise the distribution of the Medicare Claims Synthetic Public Use Files (SynPUFs) data after using PCA and visualising the dataset in 2D. The Elliptic Envelope technique was then used to discover anomalies in the dataset. We discovered that the algorithm detected 0.1% of the data as anomalous. The Elliptic Envelope algorithm detected abnormalities in the dataset, and the contamination rate of 0.1% shows that the dataset is generally clean. However, it should be noted that this analysis only covers a part of the Medicare claims data, and bigger datasets should be analysed to corroborate these findings. More research is needed to confirm these findings and uncover potential outliers in larger datasets. Furthermore, before using PCA, it is critical to thoroughly analyse the trade-offs of dimensionality reduction. Figure 2.4 shows the results of the algorithm.

Recent research talks about the applications of such systems in detail. Machine learning is used in a variety of medical fields; including neuroimaging, bridge damage diagnosis, ulcerative colitis diagnosis, sleep posture recognition, autism detection, EEG emotion recognition, lithium-ion battery health prognostics, heart failure medication phenotyping, and intrahepatic cholangiocarcinoma outcome prediction [29–32]. Although each research focuses on a distinct medical issue, they all share the use of machine learning-based algorithms [33,34] to analyse and uncover discrepancies in medical data as a common theme [35,36]. These studies show that machine learning algorithms have the potential to increase the accuracy and efficiency of medical data processing and diagnosis [37].

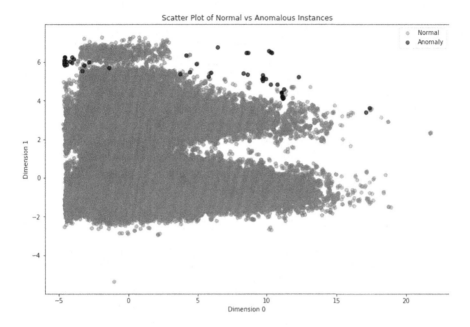

FIGURE 2.4   Scatter plot results showing inconsistency detection after PCA.

Several researchers investigate the use of machine learning in medical imaging and healthcare data identification and diagnosis. Huang et al. [38] describe a deep learning-based end-to-end multi-task system for automatic lesion diagnosis and anatomical localization in whole-body bone scintigraphy. Duman et al. [39] present a convolutional neural network technique based on deep learning for recognising the presence of taurodont teeth on panoramic radiographs. Alleman et al. [40] perform a systematic study of multimodal deep learning-based prognostication in patients with glioma. Ali et al. [41] examine time domain electronic medical record taxonomy using machine learning. DMFL_Net, a federated learning-based framework for the classification of COVID-19 from different chest disorders using X-rays, is presented by Malik et al. [42].

2.6 CONCLUSIONS

Our use of anomaly detection techniques on the Medicare Claims Synthetic Public Use Files (SynPUFs) dataset yielded encouraging results in identifying potentially fraudulent or unusual claims. We were able to visualise and locate abnormalities in the data by using PCA for dimensionality reduction and Elliptic Envelope for anomaly identification [43–45]. Further examination and development of the methodologies used could lead to more accurate and efficient detection of fraudulent claims, ultimately increasing the Medicare program's integrity and sustainability.

2.7 FUTURE SCOPES

There are various potential areas of further research for the suggested research on unsupervised anomaly detection methods in the SynPUFs dataset. Further investigation is required to validate or disprove the suspicion of fraud for each discovered anomaly, and future work can build a systematic approach to investigating the reported anomalies and determining the actual number of fraudulent claims. To improve the accuracy of medical fraud detection, comparisons with supervised learning systems and testing on larger datasets can be performed [46–48]. Furthermore, the addition of new features and the development of real-time monitoring systems may give a more complete approach to detecting and combating medical fraud in the future [49].

REFERENCES

1. Anand, R., Daniel, A. V., Fred, A. L., Jaiswal, T., Juneja, S., Juneja, A., & Gupta, A. (2023). Building integrated systems for healthcare considering mobile computing and IoT. In Integration of IoT with Cloud Computing for Smart Applications (pp. 203–225). New York: Chapman and Hall/CRC Press.
2. Anand, R., Jain, V., Singh, A., Rahal, D., Rastogi, P., Rajkumar, A., & Gupta, A. (2023). Clustering of big data in cloud environments for smart applications. In Integration of IoT with Cloud Computing for Smart Applications (pp. 227–247). New York: Chapman and Hall/CRC Press.
3. Arora, S., Sharma, S., & Anand, R. (2022, July). A survey on UWB textile antenna for wireless body area network (WBAN) applications. In Artificial Intelligence on Medical Data: Proceedings of International Symposium, ISCMM 2021 (pp. 173–183). Singapore: Springer Nature Singapore.
4. Gupta, A., Anand, R., Pandey, D., Sindhwani, N., Wairya, S., Pandey, B. K., & Sharma, M. (2021). Prediction of breast cancer using extremely randomized clustering forests (ERCF) technique: Prediction of breast cancer. International Journal of Distributed Systems and Technologies (IJDST), 12(4), 1–15.
5. Sindhwani, N., Sasi, G., & Meivel, S. (2022, October). Fuzzy acceptance analysis of impact of glaucoma and diabetic retinopathy using confusion matrix. In 2022 10th International Conference on Reliability, Infocom Technologies and Optimization (Trends and Future Directions)(ICRITO) (pp. 1–5). IEEE.
6. Sharma, G., Nehra, N., Dahiya, A., Sindhwani, N., & Singh, P. (2022). Automatic heart-rate measurement using facial video. In Networking Technologies in Smart Healthcare (pp. 289–307). Boca Raton, Florida, USA: CRC Press.
7. Sindhwani, N., Rana, A., & Chaudhary, A. (2021, September). Breast cancer detection using machine learning algorithms. In 2021 9th International Conference on Reliability, Infocom Technologies and Optimization (Trends and Future Directions) (ICRITO) (pp. 1–5). IEEE.
8. Sharma, R., Vashisth, R., & Sindhwani, N. (2023). Study and analysis of classification techniques for specific plant growths. In Advances in Signal Processing, Embedded Systems and IoT: Proceedings of Seventh ICMEET-2022 (pp. 591–605). Singapore: Springer Nature Singapore.
9. Anand, R., Sindhwani, N., & Juneja, S. (2022). Cognitive Internet of Things, its applications, and its challenges: A survey. In Indu Bala & Kiran Ahuja (Eds.), Harnessing the Internet of Things (IoT) for a Hyper-Connected Smart World (pp. 91–113). US: Apple Academic Press.

10. Cai, Y., Chen, H., Yang, X., Zhou, Y., & Cheng, K. T. (2023). Dual-distribution discrepancy with self-supervised refinement for anomaly detection in medical images. Medical Image Analysis, 86, 102794.

11. Pan, Q., Bao, Y., & Li, H. (2023). Transfer learning-based data anomaly detection for structural health monitoring. Structural Health Monitoring, 14759217221142174. https://doi.org/10.1177/14759217221142174

12. Zhou, F., Wang, G., Zhang, K., Liu, S., & Zhong, T. (2023). Semi-Supervised Anomaly Detection via Neural Process. IEEE Transactions on Knowledge and Data Engineering. 10.1109/TKDE.2023.3266755

13. Ahmed, I., Ahmad, M., Chehri, A., & Jeon, G. (2023). A smart-anomaly-detection system for industrial machines based on feature autoencoder and deep learning. Micro Machines, 14(1), 154.

14. Lei, X., Xia, Y., Wang, A., Jian, X., Zhong, H., & Sun, L. (2023). Mutual information based anomaly detection of monitoring data with attention mechanism and residual learning. Mechanical Systems and Signal Processing, 182, 109607.

15. Sridhar, N., Shanmugapriya, K., & Marimuthu, C. N. (2023). Machine learning algorithms to detect deepfakes fine tuned for anomaly detection of IoT. In Handbook of Research on Advanced Practical Approaches to Deepfake Detection and Applications (pp. 95–105). Hershey, Pennsylvania, US: IGI Global.

16. Srivastava, A., & Bharti, M. R. (2023). Hybrid machine learning model for anomaly detection in unlabelled data of wireless sensor networks. Wireless Personal Communications, 1–18. https://doi.org/10.1007/s11277-023-10253-2

17. Santhosh Kumar, S. V. N., Selvi, M., & Kannan, A. (2023). A comprehensive survey on machine learning-based intrusion detection systems for secure communication in Internet of Things. Computational Intelligence and Neuroscience, 2023. 10.1155/2023/8981988

18. Jain, V., Beram, S. M., Talukdar, V., Patil, T., Dhabliya, D., & Gupta, A. (2022). Accuracy enhancement in machine learning during blockchain based transaction classification. In 2022 Seventh International Conference on Parallel, Distributed and Grid Computing (PDGC) (pp. 536–540). IEEE.

19. Kaushik, D., Garg, M., Annu, & Gupta, A.; Sabyasachi Pramanik. (2022). Utilizing machine learning and deep learning in cybersecurity: An innovative approach. Cyber Security and Digital Forensics: Challenges and Future Trends (pp. 271–293). US: Wiley.

20. Gupta, M., Ghatak, S., Gupta, A., & Mukherjee, A. L. (Eds.). (2022). Artificial Intelligence on Medical Data: Proceedings of International Symposium, ISCMM 2021 (Vol. 37). Singapore: Springer Nature.

21. Onggirawan, C. A., Kho, J. M., Kartiwa, A. P., & Gunawan, A. A. (2023). Systematic literature review: The adaptation of distance learning process during the COVID-19 pandemic using virtual educational spaces in metaverse. Procedia Computer Science, 216, 274–283.

22. Athar, A., Ali, S. M., Mozumder, M. A. I., Ali, S., & Kim, H. C. (2023, February). Applications and possible challenges of healthcare metaverse. In 2023 25th International Conference on Advanced Communication Technology (ICACT) (pp. 328–332). IEEE.

23. Yi, T., Chen, X., Zhu, Y., Ge, W., & Han, Z. (2023). Review on the application of deep learning in network attack detection. Journal of Network and Computer Applications, 212, 103580.

24. Gómez, Á. L. P., Maimó, L. F., Celdrán, A. H., & Clemente, F. J. G. (2023). SUSAN: A deep learning based anomaly detection framework for sustainable industry. Sustainable Computing: Informatics and Systems, 100842. https://doi.org/10.1016/j.suscom.2022.100842

25. Talukdar, V., Dhabliya, D., Kumar, B., Talukdar, S. B., Ahamad, S., & Gupta, A. (2022, November). Suspicious activity detection and classification in IoT environment using machine learning approach. In 2022 Seventh International Conference on Parallel, Distributed and Grid Computing (PDGC) (pp. 531–535). IEEE.

26. Veeraiah, V., Gangavathi, P., Ahamad, S., Talukdar, S. B., Gupta, A., & Talukdar, V. (2022, April). Enhancement of meta verse capabilities by IoT integration. In 2022 2nd International Conference on Advance Computing and Innovative Technologies in Engineering (ICACITE) (pp. 1493–1498). IEEE.

27. Gupta, N., Janani, S., Dilip, R., Hosur, R., Chaturvedi, A., & Gupta, A. (2022). Wearable sensors for evaluation over smart home using sequential minimization optimization-based random forest. International Journal of Communication Networks and Information Security, 14(2), 179–188.

28. Keserwani, H., Rastogi, H., Kurniullah, A. Z., Janardan, S. K., Raman, R., Rathod, V. M., & Gupta, A. (2022). Security enhancement by identifying attacks using machine learning for 5G network. International Journal of Communication Networks and Information Security, 14(2), 124-14.

29. Jimenez-Mesa, C., Ramirez, J., Suckling, J., Vöglein, J., Levin, J., Gorriz, J. M., & Alzheimer's Disease Neuroimaging Initiative. (2023). A non-parametric statistical inference framework for deep learning in current neuroimaging. Information Fusion, 91, 598–611.

30. Xiao, H., Ogai, H., & Wang, W. (2023). A new deep transfer learning method for intelligent bridge damage diagnosis based on multi-channel sub-domain adaptation. Structure and Infrastructure Engineering, 1–16. https://doi.org/10.1080/15732479. 2023.2167214

31. Fan, Y., Mu, R., Xu, H., Xie, C., Zhang, Y., Liu, L., ... & Cai, S. (2023). Novel deep learning–based computer-aided diagnosis system for predicting inflammatory activity in ulcerative colitis. Gastrointestinal Endoscopy, 97(2), 335–346.

32. Li, X., Gong, Y., Jin, X., & Shang, P. (2023). Sleep posture recognition based on machine learning: A systematic review. Pervasive and Mobile Computing, 101752. https://doi.org/10.48550/arXiv.2301.05777

33. Islam, A., Ronco, A., Becker, S. M., Blackburn, J., Schittny, J. C., Kim, K., ... & Wexler, A. S. (2023). Lung airway geometry as an early predictor of autism: A preliminary machine learning-based study. arXiv preprint arXiv:2301.05777. https://doi.org/10.4108/eai.13-10-2021.171318

34. Zhang, X., Huang, D., Li, H., Zhang, Y., Xia, Y., & Liu, J. (2023). Self-Training Maximum Classifier Discrepancy for EEG Emotion Recognition. UK: CAAI Transactions on Intelligence Technology.

35. Ma, Y., Shan, C., Gao, J., & Chen, H. (2023). Multiple health indicators fusion-based health prognostic for lithium-ion battery using transfer learning and hybrid deep learning method. Reliability Engineering & System Safety, 229, 108818.

36. Sotomi, Y., Hikoso, S., Nakatani, D., Okada, K., Dohi, T., Sunaga, A., ... & Sakata, Y. (2023). Medications for specific phenotypes of heart failure with preserved ejection fraction classified by a machine learning-based clustering model. Heart. https://doi.org/10.1007/978-3-030-96308-8_87

37. Zhou, S. N., Jv, D. W., Meng, X. F., Zhang, J. J., Liu, C., Wu, Z. Y., ... & Zhang, N. (2023). Feasibility of machine learning-based modeling and prediction using multiple centers data to assess intrahepatic cholangiocarcinoma outcomes. Annals of Medicine, 55(1), 215–223.

38. Huang, K., Huang, S., Chen, G., Li, X., Li, S., Liang, Y., & Gao, Y. (2023). An end-to-end multi-task system of automatic lesion detection and anatomical localization in whole-body bone scintigraphy by deep learning. Bioinformatics, 39(1), btac753.

39. Duman, S., Yılmaz, E. F., Eşer, G., Çelik, Ö., Bayrakdar, I. S., Bilgir, E., ... & Orhan, K. (2023). Detecting the presence of taurodont teeth on panoramic radiographs using a deep learning-based convolutional neural network algorithm. Oral Radiology, 39(1), 207–214.

40. Alleman, K., Knecht, E., Huang, J., Zhang, L., Lam, S., & DeCuypere, M. (2023). Multimodal deep learning-based prognostication in glioma patients: A systematic review. Cancers, 15(2), 545.

41. Ali, H., Niazi, I. K., Russell, B. K., Crofts, C., Madanian, S., & White, D. (2023). Review of time domain electronic medical record taxonomies in the application of machine learning. Electronics, 12(3), 554.

42. Malik, H., Naeem, A., Naqvi, R. A., & Loh, W. K. (2023). DMFL_Net: A federated learning-based framework for the classification of COVID-19 from multiple chest diseases using X-rays. Sensors, 23(2), 743.

43. Saini, P., & Anand, M. R. (2014). Identification of defects in plastic gears using image processing and computer vision: A review. International Journal of Engineering Research, 3(2), 94–99.

44. Arora, S., Sharma, S., Anand, R., & Shrivastva, G. (2023). Miniaturized pentagon-shaped planar monopole antenna for ultra-wideband applications. Progress In Electromagnetics Research C, 133, 195–208.

45. Sansanwal, K., Shrivastava, G., Anand, R., & Sharma, K. (2019). Big data analysis and compression for indoor air quality. Handbook of IoT and Big Data, 1. www.taylorfrancis.com/chapters/edit/10.1201/9780429053290-1/big-data-analysis-compression-indoor-air-quality-khushboo-sansanwal-gulshan-shrivasta-va-rohit-anand-kavita-sharma

46. Meivel, S., Sindhwani, N., Valarmathi, S., Dhivya, G., Atchaya, M., Anand, R., & Maurya, S. (2022). Design and method of 16.24 GHz microstrip network antenna using underwater wireless communication algorithm. In Cyber Technologies and Emerging Sciences: ICCTES 2021 (pp. 363–371). Singapore: Springer Nature Singapore.

47. Gupta, A., Asad, A., Meena, L., & Anand, R. (2022, July). IoT and RFID-based smart card system integrated with health care, electricity, QR and banking sectors. In Artificial Intelligence on Medical Data: Proceedings of International Symposium, ISCMM 2021 (pp. 253–265). Singapore: Springer Nature Singapore.

48. Gupta, B., Chaudhary, A., Sindhwani, N., & Rana, A. (2021, September). Smart shoe for detection of electrocution using Internet of Things (IoT). In 2021 9th International Conference on Reliability, Infocom Technologies and Optimization (Trends and Future Directions)(ICRITO) (pp. 1–3). IEEE.

49. Sindhwani, N., Anand, R., Niranjanamurthy, M., Verma, D. C., & Valentina, E. B. (2022). IoT based smart applications. Springer International Publishing AG. https://doi.org/10.1007/978-3-031-04524-0.

3 A Perspective on Improvements in Segmentation Image Processing in Healthcare Datasets

Janjhyam Venkata Naga Ramesh, Rohit Anand, Mohammed Zabeeulla, Abhilash Kumar Saxena, Mukesh Kumar, Nidhi Sindhwani, and Ankur Gupta

3.1 INTRODUCTION

3.1.1 IoT AND HEALTHCARE BASED DEPRESSION

Medical imaging has transformed disease diagnosis and treatment by enabling non-invasive visualization and investigation of interior structures and processes. However, interpreting medical images is a difficult undertaking, particularly when it comes to segmenting organs and cells. Accurate segmentation is essential for a variety of medical applications, including disease diagnosis, treatment planning, and monitoring [1–4]. Deep learning-based approaches have recently demonstrated considerable promise in medical picture segmentation, producing state-of-the-art results in a variety of applications. The success of these strategies, however, is strongly dependent on the availability of annotated data [5–7]. Annotated data is often costly and time-consuming to gather, particularly in medical imaging where specialist expertise is necessary to execute annotations. We demonstrate our method for segmenting organs and cells in medical images using the dataset in this research. Our suggested method annotates training data using RLE-encoded masks and works with 16-bit grayscale PNG images. We also add a wrapper function for easier data exploration and visualization of segmentation masks. We assess our method's performance on the specified test set and compare it to other state-of-the-art methods.

3.1.2 APPLICATIONS OF IMAGE SEGMENTATION IN AI

Numerous disciplines have seen the dominance of AI, including but not limited to:

DOI: 10.1201/9781003330523-3

- Medical diagnosis: Accurate segmentation of organs and cells in GI tract pictures can aid clinicians in the diagnosis of digestive disorders and conditions.
- Treatment planning: Precise organ and cell localization can help with treatment planning for illnesses such as tumors, inflammatory bowel disease, and polyps.
- Surgical planning: Accurate GI tract segmentation can help surgeons plan and execute surgeries with more precision and safety.
- Medical education: The dataset can be used to educate medical students and professionals about GI anatomy and pathophysiology.
- The dataset can be utilized for research purposes, such as studying the progression of diseases and ailments affecting the GI tract and developing novel treatments.
- Drug development: Precise GI tract segmentation can be utilized in drug research to evaluate the efficacy and safety of treatments for a variety of diseases.
- The information can be used to train and test new medical imaging methods and software for better visualization and analysis of the GI tract.
- Robotics: Accurate GI tract segmentation can aid in the development of robotic instruments for minimally invasive procedures.
- Telemedicine: The dataset can be utilized in telemedicine applications to help with remote diagnosis and treatment of GI tract disorders in patients.
- Public health: The dataset can be used to track and monitor the prevalence of GI tract disorders in different populations, as well as to establish public health policies and interventions.

3.1.3 ABOUT IMAGE SEGMENTATION

Image segmentation is a key step in many computer vision applications, including object detection, scene interpretation, image manipulation, and medical imaging. Segmentation is used in object identification to detect the boundaries of items in a picture, which can aid in distinguishing and recognizing various objects. Segmentation can be used in scene understanding to distinguish distinct aspects of the scene such as sky, ground, and objects, which can aid in comprehending the context of the image [8–10].

Segmentation can be used in image editing to isolate specific sections of an image for additional processing, such as deleting or replacing the background, changing the color or texture of a single object, or adding filters to specific regions of the image. Segmentation is used in medical imaging to identify and isolate various organs, tissues, and anomalies in medical images. This can aid in the diagnosis, treatment planning, and monitoring of a wide range of medical disorders. Image segmentation is an important stage in many computer vision applications since it enables us to extract meaningful information from images and accomplish tasks like object recognition, scene understanding, image manipulation, and medical imaging.

3.1.4 DIFFERENT PERSPECTIVES ON IMAGE SEGMENTATION

Image segmentation is critical for the accurate and efficient diagnosis of numerous diseases and ailments. Segmentation can assist clinicians in identifying and measuring abnormalities in medical pictures such as tumors or lesions.

Treatment planning: Segmentation can help in treatment planning for a variety of conditions, such as cancer radiation therapy. Accurate segmentation enables clinicians to pinpoint the precise position and shape of tumors, which can aid in identifying the best treatment strategy.

Surgical guidance: In surgical applications, segmentation can help the surgeon by offering guidance. Surgeons can better plan and perform surgeries with greater accuracy and safety by segmenting critical structures and landmarks in medical pictures.

Computer-aided diagnosis: Automated image segmentation can be used to aid in the detection and diagnosis of diseases in computer-aided diagnosis systems. Machine learning algorithms can learn to find patterns and anomalies in photos by analyzing massive databases of medical images.

Image segmentation can be employed in drug discovery applications as well. Researchers can identify prospective drug targets and examine the effects of medications on diverse structures by segmenting cells and other structures in medical pictures.

Monitoring disease progression: Segmentation can be used to track the progression of various diseases and ailments throughout time. Clinicians can track the growth or shrinking of tumors or other abnormalities by comparing segmented pictures from different time points.

Image segmentation can be used to generate 3D models of anatomical structures for use in virtual anatomy education and training. Students can explore and engage with anatomical structures in a virtual environment by segmenting distinct structures in medical photographs.

Prostheses and implants: Segmentation can be used to develop patient-specific models for design and manufacture in the field of prostheses and implants. Engineers can design personalized implants and prostheses that fit the patient's unique anatomy by segmenting medical photos.

Medical research can benefit from segmentation since it allows researchers to analyze and quantify specific structures or regions of interest in medical pictures. Researchers can analyze the effects of diseases or therapies on specific structures or regions by segmenting photos.

3.2 LITERATURE SURVEY

Sharma et al. [11] presented a U-Net model as the foundation for gastrointestinal tract segmentation. It beats all transfer learning models and is designed to help oncologists in treating cancer.

Using high-throughput sequencing technologies, Zhao et al. [12] investigated and forecasted the fungal microbial diversity in several areas of the gastrointestinal tract, indicating that the hindgut of Mongolian horses has a higher richness and diversity of fungus than the foregut, which may explain Mongolian horses' superior disease resistance.

Lonseko et al. [13] proposed a semi-supervised segmentation method based on generative adversarial learning for GI lesion identification in endoscopic images. It makes use of limited annotated and vast unlabeled datasets to increase lesion segmentation accuracy and reduce diagnostic errors.

Yang et al. [14] suggested a multi-scale attention fusion network for precise segmentation. It beats comparable sophisticated approaches and achieves exact surgical instrument segmentation by gathering both local and global picture information.

Jin et al. [15] suggested a unique multi-branch medical image segmentation network (MBSNet), which successfully complements the features between multiple layers to produce improved accuracy, and performs better than other competitive approaches on five datasets.

Dabass et al. [16] presented a clinically suitable computerized segmentation model, and handles vanishing gradient and resolution-degradation difficulties effectively. With increased learning capability and three proposed modules that are resistant to digital variability and can successfully address resolution-degradation and vanishing gradient concerns.

Gupta et al. [17] discuss the use of artificial intelligence (AI) on medical data, including the application of machine learning (ML) in medical image analysis and disease diagnosis, which could be useful in detecting and treating gastrointestinal (GI) tract infections.

Onggirawan et al. [18] perform literature review on the adaptation of distance learning in metaverse during the COVID-19 pandemic, which could be helpful in providing remote education to healthcare professionals to increase their knowledge and skills in the diagnosis and treatment of GI tract infections.

Athar et al. [19] discuss the potential applications and challenges of the healthcare metaverse, which include the use of AI and ML for disease diagnosis, remote patient monitoring, and training healthcare professionals, all of which could be useful in addressing the challenges of GI tract infections. EDA was not explicitly discussed in these papers.

Pan et al. [20] present the EGG-TransUNet attention-based Transformer architecture for improving feature discrimination and merging spatial and semantic information in medical picture segmentation, yielding improved results on various biomedical datasets.

Arora et al. [21] validated mucosal impedance (MI) device for real-time assessment of gastrointestinal tract mucosal health during endoscopy in 232 patients undergoing abdominal surgery.

Xiao et al. [22] propose an EA-U-Net-based segmentation that employs a U-Net network structure with attention mechanism to increase uterine cavity OCT image segmentation accuracy, outperforming earlier approaches.

Jiang et al. [23] provide an overview of deep learning lesion recognition from medical pictures, addressing current advances and identifying prospective future study areas.

Many paper on IoT or machine learning provide insight into improvements in machine learning and IoT-based solutions for healthcare datasets [24,25]. They specifically stress the potential of machine learning and IoT in improving healthcare processes such as breast cancer prediction, suspicious activity monitoring, and smart home wearable sensors [26–28]. The papers also examine the need of safe network architecture in healthcare and provide strategies for improving security in IoT-based networks [29]. These articles can give significant insights for healthcare and technology researchers, practitioners, and policymakers.

In medical image analysis, Zhan et al. [30] suggested an intelligent auxiliary framework for bone malignant tumor lesion segmentation. Wang et al. [31] created smartphone-based platforms that use image-based artificial intelligence to detect microfluidics. Ait Nasser and Akhloufi [32] reviewed recent developments in deep learning models for detecting chest illness using radiography. Chen et al. [33] carried out a bibliometric analysis on information fusion and artificial intelligence for smart healthcare. Albahri et al. [34] conducted a comprehensive assessment of trustworthy and explainable AI in healthcare, evaluating quality, bias risk, and data fusion. Chakraborty et al. [35] offered an overview of biomedical image analysis from the standpoint of deep learning. Raja et al. [36] proposed a CXR image analysis E-healthcare CAD system based on a secure QR pattern.

In the fog-assisted IoMT, Ding et al. [37] suggested a deep network for cross-site segmentation of COVID-19 infection. Hussain et al. [38] did a thorough evaluation of deep learning-based MRI diagnosis of disc degenerative disorders. BASIN, a semi-automatic method with machine learning segmentation for objective statistical analysis of biomedical and biofilm image datasets, was proposed by Hartman et al. [39] and Morales et al. [40] proposed reslicing ultrasound pictures to add data and recreate vessels. Reverse-Net, a few-shot learning with reverse teaching for deformable medical image registration, was proposed by Zhang et al. [41]. Agrawal et al. [42] conducted a thorough survey on chest radiography segmentation and classification. Wei et al. [43] studied quantum machine learning in medical picture analysis. Finally, Ma et al. [44] devised a method for efficiently segmenting images of heart diseases.

3.3 PROBLEM STATEMENT

One problem statement that may be studied using segmentation is in the field of medical imaging, where precise segmentation of organs and anomalies is critical for diagnosis and therapy planning. EDA (Exploratory Data Analysis) can aid in the segmentation process by analyzing data and detecting patterns and variations that can aid in the selection of appropriate segmentation methods and approaches. EDA can also aid in the detection of outliers and abnormalities in data, which can impair the accuracy of segmentation results.

3.4 PROPOSED WORK

Our proposed study entails creating a segmentation algorithm that can effectively identify and isolate different organs, tissues, and anomalies in gastrointestinal (GI) tract medical imaging such as X-rays, CT scans, and MRI images. This will be accomplished by using ML, as well as exploratory data analysis (EDA) tools to better preprocess and prepare the data for segmentation. The goal is to increase the accuracy and speed of segmentation, which will eventually aid in the diagnosis, treatment planning, and monitoring of numerous GI tract-related medical disorders.

3.5 RESULTS AND DISCUSSION

The process of recognizing and classifying items or regions within an image or volume is known as segmentation. Segmentation is frequently used in medical imaging to detect specific structures or tissues within the body, such as organs, blood arteries, or tumors. There are numerous ways to segmentation, including thresholding, edge detection, and region expanding. Setting a threshold value for pixel intensity and identifying all pixels above or below that value as foreground or background is what thresholding is all about. The process of detecting the borders between various regions based on variations in pixel intensity is known as edge detection. Region growth entails recognizing and grouping regions with comparable qualities.

Segmentation is done with the help of a mask, which is a binary picture that indicates the presence or absence of the target object in each pixel. The post-processing stage is critical for improving segmentation accuracy and resilience. Finally, the segmentation is evaluated using several metrics to determine the similarity between the predicted mask and the ground truth mask, such as the Dice coefficient, Jaccard index, and Hausdorff distance. Figures 3.1–3.3 show general attributes, then Figure 3.4 shows a box plot and Figures 3.5 and 3.6 show segmented images.

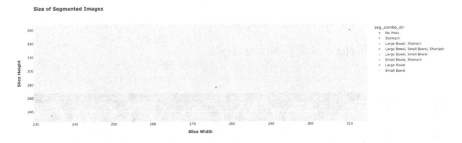

FIGURE 3.1 Size comparison of segmented images.

FIGURE 3.2 Sepal width vs sepal length of species.

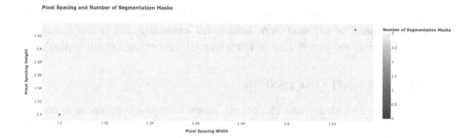

FIGURE 3.3   Pixel spacing and number of segmented images.

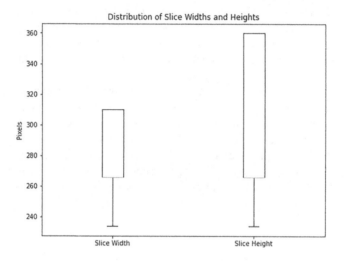

FIGURE 3.4   Box plot of slide width and heights.

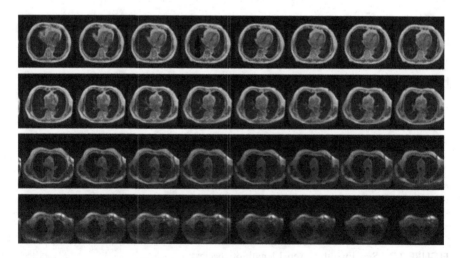

FIGURE 3.5   Segmentation sample of the images.

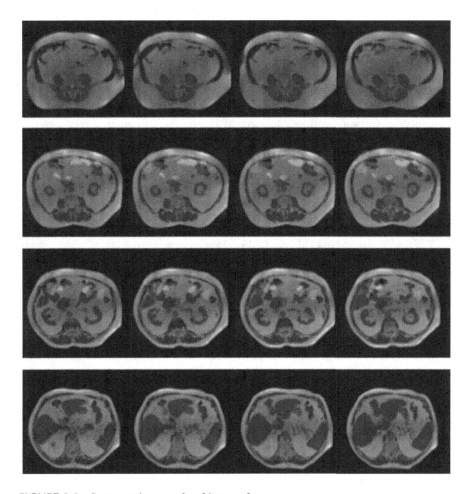

FIGURE 3.6 Segmentation sample of images 2.

3.6 CONCLUSIONS

Finally, the chapter emphasizes the potential of IoT sensors in delivering real-time and continuous health monitoring to improve overall patient care. Data analysis from IoT sensors and the healthcare system provides insights into the aspects that may influence the patient's health status and risk level [45,46]. The visualizations described in the research provide a thorough analysis of the data, which can assist healthcare providers in making educated decisions about their patients' treatment. In addition, the report emphasizes the need of adding IoT sensors into healthcare systems in order to enhance patient outcomes and lower healthcare costs. Overall, the paper's findings show the potential of IoT sensors in healthcare.

3.7 FUTURE SCOPE

Based on the suggested study, the future scope of research in this sector will include investigating more advanced segmentation approaches, such as deep learning-based methods, to increase segmentation accuracy and efficiency. Furthermore, further research can be conducted to develop automatic segmentation algorithms that can generalize well to both partially and completely unknown scenarios [47,48]. Integrating segmentation with other medical imaging techniques and analysis tools can also provide a more complete picture of medical disorders and allow for better treatment planning [49,50]. Finally, the development of more user-friendly segmentation software will enable medical practitioners to employ this sophisticated technology with simplicity and efficiency.

REFERENCES

1. Juneja, S., & Anand, R. (2018). Contrast enhancement of an image by DWT-SVD and DCT-SVD. In Data Engineering and Intelligent Computing: Proceedings of IC3T 2016 (pp. 595–603). Singapore: Springer.
2. Saini, P., & Anand, M. R. (2014). Identification of defects in plastic gears using image processing and computer vision: A review. International Journal of Engineering Research, 3(2), 94–99.
3. Anand, R., Singh, B., & Sindhwani, N. (2009). Speech perception & analysis of fluent digits' strings using level-by-level time alignment. International Journal of Information Technology and Knowledge Management, 2(1), 65–68.
4. Sindhwani, N., Rana, A., & Chaudhary, A. (2021, September). Breast cancer detection using machine learning algorithms. In 2021 9th International Conference on Reliability, Infocom Technologies and Optimization (Trends and Future Directions) (ICRITO) (pp. 1–5). IEEE.
5. Ahamad, S., Talukdar, S. B., Anand, R., Talukdar, V., Jain, S. K., & Namdev, A. (2023). Performance and analysis of propagation delay in the bitcoin network check for updates. In International Conference on Innovative Computing and Communications: Proceedings of ICICC 2023, Volume 3 (p. 123). Singapore: Springer Nature.
6. Janani, S., Sivarathinabala, M., Anand, R., Ahamad, S., Usmani, M. A., & Basha, S. M. (2023). Machine learning analysis on predicting credit card forgery. In International Conference on Innovative Computing and Communications: Proceedings of ICICC 2023, Volume 3 (p. 137). Singapore: Springer Nature.
7. Jain, N., Chaudhary, A., Sindhwani, N., & Rana, A. (2021, September). Applications of wearable devices in IoT. In 2021 9th International Conference on Reliability, Infocom Technologies and Optimization (Trends and Future Directions) (ICRITO) (pp. 1–4). IEEE.
8. Gupta, B., Chaudhary, A., Sindhwani, N., & Rana, A. (2021, September). Smart shoe for detection of electrocution using Internet of Things (IoT). In 2021 9th International Conference on Reliability, Infocom Technologies and Optimization (Trends and Future Directions)(ICRITO) (pp. 1–3). IEEE.
9. Sharma, G., Nehra, N., Dahiya, A., Sindhwani, N., & Singh, P. (2022). Automatic heart-rate measurement using facial video. In Networking Technologies in Smart Healthcare (pp. 289–307). Boca Raton, Florida, US: CRC Press.
10. Verma, S., Bajaj, T., Sindhwani, N., & Kumar, A. (2022). Design and development of a driving assistance and safety system using deep learning. In Advances in Data Science and Computing Technology (pp. 35–45). New York, US: Apple Academic Press.
11. Sharma, N., Gupta, S., Koundal, D., Alyami, S., Alshahrani, H., Asiri, Y., & Shaikh, A. (2023). U-Net model with transfer learning model as a backbone for segmentation of gastrointestinal tract. Bioengineering, 10(1), 119.

12. Zhao, Y., Wu, H., Hu, H., Cheng, C., Du, M., Huang, Y., ... & Dugarjaviin, M. (2023). Diversity and functional prediction of fungal communities in different segments of Mongolian horse gastrointestinal tracts. BMC Microbiol. https://doi.org/10.1186/s12866-023-03001-w

13. Lonseko, Z. M., Du, W., Adjei, P. E., Luo, C., Hu, D., Gan, T., ... & Rao, N. (2023). Semi-supervised segmentation framework for gastrointestinal lesion diagnosis in endoscopic images. Journal of Personalized Medicine, 13(1), 118.

14. Yang, L., Gu, Y., Bian, G., & Liu, Y. (2023). MAF-Net: A multi-scale attention fusion network for automatic surgical instrument segmentation. Biomedical Signal Processing and Control, 85, 104912.

15. Jin, S., Yu, S., Peng, J., Wang, H., & Zhao, Y. (2023). A novel medical image segmentation approach by using a multi-branch segmentation network based on local and global information synchronous learning. Scientific Reports, 13(1), 6762.

16. Dabass, M., & Dabass, J. (2023). An atrous convolved hybrid Seg-Net Model with residual and attention mechanism for gland detection and segmentation in histopathological images. Computers in Biology and Medicine, 155, 106690.

17. Gupta, M., Ghatak, S., Gupta, A., & Mukherjee, A. L. (Eds.). (2022). Artificial Intelligence on Medical Data: Proceedings of International Symposium, ISCMM 2021 (Vol. 37). Singapore: Springer Nature.

18. Onggirawan, C. A., Kho, J. M., Kartiwa, A. P., & Gunawan, A. A. (2023). Systematic literature review: The adaptation of distance learning process during the COVID-19 pandemic using virtual educational spaces in metaverse. Procedia Computer Science, 216, 274–283.

19. Athar, A., Ali, S. M., Mozumder, M. A. I., Ali, S., & Kim, H. C. (2023, February). Applications and possible challenges of healthcare metaverse. In 2023 25th International Conference on Advanced Communication Technology (ICACT) (pp. 328–332). IEEE.

20. Pan, S., Liu, X., Xie, N., & Chong, Y. (2023). EG-TransUNet: A transformer-based U-Net with enhanced and guided models for biomedical image segmentation. BMC bioinformatics, 24(1), 85.

21. Arora, P., Singh, J., Jena, A., Kumar, S., Sardana, V., Sarkar, S., ... & Dutta, U. (2023). Mucosal impedance spectroscopy: For objective real time assessment of mucosal health. Techniques and Innovations in Gastrointestinal Endoscopy, 25(3), 228–235.

22. Xiao, Z., Du, M., Liu, J., Sun, E., Zhang, J., Gong, X., & Chen, Z. (2023, January). EA-UNet based segmentation method for OCT image of uterine cavity. In Photonics (Vol. 10, No. 1, p. 73). Switzerland: MDPI.

23. Jiang, H., Diao, Z., Shi, T., Zhou, Y., Wang, F., Hu, W., ... & Yao, Y. D. (2023). A review of deep learning-based multiple-lesion recognition from medical images: classification, detection and segmentation. Computers in Biology and Medicine, 157, 106726.

24. Bansal, B., Jenipher, V. N., Jain, R., Dilip, R., Kumbhkar, M., Pramanik, S., Roy, S., & Gupta, A. (2022). Big data architecture for network security. In Cyber Security and Network Security (eds S. Pramanik, D. Samanta, M. Vinay and A. Guha). Hoboken, US: Wiley.

25. Gupta, A., Kaushik, D., Garg, M., & Verma, A. (2020). Machine learning model for breast cancer prediction. In Fourth International Conference on I-SMAC (IoT in Social, Mobile, Analytics and Cloud) (I-SMAC), Palladam, India, (pp. 472–477).

26. Talukdar, V., Dhabliya, D., Kumar, B., Talukdar, S. B., Ahamad, S., & Gupta, A. (2022, November). Suspicious activity detection and classification in IoT environment using machine learning approach. In 2022 Seventh International Conference on Parallel, Distributed and Grid Computing (PDGC) (pp. 531–535). IEEE.

27. Veeraiah, V., Gangavathi, P., Ahamad, S., Talukdar, S. B., Gupta, A., & Talukdar, V. (2022, April). Enhancement of meta verse capabilities by IoT integration. In 2022 2nd International Conference on Advance Computing and Innovative Technologies in Engineering (ICACITE) (pp. 1493–1498). IEEE.

28. Gupta, N., Janani, S., Dilip, R., Hosur, R., Chaturvedi, A., & Gupta, A. (2022). Wearable sensors for evaluation over smart home using sequential minimization optimization-based random forest. International Journal of Communication Networks and Information Security, 14(2), 179–188.

29. Keserwani, H., Rastogi, H., Kurniullah, A. Z., Janardan, S. K., Raman, R., Rathod, V. M., & Gupta, A. (2022). Security enhancement by identifying attacks using machine learning for 5G network. International Journal of Communication Networks and Information Security, 14(2), 124-14.

30. Zhan, X., Liu, J., Long, H., Zhu, J., Tang, H., Gou, F., & Wu, J. (2023). An intelligent auxiliary framework for bone malignant tumor lesion segmentation in medical image analysis. Diagnostics, 13(2), 223.

31. Wang, B., Li, Y., Zhou, M., Han, Y., Zhang, M., Gao, Z., ... & Liu, B. F. (2023). Smartphone-based platforms implementing microfluidic detection with image-based artificial intelligence. Nature Communications, 14(1), 1341.

32. Ait Nasser, A., & Akhloufi, M. A. (2023). A review of recent advances in deep learning models for chest disease detection using radiography. Diagnostics, 13(1), 159.

33. Chen, X., Xie, H., Li, Z., Cheng, G., Leng, M., & Wang, F. L. (2023). Information fusion and artificial intelligence for smart healthcare: A bibliometric study. Information Processing & Management, 60(1), 103113

34. Albahri, A. S., Duhaim, A. M., Fadhel, M. A., Alnoor, A., Baqer, N. S., Alzubaidi, L., ... & Deveci, M. (2023). A systematic review of trustworthy and explainable artificial intelligence in healthcare: assessment of quality, bias risk, and data fusion. Information Fusion, 96, 156–191.

35. Chakraborty, S., & Mali, K. (2023). An overview of biomedical image analysis from the deep learning perspective. Research Anthology on Improving Medical Imaging Techniques for Analysis and Intervention, 43–59. 10.4018/978-1-7998-2736-8.ch008

36. Raja, J., Rajeswari, J., & Jayashri, S. (2023). A secured QR pattern based E health care CAD system for CXR image analyzes. Optik, 273, 170344.

37. Ding, W., Abdel-Basset, M., Hawash, H., & Pedrycz, W. (2023). MIC-Net: A deep network for cross-site segmentation of COVID-19 infection in the fog-assisted IoMT. Information Sciences, 623, 20–39.

38. Hussain, M., Koundal, D., & Manhas, J. (2023). Deep learning-based diagnosis of disc degenerative diseases using MRI: A comprehensive review. Computers and Electrical Engineering, 105, 108524.

39. Hartman, T. W., Radichev, E., Ali, H. M., Alaba, M. O., Hoffman, M., Kassa, G., ... & Gnimpieba, E. Z. (2023). BASIN: A semi-automatic workflow, with machine learning segmentation, for objective statistical analysis of biomedical and biofilm image datasets. Journal of Molecular Biology, 435(2), 167895.

40. Morales, C., Yao, J., Rane, T., Edman, R., Choset, H., & Dubrawski, A. (2023). Reslicing ultrasound images for data augmentation and vessel reconstruction. arXiv preprint arXiv:2301.07286. https://doi.org/10.48550/arXiv.2301.07286

41. Zhang, X., Yang, T., Zhao, X., & Yang, A. (2023). Reverse-Net: Few-shot learning with reverse teaching for deformable medical image registration. Applied Sciences, 13(2), 1040.

42. Agrawal, T., & Choudhary, P. (2023). Segmentation and classification on chest radiography: A systematic survey. The Visual Computer, 39(3), 875–913.

43. Wei, L., Liu, H., Xu, J., Shi, L., Shan, Z., Zhao, B., & Gao, Y. (2023). Quantum machine learning in medical image analysis: A Survey. Neurocomputing, 525, 42–53.

44. Ma, J., & Li, W. (2023). Efficient image segmentation of cardiac conditions after basketball using a deep neural network. Electronics, 12(2), 466.

45. Gupta, A., Anand, R., Pandey, D., Sindhwani, N., Wairya, S., Pandey, B. K., & Sharma, M. (2021). Prediction of breast cancer using extremely randomized clustering forests (ERCF) technique: Prediction of breast cancer. International Journal of Distributed Systems and Technologies (IJDST), 12(4), 1–15.

46. Sharma, R., Vashisth, R., & Sindhwani, N. (2023). Study and analysis of classification techniques for specific plant growths. In Advances in Signal Processing, Embedded Systems and IoT: Proceedings of Seventh ICMEET-2022 (pp. 591–605). Singapore: Springer Nature Singapore.

47. Anand, R., Sindhwani, N., & Juneja, S. (2022). Cognitive Internet of Things, its applications, and its challenges: A survey. In Indu Bala, & Kiran Ahuja (Eds.), Harnessing the Internet of Things (IoT) for a Hyper-Connected Smart World (pp. 91–113). New York: Apple Academic Press.

48. Sansanwal, K., Shrivastava, G., Anand, R., & Sharma, K. (2019). Big data analysis and compression for indoor air quality. In Vijender Kumar Solanki, Vicente García Díaz, & J. Paulo Davim (Eds.), Handbook of IoT and Big Data (pp. 1–21). Boca Raton: CRC Press.

49. Anand, Rohit, Juneja, Sapna, Juneja, Abhinav, Jain, Vishal, & Kannan, Ramani (2023). Integration of IoT with Cloud Computing for Smart Applications. 10.1201/9781003319238.

50. Sindhwani, N., Anand, R., Niranjanamurthy, M., Verma, D. C., & Valentina, E. B. (2022). IoT based smart applications. Springer International Publishing AG. https://doi.org/10.1007/978-3-031-04524-0.

4 Health Risk Analysis Based on Embedded IoT Data and Machine Learning

Vivek Veeraiah, K Gurnadha Gupta,
G. Sindhu Madhuri, Ashendra Kumar Saxena,
Raj Sharma, Kumud Saxena, and Ankur Gupta

4.1 INTRODUCTION

4.1.1 METAVERSE AND HEALTHCARE

Clinical interviews and self-reported symptoms are often used to diagnose depression, which can be biased and may not adequately reflect the severity of the disorder. The development of objective and effective techniques for detecting depression risk based on physiological and behavioral measurements is gaining popularity. Actigraphy is a non-invasive approach that entails wearing a gadget that analyzes movement and provides data on activity levels and sleep-wake patterns over time. Actigraphy, which has shown promise as a method for predicting depression risk, has been frequently utilized in research to analyze sleep and circadian rhythms.

Machine learning is a powerful tool for analyzing massive information, and it is increasingly being utilized in healthcare to detect and forecast disease [1–3]. Machine learning algorithms have been applied to actigraphy data in recent years to detect depression risk and build personalized treatment programmes for patients suffering from depression. However, depending on the dataset and machine learning methods used, the performance of these algorithms may vary.

We present a novel approach to detecting depression risk based on machine learning algorithms applied to actigraph data from the Depression dataset in this work. The dataset includes two sets of patients: healthy controls and depressed persons, and it includes demographic and clinical information about the patients, such as age, gender, education, and MADRS scores. We employed five prominent machine learning classifiers to predict each patient's depression state based on their actigraph data. In addition, we used data analysis to identify

DOI: 10.1201/9781003330523-4

significant determinants of depression, such as age, gender, education, marital status, and employment status.

4.1.2 Applications of Machine Learning and IoT in Depression Analysis

- This study's findings can be used to create a screening tool for depression risk in clinical settings.
- Early identification of depression: The machine learning algorithms utilized in this study can assist in the early detection of depression, allowing for appropriate intervention and therapy.
- Personalized treatment plans: Based on demographic and clinical data, the study can help design personalized treatment plans for those at high risk of depression.
- Actigraph data can be collected remotely, enabling continuous monitoring of people suffering from depression and providing clinicians with insights into their activity levels and sleep-wake cycles.
- Telemedicine for depression management: The use of machine learning algorithms can enable depression management telemedicine services, making them more accessible and comfortable for patients.
- The outcomes of the study can be used to inform public health strategies on depression prevention and treatment.
- Research on depression risk factors: The study can reveal major predictors of depression, paving the way for more research on depression risk factors.
- Monitoring the efficacy of depression treatment: Actigraph data can be used to track the efficacy of depression treatment over time, allowing for treatment plan revisions as needed.
- Individuals at risk of depression may benefit from health monitoring tools that provide insights into their activity levels and sleep-wake patterns, as well as alert them to potential risk factors, according to the findings of the study.

4.1.3 Machine Learning and IoT in Healthcare

Research on depression risk factors: The study can reveal major predictors of depression, paving the way for more research on depression risk factors. Monitoring the efficacy of depression treatment where actigraph data can be used to track the efficacy of depression treatment over time, allowing for treatment plan revisions as needed. Individuals at risk of depression may benefit from health monitoring tools that provide insights into their activity levels and sleep-wake patterns, as well as alert them to potential risk factors, according to the findings of the study.

IoT devices, such as actigraphs, can collect data on individuals' activity levels and sleep-wake cycles over time in the context of depression risk assessments. Machine learning algorithms can then be applied to this data to discover depression-related trends and forecast depression risk. Machine learning algorithms can enhance depression risk prediction accuracy, allowing for earlier intervention and therapy. Furthermore, the combination of machine learning and IoT can enable remote monitoring of people suffering from depression, making it more convenient for patients and less burdensome on healthcare providers [4–8]. Actigraph data, for example, can be collected remotely and analyzed using machine learning algorithms to provide insights into people's activity levels and sleep-wake cycles.

ML and the IOT are two powerful technologies that can be utilized to address the complicated challenge of depression risk assessment. Wearables and sensors, for example, may capture vast quantities of data on people's activity levels, sleep-wake patterns, and other physiological markers that can be used to forecast depression risk. Machine learning algorithms can then be applied to this data to detect trends and risk factors for depression.

Furthermore, the application of machine learning and IoT for depression risk assessment can enable remote monitoring and telemedicine. Remote monitoring entails gathering data from IoT devices and analyzing it with machine learning algorithms to gain insights into people's activity levels and sleep-wake cycles. Telemedicine is the use of technology to deliver healthcare remotely, making it more accessible and convenient for patients.

4.1.4 WORKING

The research presents a method for detecting depression risk using machine learning algorithms and actigraph data [9] from the Depression dataset. The dataset includes two sets of patients: healthy controls and depressed persons, and it include demographic and clinical information about the patients, such as age, gender, education, and MADRS scores. We forecast each patient's depression status using several, prominent machine learning classifiers, based on their actigraph data. Patients' actigraph data includes measurements of activity throughout time, with data taken at one-minute intervals. These data are analyzed by machine learning algorithms to discover patterns related to depression. We next analyze the data to discover important determinants of depression, such as age, gender, education, marital status, and employment status. The study's findings can help to design personalized treatment regimens for people who are at high risk of depression based on demographic and clinical data.

The Depression dataset utilized in this work is a great resource for academics interested in analyzing depression risk. The dataset includes actigraph data taken from people suffering from depression and healthy people, as well as demographic and clinical information on the patients. This allows researchers to create machine learning algorithms that predict depression risk based on a variety of variables.

4.2 LITERATURE REVIEW

Lin et al. [10] investigate the feasibility of utilizing machine learning (ML) to predict the start and trajectory of depressive symptoms in home-based older individuals over a seven-year period. The researchers used data from Chinese elderly individuals to test three ML classification algorithms using a 10-fold cross-validation approach. The findings demonstrated that ML approaches can be used to forecast the onset and trajectory of depression symptoms over a 7-year period.

Shusharina et al. [11] covers interesting research areas in ML applications for the prevention and treatment of neurodegenerative and depressive illnesses. The authors emphasize the importance of a cohesive strategy to the use of expanding clinical data that takes into account the needs of medical practitioners, researchers, and government authorities.

Iyortsuun et al. [12] study analyze existing work on the diagnosis of mental diseases. Using machine learning and deep learning technologies, the researchers collected 33 papers on mental health problems. The researchers' difficulties are described, and a list of relevant public datasets is supplied.

Zhang et al. [13] attempted to classify bipolar depression (BD) and unipolar depression (UD) at the individual level by combining machine learning approaches with medical data. The study discovered that reward circuit malfunction can provide new information to aid clinical differential diagnosis, and the classifier achieved excellent classification accuracies in differentiating BD and UD patients.

Sánchez-Carro et al. [14] use supervised learning algorithms or machine learning to diagnose severe depression disorder patients based on immunometabolic and oxidative stress indicators and lifestyle factors. The support vector machine method was applied, and the importance of each immunometabolic and lifestyle variable was used to determine whether a person belonged to the patient group, the melancholic type, or the resistant depression group. The study implies that examining immunometabolic biomarkers and lifestyle factors can aid in deciphering the clinical heterogeneity of major depression.

During the COVID-19 pandemic, Bansal et al. [15] studied the function of digital technology in e-learning, which may have implications for the use of virtual education in healthcare education.

Jain et al. [16] developed a strategy to improve machine learning accuracy during blockchain-based transaction classification, which could have ramifications for safe healthcare data management.

Kaushik et al. [17] investigated the application of machine learning and deep learning in cybersecurity, which is an important part of safeguarding sensitive healthcare data. Gupta et al. [4] reported research on the use of artificial intelligence in medical data processing, which could be used to diagnose and treat depression.

Gupta et al. [18] AI was studied on medical data and can be used in the metaverse to improve healthcare. The symposium covered a wide range of topics related to the use of artificial intelligence on medical data, such as image analysis, pattern recognition, and clinical decision support.

Onggirawan et al. [19] conduct a systematic literature review of previous studies to investigate the potential of Metaverse as a tool for virtual education. The authors discovered that Metaverse has great promise in the sphere of education, but that direction from teachers and parents is still required to prevent its drawbacks.

Athar et al. [20] discuss how the Metaverse, a virtual world that mixes augmented reality and virtual reality, is changing medical communication. The paper summarizes the use of Metaverse in healthcare, as well as its future directions and potential obstacles when implementing Metaverse technology.

TJ et al. [21] suggested hybrid AI-based multimodal depression analysis approach extracts depression severity from video, audio, and text descriptors, which could be effective for automatic depression evaluation and minimizing suicide behaviors.

Chen et al. [22] study externally evaluates three depression symptom clusters, which may aid physicians in selecting the most personalized treatment for depression patients.

Vasha et al. [23] applied machine learning algorithms to social media comment data to predict depression, with the best accuracy attained using a support vector machine (SVM), emphasizing the potential of data mining and ML algorithms in readily recognizing a person's emotions.

Koops et al. [24] conduct an analysis employing a diverse set of linguistic variables, data types, and sources has yielded encouraging findings in diagnosing depression with an accuracy of up to 91%.

Bansal et al. [25] discuss big data architecture for network security. While network security is not directly related to healthcare or depression, it is important for protecting patient data and preventing data breaches that can have negative mental health consequences for patients.

Gupta et al. [26] present a machine learning model for breast cancer prediction. This paper is about healthcare since it discusses early identification and prevention of breast cancer, which can have a significant impact on a patient's mental and emotional well-being.

Talukdar et al. [27] present a machine learning approach for suspicious activity detection and classification in IoT environments. Because IoT devices are increasingly being used in the medical field, detecting suspicious activity can help prevent data breaches, which can have negative consequences for patients' mental health.

Veeraiah et al. [28] propose enhancing metaverse capabilities by integrating IoT. Because metaverse technology has the potential to be used in telemedicine and virtual mental health treatments, this paper is indirectly related to healthcare.

Gupta et al. [29] suggest using wearable sensors to evaluate a smart home framework. This work is relevant to healthcare because wearable sensors can be used for remote patient monitoring, which can improve patients' mental and emotional well-being.

Keserwani et al. [30] propose identifying threats using machine learning for 5 G network security. This study, like paper 1, is indirectly related to healthcare since network security is vital for preserving patient data and preventing data breaches, which can have significant mental health repercussions for patients.

Mijwil et al. [31] propose a deep learning model based on MobileNetV1 for reliable brain tumor classification. Using deep learning and a feature-based confidence metric, Haghpanah et al. [32] develop a real-time hand rubbing quality estimate method. Gao et al. [33] use artificial intelligence to address the problem of biological data inequality. Bao et al. [34] offer a high-throughput precision MRI evaluation system for improving preoperative prostate cancer Gleason grade prediction. Yousuf and Kadri [35] use low-cost embedded sensors and the isolation forest algorithm to create a ubiquitous architecture for wheelchair fall anomaly detection. Using resource-constrained embedded systems at the edge, Jeddi et al. [36] offer a deep learning model for post-hurricane reconnaissance of power infrastructure. Raoofi et al. [37] present a detailed assessment of machine learning-based battery status estimate methodologies for battery management.

Purnomo et al. [38] propose a deep learning-based method for monitoring Indonesian web news in order to detect COVID-19 events. Kumar et al. [39] describe a machine learning classification technique for e-healthcare cardiac disease diagnosis. Liu and Chou [40] provide a Bayesian-optimized deep learning model for segmenting deterioration patterns beneath bridge decking captured by unmanned aerial vehicle. Shuzan et al. [41] use 3D-GRF signals to create a machine learning-based categorization system for healthy and impaired gaits. Jujjavarapu et al. [42] offer a multimodal deep learning model for predicting decompression surgery using structured and unstructured health data from patients. Balch et al. [43] create a machine learning-enabled automated approach for forecasting post-operative problems.

4.3   PROBLEM STATEMENTS

This study addresses the topic of detecting and analyzing depression using embedded IoT data and machine learning approaches. The goal is to use data obtained from wearable devices to construct an autonomous system for diagnosing depression and analyzing its health hazards, as well as to compare the performance of several classifiers in the detection process.

4.4   PROPOSED WORK

The paper's planned objective is to analyze the health risk of depression using embedded IoT data and machine learning. The Depression Dataset will be used by the authors to automatically detect a person's depression condition using several machine learning classifiers such as SVM and Gaussian Naive Bayes. The study's goal is to create an accurate and dependable depression risk analysis system based on IoT and ML that can help with early detection and prevention of depression. Figures 4.1–4.4 provide some visualizations regarding the data and its possessing considering all the various attributes.

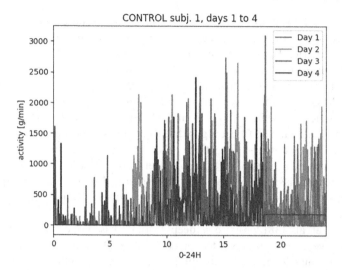

FIGURE 4.1   Time series analysis of daily activities for control subject.

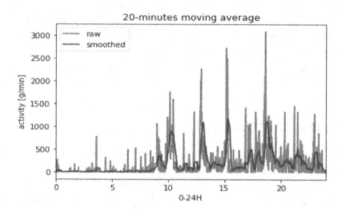

FIGURE 4.2   Time series analysis of 20 mins moving average.

4.5   RESULTS AND DISCUSSION

The findings of a comprehensive literature review indicate that Metaverse technology has the ability to improve the learning process in the educational sphere. According to survey results, students appreciate using Metaverse as learning tool and comprehend various lessons better while using Metaverse than when using traditional learning techniques. However, few studies have been conducted to determine which subjects to teach using Metaverse. The Metaverse has received considerable attention in the healthcare industry, and it is regarded as a game-changer due to its potential to address a wide range of issues.

The Metaverse has gained substantial attention in the healthcare industry because of its ability to solve a variety of issues, including virtual health

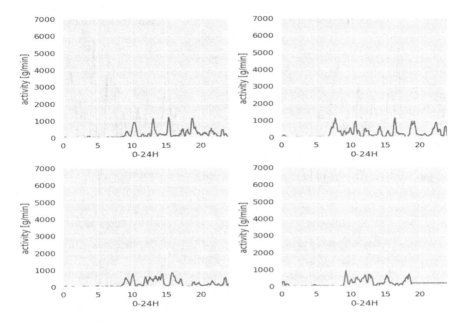

FIGURE 4.3   Activity of different sequences of the data in 24 hours.

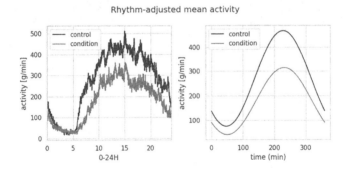

FIGURE 4.4   Rhythm adjusted mean activity.

and fitness, mental health, and health access without geographical limits. The convergence and integration of technologies in the Metaverse will help to reimagine laboratory medicine services through augmented services, user experiences, efficiency, and personalized care. However, incorporating the Metaverse into healthcare applications presents a number of challenges, including data privacy and security concerns, ethical concerns, and the requirement for trained healthcare professionals to manage the technology. Figure 4.5 shows time series analysis and Table 4.1 and Figure 4.6 show the results. Figure 4.7 shows the results of comarison w.r.t. accuracy, precision, recall and F1-score.

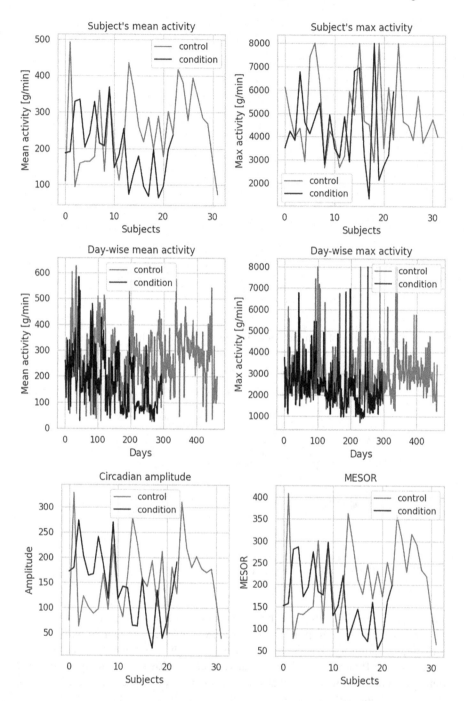

FIGURE 4.5 Time series analysis of various different features.

TABLE 4.1
Performance of Machine Learning Models

Model	Accuracy	Precision	Recall	F1 - Score
Support Vector Machine	0.73	0.70	0.61	0.65
Random Forest	0.71	0.71	0.53	0.61
K-Nearest Neighbors	0.60	0.52	0.70	0.60
Logistic Regression	0.58	0.49	0.48	0.49
Gaussian Naive Bayes	0.70	0.62	0.70	0.66

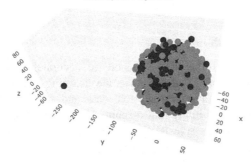

FIGURE 4.6   Data space and feature space projections.

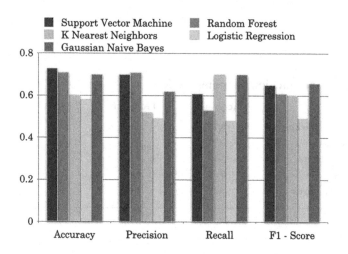

FIGURE 4.7   Comparison of accuracy chart.

4.6   CONCLUSIONS

The study demonstrated that it is possible to accurately diagnose a person's depression condition using various machine learning methods based on the proposed work employing embedded IoT data and machine learning [44–46]. The findings of this study imply that machine learning algorithms can be utilized to predict a person's depressive level using embedded IoT data. However, more research is needed to determine the applicability of the proposed strategy to diverse demographics and circumstances. Overall, the proposed method has the potential to be employed as a depression screening tool in healthcare settings.

4.7   FUTURE SCOPE

The suggested work's future scope includes investigating additional data aspects to improve the accuracy of depression identification. Furthermore, the proposed model can be extended to collect real-time data from embedded devices, allowing for continuous monitoring of depression symptoms [47,48]. Furthermore, the model is applicable to other mental health disorders such as anxiety, bipolar disorder, and schizophrenia. Finally, the model can be linked into a personal mobile application that can enable early detection and timely intervention for people suffering from depression [49,50].

REFERENCES

1. Anand, R., Sindhwani, N., & Juneja, S. (2022). Cognitive Internet of Things, its applications, and its challenges: A survey. In Indu Bala, & Kiran Ahuja (Eds.), Harnessing the Internet of Things (IoT) for a Hyper-Connected Smart World (pp. 91–113). New York: Apple Academic Press.

2. Gupta, A., Anand, R., Pandey, D., Sindhwani, N., Wairya, S., Pandey, B. K., & Sharma, M. (2021). Prediction of breast cancer using extremely randomized clustering forests (ERCF) technique: Prediction of breast cancer. International Journal of Distributed Systems and Technologies (IJDST), 12(4), 1–15.

3. Arora, S., Sharma, S., & Anand, R. (2022, July). A survey on UWB textile antenna for wireless body area network (WBAN) applications. In Artificial Intelligence on Medical Data: Proceedings of International Symposium, ISCMM 2021 (pp. 173–183). Singapore: Springer Nature Singapore.

4. Anand, R., Daniel, A. V., Fred, A. L., Jaiswal, T., Juneja, S., Juneja, A., & Gupta, A. (2023). Building integrated systems for healthcare considering mobile computing and IoT. In Integration of IoT with Cloud Computing for Smart Applications (pp. 203–225). New York: Chapman and Hall/CRC Press.

5. Sindhwani, N., Rana, A., & Chaudhary, A. (2021, September). Breast cancer detection using machine learning algorithms. In 2021 9th International Conference on Reliability, Infocom Technologies and Optimization (Trends and Future Directions) (ICRITO) (pp. 1–5). IEEE.

6. Jain, N., Chaudhary, A., Sindhwani, N., & Rana, A. (2021, September). Applications of wearable devices in IoT. In 2021 9th International Conference on Reliability, Infocom Technologies and Optimization (Trends and Future Directions) (ICRITO) (pp. 1–4). IEEE.

7. Sharma, G., Nehra, N., Dahiya, A., Sindhwani, N., & Singh, P. (2022). Automatic heart-rate measurement using facial video. In Networking Technologies in Smart Healthcare (pp. 289–307). Boca Raton: CRC Press.

8. Sansanwal, K., Shrivastava, G., Anand, R., & Sharma, K. (2019). Big data analysis and compression for indoor air quality. In Vijender Kumar Solanki, Vicente García Díaz, & J. Paulo Davim (Eds.), Handbook of IoT and Big Data (1–21). https://doi.org/10.1201/9780429053290

9. Garcia-Ceja, E., Riegler, M., Jakobsen, P., Tørresen, J., Nordgreen, T., Oedegaard, K., Fasmer, O. B. (2018). Depresjon: A motor activity database of depression episodes in unipolar and bipolar patients. In MMSys'18 Proceedings of the 9th ACM on Multimedia Systems Conference, Amsterdam, The Netherlands, June 12–15. ACM.

10. Lin, S., Wu, Y., He, L., & Fang, Y. (2023). Prediction of depressive symptoms onset and long-term trajectories in home-based older adults using machine learning techniques. Aging & Mental Health, 27(1), 8–17.

11. Shusharina, N., Yukhnenko, D., Botman, S., Sapunov, V., Savinov, V., Kamyshov, G., … & Voznyuk, I. (2023). Modern methods of diagnostics and treatment of neurodegenerative diseases and depression. Diagnostics, 13(3), 573.

12. Iyortsuun, N. K., Kim, S. H., Jhon, M., Yang, H. J., & Pant, S. (2023, January). A review of machine learning and deep learning approaches on mental health diagnosis. In Healthcare (Vol. 11, No. 3, p. 285). Switzerland: Multidisciplinary Digital Publishing Institute.

13. Zhang, A., Qiao, D., Wang, Y., Yang, C., Wang, Y., Sun, N., … & Zhang, K. (2023). Distinguishing between bipolar depression and unipolar depression based on the reward circuit activities and clinical characteristics: A machine learning analysis. Journal of Affective Disorders, 327, 46–53.

14. Sánchez-Carro, Y., de la Torre-Luque, A., Leal-Leturia, I., Salvat-Pujol, N., Massaneda, C., de Arriba-Arnau, A., … & López-García, P. (2023). Importance of immunometabolic markers for the classification of patients with major depressive disorder using machine learning. Progress in Neuro-Psychopharmacology and Biological Psychiatry, 121, 110674.

15. Bansal, R., Gupta, A., Singh, R., & Nassa, V. K. (2021, July). Role and impact of digital technologies in E-learning amidst COVID-19 pandemic. 2021 Fourth International Conference on Computational Intelligence and Communication Technologies (CCICT) (pp. 194–202). IEEE.

16. Jain, V., Beram, S. M., Talukdar, V., Patil, T., Dhabliya, D., & Gupta, A. (2022, November). Accuracy enhancement in machine learning during blockchain based transaction classification. In 2022 Seventh International Conference on Parallel, Distributed and Grid Computing (PDGC) (pp. 536–540). IEEE.

17. Kaushik, D., Garg, M., Annu, & Gupta, A.; Sabyasachi Pramanik. (2022). Utilizing machine learning and deep learning in cybersecurity: An innovative approach. Cyber Security and Digital Forensics: Challenges and Future Trends (pp. 271–293). Hoboken, New Jersey: Wiley.

18. Gupta, M., Ghatak, S., Gupta, A., & Mukherjee, A. L. (Eds.). (2022). Artificial Intelligence on Medical Data: Proceedings of International Symposium, ISCMM 2021 (Vol. 37). Singapore: Springer Nature.

19. Onggirawan, C. A., Kho, J. M., Kartiwa, A. P., & Gunawan, A. A. (2023). Systematic literature review: The adaptation of distance learning process during the COVID-19 pandemic using virtual educational spaces in metaverse. Procedia Computer Science, 216, 274–283.

20. Athar, A., Ali, S. M., Mozumder, M. A. I., Ali, S., & Kim, H. C. (2023, February). Applications and possible challenges of healthcare metaverse. In 2023 25th International Conference on Advanced Communication Technology (ICACT) (pp. 328–332). IEEE.

21. Tj, S. J., Jacob, I. J., & Mandava, A. K. (2023). D-ResNet-PVKELM: Deep neural network and paragraph vector based kernel extreme machine learning model for multimodal depression analysis. Multimedia Tools and Applications, 1–32. https://doi.org/10.1007/s11042-023-14351-y

22. Chen, Y., Stewart, J. W., Ge, J., Cheng, B., Chekroud, A., & Hellerstein, D. J. (2023). Personalized symptom clusters that predict depression treatment outcomes: A replication of machine learning methods. Journal of Affective Disorders Reports, 11, 100470.

23. Vasha, Z. N., Sharma, B., Esha, I. J., Al Nahian, J., & Polin, J. A. (2023). Depression detection in social media comments data using machine learning algorithms. Bulletin of Electrical Engineering and Informatics, 12(2), 987–996.

24. Koops, S., Brederoo, S. G., de Boer, J. N., Nadema, F. G., Voppel, A. E., & Sommer, I. E. (2023). Speech as a biomarker for depression. CNS & Neurological Disorders-Drug Targets (Formerly Current Drug Targets-CNS & Neurological Disorders), 22(2), 152–160.

25. Bansal, B., Jenipher, V. N., Jain, R., Dilip, R., Kumbhkar, M., Pramanik, S., Roy, S. and Gupta, A. (2022). Big data architecture for network security. In Cyber Security and Network Security (eds S. Pramanik, D. Samanta, M. Vinay and A. Guha). US: Wiley.

26. Gupta, A., Kaushik, D., Garg, M., & Verma,A. (2020). Machine learning model for breast cancer prediction. In Fourth International Conference on I-SMAC (IoT in Social, Mobile, Analytics and Cloud) (I-SMAC), Palladam, India, (pp. 472–477).

27. Talukdar, V., Dhabliya, D., Kumar, B., Talukdar, S. B., Ahamad, S., & Gupta, A. (2022, November). Suspicious activity detection and classification in IoT environment using machine learning approach. In 2022 Seventh International Conference on Parallel, Distributed and Grid Computing (PDGC) (pp. 531–535). IEEE.

28. Veeraiah, V., Gangavathi, P., Ahamad, S., Talukdar, S. B., Gupta, A., & Talukdar, V. (2022, April). Enhancement of meta verse capabilities by IoT integration. In 2022 2nd International Conference on Advance Computing and Innovative Technologies in Engineering (ICACITE) (pp. 1493–1498). IEEE.

29. Gupta, N., Janani, S., Dilip, R., Hosur, R., Chaturvedi, A., & Gupta, A. (2022). Wearable sensors for evaluation over smart home using sequential minimization optimization-based random forest. International Journal of Communication Networks and Information Security, 14(2), 179–188.

30. Keserwani, H., Rastogi, H., Kurniullah, A. Z., Janardan, S. K., Raman, R., Rathod, V. M., & Gupta, A. (2022). Security enhancement by identifying attacks using machine learning for 5G network. International Journal of Communication Networks and Information Security, 14(2), 124–141.

31. Mijwil, M. M., Doshi, R., Hiran, K. K., Unogwu, O. J., & Bala, I. (2023). MobileNetV1-based deep learning model for accurate brain tumor classification. Mesopotamian Journal of Computer Science, 2023, 32–41.

32. Haghpanah, M. A., Vali, S., Torkamani, A. M., Masouleh, M. T., Kalhor, A., & Sarraf, E. A. (2023). Real-time hand rubbing quality estimation using deep learning enhanced by separation index and feature-based confidence metric. Expert Systems with Applications, 218, 119588.

33. Gao, Y., Sharma, T., & Cui, Y. (2023). Addressing the challenge of biomedical data inequality: An artificial intelligence perspective. Annual Review of Biomedical Data Science, 6. 10.1146/annurev-biodatasci-020722-020704

34. Bao, J., Hou, Y., Qin, L., Zhi, R., Wang, X. M., Shi, H. B., ... & Zhang, Y. D. (2023). High-throughput precision MRI assessment with integrated stack-ensemble deep learning can enhance the preoperative prediction of prostate cancer Gleason grade. British Journal of Cancer, 128, 1–11.

35. Yousuf, S., & Kadri, M. B. (2023). A ubiquitous architecture for wheelchair fall anomaly detection using low-cost embedded sensors and isolation forest algorithm. Computers and Electrical Engineering, 105, 108518.

36. Jeddi, A. B., Shafieezadeh, A., & Nateghi, R. (2023). PDP-CNN: A Deep Learning Model for Post-hurricane Reconnaissance of Electricity Infrastructure on Resource-constrained Embedded Systems at the Edge. IEEE Transactions on Instrumentation and Measurement.

37. Raoofi, T., & Yildiz, M. (2023). Comprehensive review of battery state estimation strategies using machine learning for battery management systems of aircraft propulsion batteries. Journal of Energy Storage, 59, 106486.

38. Purnomo, H. K., Arisal, A., Rozie, A. F., Nugraheni, E., Riswantini, D., Suwarningsih, W., ... & Purwarianti, A. (2023). Monitoring Indonesian online news for COVID-19 event detection using deep learning. International Journal of Electrical and Computer Engineering, 13(1), 957

39. Kumar, S., Srivastava, S., Mongia, S., & Amsa, M. (2023). Diagnosis of heart disease using machine learning classification technique in E-healthcare. Journal of Pharmaceutical Negative Results, 14(2), 656–664.

40. Liu, C. Y., & Chou, J. S. (2023). Bayesian-optimized deep learning model to segment deterioration patterns underneath bridge decks photographed by unmanned aerial vehicle. Automation in Construction, 146, 104666

41. Shuzan, M. N. I., Chowdhury, M. E., Reaz, M. B. I., Khandakar, A., Abir, F. F., Faisal, M. A. A., ... & Alhatou, M. (2023). Machine learning-based classification of healthy and impaired gaits using 3D-GRF signals. Biomedical Signal Processing and Control, 81, 104448.

42. Jujjavarapu, C., Suri, P., Pejaver, V., Friedly, J., Gold, L. S., Meier, E., ... & Jarvik, J. G. (2023). Predicting decompression surgery by applying multimodal deep learning to patients' structured and unstructured health data. BMC Medical Informatics and Decision Making, 23(1), 2.

43. Balch, J. A., Ruppert, M. M., Shickel, B., Ozrazgat-Baslanti, T., Tighe, P. J., Efron, P. A., ... & Loftus, T. J. (2023). Building an automated machine learning-enabled platform for predicting post-operative complications. Physiological Measurement. 10.1088/1361-6579/acb4db

44. Juneja, S., Juneja, A., & Anand, R. (2019). Role of big data as a tool for improving sustainability for the betterment of quality of life in metro cities. International Journal of Control and Automation, 12, 553–557.

45. Gupta, A., Goyal, B., Dogra, A., & Anand, R. (2022). Proximity coupled antenna with stable performance and high body antenna isolation for IoT-based devices. In Communication, Software and Networks: Proceedings of INDIA 2022 (pp. 591–600). Singapore: Springer Nature Singapore.

46. Sharma, S., Rattan, R., Goyal, B., Dogra, A., & Anand, R. (2022). Microscopic and ultrasonic super-resolution for accurate diagnosis and treatment planning. In Communication, Software and Networks: Proceedings of INDIA 2022 (pp. 601–611). Singapore: Springer Nature Singapore.

47. Tripathi, A., Sindhwani, N., Anand, R., & Dahiya, A. (2022). Role of IoT in smart homes and smart cities: Challenges, benefits, and applications. In IoT Based Smart Applications (pp. 199–217). Cham: Springer International Publishing.

48. Sindhwani, N., Sasi, G., & Meivel, S. (2022, October). Fuzzy acceptance analysis of impact of glaucoma and diabetic retinopathy using confusion matrix. In 2022 10th International Conference on Reliability, Infocom Technologies and Optimization (Trends and Future Directions)(ICRITO) (pp. 1–5). IEEE.

49. Anand, Rohit, Juneja, Sapna, Juneja, Abhinav, Jain, Vishal, & Kannan, Ramani (2023). Integration of IoT with Cloud Computing for Smart Applications. 10.1201/9781003319238.

50. Sindhwani, N., Anand, R., Niranjanamurthy, M., Verma, D. C., & Valentina, E. B. (2022). IoT based smart applications. Springer International Publishing AG. https://doi.org/10.1007/978-3-031-04524-0.

5 A Comparison and Analysis of Risk Based on IoT and Healthcare

*Vivek Veeraiah, N. Beemkumar, Priyank Singhal,
Ashutosh Kr. Singh, Sumaiya Ansari, Shalini Dixit,
and Dharmesh Dhabliya*

5.1 INTRODUCTION

5.1.1 IoT and Healthcare Based Depression

With the increased usage of the Internet of Things (IoT) in healthcare, data collected by medical devices, wearable sensors, and patient health records has increased. This information can be utilized to enhance healthcare outcomes and lower expenses. However, it introduces new threats to data security and privacy [1–4]. In this study, we compare the risk associated with IoT in healthcare to the risk associated with traditional healthcare systems. We use a dataset containing daily activity levels of patients. On this dataset, we apply data analytics to uncover patterns and trends that can be used to assess the risk. We evaluate the danger of using IoT to the risk of using traditional healthcare systems based on criteria such as data security, privacy, and reliability.

5.1.2 Applications of IoT Sensor Data and Visualisations

Numerous disciplines have seen the dominance of AI, including but not limited to:

- Smart houses: Homeowners may remotely monitor and control their houses using IoT-enabled equipment such as smart thermostats, lighting systems, and security systems, making them more energy-efficient and secure.
- Industrial Automation: By monitoring machinery, managing inventory, and automating workflows, IoT can help optimize industrial processes and decrease costs.
- Agriculture: Using IoT sensors to monitor soil conditions, weather patterns, and plant health, farmers can optimize agricultural yields and minimize wastage.
- IoT devices in healthcare can assist patients and healthcare practitioners in remotely monitoring health conditions, managing chronic diseases, and improving overall patient outcomes.

DOI: 10.1201/9781003330523-5

- Transportation: Internet of Things sensors and telematics systems can be used to monitor vehicle performance, optimize logistics, and increase driver safety.
- Energy Management: By monitoring energy consumption and automatically altering settings to reduce waste, IoT can assist optimize energy usage.
- IoT sensors in retail can be used to track inventory, monitor shopper behavior, and optimize store layouts to increase sales and customer happiness.
- IoT sensors and data analytics can be used to optimize traffic flow, monitor air quality, and improve overall city services in smart cities.
- Sports and Fitness: Internet of Things-enabled wearables and sensors can be used to measure fitness and performance indicators, assisting athletes and coaches in optimizing training and improving outcomes.

5.1.3 ANALYSIS OF DEPRESSION BASED ON IoT SENSORS DATA

Depression is a frequent and dangerous mental illness that affects a vast number of people all over the world. Depression risk factors can be complex and multifaceted, encompassing genetic, environmental, and behavioral variables. Using data analytics to analyze the factors linked with depression risk and design personalized interventions for people is one strategy to address the risk of depression. The dataset offered comprises information on a group of people's physical activity levels over time. It is feasible to uncover trends in physical activity levels that are connected with depression risk by analyzing this data [5]. Individuals who routinely engage in low levels of physical activity, for example, may be more vulnerable to depression than those who engage in moderate or high levels of activity. Changes in exercise levels throughout time may potentially have a role in predicting depression risk.

The Internet of Things and healthcare technology have transformed the way we approach healthcare [6–8]. IoT technologies can be used to continuously monitor physical activity levels and other health-related metrics, allowing healthcare providers to spot patterns and trends that may be connected with depression risk. Wearable technologies, for example, can be used to track activity levels, sleep patterns, and other health indicators, which can then be analyzed to determine potential risk factors for depression. It is possible to build personalized therapies for persons at risk of depression by combining data analytics with IoT and healthcare technology. Individuals with low levels of physical activity, for example, may benefit from interventions aimed at increasing activity levels, such as exercise programmes or lifestyle adjustments.

5.1.4 APPROACHES FOR DATA ANALYTICS

We have a dataset with the following columns for persons with depression: date, n, n_non_zero, mean_act, q75_act, q90_act, q95_act, q99_act, and max_act. These columns, in order, reflect the date, the number of observations, the number of non-zero observations, the mean activity, the activity at the 75th, 90th, 95th, and 99th percentiles, and the highest activity. We have five different files for the control group, each with the following columns: date, n, mean_act, q99_act, and max_act. These columns reflect the date, number of observations, mean activity, 99th percentile activity, and highest activity, in that order. Use histograms, box plots, or density plots to visualise the distribution of activity levels for both groups. This can aid in identifying differences or similarities between the two groups' patterns of activity levels. Calculate summary statistics such as mean, median, and standard deviation for both groups' activity levels. This can provide information on the central tendency and distribution of activity levels for each group. To evaluate whether there are significant variations in activity levels between the two groups, use statistical tests such as t-tests or ANOVA [9]. This can assist determine whether the activity levels of people suffering from depression differ considerably from those of the control group.

5.2   LITERATURE SURVEY

The authors in [10] presented an overview of research contributions in multimodal interaction and Internet of Things applications. The emphasis is on recent cutting-edge breakthroughs in tackling scalability, security, privacy, and portability issues in multimodal interaction systems and IoT applications. Further [11] offered a novel method for detecting depression that integrates real-time Mobile Crowd Sensing (MCS) and task-based processes with machine learning classifiers such as Logistic Regression and Support Vector Machines (SVM). The results show that integrating information from various modalities outperforms any single modality, with SVM having the highest accuracy of 86%. In [12], there have been used IoT and fuzzy set theory of type-2 and propose a semantic framework for healthcare based mental health conditions. The authors in [13] identified the most frequent mental disorders and their incidence rates in cities, as well as methods for combining multimodal aspects for detecting and forecasting mental concerns like anxiety. The reference [14] suggested a leveraging smartphone sensing capabilities to predict depression severity using federated learning. A deep neural network model is created and evaluated in both centralized and federated learning environments, with encouraging results demonstrating federated learning's potential. The authors in [15] highlighted the potential of wearables for self-care, monitoring, and diagnosis of mental health illnesses such as anxiety and depression, which are at an all-time high.

During the COVID-19 epidemic, the authors in [16] investigated the role and impact of digital technology in e-learning. Because mental health has suffered as a result of the pandemic, the study could be tied to IoT and healthcare by looking into how e-learning platforms can assist mental health and well-being through data visualisation and analysis. By examining the potential of blockchain in securely storing and exchanging mental health data, the authors in [17] improved the accuracy of machine learning during blockchain-based transaction classification, which could be relevant to IoT and healthcare. This has the potential to improve the analysis and prediction of depression and other mental health disorders. By investigating the potential of cybersecurity in preserving sensitive medical and mental health data, the authors in [18] highlighted the use of machine learning and deep learning in cybersecurity, which could be relevant to healthcare and IoT. This may result in improved data visualisation and analysis of depression and other mental health disorders. [19] investigated how artificial intelligence might enhance the study and prediction of depression and other mental health issues through data visualisation and analysis, which could be tied to IoT and healthcare. The authors in [20] conducted a systematic review of the literature on the adaptation of distance learning in a pandemic in the metaverse, which could potentially be related to IoT and healthcare by investigating how virtual environments can be used to support mental health and well-being through data visualisation and analysis. In [21], there has been explored how virtual environments might be used to enhance mental health and well-being through data visualisation and analysis to examine the uses and potential issues of healthcare metaverse, which could be related to IoT and healthcare. The reference [22] employed machine learning models to predict depression based on brain imaging data, obtaining up to 95.74% accuracy with the densenet121 model, indicating the possibility for a multi-component model to improve accuracy. Data visualisation and analysis could aid in the identification of patterns and the improvement of model accuracy.

The authors in [23] explored the growing relevance of Internet of Things (IoT) technology in healthcare, notably in connecting doctors and patients via portable health monitoring devices. They also emphasized the significance of data security in the healthcare industry and recommend blockchain technology as a solution for boosting data management operations while safeguarding privacy. The reference [24] offered a big data architecture for network security that might be used to secure medical data in IoT devices in the healthcare area. [25] offered a machine learning approach for breast cancer prediction that requires massive dataset analysis. The visualisation and analysis of the collection could aid in the identification of patterns and traits suggestive of breast cancer, perhaps enhancing diagnosis. [26] proposed a machine learning-based solution for detecting and classifying suspicious behavior in IoT environments. This method may be useful in recognizing anomalous behavior in patients with mental health disorders, allowing healthcare workers to intervene and provide needed support. Further, [27] proposed combining IoT with metaverse capabilities, which could have uses in mental health monitoring and treatment, such as employing virtual settings to imitate therapy sessions or track patients' behavior. The authors in [28] proposed monitoring patients with mental health disorders using wearable sensors in a smart home scenario. The information gathered by these sensors might be analyzed and visualised to spot trends and changes in behavior, allowing healthcare practitioners to deliver personalized care. [29] presented a machine learning-based technique for detecting 5 G network assaults. This approach could be applied to IoT devices in the healthcare area to assure medical data security and patient privacy.

5.3   PROBLEM STATEMENT

Our purpose is to assess and contrast the risks related with IoT and healthcare [30–33]. The problem statement centers around the expanding importance of IoT and healthcare, as well as the possible hazards and obstacles associated with their use. The authors intend to identify and compare the risks related with IoT and healthcare to gain understanding of the possible impact of these risks on society and the need to minimize them.

5.4   PROPOSED WORK

The dataset provided comprises information regarding patients' activity levels throughout a specific time period. There are also four other control group datasets available for comparison. To begin performing data analytics on this dataset, we can compute some basic statistics such as mean, median, maximum, and minimum activity levels for each day. For each day, we may also compute the quartiles (25th, 50th, and 75th percentiles) and higher percentiles (90th and 99th). These statistics can be visualised using line graphs to demonstrate the trend of activity levels over time. We can also compare the patients' activity levels to those of the control groups to see whether there are any statistically significant differences.

5.5   RESULTS AND DISCUSSION

The visualisations offered in the study are intended to aid in the exploration and analysis of data obtained from IoT devices and the healthcare system. These visualisations aid in the identification of patterns, trends, and interactions within data, which can provide insights into the patients' health and risk level. The scatter plots compare distinct groups based on daily activity mean and coefficient of variation (CV). This analysis can aid in identifying discrepancies across groups as well as patterns that may contribute to disparities in health outcomes. The scatter plot with group color coding aids in easily visualising these distinctions where the point plot and box plot depict the distribution of the DeltaMADRS score in the condition group based on the various subgroups. This analysis can help to discover any changes in MADRS score change between subgroups, which can provide insights into the factors that may influence therapy outcome. The correlation matrix heatmap aids in the identification of any association between the various numerical features. This investigation can shed light on the factors that may be linked to the patient's health and risk level.

The count plots depict the distribution of categorical features within the condition group. This analysis can assist in identifying any changes in the distribution of features between subgroups, which can provide insights into the factors that may influence treatment outcome. Finally, the box plots illustrate the distribution of numerical features in the condition group. This study can assist in identifying any changes in the distribution of features between subgroups and can provide insights into the elements that may be connected with the patient's health status and risk level. Figures 5.1–5.7 provide several visualisations, Figures 5.8–5.14 provide box plots, scatter plots and plots based

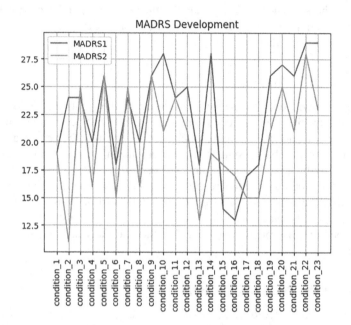

FIGURE 5.1   MADRS development analysis of different parts of dataset.

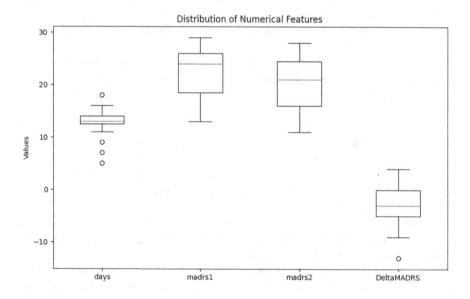

FIGURE 5.2   A box plot showing distributions of numerical features.

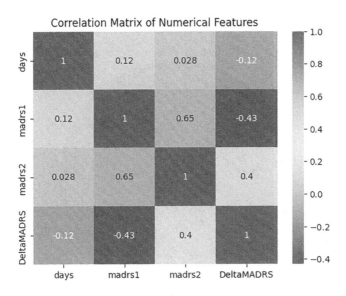

FIGURE 5.3   A heatmap showing correlation matrixes.

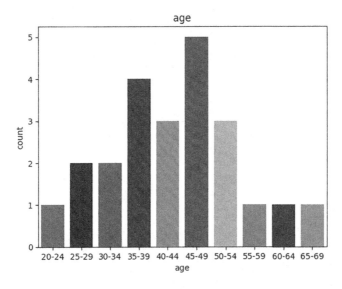

FIGURE 5.4   A bar chart showing age vs count.

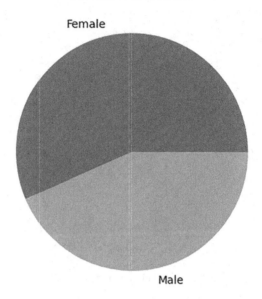

FIGURE 5.5 A pie chart for gender distribution.

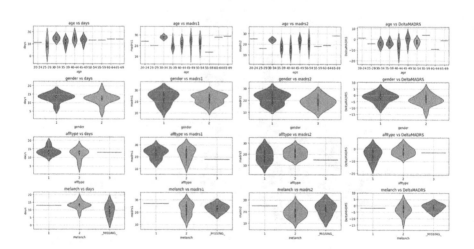

FIGURE 5.6 Boiling plots showing different features of dataset.

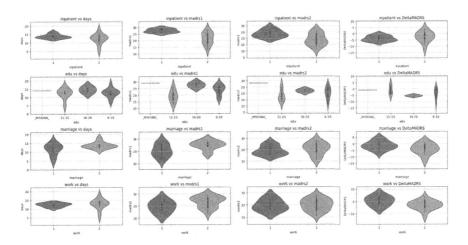

FIGURE 5.7 Boiling plots showing different features of dataset-2.

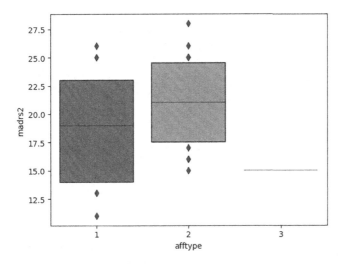

FIGURE 5.8 A box plot MADRS2 based features.

on time series based analysis. Figures 5.15 and 5.16 provide scatter plots of general dataset used.

Various techniques and applications of the Internet of Things (IoT) and blockchain technology in healthcare, particularly in medical image monitoring, health monitoring and diagnosis systems, pandemic management, and

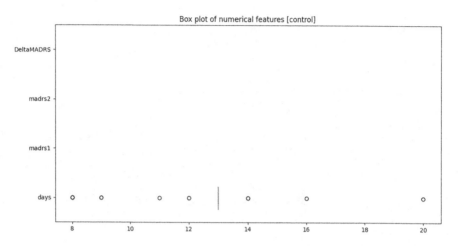

FIGURE 5.9   A box plot of numerical features.

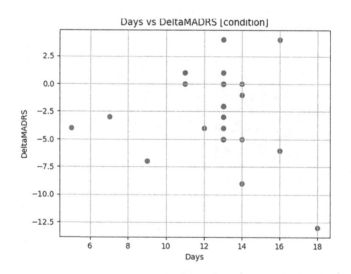

FIGURE 5.10   A scatter plot showing days vs deltaMADRS condition.

decentralized healthcare frameworks [34–38]. The papers emphasize these technologies' potential for improving healthcare services, resolving security problems, and promoting efficient decision-making procedures [39,40]. Furthermore, other studies explore the obstacles and potential trends linked

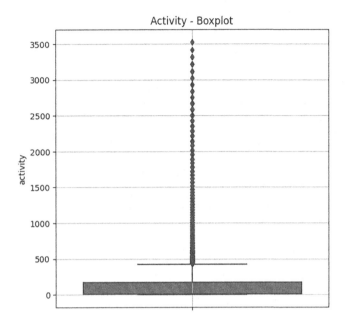

FIGURE 5.11   A box plot showing activity values.

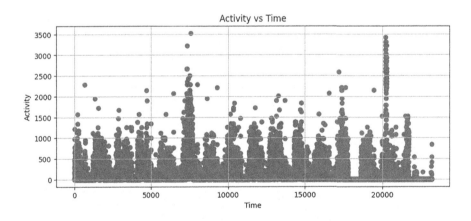

FIGURE 5.12   Time series for activity vs time.

with IoT and blockchain technology deployment in healthcare. Based on the insights provided by these papers, a comparison and study of the risk-based approach in healthcare could provide important information for healthcare practitioners, policymakers, and researchers in the field [41–43].

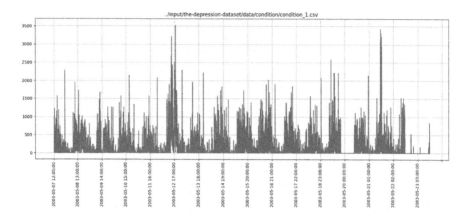

FIGURE 5.13 Time series analysis of condition 1.

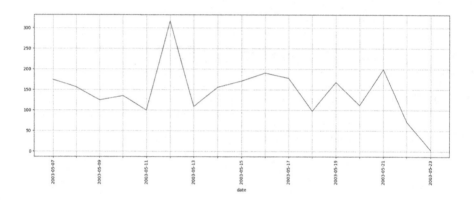

FIGURE 5.14 Plot showing time series based data for every 2 days.

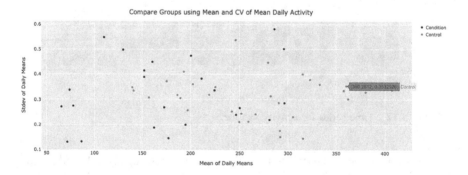

FIGURE 5.15 Scatter plot for compare groups using mean daily activities.

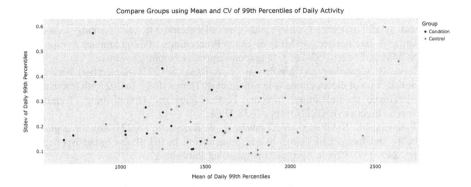

FIGURE 5.16   Scatter plot for compare groups using daily percentile activities.

5.6   CONCLUSIONS

Finally, the article emphasizes the potential of IoT sensors in delivering real-time and continuous health monitoring to improve overall patient care. Data analysis from IoT sensors and the healthcare system provides insights into the aspects that may influence the patient's health status and risk level. The visualisations described in the research provide a thorough analysis of the data, which can assist healthcare providers in making educated decisions about their patients' treatment. In addition, the report emphasizes the need of adding IoT sensors into healthcare systems in order to enhance patient outcomes and lower healthcare costs [44]. Overall, the paper's findings show the potential of IoT sensors in healthcare [45].

5.7   FUTURE SCOPE

One possibility is to expand the study to a bigger population size in order to improve the generalizability of the findings. Furthermore, additional investigation into the relationship between IoT sensor data and clinical data may provide insights into the accuracy and validity of employing IoT sensors to track mental health. Further research into the elements that may influence the change in MADRS scores such as medication and therapy that could also provide significant insights into depression treatments. Finally, using machine learning algorithms to analyze data acquired from IoT sensors could provide a more accurate and automated approach of discovering patterns and trends within data, perhaps improving depression diagnosis and therapy.

REFERENCES

1. Gupta, A., Srivastava, A., & Anand, R. (2019). Cost-effective smart home automation using Internet of Things. Journal of Communication Engineering & Systems, 9(2), 1–6.

2. Gupta, A., Asad, A., Meena, L., & Anand, R. (2022, July). IoT and RFID-based smart card system integrated with health care, electricity, QR and banking sectors. In Artificial Intelligence on Medical Data: Proceedings of International Symposium, ISCMM 2021 (pp. 253–265). Singapore: Springer Nature Singapore.

3. Gupta, B., Chaudhary, A., Sindhwani, N., & Rana, A. (2021, September). Smart shoe for detection of electrocution using Internet of Things (IoT). In 2021 9th International Conference on Reliability, Infocom Technologies and Optimization (Trends and Future Directions)(ICRITO) (pp. 1–3). IEEE.

4. Nijhawan, M., Sindhwani, N., Tanwar, S., & Kumar, S. (2022). Role of augmented reality and Internet of Things in education sector. In IoT Based Smart Applications (pp. 245–259). Cham: Springer International Publishing.

5. Garcia-Ceja, E., Riegler, M., Jakobsen, P., Tørresen, J., Nordgreen, T., Oedegaard, K., & Fasmer, O. B. (2018). Depresjon: A motor activity database of depression episodes in unipolar and bipolar patients. In MMSys'18 Proceedings of the 9th ACM on Multimedia Systems Conference, Amsterdam, The Netherlands, June 12–15. ACM.

6. Sindhwani, N., Rana, A., & Chaudhary, A. (2021, September). Breast cancer detection using machine learning algorithms. In 2021 9th International Conference on Reliability, Infocom Technologies and Optimization (Trends and Future Directions) (ICRITO) (pp. 1–5). IEEE.

7. Gupta, A., Anand, R., Pandey, D., Sindhwani, N., Wairya, S., Pandey, B. K., & Sharma, M. (2021). Prediction of breast cancer using extremely randomized clustering forests (ERCF) technique: Prediction of breast cancer. International Journal of Distributed Systems and Technologies (IJDST), 12(4), 1–15.

8. Sharma, G., Nehra, N., Dahiya, A., Sindhwani, N., & Singh, P. (2022). Automatic heart-rate measurement using facial video. In Networking Technologies in Smart Healthcare (pp. 289–307). Boca Raton: CRC Press.

9. Sansanwal, K., Shrivastava, G., Anand, R., & Sharma, K. (2019). Big data analysis and compression for indoor air quality. In Vijender Kumar Solanki , Vicente García Díaz , & J. Paulo Davim (Eds.), Handbook of IoT and Big Data (pp. 1–21). Boca Raton: CRC Press.

10. Meena, Y. K., & Arya, K. V. (2023). Multimodal interaction and IoT applications. Multimedia Tools and Applications, 82(4), 4781–4785.

11. Thati, R. P., Dhadwal, A. S., & Kumar, P. (2023). A novel multi-modal depression detection approach based on mobile crowd sensing and task-based mechanisms. Multimedia Tools and Applications, 82(4), 4787–4820.

12. Ghorbani, A., Davoodi, F., & Zamanifar, K. (2023). Using type-2 fuzzy ontology to improve semantic interoperability for healthcare and diagnosis of depression. Artificial Intelligence in Medicine, 135, 102452.

13. Alwakeel, A., Alwakeel, M., Zahra, S. R., Saleem, T. J., Hijji, M., Alwakeel, S. S., ... & Alzorgi, S. (2023). Common mental disorders in smart city settings and use of multimodal medical sensor fusion to detect them. Diagnostics, 13(6), 1082.

14. Tabassum, N., Ahmed, M., Shorna, N. J., Sowad, U. R., Mejbah, M. D., & Haque, H. M. (2023). Depression detection through smartphone sensing: A federated learning approach. International Journal of Interactive Mobile Technologies, 17(1), 40–56.

15. Ahmed, A., Aziz, S., Alzubaidi, M., Schneider, J., Irshaidat, S., Serhan, H. A., ... & Househ, M. (2023). Wearable devices for anxiety & depression: A scoping review. Computer Methods and Programs in Biomedicine Update, 100095. 10.1016/j.cmpbup.2023.100095

16. Bansal, R., Gupta, A., Singh, R., & Nassa, V. K. (2021). Role and impact of digital technologies in E-learning amidst COVID-19 pandemic. In 2021 Fourth International Conference on Computational Intelligence and Communication Technologies (CCICT) (pp. 194–202). IEEE.
17. Jain, V., Beram, S. M., Talukdar, V., Patil, T., Dhabliya, D., & Gupta, A. (2022). Accuracy enhancement in machine learning during blockchain based transaction classification. In 2022 Seventh International Conference on Parallel, Distributed and Grid Computing (PDGC) (pp. 536–540). IEEE.
18. Kaushik, D., Garg, M., Annu, & Gupta, A.; Sabyasachi Pramanik. (2022). Utilizing machine learning and deep learning in cybersecurity: An innovative approach. Cyber Security and Digital Forensics: Challenges and Future Trends (pp. 271–293). Hoboken, USA: Wiley.
19. Gupta, M., Ghatak, S., Gupta, A., & Mukherjee, A. L. (Eds.). (2022). Artificial Intelligence on Medical Data: Proceedings of International Symposium, ISCMM 2021 (Vol. 37). Singapore: Springer Nature.
20. Onggirawan, C. A., Kho, J. M., Kartiwa, A. P., & Gunawan, A. A. (2023). Systematic literature review: The adaptation of distance learning process during the COVID-19 pandemic using virtual educational spaces in metaverse. Procedia Computer Science, 216, 274–283.
21. Athar, A., Ali, S. M., Mozumder, M. A. I., Ali, S., & Kim, H. C. (2023). Applications and possible challenges of healthcare metaverse. In 2023 25th International Conference on Advanced Communication Technology (ICACT) (pp. 328–332). IEEE.
22. Mano Venkat, S., Rajendra, C., & Venu Madhav, K. (2023, March). Comparative analysis of learning models in depression detection using MRI image data. In Innovations in Bio-Inspired Computing and Applications: Proceedings of the 13th International Conference on Innovations in Bio-Inspired Computing and Applications (IBICA 2022) Held During December 15–17, 2022 (pp. 496–503). Cham: Springer Nature Switzerland.
23. Rubaeah, S., Mangkunegara, I. S., & Purwono, P. (2023). A review of Internet of Things (IoT) and blockchain in healthcare: Chronic disease detection and data security. Journal of Advanced Health Informatics Research, 1(1), 16–20.
24. Bansal, B., Jenipher, V. N., Jain, R., Dilip, R., Kumbhkar, M., Pramanik, S., Roy, S., & Gupta, A. (2022). Big data architecture for network security. In Cyber Security and Network Security (eds S. Pramanik, D. Samanta, M. Vinay and A. Guha). Hoboken, USA: WILEY.
25. Gupta, A., Kaushik, D., Garg, M., & Verma, A. (2020). Machine learning model for breast cancer prediction. In Fourth International Conference on I-SMAC (IoT in Social, Mobile, Analytics and Cloud) (I-SMAC), Palladam, India, (pp. 472–477).
26. Talukdar, V., Dhabliya, D., Kumar, B., Talukdar, S. B., Ahamad, S., & Gupta, A. (2022, November). Suspicious activity detection and classification in IoT environment using machine learning approach. In 2022 Seventh International Conference on Parallel, Distributed and Grid Computing (PDGC) (pp. 531–535). IEEE.
27. Veeraiah, V., Gangavathi, P., Ahamad, S., Talukdar, S. B., Gupta, A., & Talukdar, V. (2022, April). Enhancement of meta verse capabilities by IoT integration. In 2022 2nd International Conference on Advance Computing and Innovative Technologies in Engineering (ICACITE) (pp. 1493–1498). IEEE.

28. Gupta, N., Janani, S., Dilip, R., Hosur, R., Chaturvedi, A., & Gupta, A. (2022). Wearable sensors for evaluation over smart home using sequential minimization optimization-based random forest. International Journal of Communication Networks and Information Security, 14(2), 179–188.

29. Keserwani, H., Rastogi, H., Kurniullah, A. Z., Janardan, S. K., Raman, R., Rathod, V. M., & Gupta, A. (2022). Security enhancement by identifying attacks using machine learning for 5G network. International Journal of Communication Networks and Information Security, 14(2), 124-14.

30. Anand, R., Daniel, A. V., Fred, A. L., Jaiswal, T., Juneja, S., Juneja, A., & Gupta, A. (2023). Building integrated systems for healthcare considering mobile computing and IoT. In Integration of IoT with Cloud Computing for Smart Applications (pp. 203–225). New York: Chapman and Hall/CRC Press.

31. Anand, R., Jain, V., Singh, A., Rahal, D., Rastogi, P., Rajkumar, A., & Gupta, A. (2003). Clustering of big data in cloud environments for smart applications. In Integration of IoT with Cloud Computing for Smart Applications (pp. 227–247). New York: Chapman and Hall/CRC Press.

32. Arora, S., Sharma, S., & Anand, R. (2022, July). A survey on UWB textile antenna for wireless body area network (WBAN) applications. In Artificial Intelligence on Medical Data: Proceedings of International Symposium, ISCMM 2021 (pp. 173–183). Singapore: Springer Nature Singapore.

33. Anand, R., Sindhwani, N., Saini, A., & Shubham. (2021). Emerging technologies for COVID-19. Enabling Healthcare 4.0 for Pandemics: A Roadmap Using AI, Machine Learning, IoT and Cognitive Technologies, 163–188. https://doi.org/10.1002/978111 9769088.ch9

34. Ahuja, A., Patheja, S., & Sindhwani, N. (2022). Impact of COVID-19 on various sectors. Infectious Diseases and Microbiology, 33, 33–45.

35. Tripathi, A., Sindhwani, N., Anand, R., & Dahiya, A. (2022). Role of IoT in smart homes and smart cities: Challenges, benefits, and applications. In IoT Based Smart Applications (pp. 199–217). Cham: Springer International Publishing.

36. Jain, S., Kumar, M., Sindhwani, N., & Singh, P. (2021, September). SARS-Cov-2 detection using deep learning techniques on the basis of clinical reports. In 2021 9th International Conference on Reliability, Infocom Technologies and Optimization (Trends and Future Directions) (ICRITO) (pp. 1–5). IEEE.

37. Wenhua, Z., Qamar, F., Abdali, T. A. N., Hassan, R., Jafri, S. T. A., & Nguyen, Q. N. (2023). Blockchain technology: Security issues, healthcare applications, challenges and future trends. Electronics, 12(3), 546.

38. Harun-Ar-Rashid, M., Chowdhury, O., Hossain, M. M., Rahman, M. M., Muhammad, G., AlQahtani, S. A., ... & Hossain, M. S. (2023, January). IoT-based medical image monitoring system using HL7 in a hospital database. In Healthcare (Vol. 11, No. 1, p. 139). Switzerland: MDPI.

39. Rahman, M. Z., Akbar, M. A., Leiva, V., Tahir, A., Riaz, M. T., & Martin-Barreiro, C. (2023). An intelligent health monitoring and diagnosis system based on the Internet of Things and fuzzy logic for cardiac arrhythmia COVID-19 patients. Computers in Biology and Medicine, 154, 106583.

40. Zgheib, R., Chahbandarian, G., Kamalov, F., El Messiry, H., & Al-Gindy, A. (2023). Towards an ML-based semantic IoT for pandemic management: A survey of enabling technologies for COVID-19. Neurocomputing. https://doi.org/10.1016/j.neucom. 2023.01.007

41. Lepore, D., Dolui, K., Tomashchuk, O., Shim, H., Puri, C., Li, Y., ... & Spigarelli, F. (2023). Interdisciplinary research unlocking innovative solutions in healthcare. Technovation, 120, 102511.

42. Wan, Q., Miao, X., Wang, C., Dinçer, H., & Yüksel, S. (2023). A hybrid decision support system with golden cut and bipolar q-ROFSs for evaluating the risk-based strategic priorities of fintech lending for clean energy projects. Financial Innovation, 9(1), 1–25.

43. Goel, A., & Neduncheliyan, S. (2023). An intelligent blockchain strategy for decentralised healthcare framework. Peer-to-Peer Networking and Applications, 1, 1–12.

44. Sindhwani, N., Anand, R., Niranjanamurthy, M., Verma, D. C., & Valentina, E. B. (2022). IoT Based Smart Applications. Cham: Springer International Publishing AG.

45. Sharma, Shivam, Rattan, Ritika, Goyal, Bhawna, Dogra, Ayush, & Anand, Rohit (2022). Microscopic and Ultrasonic Super-Resolution for Accurate Diagnosis and Treatment Planning, Communication, Software and Networks,Lecture Notes in Networks and Systems (pp. 601–611). 10.1007/978-981-19-4990-6_56.

6 Biomechanics Features-Based IoT and Machine Learning for Orthopedic Patients

Vivek Veeraiah, M.S. Sowmya, Bhupesh Goyal, Madhu Yadav, Reshmi Mishra, Gulista Khan, and Dharmesh Dhabliya

6.1 INTRODUCTION

6.1.1 IoT AND HEALTHCARE-BASED DEPRESSION

Orthopedic disorders are among the most frequent health concerns in the world, impacting millions of people. The investigation of such diseases using biomechanics gives vital information about the shape and alignment of the pelvis and lumbar spine, which can aid in the diagnosis and treatment of orthopedic conditions. Advances in Internet of Things (IoT) and machine learning technology have enabled the development of novel techniques to diagnosing and treating orthopedic disorders in recent years [1–5]. We provide a study on the utilization of biomechanics-based IoT and machine learning algorithms for orthopedic patient classification based on pelvic and lumbar spine features in this paper. The work employs a dataset [6] containing biomechanics-based aspects of orthopedic patients, as well as the usage of various machine learning algorithms for classification tasks. We also do exploratory data analysis to acquire insight into the links between different attributes and their impact on categorization outcomes. Our findings demonstrate the possibility of using IoT and machine learning technology for accurate orthopedic patient classification, which can aid in early diagnosis and personalized treatment.

6.1.2 APPLICATIONS OF IoT SENSOR DATA AND VISUALIZATIONS

Numerous disciplines have seen the dominance of AI, including but not limited to:

- Early identification of orthopedic problems: Using machine learning to analyze biomechanical traits, doctors may be able to diagnose orthopedic disorders in patients at an early stage, allowing for rapid treatment and management.

DOI: 10.1201/9781003330523-6

- Personalized treatment plans: Machine learning algorithms can analyze each patients' biomechanical traits and develop personalized treatment programmes based on their specific needs.
- Remote patient monitoring: Using IoT, clinicians may remotely monitor the biomechanical aspects of orthopedic patients, ensuring that they are adhering to their treatment regimens and progressing.
- Tracking the development of patients undergoing rehabilitation: Machine learning algorithms can track the progress of patients undergoing rehabilitation, finding areas for improvement and changing treatment programmes as appropriate.
- Predictive maintenance of orthopedic equipment: Machine learning algorithms can anticipate when orthopedic equipment will require repair or replacement by analyzing biomechanical data from the equipment.
- Improved surgical planning: Machine learning algorithms can analyze biomechanical data from patients, assisting doctors in more successfully planning procedures and lowering the likelihood of problems.
- Predictive modeling of disease progression: Machine learning algorithms can anticipate how orthopedic problems will proceed in specific individuals by analyzing biomechanical data over time.
- Orthopedic device quality control: Machine learning algorithms may analyze biomechanical data from orthopedic devices to ensure that they meet quality requirements and work as intended.
- Real-time patient monitoring: Using IoT, clinicians may monitor the biomechanical characteristics of orthopedic patients in real time, allowing for quick adjustments if necessary.

6.1.3 Use of IoT-based Data for Biomechanical Features

Because of its capacity to provide real-time monitoring and analysis of patient health, the use of IoT-based data in orthopedic patient care is becoming increasingly popular. Patients can be remotely monitored via IoT devices such as wearables, and their health data can be automatically collected and delivered to healthcare specialists for study. Machine learning algorithms can then be used to find patterns and forecast outcomes in this data. Orthopedic medical care can be made more personalized and efficient by combining IoT-based data with machine learning. Clinicians may monitor patients' progress in real time, alter treatment regimens as needed, and intervene early if needed. Furthermore, machine learning algorithms can assist identify patients who are more likely to develop issues, allowing for intervention and potentially saving costly hospital readmissions.

The use of IoT-based data in orthopedics has the potential to bring considerable advantages, such as continuous monitoring of patient biomechanics and early detection of abnormalities or deviations from the norm [7,8]. To collect data on patient motions and pressure locations, IoT sensors can be installed on various orthopedic devices such as braces or prosthesis. This information can then be analyzed using machine learning techniques to uncover patterns and indicate potential problems. Furthermore, the application of IoT in orthopedics can result in more personalized and targeted treatment strategies. Doctors may personalize treatment plans to specific needs and change them in real-time based on data received by IoT sensors with a better grasp of a patient's biomechanics. This can result in better patient outcomes and lower healthcare expenses.

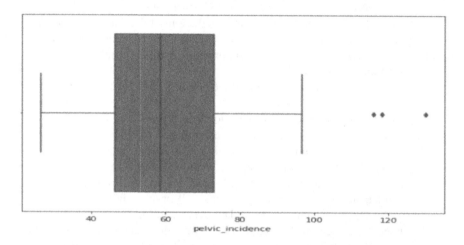

FIGURE 6.1   Box plot showing pelvic incidence.

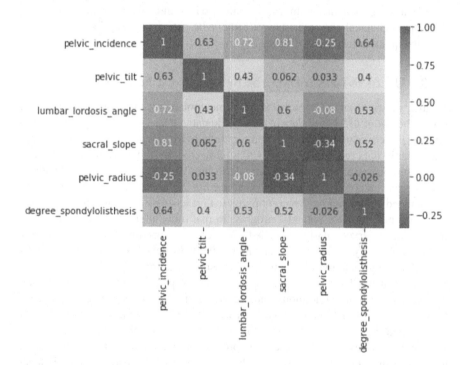

FIGURE 6.2   A heatmap showing correlation matrices.

6.1.4 USE OF MACHINE LEARNING FOR BIOMECHANICAL FEATURES

Various classifiers, Logistic regression, for example, is a simple and fast model that works well with binary outcomes, whereas decision trees and random forests are better suited for dealing with non-linear connections and variable interactions. Support vector machines are well-known for their capacity to handle high-dimensional data and outliers, but artificial neural networks excel at dealing with complex and non-linear correlations between variables.

Machine learning has demonstrated significant promise in analyzing bio-mechanical data for orthopedic patients. It enables the construction of predictive models capable of accurately categorizing patients based on their biomechanical properties. This can help with early detection and diagnosis of orthopedic disorders, resulting in more effective therapies and better patient Figures 6.1–6.3 give visualization of the dataset features.

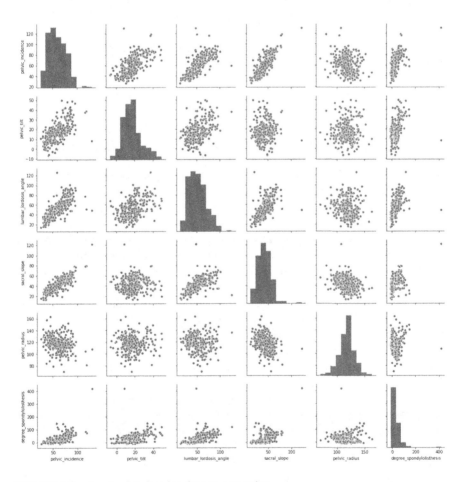

FIGURE 6.3 A pair plot showing feature correction.

6.2 LITERATURE SURVEY

Young-Shand et al [9] provided a machine learning-based clustering approach for identifying knee osteoarthritis patient phenotypes based on demographic and knee kinematic data during gait, which could aid in creating tailored treatments and assessing total knee arthroplasty treatment efficacy. Jacobs et al [10] used a claims database to evaluate the incidence of osteoarthritis diagnosis between multiple ligament knee injuries (MLKI) and anterior cruciate ligament (ACL) injuries, and then use a ML approach to identify risk factors. Krivicich et al. [11] undertook a systematic analysis of research that employs machine learning for orthopedic procedures and conclude that such algorithms have good discriminatory performance but require external validation. Yosibash et al [12] created a machine learning method that predicts the likelihood of hip fracture in type 2 diabetes patients using autonomous finite element studies and patient data from CT scans. Kim et al. [13] created with excellent to acceptable accuracy based on foot posture index and the need for various supports. During the COVID-19 epidemic, Bansal et al. [14] investigated the role and influence of digital technology in e-learning, emphasizing the obstacles and opportunities posed by the shift to online education.

Jain et al. [15] offered a method for improving machine learning accuracy for blockchain-based transaction classification, emphasizing the potential benefits of merging these technologies. Kaushik et al. [16] examined the application of machine learning and deep learning in cybersecurity, delving into the challenges and opportunities that come with using these technologies to fight against cyber threats. Gupta et al. [17] and colleagues edited a book on the use of artificial intelligence in medical data, which included contributions from a variety of professionals in the field. Onggirawan et al. [18] performed a systematic assessment of the literature on virtual education utilizing virtual education in the metaverse, examining the benefits and drawbacks of various techniques. Athar et al. [19] examined the potential of healthcare metaverse technology to alter healthcare delivery and enhance patient outcomes, as well as its applications and potential difficulties. When deciding on bilateral hip arthroscopic surgery, Owusu-Akyaw et al. [20] emphasized the importance of considering individual patient variability and functional goals, as delays may result in poor patient outcomes and the persistence of microinstability and/or femoroacetabular impingement may limit recovery of the other hip. Snyder et al. [21] presented a framework for predicting knee adduction moment variables during walking with high accuracy and low error, potentially facilitating low cost clinical analysis of knee moment in healthy individuals.

Sebro et al. [22] proposed utilizing machine learning models to predict osteoporosis/osteopenia using trabecular bone attenuation acquired from knee CT images, which showed greater predictive capacity than using CT attenuation of a single bone. To address the existing diagnostic problem in osteoarthritis (OA), Xuan et al. [23] proposed combining reliable machine learning-based predictive models with imaging modalities sensitive to early alterations in OA prior to the appearance of clinical characteristics. Tan et al. [24] proposed using portable sensing technologies such as wearables and cameras outside of the lab to identify ACL injury risk factors prevent high-risk movements prior to damage, and optimize therapy paradigms. Park et al. [25] proposed using machine learning methods with related risk variables to predict the occurrence of ramp lesions in ACL-deficient knees, which might be utilized as an additional diagnostic tool for ACL-injured knees with ramp lesions. Talukdar et al. [26] developed a machine learning strategy for suspicious activity identification and categorization in an IoT environment, which can be used to detect and mitigate potential security breaches in orthopedic patients. Veeraiah et al. [27] advocated combining IoT and metaverse capabilities to improve the monitoring and visualization of orthopedic patient data. Gupta et al. [28] evaluated wearable sensors and machine learning in a smart home, giving a non-invasive method of monitoring patient activity and rehabilitation. Keserwani et al. [29] suggested a machine learning strategy for detecting attacks and improving security in 5 G networks, which can be used to mitigate potential cyber assaults in orthopedic patient data management.

6.3 PROBLEM STATEMENT

A problem statement for a paper based on biomechanics features and IoT and machine learning for orthopedic patients could be to develop a predictive model that can accurately classify patients with orthopedic conditions such as disc hernia or spondylolisthesis based on biomechanical attributes derived from the pelvis and lumbar spine. The goal could be to provide an early identification of these disorders, allowing for timely intervention and therapy and enhancing orthopedic patients' quality of life.

6.4 PROPOSED WORK

The proposed effort entails employing exploratory data analysis (EDA) approaches to gain insights into the correlations between biomechanical characteristics and the existence of orthopedic problems in patients. We then used a dataset to train machine learning classification algorithms to predict the presence of orthopedic disorders based on the six biomechanical parameters. The goal is to compare the models that are both accurate and efficient for use in the diagnosis and treatment of orthopedic disorders in patients.

6.5 RESULTS AND DISCUSSION

In this study, we used the spine dataset from the UCI Machine Learning Repository to compare the classification performance of three machine learning algorithms on two separate classification tasks. The first job involved categorizing patients into three groups: normal, disc hernia, and spondylolisthesis, while the second entailed categorizing patients into two groups: normal and abnormal. According to our findings, SVM linear had the highest accuracy of 91% on the first task, while SVM rbf, RF, and KNN had the maximum accuracy of 86% on both tests. On the first challenge, DT earned an accuracy of 83%, whereas

AdaBoost and XGB achieved an accuracy of 81% on both tasks. On both challenges, NB obtained an accuracy of 80%.

The findings imply that machine learning algorithms can be useful in categorizing spine patients based on their biomechanical characteristics. SVM linear performed the best in the first task, demonstrating that linear classification can be beneficial in discriminating between patients with Normal, Disc Hernia, and Spondylolisthesis. Two Models getting the highest accuracy could be because sophisticated algorithms can detect underlying patterns in data and make accurate predictions based on them. Previous research has concentrated on breakthroughs in hip implant failure diagnosis, joint pathology diagnosis utilizing acoustic emissions, and knee cartilage lesion categorization using deep learning [30–32]. The papers also cover the application of machine learning and explainable artificial intelligence in assessing posture factors, as well as new strategies for tibiofibular syndesmosis stabilization [33]. Methods for biomechanical assessment of posterior malleolar fractures in ankle fractures are investigated in a comprehensive review. These papers emphasize the expanding significance of technology and machine learning in the healthcare industry, and they provide insights that may be used to develop healthcare-based human activity recognition and transportation mode detection utilizing IoT sensors [34–36]. Recent research has concentrated on many areas of using technology and artificial intelligence (AI) to improve patient outcomes. These include advances in the diagnosis of joint pathology, fracture stabilization, spinal injury categorization, and the identification of knee osteoarthritis using synthetic CT [37–39]. Furthermore, the papers investigate the use of motion technologies to assist athletes and the potential of GPT-4 in biomedical engineering. They also emphasize the growing importance of unsupervised machine learning approaches in healthcare, as well as the possibility of synthetic data to speed the development of generalizable learning-based algorithms for X-ray image processing [39–41]. Research provides useful insights into the application of technology in healthcare and highlights its potential for improving healthcare-based human activity recognition and transportation mode detection utilizing IoT sensors. Table 6.1 gives the results of ML models followed by graph in Figure 6.4.

TABLE 6.1

Accuracy of the Machine Learning Models

Logistic Regression	0.91
Linear Discriminant Analysis	0.84
Naive Bayes	0.80
K-Nearest Neighbors	0.80
Decision Tree	0.83
Support Vector Machine	0.86
Radial Basis Function	0.91
Random Forest	0.86
Adaptive Boosting	0.81
Extreme Gradient Boosting	0.81

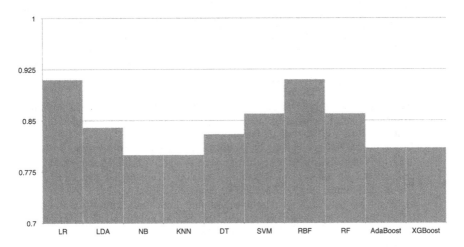

FIGURE 6.4 Graph of accuracy of the machine learning models.

6.6 CONCLUSIONS

The findings imply that machine learning algorithms can be useful in categorizing spine patients based on their biomechanical characteristics. SVM linear performed the best in the first task, demonstrating that linear classification can be beneficial in discriminating between patients with Normal, Disc Hernia, and Spondylolisthesis.

The findings of this study demonstrated that machine learning models may efficiently classify patients into different groups based on biomechanical characteristics of the pelvis and lumbar spine. In the two-class classification task, the SVM linear model scored the maximum accuracy of 91%, while the DT model achieved the highest accuracy of 83%.

6.7 FUTURE SCOPE

The scope of this work could be expanded in the future by integrating more patients and incorporating new features that may increase the classification algorithms' accuracy. Furthermore, the models can be evaluated for generalizability using data from different medical centers. Furthermore, the classification model outputs can be used to create a decision support system for physicians to aid in the diagnosis and treatment planning of orthopedic patients [42–46]. Finally, the outcomes of this study can spur additional research into IoT and machine learning applications in orthopedics, resulting in the creation of more advanced and personalized healthcare solutions [47,48].

REFERENCES

1. Sansanwal, K., Shrivastava, G., Anand, R., & Sharma, K. (2019). Big data analysis and compression for indoor air quality. Handbook of IoT and Big Data, 1.

2. Gupta, A., Srivastava, A., & Anand, R. (2019). Cost-effective smart home automation using internet of things. Journal of Communication Engineering & Systems, 9(2), 1–6.
3. Gupta, A., Asad, A., Meena, L., & Anand, R. (2022, July). IoT and RFID-based smart card system integrated with health care, electricity, QR and banking sectors. In Artificial Intelligence on Medical Data: Proceedings of International Symposium, ISCMM 2021 (pp. 253–265). Singapore: Springer Nature Singapore.
4. Sharma, G., Nehra, N., Dahiya, A., Sindhwani, N., & Singh, P. (2022). Automatic heart-rate measurement using facial video. In Networking Technologies in Smart Healthcare (pp. 289–307). CRC Press.
5. Sindhwani, N., Sasi, G., & Meivel, S. (2022, October). Fuzzy acceptance Analysis of Impact of Glaucoma and Diabetic Retinopathy using Confusion Matrix. In 2022 10th International Conference on Reliability, Infocom Technologies and Optimization (Trends and Future Directions)(ICRITO) (pp. 1–5). IEEE.
6. Lichman, M. (2013). UCI Machine Learning Repository [http://archive.ics.uci.edu/ml]. Irvine, CA: University of California, School of Information and Computer Science.
7. Anand, R., & Chawla, P. (2016, March). A review on the optimization techniques for bio-inspired antenna design. In 2016 3rd International conference on computing for sustainable global development (INDIACom) (pp. 2228–2233). IEEE.
8. Arora, S., Sharma, S., & Anand, R. (2022, July). A survey on UWB textile antenna for Wireless Body Area Network (WBAN) applications. In Artificial Intelligence on Medical Data: Proceedings of International Symposium, ISCMM 2021 (pp. 173–183). Singapore: Springer Nature Singapore.
9. Young-Shand, K. L., Roy, P. C., Dunbar, M. J., Abidi, S. S., & Astephen Wilson, J. L. (2023). Gait biomechanics phenotypes among total knee arthroplasty candidates by machine learning cluster analysis. Journal of Orthopaedic Research, 41(2), 335–344.
10. Jacobs, C., Conley, C., Johnson, D., Landy, D., & Stone, A. (2023). Machine Learning Approach To Identify Risk Factors For Post-Traumatic Osteoarthritis After Multiligament Knee Reconstruction. Osteoarthritis and Cartilage, 31, S74.
11. Krivicich, L. M., Jan, K., Kunze, K. N., Rice, M., & Nho, S. J. (2023). Machine Learning Algorithms Can Be Reliably Leveraged to Identify Patients at High Risk of Prolonged Postoperative Opioid Use Following Orthopedic Surgery: A Systematic Review. HSS Journal®, 15563316231164138.
12. Yosibash, Z., Trabelsi, N., Buchnik, I., Myers, K. W., Salai, M., Eshed, I., ... & Tripto-Shkolnik, L. Hip fracture risk assessment in elderly and diabetic patients: combining autonomous finite element analysis and machine learning. Journal of Bone and Mineral Research.
13. Kim, J. K., Choo, Y. J., Park, I. S., Choi, J. W., Park, D., & Chang, M. C. (2023). Deep-Learning Algorithms for Prescribing Insoles to Patients with Foot Pain. Applied Sciences, 13(4), 2208.
14. Bansal, R., Gupta, A., Singh, R., & Nassa, V. K. (2021). Role and impact of digital technologies in E-learning amidst COVID-19 pandemic. 2021 Fourth International Conference on Computational Intelligence and Communication Technologies (CCICT) (pp. 194–202). IEEE.
15. Jain, V., Beram, S. M., Talukdar, V., Patil, T., Dhabliya, D., & Gupta, A. (2022). Accuracy enhancement in machine learning during blockchain based transaction classification. In 2022 Seventh International Conference on Parallel, Distributed and Grid Computing (PDGC) (pp. 536–540). IEEE.
16. Kaushik, D., Garg, M., Annu, & Gupta, A.; Sabyasachi Pramanik. (2022). Utilizing Machine Learning and Deep Learning in Cybersecurity: An Innovative Approach. Cyber Security and Digital Forensics: Challenges and Future Trends, Wiley, 2022, (pp. 271–293). Wiley.

17. Gupta, M., Ghatak, S., Gupta, A., & Mukherjee, A. L. (Eds.). (2022). Artificial Intelligence on Medical Data: Proceedings of International Symposium, ISCMM 2021 (Vol. 37). Springer Nature.

18. Onggirawan, C. A., Kho, J. M., Kartiwa, A. P., & Gunawan, A. A. (2023). Systematic literature review: The adaptation of distance learning process during the COVID-19 pandemic using virtual educational spaces in metaverse. Procedia Computer Science, 216, 274–283.

19. Athar, A., Ali, S. M., Mozumder, M. A. I., Ali, S., & Kim, H. C. (2023, February). Applications and Possible Challenges of Healthcare Metaverse. In 2023 25th International Conference on Advanced Communication Technology (ICACT) (pp. 328–332). IEEE.

20. Owusu-Akyaw, K. A. (2023). Editorial Commentary: Prolonged Delays in Staging Bilateral Hip Arthroscopic Surgery for Femoroacetabular Impingement May Result in Inferior Patient Outcomes: Two Halves of One Problem. Arthroscopy: The Journal of Arthroscopic & Related Surgery, 39(3), 738–739.

21. Snyder, S. J., Chu, E., Um, J., Heo, Y. J., Miller, R. H., & Shim, J. K. (2023). Prediction of knee adduction moment using innovative instrumented insole and deep learning neural networks in healthy female individuals. The Knee, 41, 115–123.

22. Sebro, R., & Elmahdy, M. (2023). Machine Learning for Opportunistic Screening for Osteoporosis and Osteopenia Using Knee CT Scans. Canadian Association of Radiologists Journal, 08465371231164743.

23. Xuan, A., Chen, H., Chen, T., Li, J., Lu, S., Fan, T., ... & Zhu, Z. (2023). The application of machine learning in early diagnosis of osteoarthritis: a narrative review. Therapeutic Advances in Musculoskeletal Disease, 15, 1759720X231158198.

24. Tan, T., Gatti, A. A., Fan, B., Shea, K. G., Sherman, S. L., Uhlrich, S. D., ... & Chaudhari, A. S. (2023). A scoping review of portable sensing for out-of-lab anterior cruciate ligament injury prevention and rehabilitation. npj Digital Medicine, 6(1), 46.

25. Park, Y. B., Kim, H., Lee, H. J., Baek, S. H., Kwak, I. Y., & Kim, S. H. (2023). The Clinical Application of Machine Learning Models for Risk Analysis of Ramp Lesions in Anterior Cruciate Ligament Injuries. The American Journal of Sports Medicine, 51(1), 107–118.

26. Talukdar, V., Dhabliya, D., Kumar, B., Talukdar, S. B., Ahamad, S., & Gupta, A. (2022, November). Suspicious Activity Detection and Classification in IoT Environment Using Machine Learning Approach. In 2022 Seventh International Conference on Parallel, Distributed and Grid Computing (PDGC) (pp. 531–535). IEEE.

27. Veeraiah, V., Gangavathi, P., Ahamad, S., Talukdar, S. B., Gupta, A., & Talukdar, V. (2022, April). Enhancement of meta verse capabilities by IoT integration. In 2022 2nd International Conference on Advance Computing and Innovative Technologies in Engineering (ICACITE) (pp. 1493–1498). IEEE.

28. Gupta, N., Janani, S., Dilip, R., Hosur, R., Chaturvedi, A., & Gupta, A. (2022). Wearable Sensors for Evaluation Over Smart Home Using Sequential Minimization Optimization-based Random Forest. International Journal of Communication Networks and Information Security, 14(2), 179–188.

29. Keserwani, H., Rastogi, H., Kurniullah, A. Z., Janardan, S. K., Raman, R., Rathod, V. M., & Gupta, A. (2022). Security Enhancement by Identifying Attacks Using Machine Learning for 5G Network. International Journal of Communication Networks and Information Security, 14(2), 124-14

30. Ampadi Ramachandran, R., Chi, S. W., Srinivasa Pai, P., Foucher, K., Ozevin, D., & Mathew, M. T. (2023). Artificial intelligence and machine learning as a viable solution for hip implant failure diagnosis—Review of literature and in vitro case study. Medical & Biological Engineering & Computing, 1–17.

31. Nsugbe, E., Olorunlambe, K., & Dearn, K. (2023). On the Early and Affordable Diagnosis of Joint Pathologies Using Acoustic Emissions, Deep Learning Decompositions and Prediction Machines. Sensors, 23(9), 4449.

32. Zhang, L., Che, Z., Li, Y., Mu, M., Gang, J., Xiao, Y., & Yao, Y. (2023). Multi-level classification of knee cartilage lesion in multimodal MRI based on deep learning. Biomedical Signal Processing and Control, 83, 104687.

33. Dindorf, C., Ludwig, O., Simon, S., Becker, S., & Fröhlich, M. (2023). Machine Learning and Explainable Artificial Intelligence Using Counterfactual Explanations for Evaluating Posture Parameters. Bioengineering, 10(5), 511.

34. Stake, I. K., Douglass, B. W., Husebye, E. E., & Clanton, T. O. (2023). Methods for Biomechanical Testing of Posterior Malleolar Fractures in Ankle Fractures: A Scoping Review. Foot & Ankle International, 44(4), 348–362.

35. Zhu, N., Zhong, Q., Zhan, J., Zhang, S., Liu, W., Yao, Y., & Jing, J. (2023). A new type of elastic fixation, using an encircling and binding technique, for tibiofibular syndesmosis stabilization: comparison to traditional cortical screw fixation. Journal of Orthopaedic Surgery and Research, 18(1), 1–8.

36. Aresta, S., Musci, M., Bottiglione, F., Moretti, L., Moretti, B., & Bortone, I. (2023). Motion Technologies in Support of Fence Athletes: A Systematic Review. Applied Sciences, 13(3), 1654.

37. Cheng, K., Guo, Q., He, Y., Lu, Y., Gu, S., & Wu, H. (2023). Exploring the Potential of GPT-4 in Biomedical Engineering: The Dawn of a New Era. Annals of Biomedical Engineering, 1–9.

38. Gao, C., Killeen, B. D., Hu, Y., Grupp, R. B., Taylor, R. H., Armand, M., & Unberath, M. (2023). Synthetic data accelerates the development of generalizable learning-based algorithms for X-ray image analysis. Nature Machine Intelligence, 1–15.

39. Naguib, S. M., Hamza, H. M., Hosny, K. M., Saleh, M. K., & Kassem, M. A. (2023). Classification of Cervical Spine Fracture and Dislocation Using Refined Pre-Trained Deep Model and Saliency Map. Diagnostics, 13(7), 1273.

40. Eckhardt, C. M., Madjarova, S. J., Williams, R. J., Ollivier, M., Karlsson, J., Pareek, A., & Nwachukwu, B. U. (2023). Unsupervised machine learning methods and emerging applications in healthcare. Knee Surgery, Sports Traumatology, Arthroscopy, 31(2), 376–381.

41. Arbabi, S., Foppen, W., Gielis, W. P., van Stralen, M., Jansen, M., Arbabi, V., ... & Seevinck, P. (2023). MRI-based synthetic CT in the detection of knee osteoarthritis: Comparison with CT. Journal of Orthopaedic Research®.

42. Gupta, A., Anand, R., Pandey, D., Sindhwani, N., Wairya, S., Pandey, B. K., & Sharma, M. (2021). Prediction of breast cancer using extremely randomized clustering forests (ERCF) technique: prediction of breast cancer. International Journal of Distributed Systems and Technologies (IJDST), 12(4), 1–15.

43. Sindhwani, N., Rana, A., & Chaudhary, A. (2021, September). Breast cancer detection using machine learning algorithms. In 2021 9th International conference on reliability, Infocom technologies and optimization (trends and future directions) (ICRITO) (pp. 1–5). IEEE.

44. Sindhwani, N., Anand, R., Niranjanamurthy, M., Verma, D. C., & Valentina, E. B. (2022). IoT Based Smart Applications. Springer International Publishing AG.

45. Kaur, J., Jaskaran, Sindhwani, N., Anand, R., & Pandey, D. (2022). Implementation of IoT in various domains. In IoT Based Smart Applications (pp. 165–178). Cham: Springer International Publishing.

46. Jain, S., Kumar, M., Sindhwani, N., & Singh, P. (2021, September). SARS-Cov-2 detection using Deep Learning Techniques on the basis of Clinical Reports.

In 2021 9th International Conference on Reliability, Infocom Technologies and Optimization (Trends and Future Directions)(ICRITO) (pp. 1–5). IEEE.

47. Gupta, Anupma, Goyal, Bhawna, Dogra, Ayush, & Anand, Rohit (2022). Proximity Coupled Antenna with Stable Performance and High Body Antenna Isolation for IoT-Based Devices, Communication, Software and Networks,Lecture Notes in Networks and Systems (pp. 591–60010.1007/978-981-19-4990-6_55.

48. Gupta, Deena Nath, Anand, Rohit, Ahamad, Shahanawaj, Patil, Trupti, Dhabliya, Dharmesh, & Gupta, Ankur (2023). Phonocardiographic Signal Analysis for the Detection of Cardiovascular Diseases, Intelligent Data Engineering and Analytics,Smart Innovation, Systems and Technologies (pp. 529–53810.1007/978-981-99-6706-3_47.

7 Healthcare-based Human Activity Recognition and Transportation Mode Detection Using IoT Sensors

R. Dilip, M.G. Shalini, M.G. Manasa, N. Tejashwini, L. Chandrashekhar, and Bhagirathi Bai V.

7.1 INTRODUCTION

7.1.1 ARTIFICIAL INTELLIGENCE

The study emphasizes the application of AI and IoT sensors in healthcare. Healthcare professionals can monitor patient behaviors and spot potential health problems by accurately recognizing human activities and modes of transportation. AI models can be used to send timely notifications to patients or healthcare professionals, assisting them in making decisions regarding their own health. The study highlights the significance of machine learning methods for classification problems, including logistic regression, decision trees, and random forests [1–5]. These methods can be modified and expanded for a variety of healthcare applications, such as disease detection, medication development, and individualized care. These methods can be used to create AI models that may enhance patient quality of life and healthcare outcomes. Figure 7.1 shows the applications of AI in Human Activity Recognition.

7.1.2 APPLICATIONS OF HUMAN ACTIVITY RECOGNITION

Numerous disciplines have seen the dominance of AI, including but not limited to:

- Disease classification: Based on the patient's level of physical activity and mode of transportation, the data can be used to train machine learning models that can identify and categorize different diseases.

DOI: 10.1201/9781003330523-7

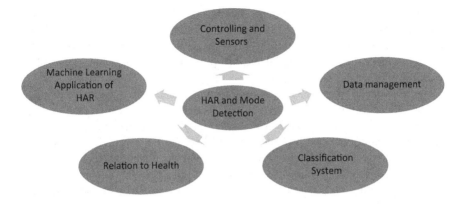

FIGURE 7.1 Applications of AI in human activity recognition.

- Personalized treatment regimens: can be made for each patient depending on their levels of physical activity and means of transportation by analyzing the data, potentially enhancing the effectiveness of the treatment.
- Health risk assessment: Using the patient's degree of physical activity and method of transportation, the data can be utilized to determine the patient's health risks and offer insights into prospective health issues.
- Falls prevention: By identifying individuals who are at high risk of falling, the data can be used by healthcare professionals to take preventative action and lessen the possibility of a fall.
- Management of chronic diseases: Through data analysis, healthcare professionals can track the levels of physical activity and modes of transportation used by patients with long-term conditions like diabetes or heart disease and modify their treatment strategies accordingly.
- Remote patient monitoring: The information can be used to track patients' levels of physical activity and modes of mobility, enabling healthcare professionals to give ongoing care and support, especially for those with chronic ailments.
- Healthcare professionals can involve patients in their treatment plans and potentially improve patient satisfaction and health outcomes by soliciting feedback from patients regarding their levels of physical activity and means of mobility.

7.1.3 MACHINE LEARNING AND HUMAN ACTIVITY RECOGNITION

Machine learning and human activity identification have the potential to provide various benefits in a wide range of disciplines, from healthcare to sports and fitness. One of the most important advantages of machine learning in human activity detection is its ability to identify human activities properly based on sensor data. Machine learning algorithms can detect patterns and traits that are indicative of specific activities by processing huge amounts of sensor data, allowing for precise recognition and classification [6–8]. This is especially relevant in healthcare, where machine learning and human activity identification may be used to track patient activity levels, identify potential health problems, and provide personalized treatment regimens.

The capacity to give real-time monitoring and feedback is another advantage of machine learning and human activity recognition. Machine learning algorithms can process sensor data in real-time, providing individuals, coaches, or healthcare practitioners with immediate feedback and alarms. This can serve to improve athletic and fitness performance, as well as enable rapid treatments in hospital situations. Individual activity tracking can also be personalized using machine learning and human activity identification [8]. Machine learning algorithms can develop personalized activity profiles that better reflect each individual's unique needs and goals by accounting for variances in physical abilities, age, and other characteristics. This can lead to more accurate physical activity tracking and monitoring, as well as more effective interventions and therapies.

Machine learning algorithms can help to modify behavior and encourage healthy habits by finding patterns in human activity and offering feedback to individuals. This is especially relevant in healthcare, where machine learning and human activity recognition can be used to track patient adherence to treatment schedules, identify potential health hazards, and provide personalized feedback and assistance. Furthermore, behavior modification techniques can be used to assist individuals in developing new habits and maintaining healthy behaviors over time. This can result in better health outcomes, lower healthcare expenditures, and a higher quality of life for individuals [7,8]. Behavior modification strategies can be used in sports and fitness to assist individuals in setting and achieving fitness goals, improving athletic performance, and preventing injuries. Figure 7.2 shows the correlation of Features in the Dataset and Figure 7.3 shows the average values of various sensors in the dataset that we use.

The combination of machine learning and human activity identification has the potential to transform the way we monitor, track, and modify human behavior, resulting in improved health outcomes, higher athletic performance, and a better knowledge of human behavior The detection of transport modes can have a considerable impact on urban planning. Urban planners can build more efficient and sustainable transportation networks by collecting data on transportation patterns. Machine learning algorithms can be used to classify modes of transportation and discover trends and patterns in transportation behavior, giving city planners useful information. Data on transportation modes, for example, can be used to optimize public transportation routes, improve pedestrian and bicycle infrastructure, and minimize road congestion [9–11]. Machine learning algorithms can also be used to improve urban traffic flow. Transportation management systems can react in real-time to alleviate congestion and increase safety by monitoring and anticipating traffic trends. For example, traffic lights can be modified to improve traffic flow, and drivers can receive real-time traffic reports to help them avoid crowded regions.

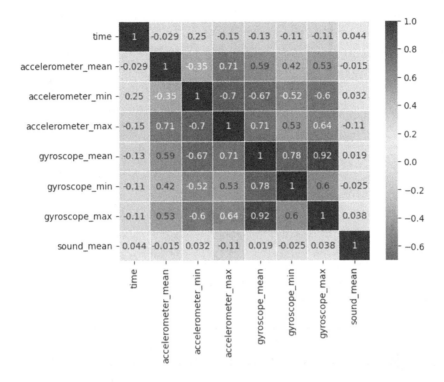

FIGURE 7.2   Correlation of features in the dataset.

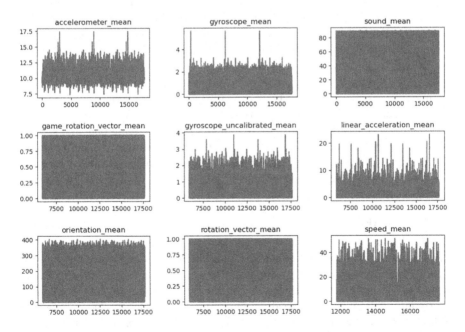

FIGURE 7.3   Average values of various sensors in the dataset.

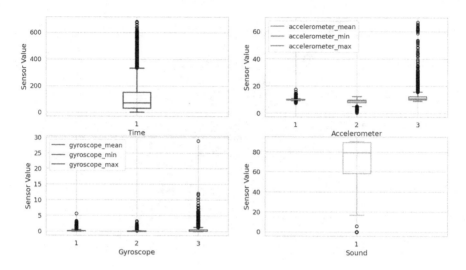

FIGURE 7.4 A box plot showing mean values of different sensors.

Transportation mode detection can also be used to improve workplace wellbeing. Machine learning algorithms can improve employee wellbeing and lower healthcare expenses by tracking employee transportation modes and giving incentives and feedback to encourage healthy commute behaviors. Employees who walk or cycle to work, for example, may be eligible for discounts on gym memberships or other wellness programmes. Transportation mode identification can be used in the insurance sector to price insurance policies depending on transportation behaviors. Insurance companies can offer more personalized and equitable insurance pricing by categorizing transportation modes and calculating the risk associated with each mode. Individuals who frequently use public transportation, for example, may be offered lower insurance rates than those who frequently drive cars. Transportation mode detection can also be used to improve public transit security. Machine learning algorithms, by classifying transportation modes and identifying potential security concerns, might enable a faster and more effective reaction to security issues. Security personnel, for example, can be dispatched to the right place based on the prospective threat's mode of transit. Figure 7.4 shows a box plot of the average values of all the sensors.

7.1.3.1 Working

After gathering the data, it can be divided into training and testing sets. The training set is used to train the machine learning model, whereas the testing set is used to assess the model's performance. The sensor data is then used to extract features. These are data qualities relevant for classification, such as the mean or maximum value of a sensor reading. Feature extraction is significant because it reduces data dimensionality and aids in the removal of noise and useless information. Following feature extraction, a classification algorithm, such as

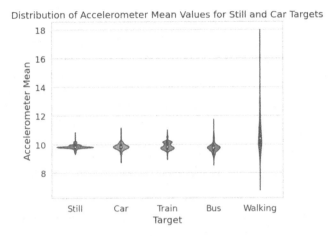

FIGURE 7.5   A plot showing distributions of target variables.

support vector machines (SVM), k-nearest neighbors (KNN), or random forest, is used to train the machine learning model among other classifiers of our choice. After training, the model can be evaluated using the testing set. The testing set is used to assess the model's performance by comparing predicted labels to actual labels. Metrics including accuracy, precision, recall, and F1 score can be used to assess the model's performance. The learned model can be applied to new sensor data. To forecast a new activity, the sensor data is first preprocessed to extract the appropriate features, and then the model is applied to the features. The accuracy of the classification is determined by the quality of the retrieved features as well as the efficiency of the classification algorithm utilized. Figure 7.5 is for visualizing the target variables.

7.1.4   APPLICATIONS OF HUMAN ACTIVITY RECOGNITION IN HEALTHCARE

The operation of a classifier for human activity detection in healthcare follows the same basic processes as in general. However, some specific considerations must be made to ensure that the classifier is effective and accurate for healthcare applications. To begin, sensor selection is critical in healthcare applications. Sensors must be chosen based on the specific requirements of the healthcare application. Sensors that measure acceleration and orientation, for example, may be more appropriate if the purpose is to monitor the physical activity levels of patients. Sensors that detect heart rate, blood pressure, and respiration rate may be more suited if the application is to monitor vital signs. Once trained, the classifier can be used to classify new sensor data in real-time. For example, the classifier can be used to monitor patients' physical activity levels, recognize falls or other irregularities, and inform healthcare personnel as needed. The accuracy of the classifier is critical in healthcare applications since it can affect patient safety and care. To ensure accuracy, the classifier may need to be tested on large and diverse datasets and assessed using metrics like sensitivity, specificity, and accuracy.

7.2   LITERATURE REVIEW

Patricia, et al. [12] demonstrate using a prediction model that used classification techniques and feature selection to accurately track the daily living activities of elderly or disabled people in indoor surroundings. The model was validated using three datasets, and twelve classifiers were developed. The Classification through Regression and OneR classifiers produced the best results, with quality metrics greater than 90%, even when occupation and number of activities varied. The study indicates that the classification-based predictive model is effective at properly detecting everyday life activities and has potential uses in healthcare to improve the quality of life of the aged and disabled.

Gonzalez et al. [13] explores advancements in human activity recognition (HAR) using cellphones and machine learning algorithms. Unlike earlier investigations, the dataset used in this study was collected in a real-life setting with participants having practically complete freedom. Tree-based models, such as Random Forest, outperformed other strategies in studies employing multiple machine learning algorithms and hyperparameters. The study also looks at how gyroscope data affects the final outcome. This work has resulted in a significant improvement in the accuracy of HAR models in real-world settings.

Gattulli et al. [14] presents a brief review of the state-of-the-art in Human Activity Recognition (HAR), highlighting the use of sensors in smartphones and smartwatches such as accelerometers, gyroscopes, and magnetometers to track users' physical and psychological states. It also highlights prior studies that focused on differentiating activities in laboratory settings, whereas this effort tries to improve HAR in a real-life context and apply it in conjunction with a cyberbullying/ bullying questionnaire.

Park et al. [15] explore the significance of human activity recognition (HAR) in human-centered IoT applications and model MultiCNN-FilterLSTM for HAR, which integrates multihead CNN with LSTM via a residual link. On two publicly available datasets, the proposed model performs better than many others in terms of classification accuracy while requiring fewer operations and being suitable for deployment in IoT systems.

Dua et al. [16] The study discusses human activity recognition (HAR) and its applications in sectors such as healthcare, fitness tracking, and smart surveillance systems. It also examines the use of deep learning techniques for HAR, common benchmark datasets, field problems, and future possibilities for HAR research.

Singh, et al. [17] presents a review of modern approaches utilized in video activity detection, including classical and automatic feature extraction methods. The report divides these approaches into groups and covers their methodologies, accuracy, classifiers, and datasets.

Khodabandelou et al. [18] study a unique fuzzy-based deep learning-based system for predicting future sequences of activities from everyday living activities of a subject wearing a lower limb exoskeleton, with good accuracy for estimating the transition between gait modes.

Soni et al. [19] study human activity recognition, a deep neural network with a bidirectional gated recurrent unit and two convolutional layers is presented, with higher reliability and identification capability than previous discoveries.

Zhang et al. [20] study a location-independent HAR system based on CSI and Parallel Convolutional Networks is suggested to improve inter-class differences and generalization ability of activity identification, attaining an average recognition accuracy of 91.7%.

Yi-Fei et al. [21] show that despite the battery issue with on-body sensors, sensor-based activity recognition algorithms are becoming more common in elderly care due to their lightweight nature and ubiquity.

Several other studies explore human activity recognition in the context of machine learning and deep learning, Human Activity Recognition (HAR) is accomplished through the use of machine learning [22,23], notably deep learning algorithms [24,25]. They all propose new or improved HAR models employing various strategies such as attention mechanisms and Adaboost classifiers. Other studies stress the necessity of precise activity recognition [26–28] in a variety of applications such as classification [29,30] healthcare, IoT, and they compare the performance of various models and datasets.

7.3 PROBLEM STATEMENT

Healthcare practitioners and policymakers must design effective interventions and policies based on data collected by IoT devices. Collaboration is required among academics, healthcare providers, policymakers, and other stakeholders to guarantee that data obtained from IoT sensors is used effectively to encourage healthy habits, reduce healthcare costs, and increase environmental sustainability. Although the use of IoT sensors and various classifiers shows promise in addressing these challenges, there are still significant challenges that must be addressed to ensure effective healthcare monitoring and transportation mode detection.

7.4 PROPOSED WORK

The growing usage of IoT sensors in healthcare and transportation opens up new possibilities for tracking human activity and promoting healthy habits. However, accurate and dependable machine learning algorithms that can classify human activities and transportation modes based on sensor data are required. In this study, we offer a system for monitoring physical activity levels, detecting falls, and classifying transportation modes using a combination of sensors and machine learning techniques. Our Study includes data collection, feature extraction, machine learning training, and real-time sensor data classification. We collect information from a varied set of participants using mobile devices. We extract essential variables from sensor data, such as mean and maximum values of acceleration and orientation, and classify the target variables using ML.

7.5   RESULTS AND DISCUSSION

According to the results, the Random Forest classifier performed the best, with a precision of 0.9966. The K-Nearest Neighbors classifier came in second with an accuracy of 0.7098, followed by the MLP classifier with an accuracy of 0.6772. The accuracies of the Logistic Regression and Gaussian Naive Bayes classifiers were 0.5109 and 0.5581, respectively. The Support Vector Classifier had the highest accuracy, 0.4762, while the Stochastic Gradient Descent Classifier had the lowest, 0.2928. The best classifier, Random Forest, is a powerful ensemble learning method that works well with complicated datasets, while the second-best classifier, K-Nearest Neighbors, is a simple, non-parametric method that performs well with tiny datasets. The third-best performer, the MLP classifier, is a neural network-based approach that can handle huge datasets but may require significant processing resources. The other classifiers have lower accuracies and may not be suitable for this purpose. Figure 7.6 gives features of some sensor using a visualization.

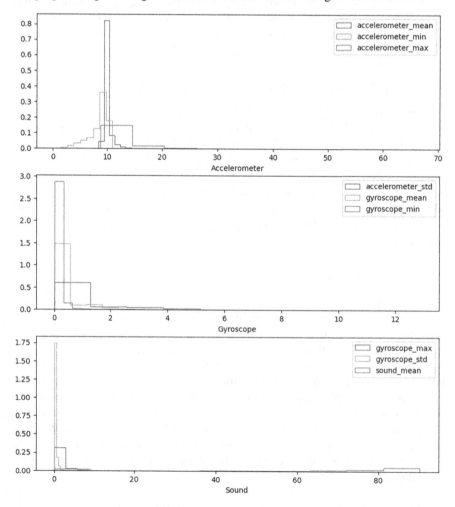

FIGURE 7.6   Activity of the 3 main sensors.

Several researchers discuss the scope of similar mechanisms. This paragraph discusses human activity recognition and machine learning algorithms in [31,32]. A big data architecture for network security is proposed in [33]. The study [34] describes a machine learning algorithm for predicting breast cancer. The paper [35] offers a machine learning strategy for detecting and classifying suspicious behavior in an IoT environment. The article [36] explains how IoT can be used to improve meta-verse capabilities. The paper [37] describes a wearable sensor assessment system for a smart home that employs a random forest based on sequential minimization optimization; presents a machine learning-based security upgrade for 5 G network attack detection. Technology and machine learning are increasingly being used in a variety of fields, including healthcare, smart cities, and safety and security [38–41] Recent research papers have emphasized the potential benefits of adopting such technology into a variety of applications. Exergaming, for example, can benefit from the use of body-worn sensors and deep learning models in recognizing physical sports activities, which can assist promote physical activity and fitness. Furthermore, federated learning has emerged as a potential approach for smart cities, allowing data exchange while maintaining anonymity [42,43]. In the IoT arena, graph-powered learning methods have also showed promise, allowing for more efficient data processing and analysis. Meanwhile, novel photonic sensors for safety and security, such as in infrastructure and ground transportation systems, have been developed [44]. Figure 7.7 shows a graphical depiction of the values.

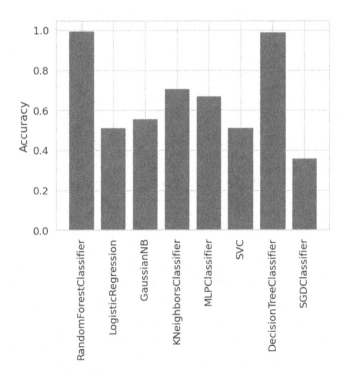

FIGURE 7.7 Performance graph of various classifiers.

7.6   CONCLUSIONS

The results show that machine learning models can reliably categorize targets in human activity detection, especially in the context of transformation mode detection. The lower accuracy scores of LogisticRegression, GaussianNB, MLPClassifier, and SVC indicate that these models may be less well-suited for this task. Further research can be conducted to investigate other machine learning models and techniques, as well as to assess their performance on similar datasets.

7.7   FUTURE SCOPE

Using IoT sensors and machine learning techniques, our proposed system shows potential for healthcare monitoring and transportation mode detection. Future research can look into the potential applications of our framework in other fields like tourism and insurance. The creation of precise and dependable ML algorithms for HAR and transportation mode detection has the potential to have a substantial influence on promoting healthy habits, lowering healthcare expenses, and enhancing environmental sustainability [45–47].

REFERENCES

1. Gupta, A., Anand, R., Pandey, D., Sindhwani, N., Wairya, S., Pandey, B. K., & Sharma, M. (2021). Prediction of breast cancer using extremely randomized clustering forests (ERCF) technique: Prediction of breast cancer. International Journal of Distributed Systems and Technologies (IJDST), 12(4), 1–15.
2. Sindhwani, N., Rana, A., & Chaudhary, A. (2021, September). Breast cancer detection using machine learning algorithms. In 2021 9th International conference on reliability, Infocom technologies and optimization (trends and future directions) (ICRITO) (pp. 1–5). IEEE.
3. Arora, S., Sharma, S., Anand, R., & Shrivastva, G. (2023). Miniaturized pentagon-shaped planar monopole antenna for ultra-wideband applications. Progress in Electromagnetics Research C, 133, 195–208.
4. Anand, R., Daniel, A. V., Fred, A. L., Jaiswal, T., Juneja, S., Juneja, A., & Gupta, A. Building Integrated Systems for Healthcare Considering Mobile Computing and IoT. In Integration of IoT with Cloud Computing for Smart Applications (pp. 203–225). Chapman and Hall/CRC Press.
5. Sharma, G., Nehra, N., Dahiya, A., Sindhwani, N., & Singh, P. (2022). Automatic heart-rate measurement using facial video. In Networking Technologies in Smart Healthcare (pp. 289–307). CRC Press.
6. Chaudhary, A., Bodala, D., Sindhwani, N., & Kumar, A. (2022, March). Analysis of Customer Loyalty Using Artificial Neural Networks. In 2022 International Mobile and Embedded Technology Conference (MECON) (pp. 181–183). IEEE.
7. Verma, S., Bajaj, T., Sindhwani, N., & Kumar, A. (2022). Design and Development of a Driving Assistance and Safety System Using Deep Learning. In Advances in Data Science and Computing Technology (pp. 35–45). Apple Academic Press.
8. Ahuja, A., Patheja, S., & Sindhwani, N. (2022). Impact of COVID-19 on various sectors. Infectious Diseases and Microbiology, 33.
9. Anand, R., & Chawla, P. (2016, March). A review on the optimization techniques for bio-inspired antenna design. In 2016 3rd International conference on computing for sustainable global development (INDIACom) (pp. 2228–2233). IEEE.

10. Chawla, P., & Anand, R. (2017). Micro-switch design and its optimization using pattern search algorithm for applications in reconfigurable antenna. Modern Antenna Systems, 10, 189–210.

11. Anand, R., Arora, S., & Sindhwani, N. (2022, January). A miniaturized UWB antenna for high speed applications. In 2022 International Conference on Computing, Communication and Power Technology (IC3P) (pp. 264–267). IEEE.

12. Patricia, A. C. P., Enrico, V., Shariq, B. A., Emiro, D. L. F., Alberto, P. M. M., Isabel, O. C. A., ... & Fulvio, P. (2023). Machine learning applied to datasets of human activity recognition: Data analysis in health care. Current Medical Imaging, 19(1), 46–64.

13. Garcia-Gonzalez, D., Rivero, D., Fernandez-Blanco, E., & Luaces, M. R. (2023). New machine learning approaches for real-life human activity recognition using smartphone sensor-based data. Knowledge-Based Systems, 110260.

14. Gattulli, V., Impedovo, D., Pirlo, G., & Sarcinella, L. (2023). Human activity recognition for the identification of bullying and cyberbullying using smartphone sensors. Electronics, 12(2), 261.

15. Park, H., Kim, N., Lee, G. H., & Choi, J. K. (2023). MultiCNN-FilterLSTM: Resource-efficient sensor-based human activity recognition in IoT applications. Future Generation Computer Systems, 139, 196–209.

16. Dua, N., Singh, S. N., Challa, S. K., Semwal, V. B., & Sai Kumar, M. L. S. (2023, January). A Survey on Human Activity Recognition Using Deep Learning Techniques and Wearable Sensor Data. In Machine Learning, Image Processing, Network Security and Data Sciences: 4th International Conference, MIND 2022, Virtual Event, January 19–20, 2023, Proceedings, Part I (pp. 52–71). Cham: Springer Nature Switzerland.

17. Singh, R., Kushwaha, A. K. S., & Srivastava, R. (2023). Recent trends in human activity recognition–A comparative study. Cognitive Systems Research, 77, 30–44.

18. Khodabandelou, G., Moon, H., Amirat, Y., & Mohammed, S. (2023). A fuzzy convolutional attention-based GRU network for human activity recognition. Engineering Applications of Artificial Intelligence, 118, 105702.

19. Soni, V., Jaiswal, S., Semwal, V. B., Roy, B., Choubey, D. K., & Mallick, D. K. (2023, January). An Enhanced Deep Learning Approach for Smartphone-Based Human Activity Recognition in IoHT. In Machine Learning, Image Processing, Network Security and Data Sciences: Select Proceedings of 3rd International Conference on MIND 2021 (pp. 505–516). Singapore: Springer Nature Singapore.

20. Zhang, Y., Yin, Y., Wang, Y., Ai, J., & Wu, D. (2023). CSI-based location-independent Human Activity Recognition with parallel convolutional networks. Computer Communications, 197, 87–95.

21. Yi-Fei, T., Soon-Chang, P., Ooi, C. P., & Tan, W. H. (2023). Human activity recognition with self-attention. International Journal of Electrical and Computer Engineering, 13(2).

22. Tasnim, N., & Baek, J. H. (2023). Dynamic edge convolutional neural network for skeleton-based human action recognition. Sensors, 23(2), 778.

23. Panja, A. K., Rayala, A., Agarwala, A., Neogy, S., & Chowdhury, C. (2023). A hybrid tuple selection pipeline for smartphone based human activity recognition. Expert Systems with Applications, 119536.

24. Malik, N. U. R., Abu-Bakar, S. A. R., Sheikh, U. U., Channa, A., & Popescu, N. (2023). Cascading pose features with CNN-LSTM for multiview human action recognition. Signals, 4(1), 40–55.

25. Bhavanasi, G., Werthen-Brabants, L., Dhaene, T., & Couckuyt, I. (2023). Open-Set Patient Activity Recognition with Radar Sensors and Deep Learning. IEEE Geoscience and Remote Sensing Letters.

26. Çalışkan, A. (2023). Detecting human activity types from 3D posture data using deep learning models. Biomedical Signal Processing and Control, 81, 104479.

27. Mata, O., Méndez, J. I., Ponce, P., Peffer, T., Meier, A., & Molina, A. (2023). Energy savings in buildings based on image depth sensors for human activity recognition. Energies, 16(3), 1078.

28. Islam, M. S., Jannat, M. K. A., Hossain, M. N., Kim, W. S., Lee, S. W., & Yang, S. H. (2023). STC-NLSTMNet: An improved human activity recognition method using convolutional neural network with LSTM from WiFi CSI. Sensors, 23(1), 356.

29. Karayaneva, Y., Sharifzadeh, S., Jing, Y., & Tan, B. (2023). Human activity recognition for AI-enabled healthcare using low-resolution infrared sensor data. Sensors, 23(1), 478.

30. Rajamoney, J., & Ramachandran, A. (2023). Representative-discriminative dictionary learning algorithm for human action recognition using smartphone sensors. Concurrency and Computation: Practice and Experience, 35(2), e7468.

31. Carpineti C., Lomonaco V., Bedogni L., Di Felice M., Bononi L. Custom Dual Transportation Mode Detection by Smartphone Devices Exploiting Sensor Diversity. In Proceedings of the 14th Workshop on Context and Activity Modeling and Recognition (IEEE COMOREA 2018), Athens, Greece, March 19-23, 2018.

32. Bansal, B., Jenipher, V. N., Jain, R., Dilip, R., Kumbhkar, M., Pramanik, S., Roy, S. and Gupta, A. (2022). Big Data Architecture for Network Security. In Cyber Security and Network Security (edsS. Pramanik, D. Samanta, M. Vinay and A. Guha).

33. Gupta, A., Kaushik, D., Garg, M., & Verma, A. (2020). Machine Learning model for Breast Cancer Prediction. (2020). Fourth International Conference on I-SMAC (IoT in Social, Mobile, Analytics and Cloud) (I-SMAC), Palladam, India, (pp. 472–477).

34. Talukdar, V., Dhabliya, D., Kumar, B., Talukdar, S. B., Ahamad, S., & Gupta, A. (2022, November). Suspicious Activity Detection and Classification in IoT Environment Using Machine Learning Approach. In 2022 Seventh International Conference on Parallel, Distributed and Grid Computing (PDGC) (pp. 531–535). IEEE.

35. Veeraiah, V., Gangavathi, P., Ahamad, S., Talukdar, S. B., Gupta, A., & Talukdar, V. (2022, April). Enhancement of meta verse capabilities by IoT integration. In 2022 2nd International Conference on Advance Computing and Innovative Technologies in Engineering (ICACITE) (pp. 1493–1498). IEEE.

36. Gupta, N., Janani, S., Dilip, R., Hosur, R., Chaturvedi, A., & Gupta, A. (2022). Wearable sensors for evaluation over smart home using sequential minimization optimization-based random forest. International Journal of Communication Networks and Information Security, 14(2), 179–188.

37. Keserwani, H., Rastogi, H., Kurniullah, A. Z., Janardan, S. K., Raman, R., Rathod, V. M., & Gupta, A. (2022). Security enhancement by identifying attacks using machine learning for 5G network. International Journal of Communication Networks and Information Security, 14(2), 124–141.

38. Afsar, M. M., Saqib, S., Aladfaj, M., Alatiyyah, M. H., Alnowaiser, K., Aljuaid, H., ... & Park, J. (2023). Body-worn sensors for recognizing physical sports activities in Exergaming via deep learning model. IEEE Access, 11, 12460–12473.

39. Bhosale, S. A. (2023). Artificial intelligence and IoT for smart cities. Smart Urban Computing Applications, 7, 207.

40. Pandya, S., Srivastava, G., Jhaveri, R., Babu, M. R., Bhattacharya, S., Maddikunta, P. K. R., ... & Gadekallu, T. R. (2023). Federated learning for smart cities: A comprehensive survey. Sustainable Energy Technologies and Assessments, 55, 102987.

41. Li, Y., Xie, S., Wan, Z., Lv, H., Song, H., & Lv, Z. (2023). Graph-powered learning methods in the Internet of Things: A survey. Machine Learning with Applications, 11, 100441.

42. Romagnano, M. G., & Lépez, H. (2023). Technological integration to reactivate paralyzed organizations. Journal of Computer Science & Technology, 23.

43. Minardo, A., Bernini, R., Berruti, G. M., Breglio, G., Bruno, F. A., Buontempo, S., ... & Cutolo, A. (2023). Innovative photonic sensors for safety and security, Part I: Fundamentals, Infrastructural and ground transportations. Sensors, 23(5), 2558.

44. Ghorbani, F., Ahmadi, A., Kia, M., Rahman, Q., & Delrobaei, M. (2023). A decision-aware ambient assisted living system with IoT embedded device for in-home monitoring of older adults. Sensors, 23(5), 2673.

45. Jain, S., Sindhwani, N., Anand, R., & Kannan, R. (2021, December). COVID Detection Using Chest X-Ray and Transfer Learning. In International Conference on Intelligent Systems Design and Applications (pp. 933–943). Cham: Springer International Publishing.

46. Singh, H., Pandey, B. K., George, S., Pandey, D., Anand, R., Sindhwani, N., & Dadheech, P. (2022, July). Effective Overview of Different ML Models Used for Prediction of COVID-19 Patients. In Artificial Intelligence on Medical Data: Proceedings of International Symposium, ISCMM 2021 (pp. 185–192). Singapore: Springer Nature Singapore.

47. Saini, P., & Anand, M. R. (2014). Identification of defects in plastic gears using image processing and computer vision: A review. International Journal of Engineering Research, 3(2), 94–99.

8 A Study of Metaverse on Medicare Analysis Using Healthcare Analysis

Himangi

8.1 INTRODUCTION

8.1.1 METAVERSE AND HEALTHCARE

Healthcare has always been data-driven, with a rising amount of data generated and collected from many sources. With the rise of big data and advanced analytics, the industry now has a new opportunity to use data to improve patient outcomes and reduce costs. Traditional data visualization and analysis methods, on the other hand, may be incapable of completely capturing the complexity of healthcare data and the insights that might be gleaned from it [1–4]. Metaverse technology creates an immersive virtual world in which users can engage in real time with a simulated environment. Metaverse can provide deeper insights into patterns and trends by enabling more natural and interactive ways of visualizing and studying healthcare data.

The purpose of this research is to investigate the possibilities of metaverse technology for healthcare data analysis, with an emphasis on Medicare. The Medicare dataset includes statistics on the use and payment for treatments as well as all physician and other supplier procedures and services, are included in the dataset. We provide an overview of the Medicare dataset that was utilized in this study and look at how metaverse technology can be used to assess healthcare data. The purpose of this paper is to add to the conversation about the potential benefits of metaverse technology for healthcare data analysis and to promote its adoption in the healthcare industry.

8.1.2 APPLICATIONS OF METAVERSE IN MEDICARE ANALYSIS

- Telemedicine: Metaverse can be utilized to construct immersive virtual environments for telemedicine consultations, allowing patients to interact more naturally and engagingly with healthcare practitioners.
- Medical training: Using metaverse technology, healthcare practitioners can build realistic simulations of medical procedures and surgeries, allowing them to practise and develop their abilities in a safe and controlled environment.

DOI: 10.1201/9781003330523-8

- Patient education: Metaverse can be used to develop interactive educational experiences that assist patients comprehend their medical issues and treatments, allowing them to become more involved in their healthcare.
- Remote patient monitoring: Metaverse can be used to develop virtual environments for remote patient monitoring, allowing healthcare personnel to remotely monitor patients' health and well-being.
- Rehabilitation: Using metaverse technology, immersive rehabilitation programmes for patients recovering from injuries or surgeries can be created, allowing them to practise motions and exercises in a virtual environment.
- Mental health: Metaverse can be used to construct virtual treatment environments for mental health patients, making therapy and counseling more interesting and participatory.
- Health and wellness: Metaverse technology can be utilized to create immersive health and wellness experiences such as virtual fitness courses and meditation sessions.
- Disease management: Metaverse can be used to construct virtual support communities for patients suffering from chronic conditions, allowing them to interact with people who understand their situation and receive help and guidance.

8.1.3 Rise of Metaverse in Healthcare and Medicare Sectors

The concept of a metaverse has received a lot of attention in the healthcare and Medicare industries in recent years. Metaverse technology creates a simulated environment in which people may interact with each other and virtual items in real time, thus establishing a new universe in which healthcare and Medicare services can be more easily accessed and delivered. The capacity to give remote care is one of the primary advantages of the metaverse in healthcare. Patients can save time and money by attending virtual meetings and consultations with healthcare experts from the comfort of their own homes, thanks to virtual reality technology. This technology also allows for the cost-effective delivery of medical training and instruction to a greater audience. The production of virtual medical simulations is another potential application of the metaverse in healthcare [5]. Before performing treatments and surgeries on real patients, medical students can practise them in a simulated environment. This enables them to gain the essential skills and confidence for these treatments, potentially improving patient outcomes and safety [6].

The metaverse can be used in clinical trials and research studies, allowing researchers to simulate different patient scenarios and test different treatments in a safe and controlled environment. This has the potential to hasten the development of new therapies while also lowering the expense of clinical trials. The metaverse can be used to build virtual support groups for people suffering from similar medical conditions, giving them a sense of community and support that they may not have in the actual world [7]. This can aid in the improvement of patient mental health and well-being, which is critical for overall health results.

The metaverse can also be utilized to better manage medical records and patient data. EHRs can be converted into a virtual environment where healthcare providers can view and edit patient information in real time. This can aid in improving the accuracy and efficiency of patient data management, ultimately leading to better patient outcomes.

Healthcare professionals can use the metaverse to construct virtual training and simulation environments [8–10]. This has the potential to improve the quality and consistency of healthcare delivery, as well as reduce medical errors and improve patient safety.

Telemedicine is another potential application of the metaverse in healthcare [11,12]. Virtual reality technology can be used by healthcare providers to perform remote operations and other medical procedures, allowing patients in distant or underdeveloped areas to obtain healthcare treatments that would otherwise be unavailable to them.

8.1.4 WORKING

The purpose of this article is to investigate and analyze the public dataset of the Centres for Medicare & Medicaid Services [13], as well as to investigate the potential of metaverse technology in the healthcare industry, specifically in Medicare analysis. The article will employ visualizations and data exploration to discover patterns and trends in Medicare beneficiaries' utilization and payments for procedures, services, and prescription medicines. The potential applications of metaverse technology in Medicare analysis are highlighted, and various visualizations will be employed to display the dataset's insights. The workings of such a paper include data gathering and cleaning from the dataset, data analysis using various visualizations, and examination of potential uses of metaverse technology in the healthcare industry.

8.2 LITERATURE REVIEW

Hu et al. [14] explained how the metaverse and associated technologies have the potential to disrupt existing medical care paradigms by providing a platform for full-scene interactivity and virtual surgical micro-manipulation. The study emphasizes the significance of strengthening grassroots medical care and promoting the notion of metaverse in order to facilitate the viability and generalization of virtual medical care at the grassroots level.

Chang, et al. [15] looked into the possible applications of metaverse technology in surgical and cosmetic dermatology, such as mixed reality (MR). It emphasizes the advantages of incorporating metaverse technology into medical education and clinical training, surgery planning, patient participation, and telemedicine.

Pandey et al. [16] discussed the potential of Metaverse technology to improve healthcare, particularly in India, where the COVID-19 pandemic has exposed its shortcomings. The author emphasizes Metaverse's multiple benefits, such as improving treatment and education facilities, and its potential to revolutionize the healthcare business.

Shao et al. [17] discussed the potential of metaverse technology in the healthcare business, with a focus on its ability to improve diagnosis, education, and treatment through the integration of artificial intelligence, virtual reality, augmented reality, and other related technologies. The authors examine the numerous metaverse technologies and uses, as well as the existing problems and potential solutions for future deployment.

AL Otaibi et al. [18] studied the metaverse concept and its potential as an immersive internet platform. It offers a thorough assessment of previous studies on metaverse architecture and limits, as well as a framework for developing a metaverse platform.

Soni et al. [19] presented an overview of the metaverse and immersive technologies such as augmented reality, virtual reality, and augmented reality (AR, VR, and MR). It addresses the metaverse's current level of development, difficulties, and potential future directions.

Pandey et al. [20] suggested a method for anonymous data transfer based on component analysis and steganography, which might be utilized to secure healthcare data communication in the metaverse.

Veeraiah et al. [21] proposed a biometric system application to improve security in the virtual world, which can be utilized in healthcare-related virtual settings.

Bansal et al. [22] investigated the use and impact of digital technology in e-learning during the COVID-19 pandemic, which may have implications for the use of virtual education in healthcare education.

Jain et al. [23] advocated improving machine learning accuracy during blockchain-based transaction classification, which might be used in the secure sharing of healthcare data in the metaverse.

Kaushik et al. [24] introduced a novel strategy to using machine learning and deep learning in cybersecurity, which could have applications in the safeguarding of healthcare-related data in virtual environments.

Gupta et al. [25] was studied on medical data and can be used in the metaverse to improve healthcare. The symposium covered a wide range of topics related to the use of artificial intelligence on medical data, such as image analysis, pattern recognition, and clinical decision support.

Onggirawan et al. [26] conducted a systematic literature review of previous studies to investigate the potential of Metaverse as a tool for virtual education. The authors discovered that Metaverse has great promise in the sphere of education, but that direction from teachers and parents is still required to prevent its drawbacks.

Athar et al. [27] discussed how the Metaverse, a virtual world that mixes augmented reality and virtual reality, is changing medical communication. The paper summarizes the use of Metaverse in healthcare, as well as its future directions and potential obstacles when implementing Metaverse technology.

Gruson et al. [28] investigated the Metaverse's impact on laboratory medicine. The authors undertook a review of available evidence, literature, and reports, as well as an analysis of the Metaverse's various viewpoints.

Shetty et al. [29] highlighted the potential of the Metaverse to influence healthcare owing to the intersection of three current primary technical advances, including telepresence, digital twinning, and blockchain. The paper focuses on the ethical concerns brought by advances in digital healthcare.

8.3 PROBLEM STATEMENT

With the introduction of new technologies such as the metaverse, the healthcare business has undergone a digital transition[30]. However, the metaverse's potential impact on healthcare has yet to be investigated, and there is a lack of analysis on how visualizations can be used to assess its potential applications in healthcare, particularly in the context of Medicare. As a result, there is a need to research the possible applications of the metaverse in healthcare utilizing visualizations and to investigate the influence on Medicare. With the rapid advancement of Metaverse technology, there is a growing interest in investigating its possible uses in healthcare. However, the lack of a comprehensive analysis of Metaverse's impact on healthcare is a significant impediment to its adoption in the medical industry; the benefits like constraints, and ethical implications of integrating Metaverse technology into healthcare, employing visualizations to analyze data and help decision-making, must be investigated.

8.4 PROPOSED WORK

The proposed research will investigate applications specifically in the context of Medicare. The analysis will include the use of visualizations to show the impact of the metaverse on healthcare and to identify any difficulties and possibilities that may develop as a result of Medicare's use of metaverse technology. The purpose is to provide healthcare practitioners and policymakers with insights and recommendations on how to use metaverse technology to improve healthcare delivery and patient outcomes.

8.5 RESULTS AND DISCUSSION

The findings of a comprehensive literature review indicate that Metaverse technology has the ability to improve the learning process in the educational sphere. According to survey results, students appreciate using Metaverse as learning tool and comprehend various lessons better while using Metaverse than when using traditional learning techniques. However, few studies have been conducted to determine which subjects to teach. The Metaverse has received considerable attention in the healthcare industry, and it is regarded as a game-changer due to its potential to address a wide range of issues. The Metaverse has gained substantial attention in the healthcare industry because to its ability to solve a variety of issues. However, incorporating the Metaverse into healthcare applications presents a number of challenges, including data privacy and security concerns, ethical concerns, and the requirement for trained healthcare professionals to manage the technology. Figures 8.1–8.3

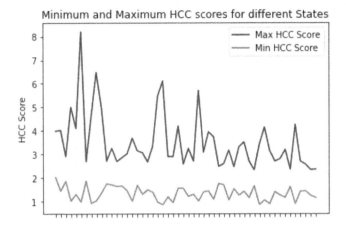

FIGURE 8.1   HCC scores for different states.

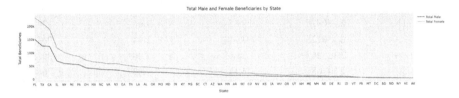

FIGURE 8.2   Total male and female beneficiaries in states.

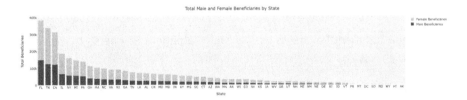

FIGURE 8.3   Total beneficiaries in different states.

give general visualizations while Table 8.1 gives HCC scores to various states facilities.

Based on data from the 2014 CMS Medicare home health agencies dataset in Figure 8.1 the table provides the average, maximum, and minimum Home Health Resource Group (HHRG) score by state, as well as the total number of facilities in each state. The states with the highest average HHRG scores are DC, New York, and New Jersey, while the states with the lowest scores are West Virginia, North Carolina, and South Carolina.

Figure 8.4 depicts the link between average inpatient and outpatient payments by healthcare providers. This process can potentially be improved with advancement in metaverse and decentralized payment methods [31].

TABLE 8.1
CMS-HCC Scores Analysis

S.no	State	Avg_Hcc_Score	Max_Hcc_Score	Min_Hcc_Score	Total Facilities
1.	DC	2.705556	3.98	2.01	18
2.	NY	2.326087	4.01	1.43	138
3.	NJ	2.306739	2.90	1.85	46
4.	OH	2.302719	5.00	1.01	526
5.	IN	2.293204	4.10	1.29	206
6.	TX	2.282303	8.20	0.97	2340
7.	HI	2.252143	2.68	1.86	14
8.	MI	2.240164	4.61	0.91	610
9.	CA	2.237322	6.48	1.02	1135
10.	AZ	2.226165	4.97	1.35	113
11.	DE	2.211250	2.70	1.74	16
12.	RI	2.197500	3.25	1.69	28
13.	GA	2.186275	2.68	1.63	102
14.	TN	2.180970	2.85	1.65	134
15.	LA	2.158128	3.01	1.44	203
16.	PA	2.153267	3.68	1.00	303
17.	SC	2.147031	3.14	1.67	64
18.	NC	2.137778	3.05	1.29	171
19.	WV	2.137143	2.66	1.48	56
20.	CT	2.132375	3.34	1.38	80

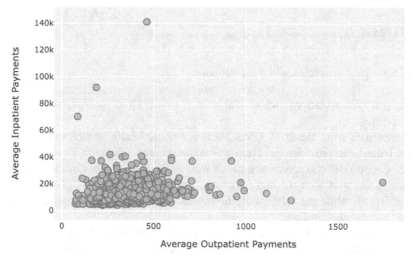

FIGURE 8.4 Payments in Medicare data using a scatter plot.

Metaverse can be used for network security [32], machine learning models can be used for breast cancer prediction [33], suspicious activity detection and classification in IoT environments can be achieved using machine learning [34], metaverse capabilities can be enhanced through IoT integration [35], wearable sensors can be evaluated over a smart home using random forest [36,37], and security for 5 G networks can be enhanced by identifying attacks using machine learning. All of these technologies can be used to improve patient care and outcomes in the metaverse by ensuring secure and efficient data transfer, accurate disease prediction and early detection, and effective patient health monitoring using wearable sensors in a secure and reliable manner.

Social networks, artificial intelligence (AI), virtual reality, remote cooperation, hunger alleviation, and education are among the issues covered in research. These papers provide insights into the most recent research and advancements in these fields [38–40], emphasizing the potential benefits for various facets of human life. A qualitative study on older individuals' online interactions during the COVID-19 epidemic, for example, gives information on trust and vulnerability issues in virtual spaces. In the meantime, a large-scale field intervention study shows that experiencing herd immunity in virtual reality increases COVID-19 vaccination intention [40,41]. Other publications investigate the importance of artificial intelligence and big data in company growth, as well as the mainstreaming of video-mediated distant cooperation during the epidemic [42].

8.6 CONCLUSIONS

The proposed study intends to fill a gap in the literature by investigating how visualizations might be used to analyze the impact of metaverse technology on healthcare and identify any issues and possibilities that may develop as a result of its adoption in the medical business. Through the use of metaverse technology, this study can contribute to the improvement of healthcare delivery and patient outcomes by providing insights and recommendations for healthcare practitioners and policymakers. The outcomes of this study can also contribute to a better understanding of the benefits, limitations, and ethical issues of incorporating metaverse technology into healthcare [43–46].

8.7 FUTURE SCOPE

Future research could look into the usage of metaverse technologies in telemedicine and remote patient monitoring. Furthermore, more research could be conducted on the ethical and legal implications of using the metaverse in healthcare, including data privacy and security concerns. Finally, future research could look into how metaverse technology affects healthcare disparities and access to care, especially for underserved populations. These lines of investigation could help to broaden our understanding of the potential benefits and challenges of incorporating the metaverse into healthcare, as well as inform the development of policies and guidelines for its use.

REFERENCES

1. Sansanwal, K., Shrivastava, G., Anand, R., & Sharma, K. (2019). Big data analysis and compression for indoor air quality. Handbook of IoT and Big Data, 1.
2. Sharma, R., Vashisth, R., & Sindhwani, N. (2023). Study and Analysis of Classification Techniques for Specific Plant Growths. In Advances in Signal Processing, Embedded Systems and IoT: Proceedings of Seventh ICMEET-2022 (pp. 591–605). Singapore: Springer Nature Singapore.
3. Sindhwani, N., Rana, A., & Chaudhary, A. (2021, September). Breast cancer detection using machine learning algorithms. In 2021 9th International conference on reliability, Infocom technologies and optimization (trends and future directions) (ICRITO) (pp. 1–5). IEEE.
4. Gupta, B., Chaudhary, A., Sindhwani, N., & Rana, A. (2021, September). Smart shoe for detection of electrocution using Internet of Things (IoT). In 2021 9th International Conference on Reliability, Infocom Technologies and Optimization (Trends and Future Directions)(ICRITO) (pp. 1–3). IEEE.
5. Mozumder, M. A. I., Armand, T. P. T., Imtiyaj Uddin, S. M., Athar, A., Sumon, R. I., Hussain, A., & Kim, H. C. (2023). Metaverse for digital anti-aging healthcare: An overview of potential use cases based on artificial intelligence, blockchain, IoT technologies, its challenges, and future directions. Applied Sciences, 13(8), 5127.
6. Garcia-Gonzalez, D., Rivero, D., Fernandez-Blanco, E., & Luaces, M. R. (2023). New machine learning approaches for real-life human activity recognition using smartphone sensor-based data. Knowledge-Based Systems, 110260.
7. Ahuja, A. S., Polascik, B. W., Doddapaneni, D., Byrnes, E. S., & Sridhar, J. (2023). The digital metaverse: Applications in artificial intelligence, medical education, and integrative health. Integrative Medicine Research, 12(1), 100917.
8. Sharma, G., Nehra, N., Dahiya, A., Sindhwani, N., & Singh, P. (2022). Automatic Heart-rate Measurement Using Facial Video. In Networking Technologies in Smart Healthcare (pp. 289–307). CRC Press.
9. Saini, P., & Anand, M. R. (2014). Identification of defects in plastic gears using image processing and computer vision: A review. International Journal of Engineering Research, 3(2), 94–99.
10. Gupta, A., Anand, R., Pandey, D., Sindhwani, N., Wairya, S., Pandey, B. K., & Sharma, M. (2021). Prediction of breast cancer using extremely randomized clustering forests (ERCF) technique: Prediction of breast cancer. International Journal of Distributed Systems and Technologies (IJDST), 12(4), 1–15.
11. Arora, S., Sharma, S., & Anand, R. (2022, July). A Survey on UWB Textile Antenna for Wireless Body Area Network (WBAN) Applications. In Artificial Intelligence on Medical Data: Proceedings of International Symposium, ISCMM 2021 (pp. 173–183). Singapore: Springer Nature Singapore.
12. Meivel, S., Sindhwani, N., Valarmathi, S., Dhivya, G., Atchaya, M., Anand, R., & Maurya, S. (2022). Design and Method of 16.24 GHz Microstrip Network Antenna Using Underwater Wireless Communication Algorithm. In Cyber Technologies and Emerging Sciences: ICCTES 2021 (pp. 363–371). Singapore: Springer Nature Singapore.
13. https://console.cloud.google.com/bigquery?p=bigquery-public-data&d=cms_medicare. Accessed 10 Feb 2023.
14. Hu, Y., & Pang, J. (2023). Research on the new path of deepening grassroots medical care from the perspective of metaverse. Academic Journal of Management and Social Sciences, 2(1), 81–84.

15. Chang, Y. F., & Chen, L. C. (2023). Introduction to metaverse: Future of surgical and cosmetic dermatology. The Journal of Clinical and Aesthetic Dermatology, 16(3), 20.

16. Pandey, A., Chirputkar, A., & Ashok, P. (2023, March). Metaverse: An innovative model for healthcare domain. In 2023 International Conference on Innovative Data Communication Technologies and Application (ICIDCA) (pp. 334–337). IEEE.

17. Shao, L., Tang, W., Zhang, Z., & Chen, X. (2023). Medical metaverse: Technologies, applications, challenges and future. Journal of Mechanics in Medicine and Biology, 23(02), 2350028.

18. Al Otaibi, M., Alharbi, E., Wadee Alhalabi, W., & Areej Malibari, A. (2023). Exploring the design elements and limitations of metaverse platform for Saudi vision 2030. Eaman and Wadee Alhalabi, Wadee and Areej Malibari, Areej, Exploring the Design Elements and Limitations of Metaverse Platform for Saudi Vision, 2030.

19. Soni, L., Kaur, A., & Sharma, A. (2023, February). A review on metaverse and immersive technologies. In 2023 Third International Conference on Artificial Intelligence and Smart Energy (ICAIS) (pp. 924–928). IEEE.

20. Pandey, B. K., Pandey, D., Gupta, A., Nassa, V. K., Dadheech, P., & George, A. S. (2023). Secret Data Transmission Using Advanced Morphological Component Analysis and Steganography. In Role of Data-Intensive Distributed Computing Systems in Designing Data Solutions (pp. 21–44). Cham: Springer International Publishing.

21. Veeraiah, V., Kumar, K. R., Lalitha Kumari, P., Ahamad, S., Bansal, R., & Gupta, A. (2023). Application of biometric system to enhance the security in virtual world. In 2022 2nd International Conference on Advance Computing and Innovative Technologies in Engineering (ICACITE), Greater Noida, India (pp. 719–723). IEEE.

22. Bansal, R., Gupta, A., Singh, R., & Nassa, V. K. (2021, July). Role and impact of digital technologies in E-learning amidst COVID-19 pandemic. 2021 Fourth International Conference on Computational Intelligence and Communication Technologies (CCICT) (pp. 194–202). IEEE.

23. Jain, V., Beram, S. M., Talukdar, V., Patil, T., Dhabliya, D., & Gupta, A. (2022, November). Accuracy enhancement in machine learning during blockchain based transaction classification. In 2022 Seventh International Conference on Parallel, Distributed and Grid Computing (PDGC) (pp. 536–540). IEEE.

24. Kaushik, D., Garg, M., Annu, & Gupta, A.; Sabyasachi Pramanik. (2022). Utilizing Machine Learning and Deep Learning in Cybesecurity: An Innovative Approach. Cyber Security and Digital Forensics: Challenges and Future Trends, Wiley, 2022, (pp. 271–293). Wiley.

25. Gupta, M., Ghatak, S., Gupta, A., & Mukherjee, A. L. (Eds.). (2022). Artificial Intelligence on Medical Data: Proceedings of International Symposium, ISCMM 2021 (Vol. 37). Springer Nature.

26. Onggirawan, C. A., Kho, J. M., Kartiwa, A. P., & Gunawan, A. A. (2023). Systematic literature review: The adaptation of distance learning process during the COVID-19 pandemic using virtual educational spaces in metaverse. Procedia Computer Science, 216, 274–283.

27. Athar, A., Ali, S. M., Mozumder, M. A. I., Ali, S., & Kim, H. C. (2023, February). Applications and possible challenges of healthcare metaverse. In 2023 25th International Conference on Advanced Communication Technology (ICACT) (pp. 328–332). IEEE.

28. Gruson, D., Greaves, R., Dabla, P., Bernardini, S., Gouget, B., & Öz, T. K. (2023). A new door to a different world: Opportunities from the metaverse and the raise of meta-medical laboratories. Clinical Chemistry and Laboratory Medicine (CCLM), (0).

29. Shetty, A., Kulkarni, G. S., SN, R. B., & Paarakh, P. M. (2023). A review on metaverse in health care and pharma. Journal of Community Pharmacy Practice (JCPP) 2799–1199, 3(01), 1–11.

30. Bhattacharya, S., Hegde, P., & Maddikunta, P. K. R. Metaverse for Healthcare: A Survey on Potential Applications, Challenges and Future Directions. 10.1109/ ACCESS.2023.3241628.

31. Hollensen, S., Kotler, P., & Opresnik, M. O. (2022). Metaverse–The new marketing universe. Journal of Business Strategy, (ahead-of-print).

32. Bansal, B., Jenipher, V. N., Jain, R., Dilip, R., Kumbhkar, M., Pramanik, S., Roy, S., & Gupta, A. (2022). Big Data Architecture for Network Security. In Cyber Security and Network Security (edsS. Pramanik, D. Samanta, M. Vinay and A. Guha).

33. Gupta, A., Kaushik, D., Garg, M., & Verma,A. (2020). Machine learning model for breast cancer prediction. (2020). Fourth International Conference on I-SMAC (IoT in Social, Mobile, Analytics and Cloud) (I-SMAC), Palladam, India, (pp. 472–477).

34. Talukdar, V., Dhabliya, D., Kumar, B., Talukdar, S. B., Ahamad, S., & Gupta, A. (2022, November). Suspicious activity detection and classification in iot environment using machine learning approach. In 2022 Seventh International Conference on Parallel, Distributed and Grid Computing (PDGC) (pp. 531–535). IEEE.

35. Veeraiah, V., Gangavathi, P., Ahamad, S., Talukdar, S. B., Gupta, A., & Talukdar, V. (2022, April). Enhancement of meta verse capabilities by IoT integration. In 2022 2nd International Conference on Advance Computing and Innovative Technologies in Engineering (ICACITE) (pp. 1493–1498). IEEE.

36. Gupta, N., Janani, S., Dilip, R., Hosur, R., Chaturvedi, A., & Gupta, A. (2022). Wearable sensors for evaluation over smart home using sequential minimization optimization-based random forest. International Journal of Communication Networks and Information Security, 14(2), 179–188.

37. Keserwani, H., Rastogi, H., Kurniullah, A. Z., Janardan, S. K., Raman, R., Rathod, V. M., & Gupta, A. (2022). Security enhancement by identifying attacks using machine learning for 5G network. International Journal of Communication Networks and Information Security, 14(2), 124–141.

38. Kim, K. D., Funk, R. J., & Zaheer, A. (2023). Structure in context: A morphological view of whole network performance. Social Networks, 72, 165–182.

39. Saxena, A. (2023). The AI Factor: How to Apply Artificial Intelligence and Use Big Data to Grow Your Business Exponentially. Post Hill Press.

40. Plechatá, A., Vandeweerdt, C., Atchapero, M., Luong, T., Holz, C., Betsch, C., … & Makransky, G. (2023). Experiencing herd immunity in virtual reality increases COVID-19 vaccination intention: Evidence from a large-scale field intervention study. Computers in Human Behavior, 139, 107533.

41. Volmar, A., Kindervater, C., Randerath, S., & Mniestri, A. (2023). Mainstreaming Zoom: Covid-19, Social Distancing, and the Rise of Video-Mediated Remote Cooperation. In Varieties of Cooperation: Mutually Making the Conditions of Mutual Making (pp. 99–133). Wiesbaden: Springer Fachmedien Wiesbaden.

42. Parks, A., & Rauchwerger, J. (2023). First Food Responders: People are Hungry. Feed Them Now! Here's How. Morgan James Publishing.

43. Arora, S., Sharma, S., Anand, R., & Shrivastva, G. (2023). Miniaturized Pentagon-Shaped Planar Monopole Antenna for Ultra-Wideband Applications. Progress In Electromagnetics Research C, 133, 195–208.

44. Chawla, P., & Anand, R. (2017). Micro-switch design and its optimization using pattern search algorithm for applications in reconfigurable antenna. Modern Antenna Systems, 10, 189–210.

45. Sindhwani, N., Anand, R., Vashisth, R., Chauhan, S., Talukdar, V., & Dhabliya, D. (2022, November). Thingspeak-based environmental monitoring system using IoT. In 2022 Seventh International Conference on Parallel, Distributed and Grid Computing (PDGC) (pp. 675–680). IEEE.

46. Badotra, S., Tanwar, S., Rana, A., Sindhwani, N., & Kannan, R. (Eds.). (2023). Handbook of Augmented and Virtual Reality (Vol. 1). Walter de Gruyter GmbH & Co KG.

9 Blockchain and IoT Sensors in Healthcare 5.0

Lipsa Das, Vimal Bibhu, Bhuvi Sharma,
Khushi Dadhich, and Akanksha Singh

9.1 INTRODUCTION

In order to considerably increase the job of doctors and more accurately treat various ailments, researchers have been attempting to merge IoT, AI and ML, Blockchain technology, and computer vision applications in the sector of e-health or intelligent medical care over the last few years [1–4]. IoT has the potential to dramatically change the healthcare sector. In medicine, Internet-connected devices may be used for a variety of purposes, such as: enhancing the accuracy and effectiveness of medical diagnosis and testing – enhancing the quality of medical care – expanding patient (and caregiver) access to medical information – which improves the standard of care for patients by giving more information to doctors and other healthcare professionals – modifying the process of care for patients by offering better coordination of care [4].

The only time a doctor and patient interacted was during hospital visits before the Internet of Things (IoT). Without actually seeing the patient, the doctor was unable to assess their condition and provide suggestions in accordance with that information. However, IoT-enabled devices have made this possible in the healthcare industry, allowing patients to receive doctor care while remaining safe and without endangering their health. IoT has improved the efficiency and ease of communication between patients and doctors. It contributes to less hospital stays, lower healthcare expenses, and simultaneous improvement of care [5–7].

Along with the previously mentioned benefits for patients, doctors, and caregivers, sensor networks are the cornerstone of operational excellence in hospitals. In many processes, sensor networks can encourage automation and minimize human involvement, which lowers costs and boosts productivity. By incorporating sensors and actuators for tracking and monitoring into patients' medications as well as their bodies. In healthcare applications, smart healthcare is essential. The IoT is used in medical supervision to collect and analyze patient information remotely from processing centers so that the necessary steps can be taken [7]. Clinical care can now use sensors to remotely check on a patient's physiological status. The adoption of wearable technology with sensors is beneficial not just for patients but also for regular people to monitor their health.

DOI: 10.1201/9781003330523-9

Patients diagnosed whose physiological status needs near monitoring can be supervised continually by IoT-driven, non-invasive technology. Sensors are progressively being integrated into more aspects of our lives through downsizing, personalization, and digital signal processing. This kind of technology employs sensors to gather detailed physiological information, after then determines and keeps it via gateways and the cloud prior transmitting the processed information wirelessly to caregivers for extra evaluation and analysis. As well as allowing individuals to be better informed about their conditions and improvements, the data acquired by sensors can aid medical practitioners in understanding life-or-death situations more quickly and precisely. Invasive and non-invasive sensors are sending localized data and information to the cloud for the benefit of patients and the medical sector, from monitoring dialysis equipment to monitoring blood pressure, from monitoring blood pressure to monitoring dialysis equipment [7].

By carefully measuring and supervising, and a different medical status information, smart sensors, who combines a sensor and a microcontroller, making it feasible to reap the benefits of the IoT's potential for medical care. These can include common vital signs like blood pressure and heart rate, as well as measurements of blood sugar or oxygen saturation. Even pill bottles can have smart sensors installed within them that are network-connected to track whether a patient has received the prescribed amount of medication. Through a variety of multimedia techniques, healthcare organizations all over the world are evolving into more effective, coordinated, and user-centered systems. IoT-generated medical data is delicate and vital, and any unwanted access might be dangerous. Since the patient's life is directly impacted by this information, it should be properly preserved. Since the medical industry is embracing IoT, security risks are highlighted more there and require special attention [6,7]. The handling of such a vast amount of data, including the reports and pictures of each lead, is difficult and raises both security threats and the demands placed on human resources. The best technique for ensuring the privacy and safety of the control systems under real-time situations has been found to be Blockchain technology, which can help to resolve these problems.

Peer-to-peer technology known as blockchain ensures that all transactions that have already been verified are unchangeable and creates a worldwide consensus. Several blocks that are connected to one another to form a long chain make up a blockchain in its fundamental form. By utilizing this technique, all information and data that enters the block cannot be changed or altered. In many computers, it is employed to keep the data secure. Blockchain technology is utilized in the medical care industry to store and interchange clients information between hospitals, labs, pharmacies, and doctors. This program is used to stop any serious or harmful error that might happen in a patient's data and affect how that patient is treated [8].

The development in the field of healthcare is increasing at a very fast rate. The requirement for the medical facilities which are very high in quality is increasing which need the support of modern technology. Blockchain can be considered as one of the modern technology which is widely used in the sector of healthcare.

The framework of complete healthcare system is being modified according to the patient use and requirement which has major two key components that are the patient data should be easily accessible by the user and the data should be secured [9–11].

As a result, the transmission of medical data throughout the healthcare system might be more effective, secure, and transparent thanks to blockchain technology. Blockchain technology is maximally used for IoT and healthcare information management activities, mainly to enhance information security, including data integrity, access control, and privacy reservation [12,13].

Personalized healthcare is defined as the practise of well-being, healthcare, and patient assistance that is tailored to a patient's particular biological, behavioral, and cultural traits. Every person is empowered by following the fundamental principle of medical, "the medical supervision for the correct individual at the right time," which also leads to more desirable outcomes, higher satisfaction levels, and cost-effective healthcare. An efficient healthcare system should prioritize protection, detection of disease in beginning stage, and homecare rather than pricy medical care. IoT guarantees the personalization of healthcare services by safeguarding each patient's digital identity. Many health conditions have gone undiagnosed in traditional healthcare systems because there aren't many accessible treatment solutions. But it is now simple to track and evaluate patient data thanks to smart, pervasive IoT-based sensors. IoT-based healthcare systems enable the gathering, archival, and analysis of enormous data streams in various innovative forms as well as the triggering of context-sensitive alarms by using a number of dispersed devices to collect, evaluate, and send valid medical data to cloud.

9.2 APPLICATION OF IOT IN HEALTHCARE

RPM expanded as "Remote physiological monitoring," which is also called remote patient monitoring, tracks patients' vital signs while they are at home and is able to take essential action when necessary with the aid of digital technologies. The field of RPM is seeing new opportunities because to developments in sensor technology, the widespread usage of cellular technology, and the falling price of implanted interacting devices. Organizations can enhance clinical results and service quality affordably. The elderly notably benefit from it because it makes going to hospitals easier. To give appropriate medical advice, remote monitoring of key physiological indicators like weights, BP, pulse rate, sugar levels, and others may be done [14]. Figure 9.1 shows the enablers of Remote Patient Monitoring System.

By altering how equipment and people interact while delivering healthcare solutions, IoT is without a doubt revolutionizing the healthcare industry [15]. There are various advantages of IoT implementation in the sector of healthcare which are discussed below:

- **IoT for Patients** – With the use of wirelessly connected blood pressure and heart rate monitor cuffs, glucometers, and other wearable devices like fitness bands, patients can access individualized care. These devices have the ability to be configured to remind users to monitor their BP changes, appointments, and a variety of other things.

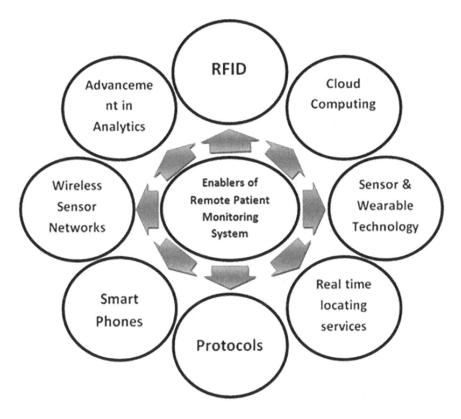

FIGURE 9.1   Enablers of remote patient monitoring system.

By enabling the ongoing monitoring of medical conditions, IoT has changed people's lives, especially those of older patients. Families and one-person households are significantly impacted by this. An individual's alarm system alerts concerned relatives and healthcare professionals to any disturbances or variations in their regular activities.

- **IoT for Physicians** – Through the use of smartwatches and some other IoT-enabled personal tracking devices, experts may more efficiently monitor their clients' health. They also can store tabs on a client's acquiescence with their treatment regimen and any other instant medical need. Grateful to IoT, Medical professionals can now actively engage with patients and maintain increased vigilance. Information from the IoT can assist physicians in selecting the appropriate therapeutic strategy for each patient and obtaining targeted outcomes.
- **IoT for Hospitals** – Hospitals can deploy IoT for a broad range of other reasons in addition to patient health supervision. The actual-time location of health instruments, like walkers, defibrillators, nebulizer treatments, oxygen pumps, and other surveillance instrument, is tracked using IoT gadgets tagged with sensors. It is also feasible to assess how well medical workers are positioned at various sites in real time. The transmission of

pathogens is a major worry for hospital patients. IoT-enabled hygiene monitoring devices can help prevent a patient infection. IoT devices can be useful for asset management tasks like managing medication inventory, keeping an eye on refrigerator temperatures, and controlling environmental humidity and temperature.

- **For Health Insurance Companies** – These companies provide a huge variety of choices for the healthcare machineries or equipment which are connected to IoT. For the claims these insurance companies collect the information from these health monitoring devices. All these information which are collected helps them to identify any kind of fraud claim. By IoT-based devices the communication between the insurance provider companies and the customer become very much easier, and the transparency also get increased. The process of pricing, claim handling and risk management also become easier. In this process the visibility of the decision and outcome of each procedure become very clear to the customer.

Insurance company clients may receive payment for using and disclosing health information produced by IoT devices. Customers can benefit from tracking their regular activities, adherence to treatment programs, and overall health metrics utilizing IoT devices. There will be far fewer insurance claims as a result. Insurance companies might be able to confirm claims using IoT technology and the data they gather.

9.3   IOT SENSORS

These IoT sensors can be sewn onto a patient's clothing, incorporated into a watch, shoe, piece of clothing, mattress, etc., or installed in a home as a motion sensor [16]. Medical-based detectors can be divided into two categories: sensors that detect physiological factors and ambient sensors, which measure the outside environment. The physiological sensors, which assess vital signs including temperature, blood oxygen saturations, pulse rate, and BP, can either be worn on the body or implanted. The room temperature, light, sound, and fall detection are just a few of the variables that the ambient sensors measure.

- **Accelerometer:** An accelerometer is a tool that calculates the speed of a moving object. It is used to watch and document the patient's body poster in healthcare applications. Additionally, it can detect falls, which is particularly useful for clients who are confined to beds.
- **Humidity and temperature sensors:** Both the outside temperature and the patient's body warmth can be measured using these sensors. Touch or contactless sensors can be used to measure temperature.
- **Sweat sensor:** Data on sodium, chloride, potassium, glucose, amino acids, etc. can be obtained from the biomarkers found in sweat. When used to diagnose disorders like cystic fibrosis, it is quite effective. Athletes and patients have employed wearable sensors that are built into textiles in numerous instances to collect data from their body fluids.

- **Respiration sensor:** During magnetic resonance imaging scanning, a patient's breathing can be monitored using a respiration sensor, an optical sensor. Monitoring disorders like sleep apnea or Chronic Obstructive Pulmonary Disease with respiratory rate monitoring is very useful for ambulatory assessments (COPD).
- **Blood glucose sensor:** For diabetes patients to repetitively supervise the glucose level in interstitial fluids, glucose monitoring sensors are essential. These devices can be non-invasive ones that use ultrasonic, infrared, or optical sensors, or they can be bio-implants that are inserted beneath the skin.
- **Blood pressure sensor:** Since high BP enhances the chances of cardiac arrests, strokes, and other conditions, it is essential to monitor blood pressure constantly. As opposed to the conventional inspection method, sensors that can be weared uses the pulse wave method provide correct readings [17].
- **Electrocardiogram sensor:** An ECG sensor measures the electrical impulse that passes through the cardiac muscles. Electrodes used by ECG sensors must make skin contact in order to function.
- **Pulse oximetry sensor:** This sensor measures the amount of oxygenated hemoglobin in the blood using a non-invasive manner. It is fastened to the patient's fingertip, through which the light wave travels to the blood vessels. The SpO2 measurement is made possible by variations in the light wave that passes through.

9.3.1 AMBULANCE FITTED WITH SENSORS

It can be quite challenging to diagnose and treat patients while an ambulance is being transported in many emergency situations. As a result, the patient's diagnosis and treatment are delayed until they are admitted to the hospital. Patients frequently die while being transported in an ambulance because there aren't adequate support mechanisms in place. Recent improvements in healthcare, lower communication costs, and much research in the field have improved the standard of care given to patients.

One such development is ambulance telemetry, which allows for the automatic measurement and wireless transfer of key information about patients within an ambulance so that doctors or medical facilities can use it to make important treatment-related choices. The patient receives the essential care while still in the ambulance thanks to sensors that have been installed on the ambulance and that can collect data.

While a seriously ill patient is being carried to the hospital by ambulance, telemetry technology is used to remotely treat the patient and monitor their vital signs [18].

- Polycam/Web Camera: A polycam is one of the tools that is highly helpful for consulting at a distance. In order to check or observe the patient vital signs, for example, pulse or heart rate, etc. these web cameras are attached to the network line and TV at a hospital or an ambulance. A webcam is frequently used instead of a polycam.

- Internet: When the hospital's portal receives the patient's vital signs from the ambulance, it can be utilized to schedule an online consultation with a doctor to ensure that the critically ill patient receives prompt care while traveling to the hospital.
- Wireless communication: In IoT-based systems, where devices connect with one other from faraway locations, wireless technology has become a crucial component. Smartphones, GPS (Global Positioning System) units, Zigbee technology, Wi-Fi, Bluetooth, and other communication devices are some examples. Data gathered from the sensor nodes is communicated by wireless communication technologies like Zigbee or low-power in a remote patient monitoring system.

The information is then collected further and transmitted over Bluetooth to the concentrator or IoT gateway where it will be analyzed in the cloud [19]. With its low energy usage and extended battery life, Zigbee is the most popular platform for distant monitoring and sensing applications.

9.3.2 SOCIAL SENSORS

Social network integration with sensor network technology offers users information-rich solutions that can recognize context. Social sensing can increase the value of the rapidly growing real-time data generated every day by social networking sites and mobile devices. Applications of social sensing present a variety of research issues.

Few difficulties which are faced by these social sensors are discussed below [20,21]:

- **Privacy Issue**: It is essential to adopt privacy-sensitive approaches before using social data obtained from sensors for analysis because the data may contain sensitive information (such as location data). The most common method for hiding the real data is to add noise or aggregate the original data. PoolView is such a delicate method for gathering and using mobile sensor data. The majority of privacy-preservation strategies undermine data dependability, but trust is predicated on strong data reliability. Even though the topic of privacy-preserving data mining has been extensively studied, dealing with the interconnected multi-dimensional time-series data provided by sensor data poses a fresh set of challenges. These correlations in sensor data streams create new opportunities for privacy breaches, demanding the creation of creative tactics.
- **Trust issues**: Smartphones and sensors may generate enormous amounts of data. The location information of users and devices may be tracked by a patient or equipment tracking system. To handle such enormous data, design strategies that can compress and process large amounts of data are needed. Sensor data are frequently prone to errors or inputs without any form of validation, which raises questions about the reliability of the data being gathered.

- **Battery life**: Mobile and wearable electronics are powered by batteries, which have a finite lifespan. These gadgets have sensors, which can quickly deplete the battery life due to their involvement in constant data collection. Battery life is still a major constraint, thus the infrastructural design should be conscious of the trade-offs and focus on increasing efficiency without sacrificing the application's goals.

9.4 CHALLENGES AND SOLUTIONS OF IOT HEALTHCARE

IoT is used in many different applications that serve the healthcare system in many ways, including patient monitoring and smart home systems. These are a few of the major issues that the healthcare system is now facing:

1. IoT offers the door for high flexibility; for example, a patient who needs ongoing care can live at home instead of a hospital and be constantly checked on thanks to IoT technology. Certain wearable technology, including sensors, might be painful for patients bodies.
2. Data that is transmitted over noise from detector to the control device and finally to the monitoring center. Better architecture makes it easier to convey data while maintaining its integrity. Techniques for removing background noise can also improve the data signal.
3. The majority of the ECG monitoring techniques now in use utilize guided signal analysis. This raises the price and raises the possibility of a detection error. The signal can be analyzed using machine learning, which increases productivity and lowers costs.
4. As there are more sensors and devices, more energy is needed to process them, which increases power loss and energy use. To consume less energy, an optimization algorithm can be utilized.
5. Keeping track of large numbers of IoT users takes more mainframe and storage space, which can be avoided by putting the data on the cloud. However, the complexity rises as a result of IoT integration with the cloud.
6. Since the gadgets are more susceptible to attack, privacy is a significant issue with the IoT. Due to their modest resource requirements, these devices are challenging to encrypt on [22].
7. Because hackers or intruders can quickly access sensor data, security has been a big problem in the IoT. It is therefore important to look at novel security measures. IDP was created in [23] as a data placement technique for the IoT that preserves privacy. The major goal of the suggested method is to maximize data access speed, maximize resource use, and minimize energy use while upholding data privacy laws.

9.5 BLOCKCHAIN TECHNOLOGY IN HEALTHCARE

Blockchain provides a promising new stage to enhance and promote the combination of health data into a variety of applications and stakes. Real-time records and blockchain manipulation resistance provide special advantages in the healthcare industry. Real-time data sharing between individuals and companies is possible when using blockchain technology. Each transaction or event is time-stamped in order to be added to a lengthy chain or permanent record that cannot be changed later. On an unlicensed blockchain, all records may be evaluated by all stakeholders. By deciding where and by whom to look for transactions on a blockchain, data safety can be ensured while protecting the identities of both parties. As a result, the blockchain turns the various pieces of information that one owner possesses into the full history of the asset. This technology has various applications in the field of healthcare, but it is not yet a fully developed technology or one that will soon be put into use as a panacea. The management of individual medical and service-based patients will continue to be based on blockchain technology [24].

Figure 9.2 shows the architecture of medical blockchain.

A. *Issue, preservation and medical data sharing are three key roles in medical blockchain.*
   1. Medical records creation or test results are produced for patients when they visit a medical facility (medical data release, or MDR). The doctor generates digest and hash-medical information once it is generated, enters the issuer's private key, and sends this to the blockchain. At the same time, symmetrical keys are used to encrypt medical data codes and public keys are also used to encrypt medical data. We are both delivered to the patient at the same time.

| Medical information service platform, Insurance |

| Patients | 3rd party agencies | Medical institutions |

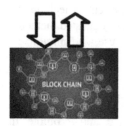

FIGURE 9.2   The architecture of medical blockchain.

2. Medical data storage (MDS): After the medical institution receives the data, the patient confirms the institution's signature. He creates a new encryption key to store medical data and a cloud signature and utilizes a private key to decrypt, encrypt, and sign original medical data.

3. Sharing of medical data: The user may grant some of their medical information to a third party through the access control system and may also withdraw their permission at any moment. The club storage management, third-party agency decryption key rights of use, and expiration date will all be recorded on the medical blockchain. A lot of people are now interested in using blockchains to provide secure healthcare data, exchange biomedical and e-health information, simulate the human brain, and think. A P2P network is present alongside blockchain. In order to get beyond the limits of traditional distributed database synchronization employing techniques of distributed consensus, this principally consists of P2P multi-field network architecture made up of algorithms, cryptography, and math. Transparent, decentralized, autonomous, immortal, anonymous, and open-source are the six main characteristics of blockchain technology.

B. *Essential elements of blockchain technology*

1. **Decentralized**: A database system that allows anyone connected to the network to access it using an open access control mechanism. Data may be accessed, tracked, stored, or updated by several systems.

2. **Transparency**: A blockchain's recorded and saved data is open to potential users and simple to update. The transparency of blockchains should prevent data from being changed or stolen.

3. **Immutable**: Records that have been stored will always be stored and are difficult to change without concurrent control of more than 51% of the nodes.

4. **Autonomy**: Because the blockchain system is autonomous and independent, each node can access, transfer, store, and update data privately and without intervention from third parties.

5. **Open Source**: Blockchain technology is made to give everyone with a network connection access to the open-source. This limitless adaptability not only enables public document inspection but also the development of countless impending applications.

6. **Anonymity**: The system is safer and more dependable because no one's identity is revealed while data is exchanged between nodes. In this network, a person must verify each new transaction that is made. Every transaction becomes progressively unaltered as each block of a blockchain is verified by every node in the network. The workflow for using blockchain in healthcare is depicted in Figure 9.3.

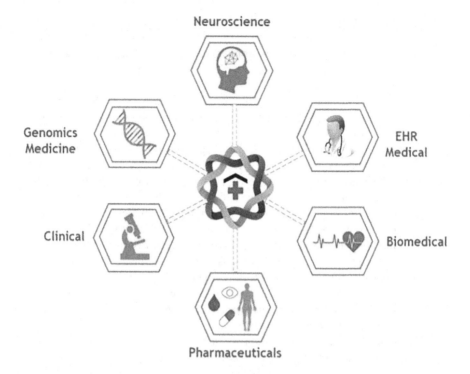

Neuroscience

Genomics
Medicine

EHR
Medical

Clinical

Biomedical

Pharmaceuticals

FIGURE 9.3 Workflow for using blockchain in healthcare.

9.6 APPLICATIONS OF BLOCKCHAIN TECHNOLOGY IN HEALTHCARE

1. **Electronic Health Records**: It is guaranteed that EHR software will be integrated into a centralized blockchain directory from the point of data generation to the point of data recovery without the need for human intervention.
2. **Clinical Research**: Blockchain created a decentralized secure platform for all potential information partnerships in clinical research. This makes it possible for research teams to safely communicate data.
3. **Medical Fraud Detection**: Blockchain, which has a permanent feature, aids in the detection of fraud and, in the end, creates a transparent and safe transaction by forbidding transaction repetition and modification.
4. **Neuroscience Research**: Blockchain's innovation has a number of potential uses for enhancing the brain, reproducing the brain, and thinking the brain. It is obvious that a platform is needed to store the entire human brain, and here is where blockchain technology shines.
5. **Pharmaceutical Industry and Research**: Using the potential of precise traceability, blockchain keeps an eye on every step of the pharmaceutical

supply chain. In order to avoid counterfeiting and theft of goods, the origin, composition, and ownership of medicines are frequently documented at every stage.

9.7 CHALLENGES OF BLOCKCHAIN IN HEALTHCARE

9.7.1 PRIVACY AND SECURITY OF DATA

A patient must designate one or more representatives who, in the event of an emergency, may access the patient's information and medical history without the third party's consent. Now that the agent can allow a number of persons to access a patient's records, the privacy and security of information are seriously threatened. In practise, high-security data mechanisms would make it challenging for users to access partial or restricted data transmissions block by block. An assault known as a 51% might compromise the security of blockchain networks. A group of miners with a network that is more than 50% blockchain are involved in this attack. Miners are given network authority, and by withholding their assent, they have the power to stop any further transactions. According to CoinDesk, this current assault affected five different crypto currencies. Additionally, a patient record can contain incorrect or sensitive data.

9.7.2 MANAGING STORAGE CAPACITY

Another issue is the control of storage capacity. Blockchain was created to store and process confidential transaction data, eliminating the need for a significant amount of storage. As the storage problems spread throughout the healthcare sector, they became more obvious. In the healthcare sector, a large amount of information must be managed each day. All information, comprising health records, medical backgrounds, and trials in addition to X-rays, MRI scans, and certain other medical images, is available to all chain nodes in the blockchain scenario. All of them are reachable. Because blockchain apps are also transaction-based, the databases used for this application are quick. The record level access and search has decreased as database size has increased, which is extremely undesirable in terms of transaction performance. Therefore, a scalable and reliable blockchain solution must be sought.

9.7.3 INTEROPERABILITY ISSUES

Interoperability, or having blockchains connect with one another accurately and perfectly by a variety of communication providers, is another problem blockchain faces. This issue makes it difficult to successfully share data.

9.7.4 STANDARDIZATION CHALLENGES

The standardization of medical and healthcare is likely to encounter challenges with blockchain technology, which is still in its infancy. A variety of well-authenticated and approved standards would also be developed by the worldwide standardization organizations. These pre-established standards may be used to determine the size, kind, and structure of information exchanges in blockchain applications. Such restrictions should act as safety precautions in addition to evaluating shared data [25,26].

9.8 SOLUTIONS FOR HEALTHCARE USING BLOCKCHAIN TECHNOLOGY

9.8.1 Burst IQ

Burst IQ offers an interactive platform for exchanging large amounts of data among individuals, researchers, and organizations. It encourages the gathering of additional health data and meets with the criteria of HIPAA, GDPR, and NIST compatibility. Additionally, Burst IQ processes enormous amounts of data using machine learning.

They offer a variety of services, mostly data-driven solutions for healthcare based on blockchain. They offer the user an ecosystem for managing data. They create individual life graphs based on user data and put them in a healthy wallet. User has the ability to supply, manage, share, and sell personal data.

9.8.2 MedRec

MedRec offers a full platform for stakeholders to share and authenticate patient data. They employed PoW (proof of work) mining to get the backing of scientists, health authorities, and individuals. Additionally, incentives for efficient data sharing and validation have been put in place. For data interchange, a simple audibility log is offered. Together, MIT Media Lab and Beth Israel Dracones Health Center are creating the "MedRec" blockchain platform.

In the present, situations include Data Infringement Code violations and other potential crimes involving healthcare data, such as confidentiality and authentication. The goal of MedRec is to meet all relevant requirements. In contrast to traditional methods of data storage, it stores health information in a unique way.

9.8.3 Health Combix

The fundamental goal of this platform is to use PP communication to build a decentralized ecosystem in real time. HC is a platform for managing patient data that relies on token privacy. This paradigm encourages the prediction of diseases based on huge data studies and open risk-related asset monetization. In this project, a framework for research collaboration is built using a private blockchain.

9.8.4 IBM Blockchain

IBM also offers further blockchain applications to numerous healthcare facilities. Automated trials and open sharing of health records are the two primary components of IBM blockchain in healthcare. The blockchain solutions are scalable, quick, and built for a multicloud world.

9.8.5 YOUBASE

Presented an HD-based wallet (hierarchic deterministic). The wallet manages data access and has a central tree-like structure. The fact that this Youbase will hold information individually according on the specific data type because it has several branches is a huge advantage (parent or child chains) An approach used to comply with data protection laws is data anonymization.

9.9 FUTURE SCOPE

The healthcare industry will be greatly benefitted from blockchain technology. Blockchain technology is most likely to have an impact on how medical research is conducted in the future, much to how the Internet changed medical treatment and made telemedicine possible by cutting data processing cost, setup, and central server management. Despite the transparency of the transmission ledger, the usage of medical blockchains greatly minimizes processing times because the entire infromation collection is accessible the moment a patient enrolls in a trial.

In reality, because of their access to original, accurate, and trustworthy data in real time, doctors are not concerned with providing the patient with an accurate medical history [27–30]. Similar to how patients won't need to consider getting a second opinion from a different doctor because of data transparency. The majority of individuals in the world have their medical records saved in blockchain networks, which can help patients connect with others who are dealing with similar conditions and feel welcomed, motivated, and reinforced in their desire to fight the disease. Patients make their own privacy decisions and are entirely autonomous [30]. In general, blockchain has the ability to broaden the scope of healthcare and change the direction of research.

9.10 CONCLUSION AND DISCUSSION

Recent developments in sensor, cloud, wireless sensor network (WSN), and big data technologies offer a platform for the optimal utilization of medical devices and personalized care delivery when combined in healthcare to build a linked system. A networked healthcare system effectively keeps track of the patients, personnel, and hospital instruments from a distant, reducing the need for on-site supervision and saving money. Security and confidentiality are among the many issues raised in this section and are of the utmost relevance given the nature of healthcare systems and the enormous volumes of sensitive information they handle [31–33].

The WSN can be combined with cloud computing technology to improve availability and dependability. However, while integrating technology, system security should be given top priority. To further enhance the interoperability, scalability, and effective deployment of WSN in healthcare applications, even cloud sensor framework can be used. In-depth information about a patient's course of treatment from start to finish can be provided via collaborative IoT systems that exchange data with other healthcare organizations and labs.

By utilizing smart monitoring devices, healthcare organizations can establish subscription plans for their patients, allowing them to pay a monthly charge for the use of a certain set of remote monitoring services. As a result, the patient will be able to participate more actively, preventing issues that could worsen their health and increasing the cost of their care. The fusion of various data sources, more advanced algorithms for finding patterns in data, and cognitive computing will continue to raise the standard of patient care and support doctors in making more accurate clinical judgments. IoT will undoubtedly alter how healthcare companies operate by enabling new business models as a result of ongoing technological improvement and based on the vast amounts of real-time data that sensors are gathering.

The patient will be at the heart of the healthcare ecosystem thanks to blockchain technology, which will also enhance the security, privacy, and interoperability of patient data. Through more effective, disintermediated, and secure electronic medical records, this technology may offer a new model for HIE (health information exchanges). In this study, we describe blockchain, assess the digital revolution of healthcare using it, and discuss some of its uses. Despite being a relatively young technology, its uses in the financial industry have multiplied dramatically and have spread to other fields including medical. Blockchain technology presents exceptional opportunities for simplifying complex processes, enabling trustless collaboration, and ensuring secure and unalterable data [34,35].

Blockchain-based methods will use encryption to confirm patients' identities and boost data integrity. Blockchain records can be shared by authorized users who have the ability to add transaction logs but not delete or modify them. Blockchain ensures network testing and transaction encryption. In this chapter, we primarily concentrate on a thorough analysis of blockchain technology in healthcare, its difficulties, and potential solutions that can be developed to provide fully functional medical information storing and sharing in the future.

REFERENCES

1. Saini, P., & Anand, M. R. (2014). Identification of defects in plastic gears using image processing and computer vision: A review. International Journal of Engineering Research, 3(2), 94–99.
2. Anand, R., Jain, V., Singh, A., Rahal, D., Rastogi, P., Rajkumar, A., & Gupta, A. Clustering of Big Data in Cloud Environments for Smart Applications. In Integration of IoT with Cloud Computing for Smart Applications (eds. R. Anand, S. Juneja, A. Juneja, V. Jain and R. Kannan) (pp. 227–247). Chapman and Hall/CRC Press.
3. Arora, S., Sharma, S., Anand, R., & Shrivastva, G. (2023). Miniaturized Pentagon-Shaped Planar Monopole Antenna for Ultra-Wideband Applications. Progress In Electromagnetics Research C, 133, 195–208.

4. Gupta, A., Srivastava, A., & Anand, R. (2019). Cost-effective smart home automation using Internet of Things. Journal of Communication Engineering & Systems, 9(2), 1–6.
5. Gupta, A., Anand, R., Pandey, D., Sindhwani, N., Wairya, S., Pandey, B. K., & Sharma, M. (2021). Prediction of breast cancer using extremely randomized clustering forests (ERCF) technique: Prediction of breast cancer. International Journal of Distributed Systems and Technologies (IJDST), 12(4), 1–15.
6. Sindhwani, N., Rana, A., & Chaudhary, A. (2021, September). Breast cancer detection using machine learning algorithms. In 2021 9th International Conference onReliability, Infocom Technologies and Optimization (Trends and Future Directions) (ICRITO) (pp. 1–5). IEEE.
7. Jain, N., Chaudhary, A., Sindhwani, N., & Rana, A. (2021, September). Applications of wearable devices in IoT. In 2021 9th International Conference on Reliability, Infocom Technologies and Optimization (Trends and Future Directions) (ICRITO) (pp. 1–4). IEEE.
8. Khezr, S., Moniruzzaman, M., Yassine, A., & Benlamri, R. (2019). Blockchain technology in healthcare: A comprehensive review and directions for future research. Applied Science, 9(9), 1736
9. Hölbl, M., Kompara, M., Kamišalić, A., & Nemec Zlatolas, L. (2018, October). A systematic review of the use of blockchain in healthcare. Symmetry, 10(10), 470
10. Farouk, A., Alahmadi, A., Ghose, S., & Mashatan, A. (2020, March 15). Blockchain platform for industrial healthcare: Vision and future opportunities. Computer Communications, 154, pp. 223–235
11. Ekblaw, A., Azaria, A., Halamka, J. D., & Lippman, A. (2016, August 13). A Case Study for Blockchain in Healthcare: "MedRec" prototype for electronic health records and medical research data. In Proceedings of IEEE Open & Big Data Conference, vol. 13, p. 13
12. Evans, D. (2011). The Internet of Things: How the next Evolution of the Internet is Changing Everything CISCO. San Jose, CA: White Paper.
13. Atzori, L., Iera, A., & Morabito, G. (2010). The Internet of Things: A survey. Computer Networks, 54, 2787–2805
14. Want, R. (2006, January–March). An introduction to RFID technology. IEEE Pervasive Computing, 5(1), 25–33.
15. Acampora, G., Cook, D. J., Rashidi, P., & Vasilakos, A. V. (2013). A Survey on Ambient Intelligence in Health Care. Proceedings of the IEEE, 101(12), 2470–2494. 10.1109/JPROC.2013.2262913
16. Poncholi, H. (2012). Mobile device for health care monitoring system using wireless body sensor network. International Journal of Electronics and Communication Engineering, 3(4). ISSN (Online): 2249-071X. ISSN (Print): 2278–4209
17. Abo-Zahhad, M., Ahmed, S. M., & Elnahas, O. (2014). A wireless emergency telemedicine system for patients monitoring and diagnosis. International Journal of Telemedicine and Applications, 2014, Article ID 380787, 11.
18. Gotadki, S., Mohan, R., Attarwala, M., & Gajare, M. P. (2014). Intelligent ambulance. International Journal of Engineering & Technical Research, 2(4). ISSN: 2321-0869
19. Hassanalieragh, M., et al. Health monitoring and management using Internet-of-Things (IoT) sensing with cloud-based processing: opportunities and challenges. In: 2015 IEEE International Conference on Services Computing
20. Ould-Yahia, Y., Banerjee, S., Bouzefrane, S., & Boucheneb, H. (2017). Exploring Formal Strategy Framework for the Security in IoT Intelligence. In Internet of Things and Big Data Technologies for next Generation Healthcare (eds. C. Bhatt, N. Dey, and A. S. Ashour) (pp 63–90). Cham: Springer.

21. Xu, X., Fu, S., Qi, L., Zhang, X., Liu, Q., He, Q., & Li, S. (2018). An IoT-oriented data placement method with privacy preservation in cloud environment. The Journal of Network and Computer Applications, 124, 148–157

22. Chen, Y., & Ding, S. (2019). Blockchain-based medical records secure storage and medical service framework. Journal of Medical Systems, 43, 5. 10.1007/s10916-018-1121-4

23. Restuccia, F., & D'Oro, S. (2018, January). Blockchain for the Internet of Things: Present and Future. IEEE Internet of Things Journal, 1 (1).

24. Onik, M. M. H., & Aich, S. (2019). Blockchain in Healthcare: Challenge and Solutions. Big Data Analytics for Intelligent Healthcare Management, 10.1016/B978-0-12-818146-1.00008-8

25. Aggarwal, C., & Abdelzaher, T. (2013). Social Sensing. In: Managing and Mining Sensor Data (eds. C. C. Aggarwal). New York: Springer.

26. Moturu, S. T., et al. (2011, September). Using social sensing to understand the links between sleep, mood, and sociability. In: Proceedings of IEEE International Conference on Social Computing (SocialCom 2011), Cambridge, MA.

27. Sharma, G., Nehra, N., Dahiya, A., Sindhwani, N., & Singh, P. (2022). Automatic heart-rate measurement using facial video. In Networking Technologies in Smart Healthcare (eds. G. Sharma, N. Nehra, A. Dahiya, N. Sindhwani and P. Singh) (pp. 289–307). Boca Raton: CRC Press.

28. Sindhwani, N., Sasi, G., & Meivel, S. (2022, October). Fuzzy acceptance analysis of impact of glaucoma and diabetic retinopathy using confusion matrix. In 2022 10th International Conference on Reliability, Infocom Technologies and Optimization (Trends and Future Directions)(ICRITO) (pp. 1–5). IEEE.

29. Jain, S., Kumar, M., Sindhwani, N., & Singh, P. (2021, September). SARS-Cov-2 detection using deep learning techniques on the basis of clinical reports. In 2021 9th International Conference on Reliability, Infocom Technologies and Optimization (Trends and Future Directions)(ICRITO) (pp. 1–5). IEEE.

30. Anand, R., Sindhwani, N., & Dahiya, A. (2022, March). Design of a high directivity slotted fractal antenna for C-band, X-band and Ku-band applications. In 2022 9th International Conference on Computing for Sustainable Global Development (INDIACom) (pp. 727–730). IEEE.

31. Anand, R., Shrivastava, G., Gupta, S., Peng, S. L., & Sindhwani, N. (2018). Audio Watermarking with Reduced Number of Random Samples. In Handbook of Research on Network Forensics and Analysis Techniques (eds. G. Shrivastava, P. Kumar, B. B. Gupta, S. Bala and N. Dey) (pp. 372–394). USA: IGI Global.

32. Singh, P., Kaiwartya, O., Sindhwani, N., Jain, V., & Anand, R. (Eds.). (2022). Networking Technologies in Smart Healthcare: Innovations and Analytical Approaches. Abingdon, Oxon: CRC Press.

33. Sindhwani, N., Anand, R., Niranjanamurthy, M., Verma, D. C., & Valentina, E. B. (2022). IoT Based Smart Applications. New York City: Springer International Publishing AG.

34. Anand, R., Ahamad, S., Veeraiah, V., Janardan, S. K., Dhabliya, D., Sindhwani, N., & Gupta, A. (2023). Optimizing 6G Wireless Network Security for Effective Communication. In Innovative Smart Materials Used in Wireless Communication Technology (eds. R. Krishan, M. Kaur and S. Mehta) (pp. 1–20). USA: IGI Global.

35. Gupta, R., Shrivastava, G., Anand, R., & Tomažič, T. (2018). IoT-based Privacy Control System through Android. In Handbook of E-business Security (eds. J. Manuel, R. S. Tavares, B. K. Mishra, R. Kumar, N. Zaman, and M. Khari) (pp. 341–363). Auerbach Publications.

10 Role of Cloud Computing in Healthcare Sector

Aryan Jain, Nidhi Sindhwani, Rashmi Vashisth, and Sudhir Chauhan

10.1 INTRODUCTION

Most people today utilize cloud computing, which is also rapidly expanding. When we hear the term "Cloud Computing," we immediately think of data that is kept on a server or the Internet and is accessible to anybody with access to the server or Internet [1–6].

The importance of cloud computing is growing, and both corporate organizations and scientific fields are paying close attention to it. According to corporate organizations and scientific fields, cloud computing is the most prevalent technology out of the 10 and has been getting better over time.

According to the National Institute of Standards and Technology(NIST), Cloud computing has four distribution methods:

i. **Private Cloud:** These clouds are those that a person or an organization owns or manages. Additionally, only authorized individuals have access to data stored on private clouds. In a private cloud, the organization owns and operates processing resources such as servers, storage, and networking, giving it a high degree of control and customization over the infrastructure. This cloud service provides numerous advantages, including increased management over data protection, compliance, and speed. Organizations can tailor their infrastructure to their requirements, ensuring that their data and apps are always accessible and secure. Private clouds, on the other hand, necessitate substantial investments in hardware, software, and upkeep, making them more costly than public clouds.

   Example – VMware and HPE.

ii. **Public Cloud:** These are the clouds that anybody with an Internet connection may access a public cloud, public cloud provider makes resources like servers, cloud storage, and user-applications accessible to the public and other organizations on a pay-per-user requirement. Public cloud services are provided via a common infrastructure controlled by the service provider, which allows numerous clients to utilize the same

DOI: 10.1201/9781003330523-10

processing resources at the same time. These services are usually provided via subscription, with users paying only for the resources they use rather than investing in their own hardware and software infrastructure. Organizations can benefit significantly from public cloud services, such as scale, freedom, and cost-effectiveness. Because the resources are shared by numerous clients, they can be rapidly scaled up or down to meet shifting demand. Furthermore, the pay-per-use approach enables organizations to pay only for the resources they use, avoiding the costs of keeping and updating their own infrastructure.

Example – Amazon Web Services and Microsoft Azure.

iii. **Community Cloud:** These cloud systems are ones where several organizations pooled their resources and services based on the same operating principles. A third-party provider owns and manages the cloud hardware in a community cloud, which can be viewed by authorized community members. This cloud model permits users to share computing resources such as storage devices, processing power units, and application while keeping control over their data and adhering to specific laws and security standards. Overall, the community cloud model allows organizations and people to cooperate and share resources in a cost-effective and safe manner while keeping control over their data and ensuring conformance with laws and security requirements.

iv. **Hybrid Cloud:** These clouds come in both public and private varieties. These clouds assist businesses in storing critical information on private clouds and less critical information on public clouds that are accessible to the public. Hybrid clouds are usually made up of two or more clouds that are linked together via a safe and protected communication. Depending on the demands and standards of the company, data and apps can be moved between private and public clouds. This enables organizations to optimize job placement and use the best cloud services for each assignment. The hybrid cloud approach also allows organizations to handle their data and apps across numerous environments, increasing agility and resilience. Organizations, for example, can use their private cloud for delicate tasks requiring improved security, while using a public cloud for less sensitive workloads requiring greater scalability and cost-effectiveness. Overall, the hybrid cloud model allows organizations to utilize the advantages of both private and public clouds while retaining control over their data and apps in an adaptable and cost-effective manner.

Example – Azure Stack and Google Anthos.

On the other side Cloud Computing also offers three different service models [3–6] as:

i. **Software as a service (SaaS):** SaaS has gained increasing popularity as a cost-effective and flexible way for organizations to access and use high-quality software. This is achieved by allowing users to rent the functionality of applications from a service provider, without having to purchase, install, or execute the program themselves. The software application is hosted and maintained by a cloud service vendor, who is responsible for maintaining the software, devices, and architecture required to operate the program. SaaS applications can be accessed by clients through a web browser or mobile application, with the provider managing all the back-end activities, including security, maintenance, and upgrades. As a result, SaaS offers a scalable and affordable alternative for organizations, eliminating the need for expensive hardware and IT employees. Popular examples of SaaS programs include Salesforce, Microsoft Office 365, Dropbox, and Google Docs.

Advantage:

- Provides companies with online access to software apps, removing the need for them to handle and support the software themselves.
- Can be more cost-effective than purchasing and maintaining the software on-premises.

ii. Platform as a service (PaaS): is a cloud-based platform that enables the creation and execution of applications. Unlike IaaS, which provides virtual computer resources, and SaaS, which delivers pre-built programs, PaaS offers a comprehensive cloud-based development and deployment environment. PaaS is unique in that it provides developers with a range of tools and services that enable them to create and deploy applications without the need to maintain the underlying infrastructure. PaaS providers offer a variety of services, such as databases, application servers, operating systems, and development tools, all of which are managed by the provider. PaaS is an ideal solution for businesses looking to simplify their application development and deployment processes.

Advantage:

- Provides an application creation and deployment platform, enabling companies to concentrate on creating and delivering their apps rather than handling the core infrastructure.
- It may be less expensive than handling the technology and platform directly.

iii. Infrastructure as a service (IaaS): wherein the suppliers provide processing power and storage space as needed. IaaS offers customers with virtualized processing tools such as virtual machines, storage, and networking over the Internet. Users have full authority over the infrastructure, including the operating system, middleware, and apps, when using IaaS. As a result, IaaS is perfect for companies that require full control over their IT infrastructure.

Advantage:

- Provides users with complete control over the infrastructure, allowing them to customize and configure their IT environment to meet their specific needs.
- High levels of scalability and flexibility enable companies to quickly change computing resources to satisfy shifting demands.

Refer to Figure 10.1 that shows a model based upon cloud services.

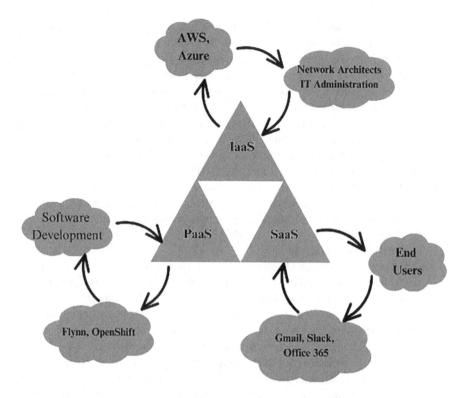

FIGURE 10.1 Model based upon cloud services.

There are main characteristics of cloud which are as follows:

a. **24×7 Availability:** It implies that cloud services are always accessible to anybody who needs them.

b. **Resource Pooling:** Cloud service providers can aggregate computing resources like processing power and storage to form a common pool of resources that can be dynamically distributed to meet the requirements of multiple users.

c. **On-demand Service:** Users can supply processing resources on-demand, such as virtual machines and storage, without requiring human interaction from a service provider.

d. **Rapid Elasticity:** Cloud computing services can be scaled up or down rapidly and easily to meet shifting demand, enabling businesses to react swiftly to changing market conditions and customer requirements.

e. **Measured Service:** Customers' purchases of services can be tallied and measured. The use of resources for both the supplier and the clients will be monitored, metered, and regulated.

f. **Service Level Agreements (SLAs):** SLAs are usually provided by cloud service providers and define the quality of service, speed, and uptime guarantees for their services.

Data Privacy is a crucial part of cloud computing since a large amount of data is kept on the cloud, which must be protected and not accessible to attackers who might hurt organizations and cause them to incur big losses, creating a bad scenario for them. At the time those users are willing or considering to moving over cloud needs to clearly identifies data objective which need to be protected and also classify the data which need to be stored over public or private cloud for security reasons and specifies the security policy for data protection as well as the policy enforcement method. There is CIA traid which assured the privacy and security of the data stored over the cloud which are 1) Confidentiality which means the data is not being shared with unauthorized. There is proper criteria for the data which need to have the confidentiality protection. 2) Integrity This implies that when data is sent from one user to the end user, it should not be modified in the middle. For this security, we may use various encryption techniques to protect the data from unwanted alteration. And 3) Availability means data stored over Internet or different locations should be available for the every user who is retrieving the information from the cloud. This is most important because of the increasing possibility of data damage or loss over the time [7–10].

Cloud integration is the process of linking cloud-based apps and services to other applications and services to facilitate data interchange. It assists firms in streamlining their processes, increasing efficiency, lowering expenses, and increasing production. Businesses can access their data from any device or platform, allowing them to make smarter choices more quickly. It also provides a secure place for partners and customers to share critical information. Businesses may swiftly build new goods and services by using current cloud resources with cloud integration [9,10].

As the organizations move there data and application over the cloud, they must ensure that there data remains the secure and confidential. The use of cloud integration also raises issues related to compliance with regulations. Companies must make sure that their data is handled in accordance with the relevant laws and regulations, such as GDPR or HIPAA. Companies must take into account the different types of data they store and how they process it in order to ensure that their users' privacy is not compromised.

10.2 REVIEW OF LITERATURE

The worry about data privacy has arisen as a key problem for enterprises globally, and it is necessary for successful management to understand the underlying elements that are contributing to this issue. Ensuring data privacy in cloud integration is vital since presently many respected firms keep their data and sensitive information on the cloud, and many more are transitioning to the cloud to take advantage of its advantages and capabilities. The purpose of this literary research is to analyze the problem of maintaining data privacy while integrating with cloud technology and to explore viable solutions for these challenges.

Predicate-Based Encryption is a security strategy and form of asymmetric encryption that emerged from Identity-Based Encryption and incorporates Attribute-Based Access Control. It is a security solution that combines ABAC with asymmetric encryption, allowing the development of a one encryptor/multiple decryptor system using a single algorithm [11].

Drawing on the study's categorization of current solutions, their individual strengths and limitations, and the examination of security and privacy concerns in cloud computing, the authors suggest three probable routes for future research to better security in the cloud environment. Ensuring the security and privacy of data is a significant problem in cloud computing, which requires for the development of increasingly complex systems [12]. In order to maintain the safety and security of cloud computing, it is important to adopt tighter rules and norms. Future study might concentrate on refining these standards to guarantee that data is safely kept, processed, and transported in the cloud while simultaneously safeguarding users' privacy.

In 2016, Sarojini presented the Enhanced Mutual Trusted Access Control Algorithm as a remedy to the security problems in cloud computing. The algorithm is aimed to strengthen the trust connection between cloud service providers and their clients by concentrating on three essential components of data security: data secrecy, data integrity, and data availability. This method may assist to boost the security of cloud computing and increase the trust of users and service providers in the safety and dependability of their data [13].

During the research of cloud integration, it has been discovered that legal and regulatory difficulties are key aspects in data protection. Using cloud services may present issues in complying with data security regulations such as GDPR and HIPAA. Organizations must ensure that they are conscious of and adhere with all pertinent laws when using cloud services to keep and handle personal data [14].

Lastly, there are ethical and moral implications of data privacy in cloud integration that have been discussed in literature. Cloud services have a huge amount of data that is stored which can be misused, mishandled, or lost which can lead to data breaches and loss of personal information. To ensure that they are utilizing these services responsibly and ethically, companies must be aware of and assess the ethical and moral implications of their usage of cloud services [15].

Overall, the literature on data privacy in cloud integration emphasizes the importance of employing encryption and other security measures, adhering to data protection regulations, carefully evaluating cloud service providers, and considering ethical and moral implications when utilizing cloud services.

10.3 CLOUD COMPUTING IN HEALTHCARE SECTOR

Recently, clinical service demand on technology has been increasing; cloud computing solutions, telemedicine, artificial intelligence, and electronic health may often deliver superior services. I completely agree with you! The healthcare industry is among the sectors that can benefit greatly from cloud computing technology. One of the significant benefits of cloud computing in healthcare is the ability to store and share electronic health records (EHRs) securely and conveniently. This can enable healthcare providers to access patient information from anywhere, at any time, leading to more efficient and coordinated care. Cloud-based medical imaging is another area where the technology has the potential to transform

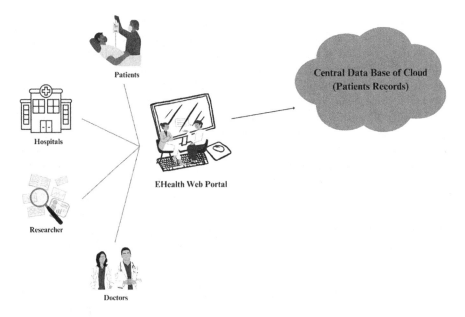

FIGURE 10.2 E-health architecture in the cloud.

the healthcare industry. With the ability to store and share medical images in the cloud, healthcare providers can collaborate with other specialists and access medical images from any location, reducing the time it takes to make a diagnosis. Furthermore, cloud computing may aid healthcare businesses in performing research and analytics more efficiently, resulting in improved healthcare results. By obtaining and studying huge volumes of healthcare data, healthcare professionals may find patterns and trends that may help them deliver more customized and effective treatment.

Overall, cloud computing has the potential to enhance patient outcomes, cut costs, and promote efficiency for healthcare providers. As cloud computing technology progresses, it will become more vital for healthcare providers to implement cloud-based solutions to stay competitive and deliver the best possible care to patients.

An E-health architecture in the cloud is understood by Figure 10.2.

10.3.1 FRAMEWORKS

The secure HIS architecture suggested in is a new way to integrating cloud computing, mobile cloud computing, and big data analytics to offer high-quality, low-cost healthcare services to patients. The framework tackles some of the fundamental difficulties confronting the healthcare sector, such as interoperability, integration, and sharing of EHRs among patients, healthcare providers, and practitioners. One of the key benefits of the framework is its capacity to harness big data analytics to evaluate patients' data and deliver relevant treatments to the right patient at the right time. By analyzing massive volumes of healthcare data, healthcare practitioners may uncover patterns and trends that might improve treatment choices, leading to better healthcare outcomes. Overall, the secure HIS architecture provided in highlights the potential of cloud computing, mobile cloud computing, and big data analytics to change the healthcare business. By offering low-cost, high-quality healthcare services to patients, the framework may enhance patient outcomes and lower costs for healthcare providers. Cloud computing is being utilized in different regions, including schooling, medical care, guard, and different fields, to give on-request admittance to shared figuring assets like organizations, servers, capacity, administrations, and applications. The specialists you referenced have presented a cloud-based cooperative media administration system that can be utilized in different regions like schooling, medical care, and safeguard. The system is intended to give a cooperative climate where different clients can access and share media assets like sound, video, and pictures, utilizing Cloud computing innovations.

Cloud computing is an ideal innovation for this system since it gives a versatile and adaptable foundation that can be handily tweaked to address the issues of various clients and applications. With Cloud computing, clients can get to registering assets on-request, without the requirement for costly equipment or programming establish-ments. This makes it simpler for associations to send and oversee cooperative media administrations, while lessening costs and expanding proficiency.

10.3.2 APPLICATIONS

Cloud computing has numerous applications in healthcare. Here are some of the most common:

1. **Electronic healthcare records:** EHRs are computerized representations of a patient's medical record, which include their medical history, diagnosis, prescriptions, allergies, and other health-related information. EHRs enable healthcare practitioners to access and exchange patient data in real time, which may increase teamwork and minimize the chance of mistakes. Cloud-based EHRs offer further advantages, since they enable healthcare practitioners to securely store and retrieve patient data from anywhere with an Internet connection. This implies that healthcare personnel may access patient data even if they are not in the same physical area as the patient, which can be very valuable in emergency circumstances. Cloud-based EHRs also allow quicker and more accurate diagnoses, treatments, and communication amongst healthcare practi-tioners, since they reduce the need for paper-based data and can give real-time updates.

   Overall, cloud-based EHRs provide considerable advantages to the healthcare sector, as they increase the accessibility and quality of patient data, while simultaneously cutting costs and enhancing efficiency for healthcare providers.

2. **Telemedicine:** Telemedicine is the process of giving healthcare treatments remotely utilizing technology, and it has grown more popular owing to its

accessibility and cost-effectiveness. Cloud computing has played a vital part in making telemedicine more accessible by offering a platform for healthcare practitioners to communicate with patients remotely. Cloud-based telemedicine solutions enable healthcare practitioners to securely contact with patients by video conferencing, texting, or other methods, offering virtual consultations, remote monitoring, and real-time communication. This may be especially valuable for individuals who reside in distant places or have trouble obtaining regular healthcare facilities. Cloud-based telemedicine solutions may also lower expenses, since they remove the need for patients to go to a physical healthcare institution, which can be time-consuming and costly.

Overall, cloud-based telemedicine is an important development in the healthcare industry, as it enables healthcare providers to provide high-quality healthcare services remotely, improving accessibility and convenience for patients, while reducing costs and increasing efficiency for healthcare providers.

3. **Medical imaging:** Medical imaging is a vital tool in the diagnosis and treatment of many medical diseases, and cloud-based technologies are making it simpler for healthcare practitioners to view and exchange medical pictures securely and effectively. Cloud-based medical imaging storage and sharing services allow healthcare practitioners to save and retrieve medical pictures (such as X-rays, MRIs, and CT scans) safely and effectively, from anywhere with an Internet connection. This enables healthcare practitioners to exchange medical pictures with other healthcare providers, independent of their physical location, which may lead to quicker and more accurate diagnosis and treatments. Cloud-based medical imaging technologies can provide other advantages, such as cutting expenses and boosting efficiency for healthcare providers. For example, cloud-based medical imaging systems remove the need for physical storage of medical pictures, decreasing the expenses involved with maintaining and administering physical storage facilities. They also enhance efficiency by letting healthcare professionals to obtain medical pictures quickly and readily, which may cut wait times and boost patient satisfaction.

Overall, cloud-based medical imaging solutions are a vital tool in the healthcare business, as they increase the accessibility, security, and efficiency of medical image storage and sharing, eventually leading to speedier diagnosis and treatments for patients.

4. **Research and analytics:** Cloud computing is playing a crucial role in helping academics and healthcare companies to analyze enormous volumes of health data to spot patterns, create novel therapies, and improve patient outcomes. loud-based research and analytics solutions allow researchers with access to powerful computer capabilities, which may be utilized to process and analyze enormous volumes of health data rapidly and effectively. This helps researchers to find patterns and trends in the data, which may be utilized to design novel therapies and enhance

patient outcomes. Cloud-based research and analytics solutions can provide other advantages, such as enhanced collaboration and cost-efficiency. For example, cloud-based solutions allow researchers to interact and exchange data more readily, regardless of their physical location. This may lead to speedier and more efficient research, as well as lower expenses associated with operating physical data storage facilities.

Overall, cloud-based research and analytics solutions are a vital tool in the healthcare business, since they allow researchers and healthcare organizations to evaluate vast volumes of health data rapidly and effectively, leading to better patient outcomes and innovative therapies.

5. **Cloud-based disaster recovery and business continuity:** Cloud-based disaster recovery and business continuity solutions are crucial for healthcare providers to guarantee that they can retain access to vital data and applications in the event of a catastrophe or other disruptive event. In the healthcare sector, interruptions may have major ramifications for patient care, which makes it vital to have a comprehensive disaster recovery and business continuity strategy in place. Some of the advantages of cloud-based disaster recovery and business continuity solutions for healthcare providers include:

   • Faster Recovery Time: Cloud-based disaster recovery and business continuity solutions may help healthcare providers restore vital data and applications considerably quicker than conventional disaster recovery approaches, which can dramatically decrease the downtime associated with a catastrophe.

   • Improved Scalability: Cloud-based solutions can be readily scaled up or down as required, which makes it simpler for healthcare providers to respond to changing situations and ensure that their disaster recovery and business continuity plans are constantly up-to-date.

   • Lower Costs: Cloud-based solutions often have lower upfront costs than conventional disaster recovery techniques, and they may also be more cost-effective in the long term, as healthcare providers simply pay for the resources they require.

   • Increased Flexibility: Cloud-based solutions are very versatile and may be adjusted to match the particular demands of healthcare providers. This makes it simpler to design disaster recovery and business continuity strategies to unique healthcare businesses.

10.3.3 BENEFITS

Cloud computing is carrying advantages to the two patients and medical services suppliers in the clinical field. The utilization of cloud frameworks can assist with lessening costs, upgrade security, and work on quiet consideration through cooperation and interoperability. One more advantage of Cloud computing in medical care is improved protection. Cloud suppliers normally offer high-level safety efforts, like encryption and multifaceted verification, to safeguard patient information. This can assist medical services suppliers with following guidelines, for example, the Healthcare coverage Transportability and Responsibility Act (HIPAA) and the Overall Information Security Guideline (GDPR).

1. **Efficient Electronic Medical Record-Keeping:** Cloud computing is assuming a huge part in making electronic clinical record-keeping more effective. Generally, electronic clinical record-keeping was finished through on-premise frameworks that necessary a great deal of equipment and programming establishments, which could be costly and tedious. Cloud-based electronic clinical record-keeping, then again, offers a few benefits. cloud-based electronic medical record-keeping allows healthcare providers to access patient records from anywhere with an Internet connection. This means that doctors and nurses can easily access patient records, even when they are not physically present in the hospital or clinic. This can improve the speed and accuracy of diagnosis and treatment.

2. **Reduced Data Storage Cost:** Laying out nearby capacity requires a direct front interest in equipment and requires buying hard drives to store information on, and extra IT foundation to keep that information secure and available consistently. Suppliers of cloud-based medical services arrangements handle the organization, development, and upkeep of cloud information capacity administrations, empowering medical care suppliers to diminish their underlying expenses and spotlight endeavors on the things they do best: really focusing on patients.

3. **Superior Data security:** Data security is a major concern in the healthcare industry, and cloud computing can offer several benefits to ensure superior data security. Cloud computing suppliers offer powerful safety efforts like encryption, multifaceted confirmation, and interruption discovery and avoidance frameworks to safeguard information. They likewise have committed security groups to screen and address security dangers. Furthermore, Cloud computing suppliers agree with different security principles like HIPAA, GDPR, and ISO 27001. Consistence with these norms guarantees that medical services associations can believe the cloud supplier's safety efforts and cycles. Cloud computing suppliers offer customary reinforcements and calamity recuperation intends to guarantee the accessibility of information in the event of a catastrophic event or digital assault. These actions help medical care associations to rapidly recuperate information and limit the effect of an information misfortune occasion.

10.4 CLOUD-RELATED SECURITY CONCERNS

Cloud computing is related with many security problems that may be divided into distinct categories.

Buyers question prospective cloud suppliers about seven important security problems before making a purchase. These include the details of user access, compliance with rules, segregation of data, recovery mechanisms, assistance for queries, and long-term sustainability [16]. Furthermore, the Cloud Security Alliance (CSA) has outlined thirteen cloud security concerns [17]. Security issues can be

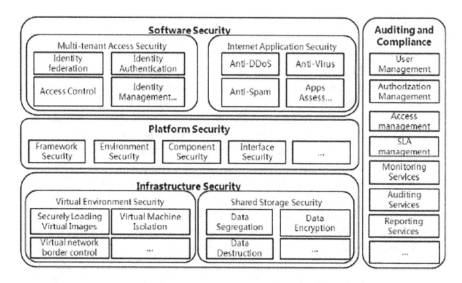

FIGURE 10.3 Security architecture of cloud computing.

found in all aspects of the infrastructure, including network, host, and application levels, concerning SPI service models, deployment techniques, and fundamental cloud characteristics.

Security Architecture of Cloud Computing is shown in Figure 10.3.

10.4.1 VIRTUALIZATION

Virtualization is a technology that generates a complete functioning image of an operating system within another operating system, allowing for full utilization of the resources of the actual operating system. A hypervisor is a essential component to execute a guest operating system as a virtual machine within a host operating system [18]. Virtualization is a critical tool in cloud computing as it enables the execution of numerous virtual computers (VMs) on a single physical machine, each with its own operating system and tools. This allows for more effective resource utilization as well as the ability to quickly transfer VMs between physical machines.

There are two main types of virtualization:

Type 1 or native or hardware level virtualization: The hypervisor leverages the hardware of the host system to supervise and manage guest virtual machines, resulting in higher performance efficiency.

Type 2 or hosted virtualization: the hypervisor runs on the host's operating system, which in turn controls the hardware and manages guest VMs.

If a hypervisor becomes susceptible, it can become the main target. If a hypervisor gets compromised, there is a risk that both the entire system and its data might be revealed. Additionally, with virtualization comes the issue of distributing and reallocating resources [19]. If the data processed by a virtual machine is retained in memory and not properly erased before allocating that memory to another virtual machine, the data may be accessible to the following virtual machine [20].

10.4.2   PUBLIC CLOUD STORAGE

Storing the data over the public cloud may encounter the following risks which include: 1) **Security risks:** which increases the data breaches, unauthorized access, and the data loss. 2) **Compliance risks:** Companies may be subject to various regulations and standards, such as HIPAA, SOC2, and PCI-DSS. To avoid potential penalties and fines, it is essential to ensure that the public cloud storage solutions implemented are in line with these requirements. 3) **Performance risks:** it may experience performance issues due to network latency, congestion or high usage. 4) **Data migration:** Migration of the data can be complex and time-consuming. To avoid these risks for particularly sensitive data, it is usually advisable to have a private cloud.

10.5   CLOUD DATA BREACH

A cloud data breach is a security incident where unauthorized individuals gain access to data that is stored in the cloud. This can occur when cloud systems are not properly secured, when user credentials are compromised, or when vulnerabilities in cloud software or infrastructure are exploited. Organizations can suffer severe repercussions as a result of cloud data breaches, such as the exposure of confidential information, monetary damages, and harm to their reputation. The type of data that is typically targeted in cloud data breaches includes personally identifiable information (PII), financial information, health information, and intellectual property.

Data leaks can occur in a variety of methods. In 2018, for example, one of the largest Aadhaar data leaks occurred when the confidential information of over one billion Aadhaar users was published online. The data revealed included personal information such as name, location, and Aadhaar number, as well as biometric information such as fingerprint and retinal images. This data was accessible for distribution on the Internet for a brief time before the Indian government took steps to have it removed. The All India Institute of Medical Sciences (AIIMS) in Delhi was struck by a ransomware assault in November 2022, causing meetings, registration, invoicing, and laboratory report production to be halted. The breach affected both the main and secondary systems at the hospital, corrupting all recorded data.

10.6   DATA SECURITY – DOES DATA INTEGRATION PUT YOUR DATA AT RISK?

It has been found that integrating data might generate a risk of data vulnerability if adequate security mechanisms are not established. Combining data from several sources raises the chance of illegal access, data loss, and breaches in data security. It's crucial to ensure that the data is safeguarded during the integration process. This may be achieved by adopting an alternative encryption mechanisms, access restrictions, and surveillance technologies. To avoid legal consequences, it's important for the integration process to adhere to data protection regulations like

GDPR and CCPA. In the end, a successful plan for integrating data should strike a balance between making data easily accessible and ensuring its security to minimize potential risks. According to a survey on data breaches in 2020, more than 300 million persons had their personal information leaked by hackers who sold it on the dark web, resulting in severe damage. Organizations should also ensure that data validation and cleaning procedures are in place to preserve data quality and accuracy.

Data Integration Concerns that should be keep up in mind – 1) **Unknown Insider Risk Threat** – It is important to be careful by individual or groups within the organization as they make more than thousands of efforts for risk the organization or the important data. 2) **Traditional Data Integration with Security Vulnerabilities** – Having an effective access control system that manages all areas of data, from management to storage, is vital to limit the risk of data difficulties throughout integration operations. This guarantees that procedures are in place to restrict data access and limit the complexity associated with it.

Strategies for Assuring Data Security during Integration – 1) **Encourage Integrity** – By prioritizing integrity in the workplace, firms may mitigate the risks associated with data integration failures. Employees that are devoted to ensuring data integrity will be more cautious and attentive while dealing with data, which may assist to avoid errors and blunders. 2) **Data Process Maps** – Process maps assist to record the movement of data through the business, from its original collection to its final use and disposal. This may assist to uncover possible gaps or vulnerabilities in the data management process, as well as chances for improvement. This may be especially crucial for organizations that operate in regulated areas, where compliance with legal and industry norms is vital. 3) **Quality Issue of Data** – Integrating data from many sources may greatly increase the chance of data quality concerns. In case the data is not adequately checked or if there are discrepancies across the many data sources, it might result in mistakes, misinterpretations, and other issues that could negatively impact the organization's operation. 4) **Software Development Lifecycle** – Implementing a suitable SDLC (Software Development Life cycle) is a fundamental method of managing data within an organization. It is essential for comprehending the regulatory procedures, data distribution, and establishing a foundation for a sustainable environment.

10.6.1 WITH HEALTHCARE

Cloud computing has changed the manner in which medical services associations store, process, and oversee information. It gives an adaptable, versatile, and financially savvy answer for overseeing huge volumes of touchy patient information. Notwithstanding, there are additionally security and protection issues related with medical care Cloud computing. Here are a portion of the key worries:

- **Information breaks:** Medical care associations are an ideal objective for programmers because of the delicate idea of patient information. Cloud computing presents extra dangers, as information is put away on outsider servers, which can be powerless against assaults. Information breaks can bring about critical monetary misfortunes, harm to notoriety, and legitimate liabilities.

- **Consistence issues:** Medical care associations are dependent upon a scope of administrative necessities, like HIPAA (Healthcare coverage Versatility and Responsibility Act) in the United States, which expect them to safeguard patient information and guarantee its privacy. Moving information to the cloud can make consistence issues on the off chance that the cloud supplier can't meet these prerequisites.
- **Information proprietorship and control:** When medical care associations move information to the cloud, they might lose a portion of the control and responsibility for information. They may likewise confront difficulties in recovering their information if they have any desire to switch cloud suppliers or end the agreement.
- **Interoperability:** Medical care associations might have to coordinate cloud-based frameworks with different frameworks, for example, electronic wellbeing records (EHRs) or clinical gadgets. Interoperability can be a test in the event that the frameworks are not intended to cooperate or on the other hand assuming that there are information configuration or security issues.
- **Insider dangers:** Cloud computing acquaints new dangers related with insider dangers, like unapproved admittance to information by cloud suppliers or representatives of the medical services association. These dangers can be especially difficult to distinguish and forestall.

10.7   CURRENT SOLUTION FOR DATA PRIVACY ISSUES

Maintaining privacy in cloud computing demands securing the flow of data over the whole lifecycle of the data inside the cloud computing service provider.

A. **Lifecycle to protect cloud data**

The most crucial part of cloud security is Data Governance. Data governance in cloud security involves implementing policies and protocols to ensure that sensitive data is managed, protected, and used in accordance with both legal requirements and organizational standards [21–23]. This includes defining procedures for data classification, access control, and retention. Additionally, monitoring and auditing data usage is necessary to ensure that it is being used appropriately and to detect any unauthorized activity. Proper data governance is essential to maintaining data privacy and security in the cloud and can help organizations meet regulatory compliance requirements and avoid significant legal and financial consequences.

B. **Legal Protection for data storage in a cloud environment**

Rules and regulations differ based on the place, whether it is a state, a nation, or a geographical region. For instance, in the United States, about 46 out of the 50 states have data protection legislation. Provisions will act as a method of restricting the capacities of the CSP to lower risk [24]. It is vital to explicitly outline the duties of the cloud provider to guarantee that they and their insurance company will answer any customer complaints and offer compensation for any damages originating from their services. It is also vital to construct thorough SLAs that identify the services to be supplied and explain the penalties for any service failures.

There are more effective ways to solve the issue of data privacy in the cloud [25–28].

- Encryption: Encrypting sensitive data both at rest and in transit is a critical step in protecting data stored in the cloud. This involves employing powerful encryption algorithms and key management practises to ensure that only authorized individuals have access to the data.
- Access controls: Implementing access restrictions such as multi-factor identification and role-based access can help ensure that only authorized individuals have access to confidential cloud data.
- Compliance with regulations: It is important for organizations to make sure they are familiar with and adhering to all relevant regulations related to data protection when using cloud-based services, including both GDPR and HIPAA.
- Third-party assurance: Organizations should carefully evaluate the security and privacy practices of cloud service providers to ensure that they meet the organization's data privacy and security requirements.
- Network segmentation: Network segmentation is another solution that helps to prevent unauthorized access to sensitive data by creating separate secure networks for different types of data and users.
- Data Loss Prevention (DLP): DLP solutions help organizations to monitor and control sensitive data across their cloud environments, preventing data breaches and ensuring compliance with various regulations such as GDPR and HIPAA.

These are just a few of the numerous options for handling the problem of data privacy in cloud integration. The particular solutions used will be determined by the organization's requirements and goals, as well as the unique risks and threats it encounters.

10.7.1 SOLUTION FOR HEALTHCARE

To defeat security and protection issues in medical services distributed computing, medical care associations can make the accompanying strides:

- **Pick a legitimate cloud supplier:** Medical services associations ought to painstakingly assess potential cloud suppliers and select one that has major areas of strength for a record in security and consistence. The supplier ought to likewise have certificates, for example, HIPAA consistence and consent to a business partner arrangement (BAA) that frames their security obligations.
- **Encode information:** Information ought to be scrambled very still and on the way to shield it from unapproved access. Medical services associations

ought to work with their cloud supplier to guarantee information encryption is executed and designed accurately.

- **Create and implement security strategies and systems:** Medical services associations ought to foster approaches and methodologies that address cloud security and protection gambles. These strategies ought to cover regions, for example, information access, information maintenance, and episode reaction. Workers ought to be prepared on these strategies and considered responsible for following them.

- **Foster an information recuperation plan:** Medical care associations ought to foster an arrangement for recuperating information if there should be an occurrence of a fiasco or information misfortune occasion. The arrangement ought to incorporate methodology for reestablishing information from reinforcements, and testing the arrangement routinely.

By following these means, medical care associations can limit security and protection chances related with distributed computing and guarantee the secrecy, respectability, and accessibility of patient information [29–31].

10.8 CONCLUSION

In conclusion, data privacy in cloud integration is a critical concern for organizations of all sizes and industries. As more and more data is being stored and processed in the cloud, it is essential that organizations take the necessary steps to protect sensitive data from unauthorized access and breaches [32,33]. There are several solutions available for addressing the issue of data privacy in cloud integration, such as encryption, access controls, compliance with regulations, third-party assurance, network segmentation, identity and access management, cloud security posture management, and data loss prevention. Organizations should carefully evaluate the security and privacy practices of cloud service providers, and implement a combination of these solutions to meet their specific data privacy and security requirements. However, it is important to note that data privacy in cloud integration is a constantly evolving field and new threats and vulnerabilities are emerging all the time [34]. Therefore, organizations must stay informed about the latest trends, developments, and solutions, and be willing to adapt their security strategies as needed to protect their sensitive data from unauthorized access and breaches.

REFERENCES

1. Anand, R., Juneja, S., Juneja, A., Jain, V., & Kannan, R. (Eds.). (2023). Integration of IoT with Cloud Computing for Smart Applications. CRC Press.
2. Nijhawan, M., Sindhwani, N., Tanwar, S., & Kumar, S. (2022). Role of Augmented Reality and Internet of Things in Education Sector. In IoT Based Smart Applications (eds. N. Sindhwani, R. Anand, M. Niranjanamurthy, D. C. Verma and E. B. Valentina) (pp. 245–259). Cham: Springer International Publishing.
3. Chauhan, Sudhir Kumar, et al. "Pareto optimal solution for fully fuzzy Bi-criteria multi-index bulk transportation problem." Mobile Radio Communications and 5G Networks:

Proceedings of Third MRCN 2022. Singapore: Springer Nature Singapore, 2023. 457–470. https://citations.springernature.com/item?doi=10.1007/978-981-19-7982-8_38

4. Sindhwani, N., Anand, R., Vashisth, R., Chauhan, S., Talukdar, V., & Dhabliya, D. (2022, November). Thingspeak-based environmental monitoring system using IoT. In 2022 Seventh International Conference on Parallel, Distributed and Grid Computing (PDGC) (pp. 675–680). IEEE.

5. Sindhwani, N., Anand, R., Meivel, S., Shukla, R., Yadav, M. P., & Yadav, V. (2021). Performance analysis of deep neural networks using computer vision. EAI Endorsed Transactions on Industrial Networks and Intelligent Systems, 8(29), e3–e3.

6. Kaur, J., Jaskaran, Sindhwani, N., Anand, R., & Pandey, D. (2022). Implementation of IoT in various domains. In IoT Based Smart Applications (pp. 165–178). Cham: Springer International Publishing. https://doi.org/10.1007/978-3-031-04524-0

7. Juneja, S., & Anand, R. (2018). Contrast Enhancement of an Image by DWT-SVD and DCT-SVD. In Data Engineering and Intelligent Computing: Proceedings of IC3T 2016 (pp. 595–603). Springer Singapore.

8. Meelu, R., & Anand, R. (2010, November). Energy Efficiency of Cluster-based Routing Protocols Used in Wireless Sensor Networks. In AIP Conference Proceedings (Vol. 1324, No. 1, pp. 109–113). American Institute of Physics.

9. Sansanwal, K., Shrivastava, G., Anand, R., & Sharma, K. (2019). Big Data Analysis and Compression for Indoor Air Quality. In Handbook of IoT and big data, (Vol. 1, first edition). CRC Press.

10. Anand, R., Jain, V., Singh, A., Rahal, D., Rastogi, P., Rajkumar, A., & Gupta, A. Clustering of Big Data in Cloud Environments for Smart Applications. In Integration of IoT with Cloud Computing for Smart Applications (eds. R. Anand, S. Juneja, A. Juneja, V. Jain and R. Kannan) (pp. 227–247). Chapman and Hall/CRC Press.

11. Nabil Giweli (2013) Enhancing Cloud Computing Security and Privacy, 20, Jan, 2019 [Online]Available: https://www.researchdirect.westernsydney.edu.au/islandora/object/uws%3AI7310/ … /view

12. Aljwari, F. K. (2022). Challenges of Privacy in Cloud Computing. Journal of Computer and Communications, 10(12), 51–61, doi: 10.4236/jcc.2022.1012004. [Online]. Available: 10.4236/jcc.2022.1012004

13. Sarojini, G. et al. (2016) Trusted and reputed services using enhanced mutual trusted and reputed access control algorithm in cloud. 2nd International Conference on Intelligent Computing, Communication & Convergence (ICCC-2016) https://www.sciencedirect.com/

14. Embracing Innovation in Government Global Trends. (2018). Aadhaar – India – Case study- Oecd. Identity, 1, 27–33.

15. Indian Railway Data Leak: 30 million Railway Customers Data for Sale on the Dark Web, Economics Times, Dec. 28, 2022 [Online], Available: https://economictimes.indiatimes.com/news/new-updates/indian-railway-data-leak-30-million-railway-customers-data-for-sale-on-the-dark-web/articleshow/96569440.cms?from=mdr. [Accessed: Apr. 15, 2023]

16. Gartner: Seven Cloud-computing Security Risks. InfoWorld. 2008-07-02. http://www.infoworld.com/d/security-central/gartner-seven-cloud-computingsecurity-risks-853

17. Cloud Security Alliance, Security Guidance for Critical Areas of Focus in Cloud Computing, V2.1, http://www.cloudsecurityalliance.org/guidance/csaguide.v2.1.pdf.

18. Pandey, A., Tugnayat, R. M., & Tiwari, A. K. (2013). Data security framework for cloud computing networks. International Journal of Computer Engineering & Technology, 4(1), 178– 181.

19. AlZain, M. A., Soh, B., & Pardede, E. (2011). Mcdb: Using multi-clouds to ensure security in cloud computing. In Proceedings of the IEEE 9th International Conference on Dependable, Autonomic and Secure Computing (DASC '11), pp. 784–791. 5.

C. P. Ram and G. Sreenivaasan, "Security as a service (sass): securing user data by coprocessor and distributing the data," in Proceedings of the 2nd International Conference on Trendz in Information Sciences and Computing, (TISC '10), pp. 152–155, IEEE, December 2010

20. Muijnck-Hughes Jan de (2011). Data Protection in the Cloud, 12 Jan, 2019 [Online], Available: https://www.ru.nl/dis

21. Deepu, N. How Secure is Your Data during Data Integration? Suyati Technologies, Sep. 16, 2021. [Online]. Available: https://suyati.com/blog/assessing-data-risks-during-data-integration/

22. Gitlin, J. 5 Data Integration Challenges to Look Out for and the Solutions for Overcoming Them. Workato, Feb. 10, 2022. [Online]. Available: https://www.workato.com/the-connector/data-integration-challenges/

23. Haufe, K., Dzombeta, S., & Brandis, K. (2014). Proposal for a security management in cloud computing for health care. The Scientific World Journal, 2014, 1–7.

24. Hossain, M. S. & Muhammad, G. (2015). Cloud-assisted speech and face recognition framework for health monitoring. Mobile Networks and Applications, 20, 391–399.

25. Saini, P., & Anand, M. R. (2014). Identification of defects in plastic gears using image processing and computer vision: A review. International Journal of Engineering Research, 3(2), 94–99.

26. Gupta, A., Srivastava, A., & Anand, R. (2019). Cost-effective smart home automation using Internet of Things. Journal of Communication Engineering & Systems, 9(2), 1–6.

27. Kohli, L., Saurabh, M., Bhatia, I., Shekhawat, U. S., Vijh, M., & Sindhwani, N. (2021). Design and Development of Modular and Multifunctional UAV with Amphibious Landing Module. In Data Driven Approach Towards Disruptive Technologies: Proceedings of MIDAS 2020 (eds. A. K. Gupta, R. Bhatt, V. Mohindru and Y. Singh) (pp. 405–421). Springer Singapore.

28. Chawla, P., & Anand, R. (2017). Micro-switch design and its optimization using pattern search algorithm for applications in reconfigurable antenna. Modern Antenna Systems, 10, 189–210.

29. Sharma, G., Nehra, N., Dahiya, A., Sindhwani, N., & Singh, P. (2022). Automatic heart-rate measurement using facial video. In Networking Technologies in Smart Healthcare (eds. P. Singh, O. Kaiwartya, N. Sindhwani, V. Jain and R. Anand) (pp. 289–307). CRC Press.

30. Sindhwani, N., Sasi, G., & Meivel, S. (2022, October). Fuzzy acceptance analysis of impact of glaucoma and diabetic retinopathy using confusion matrix. In 2022 10th International Conference on Reliability, Infocom Technologies and Optimization (Trends and Future Directions)(ICRITO) (pp. 1–5). IEEE.

31. Chaudhary, A., Bodala, D., Sindhwani, N., & Kumar, A. (2022, March). Analysis of customer loyalty using artificial neural networks. In 2022 International Mobile and Embedded Technology Conference (MECON) (pp. 181–183). IEEE.

32. Sharma, R., Vashisth, R., & Sindhwani, N. (2023). Study and Analysis of Classification Techniques for Specific Plant Growths. In: Chakravarthy, V., Bhateja, V., Flores Fuentes, W., Anguera, J., Vasavi, K.P. (eds) Advances in Signal Processing, Embedded Systems and IoT. Lecture Notes in Electrical Engineering, vol 992. Springer, Singapore. https://doi.org/10.1007/978-981-19-8865-3_53

33. Anand, R., Singh, B., & Sindhwani, N. (2009). Speech perception & analysis of fluent digits' strings using level-by-level time alignment. International Journal of Information Technology and Knowledge Management, 2(1), 65–68.

34. Anand, R., Arora, S., & Sindhwani, N. (2022, January). A miniaturized UWB antenna for high speed applications. In 2022 International Conference on Computing, Communication and Power Technology (IC3P) (pp. 264–267). IEEE.

11 Challenges Faced by AI in Healthcare and Future Opportunities

Akanchha Singh and Gurpreet Kaur

11.1 INTRODUCTION

Medical Industry might collapse if it is not provided with some transformation and structural change. WHO (World Health Organization) reckons that in spite of generating 40 million more healthcare employees by 2030, there is still going to be a shortage of nurses and physicians at the same time. Recruiting more healthcare professional is as important as it is to make sure that their skills are used in the domains of benefit which is – healthcare of patients. Automation forms the foundation of Artificial Intelligence (AI). It carries the potential to bring necessary changes to the industry and aid in tackling some matters. Artificially Intelligent makes the computer competent of carrying on tasks which seem to be done with human intelligence. With the help of AI, it is possible to ameliorate patient experience along with the effectiveness of healthcare delivery [1]. It will expedite the treatment process providing the healthcare staff more time to invest in the patient care which will furthermore enhance the staff morale. Healthcare industry has revolutionized by the introduction of automation. Since there is a decline in the ratio of healthcare workers and patients, we need to fill the hole and that can be done by trustable AI which will also lessen the chances of committing human errors. There will be a few steps of mounting AI in the healthcare industries over the time [2]. Initially, the focal point of the advancement would be to significantly lessen the time taken in tedious and repetitive organizational tasks that are traditionally performed doctors and nurses. This would improve the healthcare procedures and also promote AI's adoption in this industry [2]. There also exists Imaging solutions that are AI based and in practice in areas like radiology and ophthalmology. Further, the patient holds more authority to their care, we anticipate extra AI solutions (such as Alarm system, patient monitoring) would assist the transitional treatment which goes from the clinic to the home [3]. This phase may incorporate enlarged utilization of Natural Language Processing (NLP) aids in hospitals and at homes together with escalated AI application over an extensive range of specialities such as oncology and neurology. There will rise a high demand for merging AI and healthcare industry operations, which would furthermore demand for dynamic involvement of professionals [4]. To utilize early technology

DOI: 10.1201/9781003330523-11

effectively, there will be a requirement of clever and blended solutions. Technological breakthrough accompanied by cultural switch and expertize within a firm will help in easy adoption of AI. We can foresee witnessing additional applications of AI in clinics [5]. These developments will be driven by compelling evidence gathered from rigorous clinical trials, with a special priority on enhancing and expanding clinical decision support techniques. We look forward to AI in playing a noteworthy role/job in the healthcare domain, from learning about how to provide care to how do we enhance the care in the healthcare domain. Combination of big data with sturdy government which would work toward continuously improving the data quality and gaining trust of the healthcare firms, professionals and patients in AI techniques will be the primary requirements for AI to propose its utmost capabilities in healthcare domain [6]. Table 11.1 is showing AI applications startup companies in India.

11.2   AI APPLICATIONS STARTUP COMPANIES FOUND IN INDIA

TABLE 11.1
AI Application Startup Companies Found in India

Company	Technology	Hospital used in
Doxper	• Digitized Health records with digital Pen and paper. There is a digital pen and a coded paper. The clinical staff use this digital pen and regular coded paper to write prescriptions. The data from the digital pen is sent to the cloud, and afterward the data is sent to the hospital EMR.	1. Manipal Hospital (since 2021) 2. Wockhardt Hospitals (since 2021) 3. SAKRA World Hospital 4. KIMS Hospitals 5. Nanavati Max Hospital 6. P.D. HINDUJA Hospital 7. CK BIRLA Hospitals
Qure.ai	• Automated Chest X-ray interpretation. There are around 10,000 radiologists in India for about 1.2 billion population. We are really short of trained radiologists. This AI technology can help in sorting X-rays from normal and abnormal, providing assistance by detecting new findings and providing prior interpretation, later these things can be validated by radiologists, leading to faster processing. • Head CT scans – Identifying and prioritizing the critical situations. • Lung Nodule diagnosis – Facilitates analyzing and reporting lung disease. They claim more than 95% accuracy.	1. National Institute for Health and care research 2. PATH 3. Medica 4. Healius 5. Ericsson 6. AstraZeneca 7. Department of Health and social care 8. NHS 9. PBSP (Philippine Business for Social Care)

(Continued)

TABLE 11.1 *(Continued)*
AI Application Startup Companies Found in India

Company	Technology	Hospital used in
SIG.TUPLE (Still under research, according to data of 2022)	• DRISHTI – Used in screening diabetic Retinopathy. • SHONIT – Automatic analysis of a blood slide can be performed with this. Mimics the job of a pathologist to some level.	1. Manipal Hospitals 2. HealthCare Global Enterprises (HCG)

According to an article published by financialExpress.com, In a ground-breaking analysis titled "Revolutionary Prospects: Unveiling the Dynamics of AI in India's Healthcare Sector 2019–2025," an astute study on the Indian AI healthcare market has projected an unparalleled growth trajectory. There will be early detection of any illness, we'll be equipped with many trials during drug development, patient monitoring would become apt by new AI algorithms. From India, there will be an investment of around 11.7 billion US dollars in the healthcare sector which is anticipated to enhance India's GDP by 1 trillion US dollars by the year 2035 [7].

11.3   ANALYSIS OF AN INDUSTRY SURVEY CONDUCTED IN 2022 BY BEN LORICA AND PACO NATHAN (JOHN SNOW LABS)

11.3.1   INTENTION BEHIND THIS SURVEY

This was a 50-day long survey covering responds from 321 individuals from over 41 countries. Knowledge was gained with respect to currently used AI technologies in the healthcare domain. The responses were collected through social media, digital advertisements, industry colleagues, etc. The goal was to study contrasting ideas between – 1) Exploring and Well-developed practices over the years. 2) Technical leaders & General participants. 3) Geographic size and Company size [8].

11.3.2   DEMOGRAPHIC INFORMATION

11.3.2.1   Countries Who Gave Most Responses
It is shown in Table 11.2.

The remaining 25% are distributed throughout the world – Europe, Middle East, Africa, America, and Asia-Pacific.

TABLE 11.2

Most Number of Respondents in Country

Country	% of Respondents
USA	62
India	13

11.3.2.2   Roles of the Respondents

It is shown in Table 11.3.

TABLE 11.3

Roles of the Respondents

Role	% of Respondents
VP or CxO	8
Director or Engineering Manager	10
Architect	7
Hands on developer, engineer, data scientist	15
Researcher or Academic	13
Hobbyist or student	9
Others	37

11.3.2.3   Company Size

It is shown in Table 11.4.

TABLE 11.4

Size of the Company

Size	% of Company
<100	31
101–500	17
501–1000	13
1001–5000	12
5001–10,000	8
>10,000	18

11.3.2.4　Phase of Adopting

TABLE 11.5
Phase of Adopting

Stage	% reached
Sophisticated: Producing AI models since more than 5 years (Mature)	10
Mid-stage: Producing AI models for 3–4 years	8
Early stage adoption: AI models have been in production for less than 2 years	16
Experimenting and developing AI models but not yet in production	12
Evaluating AI use cases	20
Not actively considering AI as a business solution	34

Table 11.5 explains about different Phase of Adoption.

11.3.2.5　Technologies in Priority

AI practitioners voted for data integration to be their top priority for 2022 along with data annotation, NLP and data science platform.

11.3.2.6　Users on Target

AI application developing companies target the following users – clinicians, healthcare professionals, healthcare payers, health Information Technology, and drug developers.

11.3.2.7　Most Used Data Type, Software Used, and Model Validation

Participants from the mature organizations suggested that text data type is likely to be used broadly in AI apps. Technical leaders claimed that their favorite software is open source, and they also prefer public cloud providers. More than $2/3^{rd}$ of the technical leaders shared that they like doing evaluation in-house rather than depending on outside parties. Evaluation of Tools, Solutions, and Services is presented in Table 11.6.

11.3.2.8　Evaluation of Tools, Solutions, and Services

TABLE 11.6
Respondents and Evaluation Criteria

Respondents	Criteria
Mature Organizations	Readiness of production, scalability, accuracy, and ability to train/tune.
Technical Leaders	Ability to train/tune models, production readiness, and scalability.

For installed software, respondents claimed to prefer software that fits with their existing stack and available healthcare models and algos.

11.3.3 Observations

Startup companies of AI are in a growing environment due to which they raise fair amount of funding. Some AI health companies who could raise at least 20 million dollars funding are – BRIGHT-MD, DEEPCURE, PROTENUS, Helio, Valo, etc. Since there is great reliance on open-source technologies and public cloud, there rises a concern for the security which will ultimately have an impact on the developing process of NLP and also the use of it. According to the report of sonicwall.com/2022-cyber-threat-report, in 2021, there have been 71% increase in IoT device attack, 121% increase in malware, 218% increase in cryptojacking, and 755% spike in ransomware suggesting that healthcare industries are top targets for threats [8].

11.4 MEDICAL BENEFITS

11.4.1 Assistance in Surgery

AI has found numerous applications in the medical and dental fields. Robotic surgeries have greatly improved/enhanced the precision and effectiveness of surgeries, including oral and maxillofacial procedures. Other areas benefiting from AI include 3D printing for surgery, diabetic retinopathy, spine imaging, and radiology. Augmented reality overlays computer-generated images onto a patient's view of the actual existing world, providing a combined visual of the required surgical area [9,10]. AI-generated tele-surgical methods enable robotic-assisted surgery and senior surgeon supervision from a remote location. Perioperative instructions through video and delivery systems have proven invaluable, especially in scenarios with limited access to clinics or during pandemics [11]. AI and AR-based surgical mentorship offer a viable alternative, guiding surgeons through less invasive procedures while providing real-time consultation and feedback [9]. Surgeon progress can also be monitored using data and computer vision techniques. Trained Robots analyze patient medical data before surgery to assist in tool selection and guide the procedure. Robotic-assisted surgeries have led to shorter hospital stays due to their minimally invasive nature [12]. AI can also be utilized by robots in offering new ways to approach a surgery which will be based on the history of the patient. There is sufficiently more control over the procedure when the eye surgery is being done with the help of Da Vinci surgical robot [13].

11.4.2 Fitter Data-driven Decision That Ameliorate the Healthcare System

Decision-making process includes identification, obtaining, and assessing the problem and its remedies. With the fetched data we can point out options, and the staged process of decision making can give a helping hand in developing and deploying more cautious, thoughtful decisions. The standard of decision making now a days is highly and significantly dependent or relying on the data accumulated [14]. The data should be apt and available. In healthcare, presence of smart data contributes effectively to overcome the obstacles faced by the clinical decision makers in the path treating a patient. The data helps in better understanding and making standard informed decisions. Since the data might be unavailable, or very huge in amount for effective analysis, information is sometimes overlooked, or there may be disregarded recommendation, some judgments may fail, therefore resulting in ineffective process and clinical outcomes [15,16]. Sources of information for the AI: 1) Data of the patient. 2) Data of the hospital. 3) Data about the consumer.

11.4.3 SUPPORTS KEEPING MENTAL HEALTH STABLE OF INDIVIDUALS

AI is getting acclaimed within mental health ministration, as patients prefer easily and immediately acquired feedback [17]. Language has since very long been a key factor in assessing emotional and mental well-being, with psychiatric experts traditionally relying on therapeutic conversations and patient narratives. However, recent advancements in AI have opened up new possibilities by enabling technologies for extracting emotional meaning from a broader range of data sources [18].

Machine languages and emotions evaluation have played a crucial role in this domain. NLP is a computational linguistic mechanism that involves developing algorithms to analyze natural input of language. Interpretation of sentiments, an AI division comprehends and gives reactions to spoken data of human emotions [19]. By combining the two (NLP and sentiment analysis), data scientists designed unique algorithms capable of comprehending emotions of users from written text. These models are currently being utilized in the medical line to provide comprehensive insights into patients' level of emotional and psychological well-being or distress.

In recent years, NLP-based models got employed to spot possible self-harming ideation in patients' charts, forecasting suiciding risks online [20]. These models have in them the capacity to benefit both individual patient care and broader public health policies. For instance, NLP algorithms can corelate the behavioral health diseases/problems across the USA by collecting public health records from trusted sources like CDC. Furthermore, researchers have demonstrated impressive accuracy in predicting potential occurrence of postnatal depression among mothers based on their information available online [17,21] (Figure 11.1).

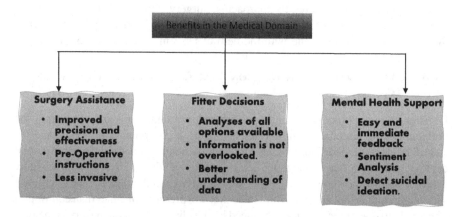

FIGURE 11.1   Health benefits of AI.

11.5   BENEFITS (IN THE DOMAIN OF ECONOMY AND SOCIETY)

11.5.1   REMOVING EXPENSES OF POST-TREATMENT PROBLEMS

In today's rapidly evolving landscape, the effective utilization of data has become paramount for making informed decisions across various industries, including healthcare. The healthcare sector is no exception to this trend. With the adoption of standardized formats for recording patient outcomes, a vast amount of data becomes readily available for analysis by AI-powered systems. These advanced systems have the capability to examine patterns of treatment outcomes and identify suitable remedial measures based on individual patient profiles. So, AI technology facilitates decision making clinically, ensuring that interventions and treatments are tailored to each patient's specific needs, thereby promoting a more personalized approach to care. The immediate outcome of this transformative approach is a significant improvement in patient outcomes, leading to the reduction of expenses associated with post-treatment complications – a prominent cost factor in healthcare ecosystems worldwide [22].

11.5.2   REDUCING EXPENSE BY DIAGNOSING EARLY

AI-powered devices have demonstrated their ability to perform repetitive and straightforward tasks with increased accuracy, such as processing CT scans and conducting specific tests. This capability mitigates the frequency of physician errors and enables swift diagnosis and on-time intervention before conditions escalate. In the field of mammography, AI has exhibited impressive precision and faster processing capabilities compared to humans. As a result, it allows for the early detection of breast cancer, significantly improving the chances of timely treatment. Additionally, AI has proven effective in identifying vertebral fractures, which are often overlooked in human diagnoses and serve as an early indicator of incipient osteoporosis. By addressing this condition at an early stage, healthcare services can substantially reduce associated expenses related to osteoporosis.

11.5.3   REDUCING COST BY ENHANCING CLINICAL TRIALS

AI possesses the remarkable capability to expedite the development of essential therapeutics, resulting in substantial cost savings for healthcare systems. By employing AI-powered programs that simulate and analyze diverse range of treatment prospects, efficacy predictions for diseases like Ebola can be generated, ultimately saving both money and, more importantly, lives. The integration of biomarker monitoring frameworks, which allow for gene-level disease detection, along with the utilization of extensive patient data, can be rapidly analyzed within seconds using convenient at-home devices. Through this process, AI has the ability to carry the potential to enhance medication optimization during clinical trials [23] (Figure 11.2).

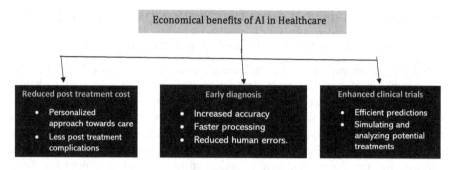

FIGURE 11.2 Economical benefits of AI in healthcare.

11.6 ADOPTION OF ARTIFICIAL INTELLIGENCE IN INDIA VS OTHER COUNTRIES

The healthcare industry is trying to inculcate AI technology to provide better and fast facilities to its patients. Since there is a shortage of medical specialists across the country, AI can be very helpful to fulfill the lacking facilities in the healthcare industries. According to an article published by *Aishwarya Banik on healthcare outlook*, India is one of the top 10 countries using AI in the healthcare sector along with the USA, China, France, Canada, Russia, the UK, Germany, Norway, and Sweden [24] Table 11.7 shows different Countries and the Corresponding AI Startups.

TABLE 11.7
Countries and the Corresponding AI Startups

Country	AI in Healthcare Industry
USA	According to a report of Sage growth partners, In the USA, 90% of the healthcare industries have adopted AI tools to help patients more efficiently. 75% of the healthcare staff have agreed that AI innovations are more useful now as the world has grappled with the new coronavirus pandemic [25]
CHINA	There will exist a remarkable surge in the integration of Artificial Intelligence. Projections give us an indication that the Chinese AI healthcare market, currently valued at $0.55 billion in 2022, is anticipated to skyrocket to a staggering $11.91 billion by 2030. This meteoric rise signifies a compelling compound annual growth rate (CAGR) of 46.72% throughout the forecast period spanning from 2022 to 2030 [26]
FRANCE	The stance of the French government remains resolute, affirming that the role of Artificial Intelligence (AI) in healthcare is complementary rather than substitutive, emphasizing its potential to support and collaborate with doctors. Among the many developing AI healthcare tools, eCerveau is a tool that is used by emergency and accident departments, it basically provides the number of available beds, information related to in service ambulance, etc. [27]

TABLE 11.7 *(Continued)*
Countries and the Corresponding AI Startups

Country	AI in Healthcare Industry
CANADA	A Toronto-based startup named Swift Medical has emerged as a trailblazer with its amazing smartphone tool powered by artificial intelligence (AI). Remarkably, Swift Medical's solution has already gained significant traction, being deployed with over 100,000 patients every month. BlueDot, an innovative organization, harnesses the power of big data to track, predict, and proactively combat the spread of infectious diseases. From the formidable Ebola and Zika viruses to the seasonal flu, BlueDot's data-driven approach equips healthcare professionals with valuable insights, enabling swift and targeted interventions [28]
Russia	Russia has 37 startup companies for AI in Healthcare. Some of them are – Botkin.AI, Webiomed, Semantic Hub, TeleMD, Cashee, ImmunoMind, Aivarix, Third Opinion, Denti.AI [29]
UK	In the UK, they have currently, 484 startup companies of AI in healthcare. Some of them are – Lifebit, Healx, Healthily, Ultromics, Charm Therapeutics, Nucleome Therapeutics, Eagle Genomics, Brainomix, HelloSelf, Causaly [30]
Germany	To provide the benefits of AI all over the world, the country is focussing on building AI-excelling central systems. The Market is expected to increase from $0.25 Billion in 2022 to $4.52 Billion by 2030, This surge represents an impressive compound annual growth rate (CAGR) of 43.42% during the forecast period spanning from 2022 to 2030 [31]
NORWAY	The National Health and Hospital plan of Norway focuses on developing more digital tools and medical devices. These tools must be very needed by the patients and must be of great service. This development should come under appropriate ethical practices. Upcoming fields include – Pathology. They established a Multi-Agency Coordination Project which aims in providing guidance in healthcare service and self-implementation of artificial intelligence. [Norwegian Centre for E-health Research]
SWEDEN	They have 55 startup companies of AI in healthcare. Some of them are – Elypta, Stardots, AIMedtech, Grace.health, Qlucore, Lytics.AI, Magnea, Smart HealthCare, Goodsomnia, Hypocampus [32,33]

11.7   CHALLENGES FACED BY AI IN INDIA

The adoption of AI in India is still in its early stages, but it is experiencing rapid growth. The healthcare industry is one particular sector where AI is being extensively embraced to bring about a transformation in care delivery. However, the successful implementation of AI in the healthcare is accompanied by several challenges that need to be addressed. The following section explores some of these challenges (Figure 11.3):

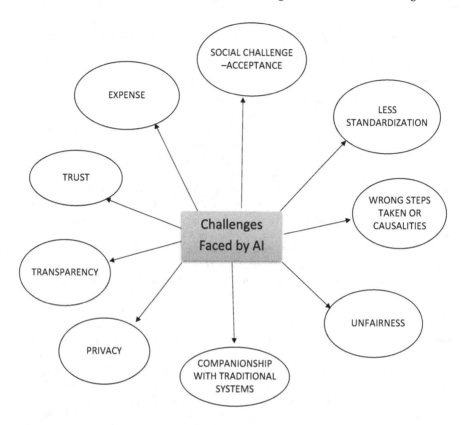

FIGURE 11.3 Challenges of AI in medical domain.

11.7.1 LESS STANDARDIZATION

One of the primary obstacles in the enforcement of AI in healthcare domain is the absence of standardized guidelines. Presently, there is a lack of consensus on how AI should be utilized within healthcare settings. This absence of standardization poses challenges for both healthcare providers and patients alike. For healthcare providers, the absence of agreed-upon standards makes it difficult to determine the effectiveness of various AI applications. As a result, valuable time and resources may be wasted on implementing AI solutions that ultimately or eventually are proving to be ineffective. On the patient side, the lack of standardization creates confusion and uncertainty regarding the quality of care they can expect. Patients may also exhibit hesitancy in utilizing AI applications if they are unsure about their efficacy. Addressing the issue of standardization is crucial for the successful adoption of AI in healthcare.

11.7.2 WRONG STEPS TAKEN OR CAUSALITIES

One among primary concerns with AI systems in healthcare is the potential for occasional inaccuracies, leading to harm or other healthcare-related issues for patients. Patient harm can occur if an AI system puts forth as a prescription an incorrect medication, proves to be inadequate to spot a tumor in the radiological examinations, or dedicates a medical hospital bed to the wrong person based on inaccurate projections. It must be noted that injuries within the healthcare system are already prevalent due to medical errors, even without employment of AI. However, AI errors may have distinct implications for several reasons.

Firstly, afflictions brought about by AI software's may provoke different responses from patients and caregivers compared to those induced by human made mistakes. Secondly, the widespread utilization of AI systems amplifies the potential impact of a flaw in the system. A single error in an AI system could potentially lead to harm for thousands of patients, whereas a human error would typically affect a smaller number of patients within a single provider's practice.

11.7.3 UNFAIRNESS

Within the realm of healthcare AI, concerns regarding prejudice and inequality arise. AI systems have the capacity to acquire biases from the data they are trained on. For instance, if the AI data predominantly originates from scholastic medical institutions, the upcoming future AI systems may have limited knowledge about and consequently provide less effective treatment to patients from communities that typically do not frequent such establishments. In the same vein, when utilizing AI-powered speech recognition for transcribing encounter jottings, the performance of the AI may be compromised in the event that the healthcare provider pertains to an underrepresented racial or gender attributes in the training data. Even when AI systems get trained on reliable and representative data, issues can arise if the underlying data shows back built-in biases and discrepancies within the healthcare system. For example, an AI system trained on healthcare records might erroneously recommend lower doses of painkillers for African-American patients due to systemic biases rather than biological realities (Lee, 2021) [14]. Moreover, AI systems involved in resource allocation have the potential to exacerbate existing inequalities by allocating limited resources to patients who are of less importance or profitable by health systems, for various reasons.

11.7.4 COMPANIONSHIP WITH TRADITIONAL SYSTEMS

One of the major impediments in incorporating AI in healthcare is incorporating it into legacy infrastructure. Legacy systems are often outdated and incompatible with newer systems, which can make it difficult to exchange data. This is a pivotal requirement for AI applications, as they are dependent on significant data quantities for training and operation. Furthermore, legacy systems often lack the necessary computing power and storage capacity to support AI algorithms. Consequently, organizations may need to invest in upgrading their legacy systems before being able to effectively adopt AI technology. Despite these challenges, the potential benefits of AI in healthcare are substantial and should not be overlooked. By approaching the integration process strategically, organizations can overcome these obstacles and leverage the transformative advantages of AI [14].

11.7.5 WORRY ABOUT OUR PRIVACY

Another set of concerns arises in relation to privacy when as regards to AI in healthcare. The inclination for extensive information sets often drives technologists to collect data from a substantial patient population. Some individuals may express concerns regarding the potential violation of their confidentiality due to data sharing between major healthcare institutions and AI companies, leading to legal action. Additionally, privacy can be compromised by AI systems that predict personal information about patients, even without being explicitly provided with that information. In factually accurate terms, the ability to infer such information is often one of the key purposes of AI in healthcare [34].

For instance, an AI system is likely to be capable of detecting, even if the affected person has never revealed it, Parkinson's disease solely based on the movements of a mouse of computer. Also, when the individual has never disclosed this information to anyone else or may not be aware of their condition. Patients perhaps perceive this as a defiance or infringement of their privacy (confidential data), primarily if the outcomes of AI system are shared with external entities such as financial institutions or companies dealing in insurances [35].

11.7.6 INABILITY TO TRUST THE ARTIFICIAL INTELLIGENCE

The adoption of AI in healthcare faces an obstacle related to the fear and lack of trust that many individuals have toward change, particularly when it involves decisions about their health. People often exhibit reluctance to embrace new approaches, even when they hold the potential to enhance their well-being. This resistance to change becomes even more pronounced when it concerns matters as personal as our health. To overcome this challenge, it is crucial to establish transparent and comprehensive communication regarding the utilization of AI in healthcare and the benefits it can offer. Building trust through the active collaboration of patients and doctors in the development and implementation of AI-based solutions is also imperative. By directly addressing these fears and concerns, we can unlock the full potential of AI in transforming healthcare.

11.7.7 EXPENSE

The issue of high costs poses a significant challenge in the embracement of AI in healthcare. Despite the numerous potential applications of AI in the healthcare domain, the expenses involved in AI development and implementation remain a major hurdle to its extensive adoption. Notably, the creation of an accurate disease-diagnosing AI system demands substantial investments in data collection, annotation, and algorithm development. The high cost of AI adoption is a major obstacle to its extensive use in healthcare. The infrastructure required to deploy AI systems in hospitals and clinics is expensive, and the cost of training and maintaining these systems is also high. As a result, many healthcare organizations are hesitant to adopt AI, even though it has the potential to improve patient care and efficiency [36].

11.7.8 SOCIAL CHALLENGES

It is feared that AI will take over the jobs of regular people. Therefore, making healthcare employees insecure and defensive about adopting the AI technologies. This insecurity leads to being reluctant to adopting AI aids. It is a mere misunderstanding among the healthcare workers. AI is not capable of taking over jobs of regular people, people who use AI are a threat to the workers who are abstaining from using AI. Existence of AI does not mean absence of job opportunities, it means that the jobs are required to be done using new technologies and a person with optimum AI knowledge can get to do that job.

11.7.9 TRANSPARENCY

The way of working and making decisions of the AI models should be easy and clear to understand. And it shall be treated as an essential and legal rule by the AI developers and strictly followed by. In order to achieve a significant level of transparency various measures can be adopted, ranging from providing information about how the AI system works, keeping records and documentation of its activities, making it auditable and traceable, and ensuring that it can be explained and interpreted [37].

11.7.9.1 Interpretability and Explaining Ability

Interpretability means to understand something and put together all the information to drive meaning. Explaining ability means the ability to present certain explanations. Interpretability is the ultimate goal, and it is achieved by going through explanations that one actor presents for interpreting by another actor. Here, transparency encompasses the whole procedure of development and use of AI systems, while interpretability focuses on how humans perceive/understand the AI system and its results [37].

11.8 NOTEWORTHY PROBLEMS ASSOCIATED WITH MACHINE LEARNING IN THE MEDICAL FIELD

11.8.1 EXISTENCE OF THE ISSUE

It is like trying to cut butter with a beam. With the easily available software on the internet, it is becoming very easy to design models which will perform high computational tasks with ease. When developers have only one aim – to create a technical solution, there are high chances of making a model that is designed to solve a problem which does not even exist. Therefore, resulting in decline of interest of general physicians in the models' answers or solutions [38]. For instance, a machine learning expert when provided with a lot of patient data who are schizophrenic, the expert will be urged to design a model to detect schizophrenia in patients. But the medical experts are already equipped with such models which can perform this detection. There is a need to develop such models which can provide medical practitioners with the information about how the patients would respond to the treatment given. Therefore, whenever there is an ML model designing process going on, it is crucial to consider the eventual users of the application. Designing projects just for the sake of computer science or statistical point should be avoided [39–41].

11.8.2 PRACTICAL ASPECT

Just like existence of a problem mentioned above, there is a concerning domain for practicality as well. Before creating a model, its compatibility with real-life environment should be considered. Sometimes the model created is not well enough to be adapting with the actual world situations. For example, a model may require such resources which are not available in the actual place of application (like clinics and other practical settings). To avoid these issues, prior acknowledgment of current environmental factors such as resources limitations, etc. where the model is to be used should be done [38,42].

11.8.3 SAMPLE SIZE RELIABILITY

When a small sample size is considered to design a solution for analysis, there might be chances of the model not being able to give accurate results. This happens because the small sample size fails to give justice to the actual clinical environment and the results given by this model may be less accurate. The models that are being build should be strong and dependable. They should give accurate results under different and new conditions. In this contemporary world, one can access a large amount of data. Algorithms that are being designed with the help of Machine Learning should be well trained with datasets that are large and contain various dimensions of information. The data should be taken from different sources and combined to create a meaningful dataset [38,43].

11.8.4 DISCRIMINATION AND BIASES

One more concerning factor with AI technologies is that they can forward the previously existing biases to the new models. This is indeed an alarming concern since it can worsen the current biases in the medical field. For instance, if a model is being built with the training dataset which has been biased toward a certain group, then the new built model will also show the same traits in the prediction toward the certain group [44]. Suggesting that the previous pattern of biasness is being carried forward. The main problem in this practice of using AI technology is that the model may show satisfactory performance for one dataset of patient but fail when it is used for another dataset. For example, there is an ML algorithm which is intended to serve as a skin disease detector and diagnose. Since there is no proper representations of racial differences in the skin type, there is a disparity in healthcare [7]. To solve this issue medical schools have started including more descriptive knowledge about different skin tones and types. When deep learning algorithms are trained, they have very low-quality images data which results in not being able to treat patients who have a darker skin tone. To improve the accuracy, it is essential to use high-quality images/datasets. This will ensure no discrimination against darker skin tones [38,45].

11.8.5 GENERALIZING THE POPULATION

In addition to the discriminations in AI algorithms, this occurs due to the acquisition of data from one specific group of people like the same country, same race, etc. As a result, the program may fail to give correct results when used on different group of people. For example, suppose we have a program that does predictions about someone's language ability based on their brain activity. Majority of the data used to train this program comes from English speaking people or people from the USA. But when we test this program with Chinese participants, we find that their brain activity is different when learning Mandarin. This means the program may not work fairly for them because it was trained on a different language and culture. To avoid these problems, it is important to have data from different places and diverse populations when training these models. This way, the programs can be more fair and accurate for everyone, no matter where they are from or what language they speak [38,46].

11.9 CONCLUSION

AI possesses the capability to not just aid in the advancement of valuable pharmaceuticals moreover enhance the effectiveness of existing ones. While AI implementation in the realm of healthcare at present is limited, the significant medical and economic benefits it offers cannot be ignored [47–50]. Forward-thinking healthcare organizations have the opportunity to leverage breakthrough technologies in high-cost sectors, thereby maintaining a competitive edge excelling their counterparts or parallels. These examples merely touch the preliminary understanding of what is achievable when the utmost possibility of AI is harnessed in medical care conveyance [51,52]. The range of possibilities are both immense and invaluable, necessitating partnership between governmental and private enterprise stakeholders to realize this potential range. The rising healthcare costs will continue to be a pressing concern for healthcare partners, given the aging global population and the increasing prevalence of chronic diseases. Maybe it is time to seek the aid of machines.

However, as we embrace these exciting technologies, we must consider their implications within the contemporary healthcare landscape. The integration of intelligent health solutions within the realm of medicine is driving noteworthy transformations within the healthcare sphere, and the decisions we make today will entail pervasive consequences for prospective patient care. It is essential for researchers and developers to approach these tools with a critical lens, acknowledging the historical context of prejudiced conduct, biases, and medical mistakes in the domain [53–56].

REFERENCES

1. Shaheen, M. Y. (2021). Applications of artificial intelligence (AI) in healthcare: A review. ScienceOpen.
2. Govindasamy, S. P. (2019). Scaling Innovations in Healthcare: A Multi-Method Analysis of Facilitators and Barriers of Innovation Adoption in Hospitals. Temple University.
3. Arora, A. (2020). Conceptualising artificial intelligence as a digital healthcare innovation: An introductory review. Medical Devices, 13, 223.
4. Apell, P., & Eriksson, H. (2021). Artificial intelligence (AI) healthcare technology innovations: The current state and challenges from a life science industry perspective. Technology Analysis & Strategic Management, 35, 1–15.
5. Shaheen, M. Y. (2021). Adoption of machine learning for medical diagnosis.ScienceOpen Preprints.
6. Shaheen, M. Y. (2021). AI in Healthcare: Medical and Socio-economic Benefits and Challenges. ScienceOpen Preprints. DOI: 10.14293/S2199-1006.1.SOR-.PPRQNI1.v1
7. Title: "Healthcare AI Advances Rapidly in India" Website: The Financial Express URL: https://www.financialexpress.com/life/technology/healthcare-ai-advances-rapidly-in-india/2937432/#:~:text=Healthcare%20applications%20of%20AI%20algorithms,US%241%20trillion%20by%202035.
8. Lorica, B., & Nathan, P. Title: "Second Annual AI in Healthcare Survey Uncovers Industry Trends, Challenges, and Best Practices in Artificial Intelligence Among Healthcare and Life Sciences Practitioners" Website: John Snow Labs URL: https://www.johnsnowlabs.com/second-annual-ai-in-healthcare-survey-uncovers-industry-trends-challenges-and-best-practices-in-artificial-intelligence-among-healthcare-and-life-sciences-practitioners/
9. Hashimoto, D. A., Ward, T. M., & Meireles, O. R. (2020). The role of artificial intelligence in surgery. Advances in Surgery, 54, 89–101.
10. Zhou, X.-Y., Guo, Y., Shen, M., & Yang, G.-Z. (2019). Artificial intelligence in surgery. ArXiv Preprint ArXiv:2001.00627.
11. Fekri, P., Setoodeh, P., Khosravian, F., Safavi, A. A., & Zadeh, M. H. (2018). Towards deep secure telesurgery. Proceedings of the International Conference on Scientific Computing (CSC), 81–86.
12. Prabu, A. J., Narmadha, J., & Jeyaprakash, K. (2014). Artificial intelligence robotically assisted brain surgery. Artificial Intelligence, 4(5), 116–117.
13. Hockstein, N. G., Nolan, J. P., O'Malley Jr, B. W., & Woo, Y. J. (2005). Robotic microlaryngeal surgery: A technical feasibility study using the daVinci surgical robot and an airway mannequin. The Laryngoscope, 115(5), 780–785.
14. Madsen, L. (2014). Data-driven healthcare: How analytics and BI are transforming the industry. https://books.google.com/books?hl=en&lr=&id=De_lBQAAQBAJ&oi=fnd&pg=PR13&dq=datadriven+decision+healthcare&ots=lEbwt52_Au&sig=QN7m-si9scdFdmQ6Rx5c9W6nqp
15. Guo, C., Engineering, J. C.-J. of S. S. and S., & 2019, undefined. (n.d.). Big data analytics in healthcare: Data-driven methods for typical treatment pattern mining. SpringerPaperpile. Retrieved September 23, 2021, from https://link.springer.com/article/10.1007/s11518-019-5437-5
16. Guo, C., & Chen, J. (2019). Big data analytics in healthcare: Data-driven methods for typical treatment pattern mining. Journal of Systems Science and Systems Engineering, 28(6), 694–714. 10.1007/S11518-019-5437-5
17. Luxton, D. D. (2016). An Introduction to Artificial Intelligence in Behavioral and Mental Health Care. In Artificial Intelligence in Behavioral and Mental Health Care (pp. 1–26). Elsevier.

18. Lovejoy, C. A. (2019). Technology and mental health: the role of artificial intelligence. European Psychiatry, 55, 1–3.
19. Graham, S., Depp, C., Lee, E. E., Nebeker, C., Tu, X., Kim, H.-C., & Jeste, D. V. (2019). Artificial intelligence for mental health and mental illnesses: an overview. Current Psychiatry Reports, 21(11), 1–18.
20. Le Glaz, A., Haralambous, Y., Kim-Dufor, D.-H., Lenca, P., Billot, R., Ryan, T. C., Marsh, J., Devylder, J., Walter, M., & Berrouiguet, S. (2021). Machine learning and natural language processing in mental health: Systematic review. Journal of Medical Internet Research, 23(5), e15708.
21. Luxton, D. D. (2014). Artificial intelligence in psychological practice: Current and future applications and implications. Professional Psychology: Research and Practice, 45(5), 332.
22. Le Nguyen, T., & Do, T. T. H. (2019). Artificial intelligence in healthcare: A new technology benefit for both patients and doctors. 2019 Portland International Conference on Management of Engineering and Technology (PICMET), 1–15.
23. Beck, J. T., Rammage, M., Jackson, G. P., Preininger, A. M., Dankwa-Mullan, I., Roebuck, M. C., Torres, A., Holtzen, H., Coverdill, S. E., & Williamson, M. P. (2020). Artificial intelligence tool for optimizing eligibility screening for clinical trials in a large community cancer center. JCO Clinical Cancer Informatics, 4, 50–59.
24. Banik, A. Title: "Top 10 Countries Actively Applying AI in Healthcare" Website: Healthcare Outlook URL: https://www.healthcareoutlook.net/top-10-countries-actively-applying-ai-in-healthcare/
25. Kent, J. Title: "90% of Hospitals Have Artificial Intelligence Strategies in Place" Website: HealthITAnalytics URL: https://healthitanalytics.com/news/90-of-hospitals-have-artificial-intelligence-strategies-in-place#:~:text=March%2011%2C%202021%20%2D%20Nine%20in,report%20from%20Sage%20Growth%20Partners.
26. Title: "China's Artificial Intelligence (AI) in Healthcare Market Analysis" Website: Insights10 URL: https://www.insights10.com/report/china-artificial-intelligence-ai-in-healthcare-market-analysis/#:~:text=Market%20Executive%20Summary-,China's%20Artificial%20Intelligence%20(AI)%20in%20the%20healthcare%20market%20is%20projected,two%2Dthirds%20of%20them%20privatized.
27. Title: "French Government Gets Ready for AI in Healthcare" Website: Healthcare in Europe URL: https://healthcare-in-europe.com/en/news/french-government-gets-ready-for-ai-in-healthcare.html#:~:text=There%20are%20several%20artificial%20intelligence,service%20and%20emergency%20department%20activity.
28. Mediaplanet, Title: "The Future of Canadian Health Care and AI" Website: Innovating Canada URL: https://www.innovatingcanada.ca/technology/the-future-of-canadian-health-care-and-ai/
29. Title: "AI in Healthcare Startups in Russia" Website: Tracxn URL: https://tracxn.com/explore/AI-in-Healthcare-Startups-in-Russia
30. Title: "AI in Healthcare Startups in United Kingdom" Website: Tracxn URL: https://tracxn.com/explore/AI-in-Healthcare-Startups-in-United-Kingdom
31. Title: "Germany Artificial Intelligence (AI) in Healthcare Market Analysis" Website: Insights10 URL: https://www.insights10.com/report/germany-artificial-intelligence-ai-in-healthcare-market-analysis/#:~:text=The%20Germany%20Artificial%20Intelligence%20(AI,forecast%20period%20of%202022%2D2030.
32. Title: "AI in Healthcare Startups in Sweden" Website: Tracxn URL: https://tracxn.com/explore/AI-in-Healthcare-Startups-in-Sweden
33. Lee, E. (2021). How do we build trust in machine learning models? Available at SSRN 3822437

34. Marwan, M., Kartit, A., & Ouahmane, H. (2018). Security enhancement in healthcare cloud using machine learning. Procedia Computer Science, 127, 388–397.

35. van der Schaar, M., Alaa, A. M., Floto, A., Gimson, A., Scholtes, S., Wood, A., McKinney, E., Jarrett, D., Lio, P., & Ercole, A. (2021). How artificial intelligence and machine learning can help healthcare systems respond to COVID-19. Machine Learning, 110(1), 1–14.

36. Kulkarni, V. Title: "Key Challenges in Adopting AI in Healthcare" Website: Times of India Blogs URL: https://timesofindia.indiatimes.com/blogs/voices/key-challenges-in-adopting-ai-in-healthcare/

37. Kiseleva, A., Kotzinos, D., & De Hert, P. (2022). Transparency of AI in healthcare as a multilayered system of accountabilities: Between legal requirements and technical limitations. Frontiers in Artificial Intelligence, 5, 879603. doi: 10.3389/frai.2022.879603

38. Doyen, S. & Dadario, N. B. (2022). 12 Plagues of AI in healthcare: A practical guide to current issues with using machine learning in a medical context. Frontier in Digital Health, 4, 765406. doi: 10.3389/fdgth.2022.765406

39. Glasser, M. F., Coalson, T. S., Robinson, E. C., Hacker, C. D., Harwell, J., Yacoub, E., et al. (2016). A multi-modal parcellation of human cerebral cortex. Nature, 536, 171–178. doi: 10.1038/nature18933

40. Dadario, N. B., Brahimaj, B., Yeung, J., & Sughrue, M. E. (2021). Reducing the cognitive footprint of brain tumor surgery. Frontier Neurology, 12, 711646. doi: 10.3389/fneur.2021.711646

41. Ren, H., Zhu, J., Su, X., Chen, S., Zeng, S., Lan, X., et al. (2020). Application of structural and functional connectome mismatch for classification and individualized therapy in Alzheimer disease. Frontier in Digital Health, 8, 584430. doi: 10.3389/fpubh.2020.584430

42. Colubri, A., Hartley, M. A., Siakor, M., Wolfman, V., Felix, A., Sesay, T., et al. (2019). Machine-learning prognostic models from the 2014-16 ebola outbreak: Dataharmonization challenges, validation strategies, and mHealth applications. EclinicalMedicine, 11, 54–64. doi: 10.1016/j.eclinm.2019.06.003

43. Roberts, M. D., Aix-Covnet, Driggs, M., Thorpe, J., Gilbey, M., Yeung, S., et al. (2021). Common pitfalls and recommendations for using machine learning to detect and prognosticate for COVID-19 using chest radiographs and CT scans. Nature Machine Intelligence, 3, 199–217. doi: 10.1038/s42256-021-00307-0

44. Louie, P., & Wilkes, R. (2018). Representations of race and skin tone in medical textbook imagery. Social Science & Medicine, 202, 38–42. doi: 10.1016/j.socscimed.2018.02.023

45. Adamson, A. S., & Smith, A. (2018). Machine learning and health care disparities in dermatology. JAMA Dermatology, 154, 1247–1248. doi: 10.1001/jamadermatol.2018.2348

46. Buolamwini, J., & Gebru, T. (2018). Gender shades: Intersectional accuracy disparities in commercial gender classification. In: Proceedings of the 1st Conference on Fairness, Accountability and Transparency, Vol. 81. PMLR (pp. 77–91). Available online at: https://proceedings.mlr.press/v81/buolamwini18a.html

47. Arora, S., Sharma, S., Anand, R., & Shrivastva, G. (2023). Miniaturized pentagon-shaped planar monopole antenna for ultra-wideband applications. Progress In Electromagnetics Research C, 133, 195–208.

48. Anand, R., Singh, B., & Sindhwani, N. (2009). Speech perception & analysis of fluent digits' strings using level-by-level time alignment. International Journal of Information Technology and Knowledge Management, 2(1), 65–68.

49. Sansanwal, K., Shrivastava, G., Anand, R., & Sharma, K. (2019). Big Data Analysis and Compression for Indoor Air Quality. Handbook of IoT and Big Data, 1.

50. Juneja, S., & Anand, R. (2018). Contrast Enhancement of an Image by DWT-SVD and DCT-SVD. In Data Engineering and Intelligent Computing: Proceedings of IC3T 2016 (pp. 595–603). Springer Singapore.

51. Sindhwani, N., Rana, A., & Chaudhary, A. (2021, September). Breast cancer detection using machine learning algorithms. In 2021 9th International Conference on Reliability, Infocom Technologies and Optimization (Trends and Future Directions) (ICRITO) (pp. 1–5). IEEE.

52. Gupta, B., Chaudhary, A., Sindhwani, N., & Rana, A. (2021, September). Smart shoe for detection of electrocution using Internet of Things (IoT). In 2021 9th International Conference on Reliability, Infocom Technologies and Optimization (Trends and Future Directions)(ICRITO) (pp. 1–3). IEEE.

53. Jain, N., Chaudhary, A., Sindhwani, N., & Rana, A. (2021, September). Applications of Wearable devices in IoT. In 2021 9th International Conference on Reliability, Infocom Technologies and Optimization (Trends and Future Directions)(ICRITO) (pp. 1–4). IEEE.

54. Sharma, G., Nehra, N., Dahiya, A., Sindhwani, N., & Singh, P. (2022). Automatic Heart-rate Measurement Using Facial Video. In Networking Technologies in Smart Healthcare (pp. 289–307). CRC Press.

55. Anand, R., Arora, S., & Sindhwani, N. (2022, January). A miniaturized UWB antenna for high speed applications. In 2022 International Conference on Computing, Communication and Power Technology (IC3P) (pp. 264–267). IEEE.

56. Anand, R., Sindhwani, N., Saini, A., & Shubham. (2021). Emerging technologies for COVID-19. Enabling Healthcare 4.0 for Pandemics: A roadmap using AI, machine learning, IoT and Cognitive Technologies, 163–188.

12 Privacy and Security Considerations in Healthcare: Navigating the Challenges of IoT and Ubiquitous Computing

Laxmi Ahuja, Rajbala Simon, and Ayush Thakur

12.1 INTRODUCTION

Privacy is a longstanding concern that has persisted in the realm of technology for decades [1]. As early as 1991, Mark Weiser identified privacy as a significant challenge in the context of IoT and ubiquitous computing devices. He foresaw a future with numerous computers capable of sensing individuals in close proximity, all interconnected by high-speed networks, raising profound questions about privacy and potential implications. Fast forward almost two decades, and while technological advancements have flourished, a universal solution for ensuring privacy in computer systems remains elusive [2]. The intricacies of privacy issues make it challenging to prescribe a single standardized approach to make a system "privacy-safe." The very definition of "privacy-safe" varies, depending on whose privacy is protected, when, and to what extent. Instead of seeking a one-size-fits-all solution, a meticulous examination of each individual system and application becomes essential to understand its functionality, implications, and how to address privacy concerns. This chapter aims to provide guidance in navigating privacy considerations, beginning with a comprehensive explanation of the privacy concept and showcasing examples of how technology can safeguard sensitive information within ubiquitous computing systems.

With the ever-expanding integration of IoT and ubiquitous computing technologies into the healthcare landscape, the importance of privacy has become even more critical [3–7]. While these innovations offer immense potential in improving patient care, they also present unique challenges in safeguarding patient data and ensuring confidentiality. In this context, the concept of privacy gains heightened

DOI: 10.1201/9781003330523-12

significance as healthcare providers and technology developers must grapple with questions surrounding the protection of patients' sensitive medical information. As well, the chapter seeks to shed light on how technology can be leveraged to protect patient privacy within healthcare IoT and ubiquitous computing systems. It underscores that this chapter does not offer a ready-made solution for specific problems; rather, it serves as a starting point for healthcare professionals and developers to recognize and address privacy concerns in the design, development, and use of IoT and ubiquitous computing applications in healthcare settings [8–12]. By exploring the intricacies of privacy in healthcare technology, readers will be equipped to navigate the complex landscape and foster a privacy-centric approach to their healthcare technology endeavors.

12.2   INTERNET OF THINGS

The Internet has revolutionized our lives, providing a vast network where devices can communicate globally through a set of communication protocols. Initially limited to fixed websites and email, the Internet has witnessed an emergence of new and diverse technologies, with smart devices becoming an integral part of our daily routines. These smart devices, seamlessly interconnected and remotely accessible, form the Internet of Things (IoT), offering an ideal solution for controlling and tracking various aspects of our lives [13]. The concept of IoT, coined by Kevin Ashton in 1999 during a talk at Proctor & Gamble, originated from the idea of connecting radio frequency identification (RFID) [14] with the Internet theme. IoT technology has evolved over the years, with projections estimating 20 billion IoT devices to be connected by 2020.

The healthcare sector has embraced the potential of IoT, leveraging its expanding array of devices with cameras, microphones, sensors, and network access to non-computer products. This convergence of technology into healthcare settings has opened new avenues for interaction, entertainment, commerce, and communication. Yet, it also poses challenges to privacy, particularly in the case of home and wearable IoT applications, where strong privacy presumptions are associated with personal spaces. The introduction of IoT devices in healthcare can blur the boundaries between private and public spheres, as they collect an increasing amount of data from our bodies and personal spaces [15,16]. As IoT devices become more ubiquitous, concerns regarding power, consent, and openness arise, necessitating a thoughtful approach to balance the benefits of IoT in healthcare with privacy protection.

The potential impact of IoT in healthcare is significant, offering exciting opportunities to improve patient care and healthcare services. But, it is essential to recognize and address the privacy implications that arise with the integration of IoT devices into healthcare settings. This chapter aims to explore the dynamic interplay between IoT and healthcare, providing insights into the challenges and opportunities that lie ahead. By examining the privacy concerns and offering strategies to ensure a privacy-centric approach, healthcare professionals and technology developers can harness the transformative power of IoT while safeguarding patient privacy and confidentiality.

12.3 UBIQUITOUS COMPUTING

Ubiquitous Computing, with its unique characteristics, has brought numerous benefits to various domains, including healthcare. As with any technology, it also presents certain challenges, particularly concerning security and privacy. In the context of healthcare, these challenges are of paramount importance, as the protection of sensitive medical data and patient privacy is critical. Two significant issues that arise in ubiquitous computing environments are Transparent Accessibility and Self-governance and Loss of Control [17].

The Transparent Accessibility problem stems from the confidentiality property of Ubiquitous Computing, which shields unnecessary information from stakeholders to foster cooperation [18]. While this promotes collaboration, it also introduces serious security concerns. During a clear access protocol, users may not be aware of what information is being accessed, how it is accessed, and by whom. This lack of visibility leads to a loss of security control, putting individuals' privacy at risk. In healthcare, where patient data confidentiality is vital, addressing this issue becomes crucial to ensuring the integrity and privacy of medical information.

To enable ease of use and user-centric experiences, Ubiquitous Computing systems adopt "context computing" which focuses on self-management and providing comfort to users [19]. But, this emphasis on user convenience may inadvertently leave the system vulnerable to unrecognized hacking attempts. The pervasive nature of ubiquitous computing, with its widespread spatial distribution and ubiquitous networking, further complicates the physical protection of the system. In the healthcare context, where patient health and well-being are at stake, safeguarding the system from potential threats becomes imperative.

Privacy in healthcare encompasses a broad range of considerations. It involves negotiating and implementing the appropriate levels and contexts in which an entity's data is revealed. Healthcare providers must be vigilant in understanding the intricacies of privacy within ubiquitous computing environments, as they handle sensitive patient information. Ensuring self-governance while maintaining a robust level of control over the system's security is vital to prevent privacy breaches and unauthorized access to patient data.

12.4 PRIVACY CONSIDERATIONS IN UBIQUITOUS HEALTHCARE

12.4.1 IMPORTANCE OF PRIVACY SAFEGUARDS IN HEALTHCARE TECHNOLOGY

Privacy is a fundamental right that individuals have when it comes to their healthcare information. It refers to the control patients have over their personal health information (PHI) and how it is used, disclosed, and protected. In healthcare, privacy involves ensuring that sensitive medical information remains confidential and secure, and that patients have autonomy over who can access and use their data. This includes protecting patients' names, addresses, medical histories, test results, insurance information, and other identifiable health data. The Health Insurance Portability and Accountability Act (HIPAA) sets national standards for protecting the privacy and security of PHI, including rules for authorized access, uses, and disclosures [20]. Healthcare providers must obtain informed consent from patients before collecting, using, or sharing their PHI, unless required by law. By safeguarding patient privacy, healthcare organizations build trust with their patients, promote better care outcomes, and avoid legal penalties associated with non-compliance.

12.4.2 TRANSPARENT ACCESSIBILITY ISSUE

One of the challenges in addressing accessibility issues in healthcare is the lack of transparency in the way that accessibility barriers are identified and addressed. Often, accessibility issues are not well-documented or communicated within healthcare organizations, leading to confusion and delays in resolving these issues [21]. Besides, patients may be hesitant to report accessibility barriers due to concerns about stigma or discrimination. To address this challenge, healthcare organizations can implement transparent policies and procedures for reporting and addressing accessibility issues. For example, they can create accessible feedback mechanisms, such as online forms or mobile apps, that allow patients to easily report accessibility barriers. They can also establish clear guidelines for responding to accessibility issues, including timelines for resolution and communication protocols for keeping patients informed. By increasing transparency around accessibility issues, healthcare organizations can foster greater accountability and improve the overall experience for patients with disabilities.

12.4.2.1 Confidentiality and Cooperation

Maintaining confidentiality and cooperating with healthcare providers are essential components of addressing accessibility issues in healthcare. Confidentiality is critical in ensuring that patients feel comfortable disclosing their accessibility needs and requesting accommodations without fear of discrimination or stigma [22]. Healthcare providers must respect patients' privacy and adhere to laws and regulations governing the release of PHI. Cooperating with healthcare providers means working together to identify and address accessibility barriers, providing necessary documentation or support, and communicating openly and honestly about patients' needs. Patients who feel heard and understood are more likely to engage in shared decision-making and adhere to treatment plans, resulting in better health outcomes. By prioritizing confidentiality and cooperation, healthcare organizations can build trust with patients and advance inclusive, patient-centered care.

12.4.2.2 Security Implications in Healthcare

The importance of confidentiality and cooperation in addressing accessibility issues in healthcare also has significant implications for security. Protecting patients' PHI is a critical aspect of healthcare delivery, and security breaches can have serious consequences for both patients and healthcare providers. Cybercriminals often target healthcare organizations because PHI contains valuable personal information that can be used for malicious purposes, such as identity theft or fraud [23]. When healthcare providers fail to address accessibility issues, they may inadvertently expose patients' PHI to unauthorized parties, compromising patients' privacy and putting them at risk of financial or reputational harm. Furthermore, HIPAA violations can result in hefty fines and reputational damage for healthcare organizations. Therefore, it is crucial for healthcare providers to prioritize accessibility and security simultaneously, implementing robust cybersecurity measures to safeguard patients' PHI and maintain their trust. By doing so, healthcare organizations can provide safer, high-quality care that respects patients' autonomy and privacy.

12.4.3 SELF-GOVERNANCE AND LOSS OF CONTROL PROBLEM

The increasing use of IoT devices and ubiquitous computing in healthcare raises significant concerns about self-governance and loss of control. As patients generate vast amounts of sensitive data through wearables, smartphones, and other connected devices, they may struggle to manage and control access to this information. Healthcare providers must ensure that patients retain agency over their data, while also complying with regulatory requirements and industry standards. The complexity of IoT ecosystems and the sheer volume of data generated can make it difficult for patients to track and govern their data effectively. Besides, the reliance on third-party vendors and cloud services further exacerbates the issue of control, as patients may unknowingly grant access to their data through terms of service agreements or default settings. To mitigate these risks, healthcare organizations should adopt transparent data management practices, provide users with granular controls over data sharing and access, and educate patients about digital literacy and data privacy best practices. By empowering patients to take an active role in managing their digital footprint, healthcare providers can help restore trust in the system and promote better health outcomes.

12.4.3.1 Context Computing and User Convenience

The integration of context computing in healthcare IoT systems also enhances user convenience by tailoring the user experience to individual preferences and circumstances. For instance, smart home systems can adjust lighting, temperature, and entertainment options based on a patient's activity patterns, mood, and interests. Wearable devices can similarly customize notifications, reminders, and recommendations according to a patient's physical activity, sleep patterns, and nutritional intake. Context computing can even optimize medication schedules and dosages based on factors like meal times, exercise routines, and vital signs. By using machine learning algorithms and real-time data analytics, healthcare IoT systems can proactively anticipate patients' needs and adapt to their unique habits and lifestyles. This personalized approach improves user satisfaction, encourages higher adherence rates, and ultimately leads to better health outcomes. What's more, context computing can enable seamless communication [24] between patients, caregivers, and healthcare professionals, facilitating remote consultations, monitoring, and interventions when needed. By enhancing user convenience and streamlining healthcare processes, context computing plays a vital role in realizing the full potential of healthcare IoT systems.

12.4.3.2 Ensuring System Security and Control in Healthcare

Healthcare organizations face unique challenges in ensuring the security and control of their systems and data [25,26]. With the increased use of electronic health records (EHRs), telemedicine, and other digital technologies, protecting patient data and preventing cyber threats has become more important than ever.

- Implement Strong Access Control Measures

  One of the most effective ways to ensure system security and control is to implement strong access control measures. This includes using secure login credentials, two-factor authentication, and role-based access control. Secure login credentials include using complex passwords that are regularly updated, while two-factor authentication adds an extra layer of security by requiring users to provide additional verification, such as a fingerprint or one-time code sent via SMS. Role-based access control limits access to sensitive data and systems to only those who need it to perform their job functions.

- Regularly Update and Patch Systems

  Another important step in ensuring system security and control is to regularly update and patch systems and software. This includes updating operating systems, applications, and firmware to fix known vulnerabilities and improve security features. Regular updates and patches can help prevent cyber attacks that exploit known weaknesses in outdated software.

- Monitor Network Traffic

  Monitoring network traffic is essential in detecting and responding to potential security threats. Healthcare organizations can monitor network traffic using intrusion detection and prevention systems (IDPS) and log analysis tools. IDPS can detect suspicious activity and alert IT staff to potential threats, while log analysis tools can help identify unusual pattern in system usage.

- Use Encryption

  Encryption is another important tool in ensuring system security and control [27]. Encrypting sensitive data, such as patient records and financial information, can prevent unauthorized access in case of a breach. Encryption can also be used to protect data in transit, such as when transmitting patient information between healthcare facilities or to remote workers.

- Implement Incident Response Plans

  Despite the best efforts to prevent security breaches, incidents can still occur. Therefore, it's essential for healthcare organizations to have incident response plans in place. These plans outline steps to be taken in case of a security incident, including how to contain the incident, assess the damage, notify affected parties, and restore systems and data. Regularly testing and updating incident response plans can help ensure that they remain effective and relevant.

- Train Employees

  Finally, training employees on system security and control is critical in preventing security breaches. Healthcare employees should be trained on best practices for password management, email phishing scams, social engineering tactics, and other types of cyber attacks. Employees should be aware of the organization's security policies and procedures and understand their roles and responsibilities in protecting patient data and systems.

12.5   SECURITY CHALLENGES IN UBIQUITOUS HEALTHCARE

This covers data exchange, remote monitoring, and electronic communication between patients and healthcare professionals. While Ubiquitous healthcare has many advantages, such as increased accessibility and convenience, it also poses a number of security risks. Defending IoT devices against hacking attempts, safeguarding data transmission and storage, and implementing strong authentication and access restrictions are the three main security issues in ubiquitous healthcare that will be covered in this section.

12.5.1   SECURING DATA TRANSMISSION AND STORAGE

One of the most significant security challenges in ubiquitous healthcare is ensuring the confidentiality, integrity, and availability of patient data during transmission and storage [28]. EHRs, medical images, and other sensitive information must be protected from unauthorized access, tampering, and cyber attacks. The following measures can help address these concerns:

- Encryption: All data transmitted electronically should be encrypted using standardized protocols like HTTPS or SFTP. This ensures that even if an attacker intercepts the data, they cannot read or modify it without the decryption key.
- Secure Sockets Layer (SSL)/Transport Layer Security (TLS): SSL/TLS certificates should be used to authenticate and encrypt data transmitted between systems. These certificates provide a secure handshake between the client and server, ensuring that only authorized parties can access the data.
- Access control lists (ACLs): ACLs should be implemented to restrict access to sensitive data based on user roles, permissions, and need-to-know principles. This ensures that only authorized personnel can view, edit, or delete patient information.
- Two-factor authentication (2FA): 2FA adds an extra layer of security by requiring users to provide two forms of verification, such as a password and biometric scan, before accessing patient data.
- Regular backups and disaster recovery plans: Data backups are essential for restoring critical information in case of system failures, natural disasters, or cyber attacks. Disaster recovery plans should be developed and tested regularly to minimize downtime and ensure business continuity.

12.5.2 PROTECTING IoT DEVICES FROM HACKING ATTEMPTS

The increasing use of IoT devices in ubiquitous healthcare has introduced new vulnerabilities that hackers can exploit. Medical devices, wearables, and mobile apps often lack adequate security features, making them susceptible to cyber attacks. To mitigate these risks, consider the following strategies:

- Implement secure boot mechanisms: Ensure that all IoT devices have secure boot mechanisms to prevent malware injection during the boot process.
- Use secure communication protocols: Implement secure communication protocols, such as end-to-end encryption, to protect data transmitted between IoT devices and central systems.
- Conduct regular firmware updates: Manufacturers should provide timely firmware updates to patch vulnerabilities and improve device security. Users should ensure their devices receive these updates automatically or manually update them whenever necessary.
- Enable strong passwords and multi-factor authentication: Each IoT device should have a unique, complex password and support multi-factor authentication to prevent unauthorized access.
- Monitor network traffic: Implement IDPS to monitor network traffic and block suspicious activity. Anomaly detection algorithms can identify unusual patterns that may indicate attempted hacking.
- Limit device exposure: Restrict public exposure of IoT devices by implementing firewalls, Network Address Translation (NAT), and Virtual Private Networks (VPNs).
- Educate users: Raise awareness among healthcare professionals and patients about the potential risks associated with IoT devices and the importance of proper usage, maintenance, and security practices.

12.5.3 ESTABLISHING AUTHENTICATION AND ACCESS CONTROLS

Authentication and access control are crucial components of ubiquitous healthcare security. Unauthorized access to patient data can lead to serious consequences, including privacy breaches, identity theft, and medical fraud. To address these concerns, follow these best practices:

- Role-based access control (RBAC): Assign unique usernames and passwords to each user, and implement RBAC to limit access to specific resources based on job responsibilities, privileges, and needs, and enforcing strict access controls [29].
- Implement attribute-based access control (ABAC): ABAC allows you to define fine-grained access policies based on attributes such as user location, time of day, and device being used. This approach enables more flexible and granular access control, reducing the risk of unauthorized access.

- Use OAuth 2.0 and OpenID Connect (OIDC): OAuth 2.0 and OIDC are widely adopted standards for authorization and authentication. They enable secure delegated access, allowing clients to access resources on behalf of users without sharing credentials [30].
- Implement single sign-on (SSO): SSO solutions allow users to access multiple applications with a single set of login credentials, reducing the number of passwords users need to remember and decreasing the likelihood of weak passwords.
- Use adaptive authentication: Adaptive authentication techniques analyze user behavior and environmental factors to determine the level of risk associated with a given access request. This approach enables more accurate decision-making when evaluating access requests, reducing false positives and false negatives.
- Machine learning and artificial intelligence (AI): Machine learning and AI can be used to detect and respond to advanced threats, such as insider attacks and sophisticated external attacks. These technologies can analyze patterns and anomalies in access requests to identify potential security incidents.
- Monitor and audit access requests: Regularly reviewing and analyzing access requests helps identify inappropriate access patterns, misconfigured access controls, or attempted security breaches. This information can be used to refine access controls and improve overall security posture.
- Train employees and contractors: Providing regular training and education on security best practices and policies helps reduce the risk of accidental or intentional breaches resulting from employee or contractor actions.
- Continuously assess and evaluate third-party vendors: Third-party vendors often have access to sensitive data and systems. It's essential to assess and evaluate their security practices regularly to ensure they meet your organization's security standards.
- Implement emergency access procedures: Establishing emergency access procedures allows authorized individuals to access critical systems and data in the event of unexpected events or system failures.
- Periodically review and update access controls: Regularly reviewing and updating access controls ensures they remain aligned with changing business requirements and evolving security threats. This helps maintain optimal security levels and reduces the risk of security breaches.

12.6 STRATEGIES FOR PRIVACY PROTECTION IN UBIQUITOUS HEALTHCARE

Ubiquitous healthcare, also known as pervasive healthcare, refers to the integration of technology into everyday life to promote health and wellness [31]. This includes wearables, mobile apps, and other devices that collect and transmit personal health data. While these technologies have the potential to revolutionize healthcare, they also raise significant privacy concerns. Here, we will discuss strategies for protecting privacy in ubiquitous healthcare, including user awareness and informed consent, encryption and data anonymization, and compliance with privacy regulations.

12.6.1 User Awareness and Informed Consent

One of the most important strategies for protecting privacy in ubiquitous healthcare is user awareness and informed consent. Users must be aware of what data is being collected, how it is being used, and who has access to it. They must also understand their rights and how to exercise them. Informed consent involves providing users with clear and concise information about the data collection process and obtaining their explicit consent before collecting any data.

To achieve user awareness and informed consent, healthcare providers and technology companies must invest in educating users about the benefits and risks of ubiquitous healthcare. This includes providing users with easy-to-understand privacy policies and terms of service agreements. Also, users should be able to opt-out of data collection at any time, and their consent should be renewed periodically to ensure that they continue to be aware of how their data is being used.

12.6.2 Encryption and Data Anonymization

Another strategy for protecting privacy in ubiquitous healthcare is encryption and data anonymization. Encryption involves converting data into a code that can only be deciphered by authorized parties. This prevents unauthorized access to data during transmission or storage. Data anonymization involves removing personally identifiable information from data sets, making it impossible to link the data to individual users.

Healthcare providers and technology companies should use end-to-end encryption to protect user data from unauthorized access. Also, they should use data anonymization techniques such as aggregation, pseudonymization, and differential privacy to minimize the risk of identifying individual users. By doing so, they can protect users' privacy while still using their data to provide personalized care and improve population health.

12.6.3 Compliance with Privacy Regulations

Finally, healthcare providers and technology companies must comply with privacy regulations such as HIPAA and GDPR. HIPAA sets national standards for protecting individually identifiable health information, while GDPR provides comprehensive data protection laws for European Union citizens. Compliance with these regulations requires implementing robust security measures, conducting regular audits, and reporting data breaches promptly.

In addition to complying with existing regulations, healthcare providers and technology companies should work together to develop new privacy standards that address the unique challenges posed by ubiquitous healthcare. This includes developing guidelines for handling sensitive health data, establishing accountability mechanisms, and promoting transparency throughout the data collection and analysis process.

12.7 MITIGATING SECURITY RISKS IN UBIQUITOUS HEALTHCARE

While these technologies have the potential to revolutionize healthcare, they also introduce new security risks that must be mitigated to protect patients' privacy and safety. In this section, we will discuss three strategies for mitigating security risks in ubiquitous healthcare: IDPS, regular firmware updates and security patches, and network segmentation and isolation.

12.7.1 INTRUSION DETECTION AND PREVENTION SYSTEMS

IDPS are security measures designed to identify and stop unauthorized access to computer systems, networks, and electronic data [32]. IDPSs monitor network traffic and analyze it for suspicious activity, alerting security personnel when potential threats are detected. These systems can be deployed in real-time to detect and prevent cyber attacks, which are becoming increasingly common in healthcare. For example, in 2017, the WannaCry ransomware attack affected healthcare organizations around the world, highlighting the need for robust security measures [33].

IDPSs can help mitigate security risks in ubiquitous healthcare by monitoring network traffic between devices and detecting unusual patterns that may indicate malicious activity. For instance, if a patient's wearable device suddenly starts transmitting large amounts of data to an unfamiliar IP address, an IDPS could flag this behavior and alert security personnel to investigate. IDPSs can also help prevent distributed denial-of-service (DDoS) attacks, which can overwhelm healthcare systems and disrupt medical services. By deploying IDPSs, healthcare organizations can proactively defend against cyber threats and protect patients' data.

12.7.2 REGULAR FIRMWARE UPDATES AND SECURITY PATCHES

Firmware updates and security patches are essential for maintaining the security of devices in ubiquitous healthcare. Outdated firmware can leave devices vulnerable to exploitation, allowing hackers to gain unauthorized access to sensitive health data. Regular firmware updates and security patches can help mitigate this risk by fixing known vulnerabilities and improving device security. For example, in 2019, the US Food and Drug Administration (FDA) recalled several models of pacemakers due to concerns that they could be hacked wirelessly [34]. The recall emphasized the importance of keeping medical devices up-to-date with the latest security patches.

Healthcare organizations should implement a policy of regular firmware updates and security patches for all devices connected to their networks. This can be achieved by partnering with vendors that provide timely updates and patches, as well as by training IT staff to apply updates quickly and efficiently. On top of that, healthcare organizations should consider implementing automated update processes to reduce the likelihood of human error. By staying up-to-date with the latest security patches, healthcare organizations can significantly reduce the risk of device compromise and protect patients' data.

12.7.3 NETWORK SEGMENTATION AND ISOLATION

Network segmentation and isolation involve dividing a network into smaller segments and isolating sensitive areas from the rest of the network [35]. This approach helps limit the spread of malware and reduces the attack surface. In ubiquitous healthcare, network segmentation and isolation can help protect sensitive health data by restricting access to authorized personnel only. For example, a hospital might segregate its network into different segments for patient data, administrative functions, and medical devices. Each segment would have its own set of access controls, limiting the movement of malware and unauthorized users.

Network segmentation and isolation can also help contain security incidents. If a device is compromised, the damage can be limited to the isolated segment, preventing the incident from spreading to other parts of the network [36]. Furthermore, network segmentation and isolation can help healthcare organizations meet regulatory requirements, such as HIPAA's requirement for secure data transmission and storage. By implementing network segmentation and isolation, healthcare organizations can better protect patients' data and reduce the risk of security breaches.

12.8 CASE STUDY AND EXAMPLES

12.8.1 CASE STUDY: KAISER PERMANENTE'S ELECTRONIC HEALTH RECORD SYSTEM

Kaiser Permanente, a leading healthcare provider in the United States, has successfully implemented an EHR system that utilizes ubiquitous computing technology [37]. The EHR system, called KP HealthConnect, allows healthcare providers to access patients' medical records and information from any location, at any time, using mobile devices or computers.

The KP HealthConnect system was rolled out in phases, starting in 2004, and was fully implemented across all Kaiser Permanente facilities by 2010. The system includes features such as online appointment scheduling, medication refill requests, and secure messaging between patients and healthcare providers [37,38].

Benefits Realized:
- Improved patient care coordination: With the ability to access patient records remotely, healthcare providers can easily coordinate care and communicate with other team members, reducing errors and improving patient outcomes.
- Enhanced patient engagement: Patients can take a more active role in managing their health through the patient portal, which allows them to view test results, schedule appointments, and communicate with their healthcare providers.
- Reduced costs: The EHR system has helped Kaiser Permanente reduce costs associated with paper records, transcription services, and manual data entry.

- Increased efficiency: The system enables healthcare providers to quickly locate patient information, reducing the time spent searching for records and increasing the amount of time spent on direct patient care.

Lessons Learned:
- Develop a comprehensive rollout plan: Kaiser Permanente took a phased approach to rolling out the EHR system, starting with small pilot programs and gradually expanding to larger groups of users. This allowed the organization to work out technical issues and ensure user adoption before scaling up.
- Provide adequate training and support: The organization invested heavily in training and support for healthcare providers, ensuring that they were comfortable using the new system and understood its full capabilities.
- Prioritize data security: Kaiser Permanente implemented strong data encryption and authentication protocols to protect patient data and ensure confidentiality.

12.8.2   CASE STUDY: COMMUNITY HEALTH SYSTEMS DATA BREACH

Community Health Systems, a healthcare organization operating in 28 states, experienced a data breach in 2014 that exposed the personal information of 4.5 million patients. The breach occurred when Chinese hackers gained access to the organization's database through a vulnerability in its VPN software [39,40].

The hackers accessed patient names, addresses, birthdays, and Social Security numbers, but not medical information or financial data. Community Health Systems reported that the breach did not result in any known misuse of patient data.

Lessons Learned:
- Keep software up-to-date: Ensure that all software, including VPN clients, is updated regularly to fix security vulnerabilities.
- Use multi-factor authentication: Require multiple forms of authentication, such as passwords and biometric scans, to increase security and reduce the risk of unauthorized access.
- Monitor for suspicious activity: Implement robust monitoring tools and procedures to detect and respond to potential security incidents promptly.
- Notify patients promptly: In the event of a breach, notify affected patients immediately and provide guidance on how they can protect themselves from further harm.

Recommendations:
- Conduct regular security audits and risk assessments to identify vulnerabilities and prioritize remediation efforts.
- Train employees on security best practices and ensure that they understand the importance of protecting patient data.
- Consider implementing advanced security technologies, such as AI and machine learning, to enhance threat detection and response capabilities.

12.9 FUTURE DIRECTIONS AND EMERGING TECHNOLOGIES

This field has been rapidly evolving in recent years, and one of its most promising applications is in healthcare. But, as with any emerging technology, there are concerns regarding privacy and security that must be addressed. This section will explore advancements in ubiquitous computing for healthcare, anticipated privacy and security challenges, and research and innovations aimed at enhancing privacy protection.

12.9.1 ADVANCEMENTS IN UBIQUITOUS COMPUTING FOR HEALTHCARE

Ubiquitous computing has already made significant strides in transforming healthcare. Wearable devices like fitness trackers and smartwatches allow individuals to monitor their vital signs, sleep patterns, and physical activity. Mobile apps enable remote consultations, telemedicine, and communication between patients and healthcare providers. Smart homes equipped with sensors and intelligent systems can assist seniors and people with disabilities in managing daily tasks and maintaining independence. Also, the IoT has enabled the creation of connected hospitals where medical devices, patient rooms, and even hospital beds are embedded with sensors and wireless connectivity.

One of the most exciting developments in ubiquitous computing for healthcare is the use of AI and machine learning algorithms. These technologies can analyze large amounts of data collected from various sources, such as wearables, medical records, and environmental sensors, to provide personalized treatment recommendations, predict patient outcomes, and streamline clinical workflows. For instance, AI-powered chatbots can help patients manage chronic conditions, while smart prosthetics equipped with sensors and AI algorithms can adapt to the user's needs and environment.

12.9.2 ANTICIPATED PRIVACY AND SECURITY CHALLENGES

While ubiquitous computing holds great promise for healthcare, it also raises significant privacy and security concerns. As more devices become interconnected, the attack surface expands, leaving sensitive patient data vulnerable to cyber threats. Hackers could potentially gain access to medical records, alter treatment plans, or even compromise medical devices, putting patients' lives at risk. Also, the increased reliance on cloud storage and transmission of health data heightens the risk of data breaches and unauthorized access.

Another concern is the potential misuse of PHI. Employers, insurance companies, and government agencies may seek access to this data, threatening individuals' privacy and autonomy. Furthermore, the use of AI and machine learning algorithms raises ethical questions about bias, discrimination, and accountability. There is a risk that these systems might perpetuate existing health disparities or make decisions that have unintended consequences.

12.9.3 RESEARCH AND INNOVATIONS FOR ENHANCED PRIVACY PROTECTION

To address these concerns, researchers and innovators are working on developing novel solutions and technologies that prioritize privacy and security in ubiquitous computing for healthcare. One such initiative is the development of blockchain technology specifically designed for healthcare applications. Blockchain can provide decentralized, secure, and transparent data management, allowing patients to control their own health data and share it only with authorized parties.

Another area of focus is the creation of privacy-preserving AI and machine learning techniques [41,42]. Techniques such as differential privacy, homomorphic encryption, and federated learning enable the analysis of health data without revealing individual identities or sensitive information. These methods can help maintain patient privacy while still deriving valuable insights from health data.

12.10 CONCLUSION AND DISCUSSIONS

This chapter has delved into the intricate world of IoT and ubiquitous computing, uncovering significant privacy and security risks that accompany these ever-connected technologies. With a particular focus on healthcare applications, we have explored the importance of safeguarding patient data and ensuring the integrity of medical information. The findings highlighted the need for user-friendly yet secure design principles in the realm of IoT, acknowledging that security remains a primary challenge in the heterogeneous environments of IoT deployment [43–45]. To preserve data confidentiality, integrity, and authenticity in IoT interactions, robust encryption algorithms and security measures are essential [46]. Further research is warranted to develop intuitive and seamlessly integrated solutions to address these security challenges effectively. By considering security measures from academic, technical, and industrial perspectives, IoT environments can offer safety assurances for users globally sharing and communicating information through IoT devices.

Throughout this study, it became evident that data security and protection must be meticulously integrated into the design of IoT devices. Implementing security by design, data minimization, and providing users with notice and choice for unexpected services are crucial aspects to enhance security in IoT devices. As healthcare organizations embrace IoT technology, they must prioritize privacy and security considerations from the onset, aligning their efforts with regulatory guidelines and industry best practices.

Yet, despite notable progress, there remain open questions and challenges that necessitate further exploration and harmonization. The complex interplay of technological, social, and policy considerations involving various stakeholders requires continued research efforts and collaboration. The continuous growth and undeniable impact of IoT in healthcare and other sectors underscore the urgency to develop effective processes for the secure and safe use of these technologies.

As we conclude, the potential of IoT is undeniable, offering exciting possibilities for healthcare innovation and improved patient outcomes. Nevertheless, a concerted and sustained focus on addressing privacy and security issues is essential to ensure that IoT remains a transformative force for good in the rapidly evolving landscape of healthcare technology. The commitment of governments, engineering, production, industry, and academia to ongoing research and proactive measures will pave the way for a future where IoT thrives securely and responsibly, benefiting society and individuals alike.

REFERENCES

1. Solove, D. J. (2008). Understanding privacy.
2. Ware, W. H. (1967, April). Security and privacy in computer systems. In Proceedings of the April 18–20, 1967, Spring Joint Computer Conference (pp. 279–282).
3. Sharma, R., Vashisth, R., & Sindhwani, N. (2023). Study and Analysis of Classification Techniques for Specific Plant Growths. In Advances in Signal Processing, Embedded Systems and IoT: Proceedings of Seventh ICMEET-2022 (pp. 591–605). Singapore: Springer Nature Singapore.
4. Gupta, B., Chaudhary, A., Sindhwani, N., & Rana, A. (2021, September). Smart shoe for detection of electrocution using Internet of Things (IoT). In 2021 9th International Conference on Reliability, Infocom Technologies and Optimization (Trends and Future Directions)(ICRITO) (pp. 1–3). IEEE.
5. Jain, N., Chaudhary, A., Sindhwani, N., & Rana, A. (2021, September). Applications of Wearable devices in IoT. In 2021 9th International Conference on Reliability, Infocom Technologies and Optimization (Trends and Future Directions)(ICRITO) (pp. 1–4). IEEE.
6. Sindhwani, N., Sasi, G., & Meivel, S. (2022, October). Fuzzy acceptance analysis of impact of glaucoma and diabetic retinopathy using confusion matrix. In 2022 10th International Conference on Reliability, Infocom Technologies and Optimization (Trends and Future Directions)(ICRITO) (pp. 1–5). IEEE.
7. Nijhawan, M., Sindhwani, N., Tanwar, S., & Kumar, S. (2022). Role of augmented reality and Internet of Things in education sector. In IoT Based Smart Applications (pp. 245–259). Cham: Springer International Publishing.
8. Gupta, A., Asad, A., Meena, L., & Anand, R. (2022, July). IoT and RFID-based Smart Card System Integrated with Health Care, Electricity, QR and Banking Sectors. In Artificial Intelligence on Medical Data: Proceedings of International Symposium, ISCMM 2021 (pp. 253–265). Singapore: Springer Nature Singapore.
9. Gupta, A., Srivastava, A., & Anand, R. (2019). Cost-effective smart home automation using Internet of Things. Journal of Communication Engineering & Systems, 9(2), 1–6.
10. Saini, P., & Anand, M. R. (2014). Identification of defects in plastic gears using image processing and computer vision: A review. International Journal of Engineering Research, 3(2), 94–99.
11. Anand, R., Jain, V., Singh, A., Rahal, D., Rastogi, P., Rajkumar, A., & Gupta, A. Clustering of Big Data in Cloud Environments for Smart Applications. In Integration of IoT with Cloud Computing for Smart Applications (pp. 227–247). Chapman and Hall/CRC Press.
12. Anand, R., Daniel, A. V., Fred, A. L., Jaiswal, T., Juneja, S., Juneja, A., & Gupta, A. Building Integrated Systems for Healthcare Considering Mobile Computing and IoT. In Integration of IoT with Cloud Computing for Smart Applications (pp. 203–225). Chapman and Hall/CRC Press.

13. Rose, K., Eldridge, S., & Chapin, L. (2015). The Internet of Things: An overview. The Internet Society (ISOC), 80, 1–50.
14. Alsinglawi, B., Elkhodr, M., Nguyen, Q. V., Gunawardana, U., Maeder, A., & Simoff, S. (2017). RFID localisation for Internet of Things smart homes: A survey. arXiv preprint arXiv:1702.02311.
15. Baker, S. B., Xiang, W., & Atkinson, I. (2017). Internet of Things for smart healthcare: Technologies, challenges, and opportunities. IEEE Access, 5, 26521–26544.
16. Sharma, M., & Ahuja, L. (2018). A data mining approach towards healthcare recommender system. In Smart and Innovative Trends in Next Generation Computing Technologies: Third International Conference, NGCT 2017, Dehradun, India, October 30–31, 2017, Revised Selected Papers, Part I 3 (pp. 199–210). Springer Singapore.
17. Lyytinen, K., & Yoo, Y. (2002). Ubiquitous computing. Communications of the ACM, 45(12), 63–96.
18. Li, Y. H., Dow, C. R., Lin, C. M., & Lin, P. J. (2012). A transparent and ubiquitous access framework for networking and embedded system laboratories. Computer Applications in Engineering Education, 20(2), 321–331.
19. Schmidt, A. (2003). Ubiquitous Computing-computing in Context. United Kingdom: Lancaster University.
20. Edemekong, P. F., Annamaraju, P., & Haydel, M. J. (2018). Health insurance portability and accountability act.
21. Cutillo, C. M., Sharma, K. R., Foschini, L., Kundu, S., Mackintosh, M., Mandl, K. D., & MI in Healthcare Workshop Working Group Beck Tyler 1 Collier Elaine 1 Colvis Christine 1 Gersing Kenneth 1 Gordon Valery 1 Jensen Roxanne 8 Shabestari Behrouz 9 Southall Noel 1. (2020). Machine intelligence in healthcare—perspectives on trustworthiness, explainability, usability, and transparency. NPJ Digital Medicine, 3(1), 47.
22. Mulligan, D. P., Petri, G., Spinale, N., Stockwell, G., & Vincent, H. J. (2021, September). Confidential computing—a brave new world. In 2021 international symposium on secure and private execution environment design (SEED) (pp. 132–138). IEEE.
23. Khan, S., & Hoque, A. (2016). Digital health data: a comprehensive review of privacy and security risks and some recommendations. Computer Science Journal of Moldova, 71(2), 273–292.
24. Yoon, C., & Kim, S. (2007). Convenience and TAM in a ubiquitous computing environment: The case of wireless LAN. Electronic Commerce Research and Applications, 6(1), 102–112.
25. Ghiasipour, M., Mosadeghrad, A. M., Arab, M., & Jaafaripooyan, E. (2017). Leadership challenges in health care organizations: The case of Iranian hospitals. Medical journal of the Islamic Republic of Iran, 31, 96.
26. Abouelmehdi, K., Beni-Hssane, A., Khaloufi, H., & Saadi, M. (2017). Big data security and privacy in healthcare: A Review. Procedia Computer Science, 113, 73–80.
27. Alshehri, S., Radziszowski, S. P., & Raj, R. K. (2012, April). Secure access for healthcare data in the cloud using ciphertext-policy attribute-based encryption. In 2012 IEEE 28th International Conference on Data Engineering Workshops (pp. 143–146). IEEE.
28. Boukerche, A., & Ren, Y. (2008). A trust-based security system for ubiquitous and pervasive computing environments. Computer Communications, 31(18), 4343–4351.
29. Sandhu, R. S. (1998). Role-based access control. In Advances in Computers (Vol. 46, pp. 237–286). Elsevier.

30. Wilson, Y., & Hingnikar, A. (2019). Solving Identity Management in Modern Applications: Demystifying OAuth 2.0, OpenID Connect, and SAML 2.0. Apress.
31. Lin, C. C., Lee, R. G., & Hsiao, C. C. (2008). A pervasive health monitoring service system based on ubiquitous network technology. International Journal of Medical Informatics, 77(7), 461–469.
32. Scarfone, K., & Mell, P. (2007). Guide to intrusion detection and prevention systems (IDPs). NIST Special Publication, 800(2007), 94.
33. Mohurle, S., & Patil, M. (2017). A brief study of wannacry threat: Ransomware attack 2017. International Journal of Advanced Research in Computer Science, 8(5), 1938–1940.
34. Sengupta, J., Storey, K., Casey, S., Trager, L., Buescher, M., Horning, M., ... & Hauser, R. G. (2020). Outcomes before and after the recall of a heart failure pacemaker. JAMA Internal Medicine, 180(2), 198–205.
35. Mhaskar, N., Alabbad, M., & Khedri, R. (2021). A formal approach to network segmentation. Computers & Security, 103, 102162.
36. Wagner, N., Şahin, C. Ş., Winterrose, M., Riordan, J., Pena, J., Hanson, D., & Streilein, W. W. (2016, December). Towards automated cyber decision support: A case study on network segmentation for security. In 2016 IEEE Symposium Series on Computational Intelligence (SSCI) (pp. 1–10). IEEE.
37. Scott, J. T., Rundall, T. G., Vogt, T. M., & Hsu, J. (2005). Kaiser Permanente's experience of implementing an electronic medical record: A qualitative study. BMJ, 331(7528), 1313–1316.
38. Chen, C., Garrido, T., Chock, D., Okawa, G., & Liang, L. (2009). The Kaiser Permanente Electronic Health Record: transforming and streamlining modalities of care. Health Affairs, 28(2), 323–333.
39. Botha, J., Grobler, M., & Eloff, M. (2017, June). Global Data Breaches Responsible for the Disclosure of Personal Information: 2015 & 2016. In European Conference on Cyber Warfare and Security (pp. 63–72). Academic Conferences International Limited.
40. Botha, J. G., Grobler, M. M., & Eloff, M. M. (2017). Global data breaches responsible for the disclosure of personal information.
41. Anand, R., Ahamad, S., Veeraiah, V., Janardan, S. K., Dhabliya, D., Sindhwani, N., & Gupta, A. (2023). Optimizing 6G Wireless Network Security for Effective Communication. In Innovative Smart Materials Used in Wireless Communication Technology (pp. 1–20). IGI Global.
42. Arora, S., Sharma, S., Anand, R., & Shrivastva, G. (2023). Miniaturized pentagon-shaped planar monopole antenna for ultra-wideband applications. Progress In Electromagnetics Research C, 133, 195–208.
43. Kohli, L., Saurabh, M., Bhatia, I., Sindhwani, N., & Vijh, M. (2021). Design and development of modular and multifunctional UAV with amphibious landing, processing and surround sense module. Unmanned Aerial Vehicles for Internet of Things (IoT) Concepts, Techniques, and Applications, 1, 207–230.
44. Anand, R., Sindhwani, N., & Dahiya, A. (2022, March). Design of a high directivity slotted fractal antenna for C-band, X-band and Ku-band applications. In 2022 9th International Conference on Computing for Sustainable Global Development (INDIACom) (pp. 727–730). IEEE.
45. Chauhan, S. K., Khanna, P., Sindhwani, N., Saxena, K., & Anand, R. (2023). Pareto Optimal Solution for Fully Fuzzy Bi-criteria Multi-index Bulk Transportation Problem. In Mobile Radio Communications and 5G Networks: Proceedings of Third MRCN 2022 (pp. 457–470). Singapore: Springer Nature Singapore.
46. Anand, R., Singh, B., & Sindhwani, N. (2009). Speech perception & analysis of fluent digits' strings using level-by-level time alignment. International Journal of Information Technology and Knowledge Management, 2(1), 65–68.

13 Empowering Harvest – Unlocking the Secrets to Optimal Health

Parth Seth and Monika Sharma

13.1 INTRODUCTION

The agricultural industry has been impacted in numerous ways by technological advances over the years. The UN predicts that there will be 9.7 billion people in 2050, an increase from the current 7.5 billion. Several countries around the world rely heavily on agriculture. Farmers will be forced to do more with less land since there will only be an additional 4% of land under cultivation by 2050. Likewise, to feed two billion more people, 60% more food will have to be produced. However, traditional methods cannot handle this demand, which forces farmers and agro-companies to look for more efficient methods [1]. In order to feed an additional two billion people by 2050, Agriculture's technological evolution is driven by artificial intelligence and other emerging technologies. In addition to improving efficiencies for farmers, AI-powered solutions will also reduce costs, ensure greater product quality, and ensure faster time-to-market [1]. Due to artificial intelligence, today's agriculture system is at a whole new level. With AI, crop production and monitoring, harvesting and processing, and marketing is becoming more efficient as well. There are various hi-tech computer-based systems designed to identify weeds, yields, crop quality, and different other parameters [2,3].

13.2 WORKING OF ARTIFICIAL INTELLIGENCE

By combining large sets of data with intelligent, iterative algorithms, artificial intelligence learns from patterns and features. By testing and measuring its own performance, AI systems develop more abilities over time [4,5]. Since AI doesn't require a break, it can handle hundreds, thousands, or even millions of tasks in record time, learning a great deal in a very short period of time.

To truly grasp how AI works, despite what many people think, it is a field of study, not just a computer application [4]. Computer systems with AI can solve complex problems by resembling human thought processes to solve complex problems [6–9]. To carry out this aim, AI systems use a variety of technologies and techniques, along with a multitude of different techniques and processes. An overview of robot functionality is shown in Figure 13.1 and brief principle of AI is indicated in Figure 13.2.

DOI: 10.1201/9781003330523-13

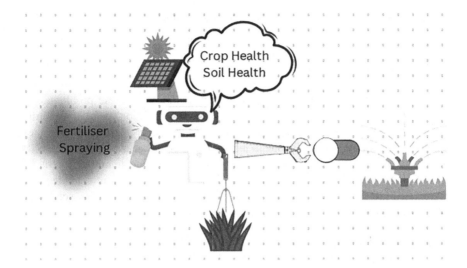

FIGURE 13.1 An overview of robot functionality.

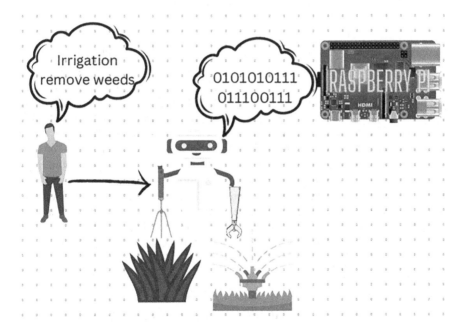

FIGURE 13.2 Putting human commands into machine language and making them actionable.

13.3 GREEN REVOLUTION

In the 1950s and 1960s, the Green Revolution increased global food production dramatically, saving a billion people from starvation. With the advent of the agricultural revolution, new technologies such as high-yielding varieties of cereals, chemical fertilizers, agro-chemicals, and improved irrigation became available. After following the lead of Europe, India adopted hybrid seeds, machinery, fertilizers, and pesticides. As a result of these practices, food shortages were resolved, but they caused several problems as well, such as excessive fertilizers and pesticides, groundwater depletion, and soil degradation. Due to a lack of training and awareness about the proper use of modern technology, these problems were exacerbated Global population is expected to grow by 2 billion by 2050, according to the UN Food and Agriculture Organization [5]. As there is a limited amount of arable land available and an exponential increase in the number of mouths to feed, a second Green Revolution is urgently needed. AI, machine learning, Internet of Things (IoT), and big data will enable an efficient, eco-friendly, and smarter green revolution [10–14]. Farmers face the following challenges from seeding to harvesting crops:

1. Infestations of crop diseases
2. Storage management Lakes
3. Control of pesticide
4. Management of weed
5. Lack of irrigation and drainage facilities.

With AI-based methods, each problem is approached separately, and instead of generalizing, customized solutions to a particular issue are provided.

Farming has been redefined by technology over the years, and technological advances have had a profound impact on agriculture. With a growing population expected to rise from 7.5 billion to 9.7 billion by 2050 [5], agriculture will maintain to be the mainstay occupation in many countries worldwide. However, by 2050 there will only be 4% more land available for cultivation. Therefore, farmers will need to produce more food with less land [15,16]. Hence, they will need to produce more food with less land. According to the same survey, food production must increase by 60% to feed an additional two billion people by 2050. Traditional methods, however, cannot meet this demand. These developments have enabled farmers and agro-companies to increase production and reduce waste. As agriculture's technological progress continues, artificial intelligence is becoming more prevalent. As the world's population grows to over nine billion, farmers will increasingly need AI-powered solutions to improve efficiencies, quality, quantity, and go-to-market speed.

13.4 AN OVERVIEW OF AGRICULTURAL LIFECYCLE

Agricultural lifecycle is shown in Figure 13.3. It is explained [17] as follows:

Getting the soil ready: When preparing soil for sowing seeds, farmers break up large soil clumps, remove debris, such as sticks, rocks, and roots, and add fertilizers and organic matter according to the type of crop.

The sowing of seeds: In this stage, two seeds must be spaced apart, and the depth at which seeds are planted must be considered. During this stage, climatic conditions such as temperature, humidity, and rainfall are important.

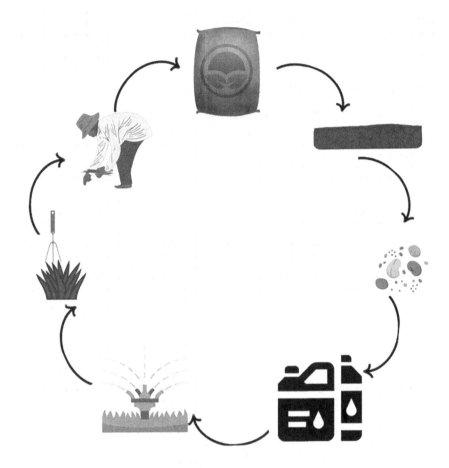

FIGURE 13.3 Agricultural lifecycle.

Feeding your garden with fertilizer: It is imperative for farmer to maintain soil fertility in order to grow nutritious and healthy crops. Plant nutrients like nitrogen, phosphorus, and potassium are contained in fertilizers, an essential element of a soil is added through fertilizer. A crop's quality is also determined during this stage.

Irrigation: Moisture and humidity are maintained in the soil during this stage. A crop can be damaged or stunted if it is overwatered or underwatered.

Protection against weeds: A weed is an unwanted plant that grows near crops or borders of farms. Weed protection is important since weeds reduce yields, increase production costs, interfere with harvest, and reduce crop quality.

Harvesting: In this stage, ripe crops are collected from the fields. The task involves many workers, making it a very labor-intensive activity. In addition, post-harvest handling takes place such as cleaning, sorting, packing, and cooling.

Storage: A phase in the post-harvest process that ensures food security when the products are not being used for agriculture. It also involves packing and transporting the products.

13.5   WHY ADOPT AI IN AGRICULTURE?

The agricultural industry perceives the use of AI to be a purely digital tool. They see no way it can be useful on the ground. Their resistance to AI is due to a lack of understanding of how it can be applied to their situation. In order to facilitate farmers' use of AI tools, technology providers still have a lot to do. As the world's population grows, urbanization continues to expand. Consumption habits are changing as disposable income rises. To meet the growing demand, farmers must increase productivity. More people will need to be fed in 30 years. Since there is a limited amount of fertile soil, we need to move beyond traditional farming methods. Agricultural risks need to be minimized or at least managed to artificial intelligence in agriculture on a global scale. AI could revolutionize agriculture, allowing farmers to achieve more results with less effort and bringing a number of other benefits [18,19]. AI, however, is not an independent technology. AI can complement already implemented technologies as the next step from traditional to innovative farming.

High value use cases

1. Precision Livestock counting (refer to Figure 13.4) – By combining industry-proven methodologies with edge computing technologies, you can eliminate error-prone manual livestock inventory.

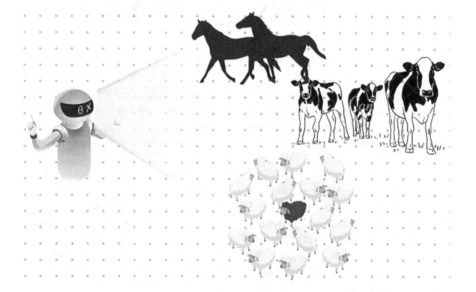

FIGURE 13.4   Livestock counting.

- Multiple locations can be monitored automatically for livestock counts and animal detection.
- Inspect the on- and off-loading of transports and the entries and exits of feedlots.
- Develop auditable data records for existing receiving processes by digitizing them.
- Other functions can be supported by re-allocating staff.
- Repeatable solutions can be easily operationalized at scale.

2. Quality assurance process for harvesting and processing – Implement vision-based best practices to ensure the quality and safety of produce.
- Maintain adherence to safety and process standards.
- Automated alerts for contaminants and risks.
- Traceability and remediation can be achieved by creating visual data records.

3. Ripeness detection for fruits and vegetables (refer to Figure 13.5) – Enhance genetics, growing, and quality control by automating the detection of fruit and vegetable maturation. Determine the level of the following vision-derived characteristics:
- It's size, shape, firmness, color, bruising, brix (fruit flavor, sweetness, etc.), and overall quality.
- Determine whether variations are due to seasonal, environmental, varietal, or management factors.
- Improve shelf life and quality by assisting genetic selection.

FIGURE 13.5 Ripeness detection.

4. Recognizing and managing crop risks – Achieve consistent, high-quality production with vision AI-based accuracy and increase knowledge and productivity.
   - Measure the volume of plants and inventory the population.
   - Analyze the health and productivity of crops.
   - Color, shape, and texture of plants should be captured.
   - The ability to detect and measure stress and disease in plants as early as possible.
   - Identification of invasive species, weeds, and pests.

13.5.1 BENEFITS

1. Decision-making is made easier with AI – There is no doubt that predictive analytics can be a significant change. Artificial intelligence enables farmers to collect and process a significant amount of data faster than they could otherwise. By using artificial intelligence, Farmers can forecast market prices, analyze market demand, and decide when to sow and harvest.
2. The use of AI reduces costs – Farmers can use artificial intelligence to identify irrigation, fertilization, and pesticide treatment needs in their fields in real time. Furthermore, vertical agriculture may help reduce resource consumption while increasing food production.
3. Labor shortages are addressed by AI – The agricultural industry faces labor shortages, which are not new. Automation can help farmers solve this problem. A few examples of how farmers may be able to get their work done without hiring more people are autonomous tractors, smart irrigation and fertilizing systems, smart spraying systems, vertical farming software, and robots based on artificial intelligence. Human farm workers cannot match the speed, accuracy, and hard work of AI-driven tools. Figure 13.6 demonstrate how AI helps in faster data collection, processing and execution.

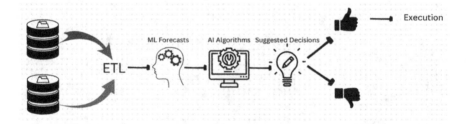

FIGURE 13.6   AI helps in collection, processing, and execution of data.

13.5.2 Challenges

1. Unawareness of evolving technologies – For emerging countries, employing AI and developing technologies in agriculture can be challenging. It will be challenging to sell these technologies in areas where no such agronomic technologies are currently being implemented [20].
2. Process of adopting technology is prolonged – The use of artificial intelligence is only one aspect of simpler technologies for collecting, processing, and monitoring field data that farmers need to understand. For AI to work, a proper technology infrastructure is required. Therefore, it can be challenging even for farms with some technology in place to move forward [21].
3. Exorbitant – Purchasing automated devices and maintaining them will cost farmers some money when they want to implement AI in fields [21].

13.6 POLICY AND REGULATORY ISSUES

The implementation of IoT in agriculture raises a number of policy and regulatory issues that need to be addressed to ensure that the technology is used effectively and responsibly. Here are some of the policy and regulatory issues related to the implementation of IoT in agriculture:

- Data ownership and access: IoT devices collect large amounts of data about agricultural production, including soil quality, crop growth, and weather patterns. It is important to establish clear policies and regulations around data ownership and access, to ensure that farmers retain control over their data and that it is not used for unintended purposes.
- Privacy concerns: IoT devices can collect personal information about farmers and their employees, such as their location and work hours. It is important to establish policies and regulations around data privacy, to ensure that this information is not misused or shared without consent.
- Potential impacts on small-scale farmers: The high cost of IoT devices and the need for reliable Internet connectivity can make it difficult for small-scale farmers to access and use these technologies. It is important to establish policies and regulations that support the adoption of IoT technologies by small-scale farmers, to ensure that they are not left behind in the digital revolution.
- Interoperability and standardization: IoT devices from different manufacturers may not be compatible with each other, which can create interoperability issues. It is important to establish standards and regulations that promote interoperability and compatibility, to ensure that farmers can use different IoT devices together seamlessly.
- Cybersecurity: IoT devices are vulnerable to cyber-attacks, which can compromise the security of agricultural production systems. It is important to establish policies and regulations that promote cybersecurity, to ensure that IoT devices are used safely and responsibly.

In conclusion, policy and regulatory issues related to the implementation of IoT in agriculture are complex and multifaceted. It is important to establish clear policies and regulations that support the responsible use of IoT technologies, while also addressing issues such as data ownership and access, privacy concerns, and potential impacts on small-scale farmers. By doing so, we can ensure that IoT technologies are used effectively and responsibly in the agriculture sector, to promote sustainable and efficient agricultural production.

13.7 PROPOSED FRAMEWORK

A solar powered, fully autonomous device that uses solar power all day. This robot can save considerable amounts of resources. Cameras can be used to target weeds, and an additional arm can be used to weed, hoe, and harvest. Fruit and vegetable ripeness can be detected by silicon photodiodes, soil moisture can be detected by volumetric moisture sensors. A device like this can be loaded with farm-related data like the size of the field, the type of soil, the type of crop, and irrigation facilities to make its use more convenient. It can be used for a season without any hassles. In the market, there are many devices, but either they are very costly or they can't do multiple tasks at once. Due to the fact that this device is made in India, it can be cost-effective, and if it gets covered by the NITI Aayog Scheme, it will be subsidized, and the main purpose of discussing it is to support farmers and cause India to reach new heights.

13.7.1 BENEFITS

1. AI and ML-based surveillance can be effective in deterring trespassers, securing distant facilities, and augmenting crops.
2. With AI robots and automated machines, land can be fully utilized with effective use of resources.
3. AI can use the pesticides and fertilizers when required, it can detect the infected plants and weeds.

13.7.2 CHALLENGES

1. Setting up the cameras and real-time monitoring system requires basic network structure to operate.
2. AI devices and automated machines are quite expensive for the small-scale farmers to opt it for their agricultural land.
3. It requires many algorithms to detect infected areas and plants, to check the ripeness of fruits and weeds.

Sensors for collecting data include temperature sensors, humidity sensors, optical sensors, ground moisture sensors, soil pH sensors, and camera modules. LCD monitors and mobile applications are used to monitor field characteristics. The solenoid valve in Figure 13.7 controls the sprayed chemicals in the plants.

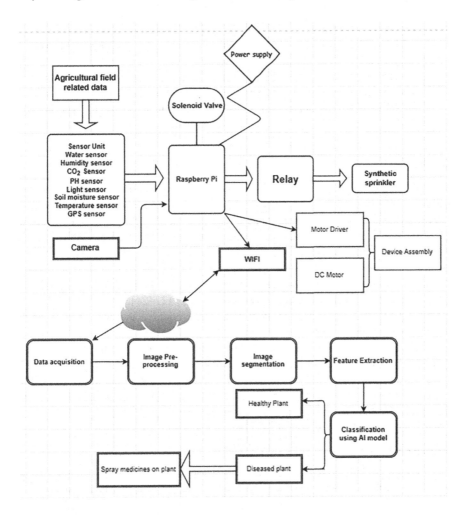

FIGURE 13.7   Process of cultivating a green and healthy life.

Using an app, farmers are able to spray pesticides or fertilizers to convert ON/OFF into water using the image taken from the camera, and this image is detected and displayed by image infection pick-up when the appropriate steps are taken after disease identification. The relay driver controls the ON/OFF of external devices. Four types of sensors are used to measure soil condition, water level, and pesticide tanks. The sensors consist of a humidity sensor, a water sensor, and a humidity sensor. Raspberry Pi is the interface for all of these sensors. DC motors and motor drivers are used to move the entire system. Different locations are monitored by the movable system.

1. By using Wi-Fi, agricultural field data will be input into the device and stored on the cloud. Raspberry Pi will be at the heart of the device. Powered by solar energy or electricity, the device will work.

2. This device uses a relay to distribute power to various components. In the field, the DC motor and motor driver will operate the device and sprinkle fertilizers.

3. The main feature of this device is that it can detect whether a plant is healthy or diseased by capturing an image of it. A camera is used to implement it. If it detects an unhealthy plant, it automatically sprinkles medicine on it.

13.8 CONCLUSION

In conclusion, farm automation devices are transforming the agriculture industry by simplifying the work of farmers. These devices are designed to perform tasks that were once time-consuming and labor-intensive, such as planting, watering, and harvesting crops. With the help of automation, farmers can now save time, reduce their workload, and improve the efficiency of their farms.

Furthermore, automation devices offer a range of benefits, including improved crop yields, reduced costs, and increased profitability [22–24]. They can also help to minimize the use of resources like water and energy, making farming more sustainable and environmentally friendly.

Overall, the use of farm automation devices is a game-changer for the agriculture industry, and it is exciting to see how technology is revolutionizing the way we produce food. As these devices continue to advance and become more accessible, we can expect to see the adoption of automation in the operations [25–30], leading to a more productive and sustainable future for farming.

REFERENCES

1. Singh, R., & Singh, G. S. (2017). Traditional agriculture: A climate-smart approach for sustainable food production. Energy, Ecology and Environment, 2, 296–316.

2. Peteinatos, G. G., Weis, M., Andújar, D., Rueda Ayala, V., & Gerhards, R. (2014). Potential use of ground-based sensor technologies for weed detection. Pest Management Science, 70(2), 190–199.

3. Lee, W. S., Alchanatis, V., Yang, C., Hirafuji, M., Moshou, D., & Li, C. (2010). Sensing technologies for precision specialty crop production. Computers and Electronics in Agriculture, 74(1), 2–33.

4. Jarrahi, M. H. (2018). Artificial intelligence and the future of work: Human-AI symbiosis in organizational decision making. Business Horizons, 61(4), 577–586.

5. Oktradiksa, A., Bhakti, C. P., Kurniawan, S. J., & Rahman, F. A. (2021). Utilization Artificial Intelligence to Improve Creativity Skills in Society 5.0. Journal of Physics: Conference Series, 1760(1), 012032.

6. Meivel, S., Sindhwani, N., Valarmathi, S., Dhivya, G., Atchaya, M., Anand, R., & Maurya, S. (2022). Design and Method of 16.24 GHz Microstrip Network Antenna Using Underwater Wireless Communication Algorithm. In Cyber Technologies and Emerging Sciences: ICCTES 2021 (pp. 363–371). Singapore: Springer Nature Singapore.

7. Anand, R., Jain, V., Singh, A., Rahal, D., Rastogi, P., Rajkumar, A., & Gupta, A. Clustering of Big Data in Cloud Environments for Smart Applications. In Integration of IoT with Cloud Computing for Smart Applications (pp. 227–247). Chapman and Hall/CRC Press.

8. Anand, R., Daniel, A. V., Fred, A. L., Jaiswal, T., Juneja, S., Juneja, A., & Gupta, A. Building Integrated Systems for Healthcare Considering Mobile Computing and IoT. In Integration of IoT with Cloud Computing for Smart Applications (pp. 203–225). Chapman and Hall/CRC Press.

9. Gupta, B., Chaudhary, A., Sindhwani, N., & Rana, A. (2021, September). Smart shoe for detection of electrocution using Internet of Things (IoT). In 2021 9th International Conference on Reliability, Infocom Technologies and Optimization (Trends and Future Directions)(ICRITO) (pp. 1–3). IEEE.

10. Anand, R., Arora, S., & Sindhwani, N. (2022, January). A miniaturized UWB antenna for high speed applications. In 2022 International Conference on Computing, Communication and Power Technology (IC3P) (pp. 264–267). IEEE.

11. Sharma, R., Vashisth, R., & Sindhwani, N. (2023). Study and Analysis of Classification Techniques for Specific Plant Growths. In Advances in Signal Processing, Embedded Systems and IoT: Proceedings of Seventh ICMEET-2022 (pp. 591–605). Singapore: Springer Nature Singapore.

12. Arora, S., Sharma, S., Anand, R., & Shrivastva, G. (2023). Miniaturized pentagon-shaped planar monopole antenna for ultra-wideband applications. Progress In Electromagnetics Research C, 133, 195–208.

13. Anand, R., Sindhwani, N., & Dahiya, A. (2022, March). Design of a high directivity slotted fractal antenna for C-band, X-band and Ku-band applications. In 2022 9th International Conference on Computing for Sustainable Global Development (INDIACom) (pp. 727–730). IEEE.

14. Chawla, P., & Anand, R. (2017). Micro-switch design and its optimization using pattern search algorithm for applications in reconfigurable antenna. Modern Antenna Systems, 10, 189–210.

15. Hobbs, P. R. (2007). Conservation agriculture: What is it and why is it important for future sustainable food production?. The Journal of Agricultural Science, 145(2), 127.

16. Hazell, P. B. (2005). Is there a future for small farms?. Agricultural Economics, 32, 93–101.

17. Audsley, E., Alber, S., Clift, R., Cowell, S., Crettaz, P., Gaillard, G., … & van Zeijts, H. (1997). Harmonisation of environmental life cycle assessment for agriculture. Final Report, Concerted Action AIR3-CT94-2028. European Commission, DG VI Agriculture, 139(1).

18. Dharmaraj, V., & Vijayanand, C. (2018). Artificial intelligence (AI) in agriculture. International Journal of Current Microbiology and Applied Sciences, 7(12), 2122–2128.

19. Smith, M. J. (2018). Getting value from artificial intelligence in agriculture. Animal Production Science, 60(1), 46–54.

20. Zhang, Q. (2023). Opinion: AI in agriculture, researchable issues. Computers and Electronics in Agriculture, 212, 108110.

21. Zha, J. (2020, December). Artificial intelligence in agriculture. Journal of Physics: Conference Series, 1693(1), 012058.

22. Sindhwani, N., Maurya, V. P., Patel, A., Yadav, R. K., Krishna, S., & Anand, R. (2022). Implementation of intelligent plantation system using virtual IoT. Internet of Things and its Applications, 2022, 305–322.

23. Anand, R., & Chawla, P. (2016, March). A review on the optimization techniques for bio-inspired antenna design. In 2016 3rd International Conference on Computing for Sustainable Global Development (INDIACom) (pp. 2228–2233). IEEE.

24. Meelu, R., & Anand, R. (2010, November). Energy Efficiency of Cluster-based Routing Protocols Used in Wireless Sensor Networks. In AIP conference Proceedings (Vol. 1324, No. 1, pp. 109–113). American Institute of Physics.

25. Anand, R., Singh, J., Pandey, D., Pandey, B. K., Nassa, V. K., & Pramanik, S. (2022). Modern technique for interactive communication in LEACH-based ad hoc wireless sensor network. In Software Defined Networking for Ad Hoc Networks (pp. 55–73). Cham: Springer International Publishing.

26. Gupta, A., Srivastava, A., & Anand, R. (2019). Cost-effective smart home automation using Internet of Things. Journal of Communication Engineering & Systems, 9(2), 1–6.

27. Gupta, A., Asad, A., Meena, L., & Anand, R. (2022, July). IoT and RFID-based Smart Card System Integrated with Health Care, Electricity, QR and Banking Sectors. In Artificial Intelligence on Medical Data: Proceedings of International Symposium, ISCMM 2021 (pp. 253–265). Singapore: Springer Nature Singapore.

28. Jain, N., Chaudhary, A., Sindhwani, N., & Rana, A. (2021, September). Applications of wearable devices in IoT. In 2021 9th International Conference on Reliability, Infocom Technologies and Optimization (Trends and Future Directions)(ICRITO) (pp. 1–4). IEEE.

29. Saini, P., & Anand, M. R. (2014). Identification of defects in plastic gears using image processing and computer vision: A review. International Journal of Engineering Research, 3(2), 94–99.

30. Anand, R., Singh, B., & Sindhwani, N. (2009). Speech perception & analysis of fluent digits' strings using level-by-level time alignment. International Journal of Information Technology and Knowledge Management, 2(1), 65–68.

14 Violence-Based Object Detection in Streets for Effective Monitoring of Safe Environments

Navneet Vishnoi, Thirukumaran Subbiramani, Mohit Kumar Sharma, Sukhvinder Singh Dari, Vikas Sagar, and Nitendra Kumar

14.1 INTRODUCTION

In today's society, ensuring the security and safety of public spaces is of utmost importance. This study article focuses on the essential issue of weapon and violence-based object identification in street circumstances in order to efficiently monitor and create secure surroundings. The goal is to create an accurate and dependable system that can quickly recognize weapons and aggressive behavior in order to support better security measures, proactive reactions, and risk reduction. This is accomplished by integrating deep learning techniques, utilizing the MobileNetV2 architecture's capabilities for feature extraction, and a modified Long Short-Term Memory (LSTM) network for sequence modeling [1–4]. This study's data collection, which was compiled to allow for thorough analysis, consists of actual incidents of violence. The dataset comprises video frames that were taken out of videos using a particular processing technique. These frames were used to train and assess the model that was created for this purpose. The dataset was divided into two classes, "Violence" and "Non-Violence," which each contained a wide collection of video clips with different street situations. The dataset comprises these frames, and one-hot encoding was used to encode the labels numerically to enable effective training and classification. Importing crucial libraries like OpenCV, TensorFlow, and Keras prepared the framework for data processing, model construction, and training [3]. The cornerstone for feature extraction was the MobileNetV2 architecture, which was pre-trained on the ImageNet dataset. To be more precise, the model's final 40 layers were made trainable, while the remaining layers were frozen to preserve the learnt weights. Using this method, the model was able to extract significant traits that are essential for accurately identifying weapons and violent crime. The model architecture was created to take into consideration temporal relationships because it was recognized that the input data were sequential. The frames were transmitted using the MobileNetV2 backbone, followed by dropout layers to avoid over-fitting. To capture temporal dependencies moving both forward and backward, a bidirectional LSTM layer was then used [5–9]. By adding more dense layers with dropout regularization, the gathered features were further honed. A softmax activation function was used to forecast the probability distribution across the classes in the final layer. The dataset was divided into training and testing sets, with 90% of the data going to training and 10% to testing. This division made sure that the model's performance was thoroughly assessed. The testing set was used to evaluate the effectiveness of the created system, while the training set was utilized to generate the model. With a validation accuracy of 91.53% and a training accuracy of 95.65%, the findings obtained demonstrated accurate and promising accuracy. These findings demonstrate the model's capacity to detect weapons and hostile behavior in urban environments. The results of this study have important ramifications, especially in the context of real-time surveillance systems meant to protect the public. By automatically identifying and detecting potential dangers, the implementation of such a system can enable proactive actions, reduce risks, and improve security measures. The field of computer vision applications for public safety, which is still growing, is aided by this study. It highlights how effective deep learning techniques may be in resolving pressing societal problems. Future studies will concentrate on evaluating the model's performance on bigger and more varied datasets. The incorporation of continuous video streams for monitoring will be investigated, and the model will be improved to work with low-powered devices. To make sure the model is effective in scenarios that occur in real life, it is essential to examine the model's scalability and adaptability in varied street environments. This research proposes a thorough method for detecting violent and weapon-based objects in urban settings. The constructed model exhibits its capability to precisely identify weapons and violent behavior by merging deep learning methods, the MobileNetV2 architecture, and a modified LSTM network. The results show how such a system may affect real-time monitoring for public safety, opening up possibilities for preventative actions and stepped-up security efforts.

14.1.1 Why Safe Environments Are Important

In the world of today, ensuring safe environments is crucial. Due to the prevalence of violence and the rising risks posed by firearms, efficient monitoring systems that can quickly identify and address possible threats are required. The critical duty of spotting weapons and other objects associated with violence on the street is the topic of this research piece. The study hopes to contribute to the creation of secure environments and enable effective monitoring to protect the public's well-being by addressing this urgent issue. The innate desire of people to live and prosper in a society that fosters security and peace gives birth to the demand for safe environments. Streets, parks, and recreational areas should all be free from intimidation and violence. Unfortunately, occurrences involving firearms and aggressive behavior can compromise the tranquility and safety of these areas, increasing dread among residents and impairing their movement and quality of life. To reduce such hazards and foster a sense of security in public settings, it is crucial to design efficient tactics and procedures. Through the use of deep learning methods, notably the MobileNetV2 architecture for feature extraction and a modified LSTM network for sequence modeling, the article addresses the problem of assuring safe settings. In computer vision, deep learning has emerged as a promising methodology that enables more precise and effective object detection tasks [7–9]. The research intends to improve the identification and recognition of weapons and violent behavior in street scenarios using this cutting-edge methodology, enabling proactive responses and prompt intervention to avoid potential injury. The collecting and processing of an extensive dataset with actual incidences of violence is a crucial component of our study. By gathering such information, the generated model may be evaluated realistically, ensuring its usefulness in real-world situations. The basis for training and assessing the model are frames from recordings that document violent incidents. The dataset is prepared for numerical representation by meticulously annotating these frames and utilizing one-hot encoding to encode the labels. This facilitates the training procedure and subsequent assessment of the model's performance. The research suggests a well-designed model architecture to solve the unique difficulties of object recognition in street contexts. The transmission of the frames is supported by the MobileNetV2 backbone, allowing the extraction of pertinent characteristics necessary for recognizing weapons and violent behavior. In order to prevent overfitting and ensure the model's generalizability, dropout layers are inserted judiciously.

Additionally, by including a bidirectional LSTM layer, it is possible to capture temporal dependencies in both forward and backward directions, taking into account the sequential nature of the input data. The acquired features are strengthened by this thorough architecture, which also includes additional dense layers and dropout, allowing the model to produce precise predictions. This study includes training and evaluation heavily. 90% of the dataset is used for training, allowing for a thorough assessment of the model's performance. The dataset is split into training and testing sets. The research provides empirical evidence of the model's efficacy in identifying weapons and aggressive behavior by training the model on the gathered dataset and evaluating its accuracy using the testing set. The model's capacity to accurately identify possible threats in urban environments is demonstrated by the validation accuracy of 91.53% and training accuracy of 95.65% attained. The constructed model has real-world applications in real-time surveillance systems, hence the ramifications of this research go beyond academic interest. Authorities can proactively respond to possible threats by incorporating the model into surveillance frameworks, greatly lowering risks and boosting security efforts. The protection of public areas and the well-being of residents are made easier by the automatic recognition and flagging of weapons and hostile behavior. The potential impact of such a system is significant since it provides security professionals and law enforcement with a powerful instrument to uphold safe surroundings and effectively prevent crime. The work tackles a significant societal issue by focusing on the crucial task of weapon and violence-based item recognition in street situations. The use of deep learning techniques highlights their significance in tackling public safety issues and displays their capacity to handle complicated situations. This study also paves the way for further investigation, including testing the model's effectiveness on bigger and more varied datasets, adding real-time video streams for continuous monitoring, and optimizing the model for use on devices with limited resources. The importance of safe environments cannot be emphasized, to sum up. By utilizing deep learning methods and model architecture design, the paper's research on weapon and violence-based object recognition in street circumstances aids in the creation of secure environments. The actual findings confirm the efficacy of the suggested methodology and show how well the model predicts future dangers. Real-time surveillance frameworks that incorporate such a system have far-reaching effects on public safety by enabling preemptive responses, lowering risks, and promoting safer urban environments. The study highlights the potential of deep learning techniques to address significant societal concerns and improves the field of computer vision applications for public safety.

14.1.2 STREET ENVIRONMENT OBJECT DETECTION

A crucial component of the research paper under discussion is object detection in urban settings. It focuses on creating a dependable and accurate system that can quickly recognize weapons and hostile behavior in public settings. Due to considerations including varying lighting, occlusions, and complicated backgrounds, detecting objects and their attributes in real-world urban situations presents special challenges. But overcoming these obstacles is essential for efficient monitoring and the creation of secure settings. Street environments are known for their dynamic nature, with many people and objects moving at once. For the sake of safeguarding public safety, it is crucial to be able to precisely detect and identify certain things, such as weapons and violent behavior. The purpose of the paper is to address the challenges of object detection in street situations using deep learning techniques. Deep learning has proven to be an effective method for computer vision, allowing for the accurate and automatic recognition of objects as well as the automatic extraction of pertinent characteristics. The study makes use of the pre-trained MobileNetV2 architecture for feature extraction, which was developed using the popular ImageNet dataset [8,9]. With the help of this architecture, which provides a solid base for gathering significant details from street situations, the model can learn to discern between the many characteristics of weapons and violent behavior. The model gains knowledge from a vast dataset by using pre-trained layers and freezing their weights, while maintaining the adaptability to the particular job at hand. The temporal component of object detection presents one of the particular difficulties in urban settings. Street scenes require the model to take into account the sequential character of the input data since they feature the movement of things and people through time. The paper uses a modified LSTM network for sequence modeling to overcome this. The model incorporates temporal dependencies in both the forward and backward directions by using a bidirectional LSTM layer, which enables a thorough understanding of object behavior and dynamics in street scenarios. To increase the model's robustness and generalization abilities, the model architecture also incorporates extra layers such dropout layers and thick layers. By haphazardly removing units during training, dropout layers lessen the effects of overfitting by preventing the model from depending excessively on particular characteristics. Dense layers further sharpen the gathered information, allowing the model to predict the presence of weapons and violent behavior with accuracy. The technique for the article entails gathering and creating a dataset that is primarily targeted at violent incidents that occur in urban settings. This dataset offers examples from real-world situations and enables thorough model training and evaluation.

The dataset enables the model to learn and recognize the geographical and temporal properties of weapons and violent behavior by annotating frames taken from videos. The classes are numerically represented using one-hot encoding, which simplifies the training process and performance evaluation of the model. The study report illustrates the efficacy of the suggested model in item recognition in street situations through training and evaluation. The testing set is used to evaluate the model's performance once it has been developed using the training set. The model's capacity to correctly recognize weapons and violent behavior in urban environments is highlighted by the validation accuracy of 91.53% and training accuracy of 95.65% that were attained. These findings confirm the model's accuracy and dependability, pointing to its potential for use in actual monitoring systems designed to keep the public safe. The effects of object detection in urban settings go beyond the scope of this study. Such a system can enable proactive reactions, lower risks, and boost the efficiency of security activities by successfully recognizing and flagging potential threats. The suggested model can be integrated into real-time surveillance systems to enable continuous monitoring and prompt responses to stop violent situations. This application helps achieve the larger objective of making safe settings, promoting public safety, and raising urban residents' quality of life. Hence, the research paper's key finding is the importance of object detection in urban settings. The paper uses deep learning methods and a properly constructed model architecture to discuss the difficulties in spotting weapons and hostile behavior in fast-paced metropolitan environments. The obtained findings confirm the model's accuracy and dependability and show its potential for use in actual monitoring systems. The study makes a contribution to the field of computer vision applications for public safety by stressing the value of object detection in maintaining secure environments and the promise of deep learning methods for tackling challenging social issues.

14.1.3 MODEL ARCHITECTURE DESIGN

A key component of the research article under discussion is the model architecture design, which establishes the groundwork for the successful detection of weapons and hostile behavior in urban settings. To handle the particular difficulties of the work at hand, the chosen architecture combines deep learning methods with customized modifications. The model's framework, the MobileNetV2 architecture, is used for feature extraction. The ImageNet dataset, which offers a wide variety of visual representations of objects, served as the pre-training data for this architecture. The model is able to extract pertinent features from street scenes, capturing differentiating traits of weapons and violent behavior by utilizing this pre-training. The model is able to maintain the information obtained from a sizable dataset while adjusting to the particular detection job by freezing the weights of the pre-trained layers and making the final 40 layers trainable. Since people and items display temporal behavior in street contexts, the sequential nature of the incoming data is an important factor to take into account. A modified LSTM network for sequence modeling is incorporated into the model design to account for this. A thorough understanding of object behavior across time is made possible by the bidirectional LSTM layer's ability to capture temporal dependencies in both the forward and backward directions. The model's capacity to identify patterns and dynamics linked to the use of weapons and violent behavior is improved by this sequential analysis, increasing prediction precision. The model architecture consists of additional elements that improve the performance and resilience of the model in addition to the LSTM layer and MobileNetV2 backbone. To reduce overfitting, a typical problem in deep learning models, dropout layers are added. Dropout layers help the model generalize to new data by randomly dropping out units during training, preventing the model from relying too heavily on particular attributes. The model's ability to manage changes and complexities in street situations is enhanced by this regularization technique, which increases the model's dependability and accuracy. After the LSTM layer, the model architecture includes thick layers to further hone the gathered characteristics. The existence of weapons and violent behavior may be accurately predicted by the model because to these deep layers that permit higher-level feature abstraction. The model's ability to learn complicated representations and retrieve pertinent information from the input data is enhanced by the combination of dropout layers and dense layers. A probability distribution across the classes is produced using a softmax activation function in the model architecture's top layer. As a result, the model can make predictions about the probability that an input image contains weapons or displays aggressive behavior. It is possible to make sure that the probabilities add up to one thanks to the softmax activation function [10–13].

The model architecture is meticulously trained and assessed using a specific dataset throughout the study paper. This dataset is built on still images taken from videos showing violent crimes occurring in public places. The machine learns to connect particular visual patterns with weapons and aggressive behavior by training on this dataset. Using an optimizer like Adam, the model's parameters are optimized during the training process, and the learning rate is changed to improve convergence. A second testing set is used to examine the model's performance, ensuring a fair assessment of its accuracy and generalization skills. With training accuracy of 95.65% and validation accuracy of 91.53%, the study paper presents excellent findings. These measures demonstrate the model's effectiveness and potential for real-world application by showing how well it can recognize weapons and violent behavior in urban settings. The study paper's model architectural design incorporates the advantages of the MobileNetV2 architecture, the LSTM network, the dropout layers, the dense layers, and the softmax activation function. Together, these elements identify pertinent characteristics, record temporal dependencies, reduce overfitting, and produce precise predictions about the existence of weapons and violent behavior. The model's dependability, accuracy, and viability for real-world implementation in surveillance systems aimed at promoting public safety in urban contexts are all influenced by the thorough design and training of the architecture.

14.1.4 SCALABILITY AND ADAPTABILITY

In the research article, scalability and adaptability are crucial factors since they address the model's capacity to function well in varied street situations and take into account various system requirements and limits [14–19]. The research acknowledges the significance of examining the model's ability to scale and adapt to various situations, assuring its effectiveness and applicability in real-world circumstances. The ability of a model to accommodate larger and more varied datasets is referred to as scalability. The research paper provides encouraging findings based on the existing dataset of actual violent incidents, but it also recognizes the need for more research to assess the model's efficacy on larger datasets. It is essential to test the model on a wide range of datasets because street surroundings might differ greatly in terms of illumination, camera angles, and object appearances. Researchers can learn more about the model's generalizability and effectiveness in detecting weapons and violent behavior in a variety of real-world circumstances by analyzing its scalability. While adaptability focuses on the model's capacity to adapt to various street environments and system requirements. In order to deploy the model on devices with constrained resources, the research article emphasizes the necessity for model improvement. Models must frequently be deployed in real-time surveillance systems on devices with limited resources, including embedded systems or edge sensors [17–19]. The model's usability and wide applicability are ensured by optimizing it for use on such devices. In order to maximize speed while using the fewest resources possible, this adaptation process may involve optimizing the model's design, lowering computational complexity, and utilizing hardware acceleration techniques. Adaptability goes beyond hardware issues. distinct locales, cities, and nations can have very distinct street environments. To remain effective, the model must be able to adjust to these changes. The report emphasizes the significance of assessing the model's adaptability to various street environments. This includes elements like regional variances in violence or hostility, cultural differences, and architectural features. Researchers may make sure that the model is effective over a wide range of real-world circumstances by assessing and fine-tuning its performance in various street contexts. Future investigations, as suggested by the research report, should incorporate real-time video streams for continuous monitoring to evaluate scalability and flexibility. As the model must process and analyze frames in real-time to successfully recognize weapons and hostile behavior, real-time video streams offer a more dynamic and difficult input for the model. Researchers can examine the model's scalability and adaptability to handle streaming data and provide real-time insights for preemptive responses by evaluating the model's performance on real-time video streams. The computational and memory needs of the model are also taken into account when examining how well it can scale and adapt. Although the research report uses the model's current implementation to show how good it is, it is crucial to assess how well it works when used widely. This involves evaluating the model's compute needs, memory usage, and inference time. Researchers can assess the model's viability in large-scale surveillance systems and its potential for deployment in actual contexts by conducting scalability tests. In conclusion, the study paper's scalability and flexibility are essential components. While adaptability refers to the model's flexibility to perform well in various street scenarios and satisfy system requirements, scalability concentrates on the model's capacity to handle larger and more diversified datasets. Researchers can guarantee the model's generalizability and efficacy across multiple real-world circumstances by assessing the model's scalability. Assuring the model's adaptability also guarantees that it will continue to be useful and effective in a variety of hardware environments, street scenarios, and cultural settings. The model's scalability and adaptability will be furthered by future studies involving real-time video streams, resource-constrained devices, and scalability tests, improving its potential for use in monitoring and upkeep of safe street environments.

14.1.5 DATASET COLLECTION AND ANNOTATION

The study report emphasizes the importance of dataset collection and annotation since they serve as the basis for training and assessment of the suggested model for weapon and violence-based item recognition in urban contexts. In order to undertake a thorough analysis and create an accurate and dependable system, the research emphasizes the significance of compiling an extensive dataset of real-world incidences of violence. Selecting and recording video files with various street sceneries that depict actual situations is part of the dataset gathering process. The dataset's main source of frames comes from these video files. The procedure of frame extraction utilizing a processing approach is described in the paper once the video files have been received. Individual images known as frames are taken from the video files and used as training data for the model. A wide variety of frames reflecting various street situations, lighting conditions, and object appearances are collected thanks to the frame extraction technique. This variety of frames is crucial for training the model to reliably recognize weapons and violent behavior in a range of real-world scenarios. In addition to gathering the dataset, labeling and categorizing the frames with annotation is a crucial step.

The dataset is divided into two categories: violence and non-violence. Annotation entails giving the frames the proper labels to indicate whether or not they contain violent incidents. In order for the model to learn and categorize frames according to their corresponding categories, the study describes the usage of one-hot encoding to numerically represent the labels. Manual work is required for the annotation process, where human annotators examine the frames and assign labels as necessary. In addition to ensuring that the dataset appropriately depicts violent incidents, this method also supplies the model with the essential ground truth for training and evaluation. Annotating a dataset takes a lot of time and requires precision and consistency. To appropriately record the presence of weapons or hostile behavior, annotators must carefully study each frame. The paper recognizes the significance of obtaining high-quality annotations in order to develop an accurate and dependable system. An unbalanced or unproductive model can result from inaccurate or inconsistent annotations. In order to ensure accuracy and uniformity across the dataset, the article emphasizes the importance of rigorous annotation and the usage of established annotation criteria. The research report also details how the dataset was split into training and testing sets. This division guarantees a fair assessment of the model's effectiveness. According to the research, 90% of the dataset is used for the training set and 10% is used for testing. This division enables thorough model training on the majority of the data while keeping a separate fraction aside for assessing the model's efficacy.

Researchers may gauge the model's ability to generalize and estimate its efficacy in spotting weapons and violent behavior in urban contexts by testing it on the testing set. The gathered and annotated dataset is the basis for developing and testing the suggested model. It gives the model the input it needs to discover and identify patterns linked to violence and non-violence. The research report recognizes the value of a high-quality dataset and the influence it has on the accuracy and dependability of the built system. The study creates a solid foundation for training a model that can properly identify weapons and aggressive behavior in urban contexts by making sure the dataset appropriately depicts real-world events and labels occurrences of violence. Gathering data and annotating it are essential components of the research article. The foundation for creating an accurate and dependable model is laid by the process of gathering a broad dataset of real-world violent incidents and street scene frames. The dataset is appropriately labeled by annotation, which divides frames into classifications for violence and non-violence. The dataset's separation into training and testing sets enables thorough model training and objective model evaluation. To train a model that can accurately and generally detect weapons and hostile behavior in urban contexts, a high-quality dataset is necessary. In order to guarantee dataset quality, the study recognizes the value of rigorous annotation and uniform labeling rules. The procedures for gathering data and annotating it represent the core of the research, allowing for the creation and assessment of an efficient system for object detection in urban settings.

14.2 LITERATURE REVIEW

Researchers and policymakers alike have paid close attention to the problem of school violence. Numerous studies have looked at the efficiency of various tactics and regulations meant to stop and deal with school violence [20]. Implementing security measures, such as the installation of security cameras in public schools, is one such strategy [21]. Increased surveillance, according to proponents, can deter potential offenders and improve overall security on school grounds. Critics draw attention to worries about privacy invasion and the scant data demonstrating the effectiveness of surveillance systems in reducing school violence [22]. The role of law enforcement in schools is another topic that receives attention in the literature. Some studies investigate the results of having police officers stationed on school grounds, looking at how they affect crime rates in schools and how they deal with criminal behavior [23]. These results support conversations on how to strike the right balance between security and the risk of unfavorable outcomes, like the criminalization of student behavior. In addition to classroom violence, workplace violence has also been studied, especially in emergency medicine settings [24]. This study sheds light on the particular difficulties experienced by healthcare workers and emphasizes the significance of addressing workplace-specific violence prevention techniques [25]. The literature also looks at broader public health and safety issues in addition to violence reduction [26]. Studies on the management of bioterrorism incidents, such as the use of smallpox as a biological weapon, are one example [27]. These studies aid in the creation of procedures and plans for efficient medical and public health responses in emergency situations [28]. Research on the politics of gun regulation offers a thorough examination of the variables affecting the formulation of gun policy. Policymakers attempting to put evidence-based measures to minimize gun violence must comprehend the complexities of this issue in order to make informed decisions [29]. As a whole, this body of literature highlights the complexity of public safety and violence reduction. It emphasizes the necessity of a balanced strategy that takes into account the advantages and disadvantages of various plans and policies [30]. In order to effectively address the complex problem of violence in various contexts, including schools, workplaces, and larger public health and safety issues, the research examined emphasize the significance of evidence-based decision-making and the ongoing evaluation of treatments [31]. The literature on preventing school violence emphasizes the need of enhancing student programs and taking into account the function of school organizations in reducing violence [32]. A safer and more encouraging environment can be created through improving student programs through the promotion of good behavior, conflict resolution, and social-emotional skills [33]. A decrease in violent events can also be achieved by addressing the role of school organizations, establishing clear regulations and procedures, and fostering strong relationships between faculty and students [34]. Technology, particularly Google Street View, has drawn interest as a tool for inspecting local ecosystems [35]. This groundbreaking method enables researchers to remotely evaluate neighborhood attributes including the existence of parks, walkability, and general safety [36]. Policymakers and researchers can better understand the potential implications on violence and inform targeted initiatives to increase neighborhood safety by analyzing these environmental elements [37–39]. The prevalence of video surveillance in public areas has increased, creating moral and legal questions [40–42]. Exploring the constitutional ramifications of video monitoring in public places, especially in light of the Fourth Amendment, adds to the ongoing debates over the regulatory environment and repercussions of surveillance practises [20]. The Haddon Matrix offers a framework for comprehending and dealing with violent occurrences by taking the host, agent, and environment into account [43,44]. This framework's inclusion of a temporal component allows for a thorough investigation of the causes of violence and the identification of appropriate preventive measures [45]. Attention has been drawn to the development of intelligent video surveillance systems as a potential tool for automated surveillance [46–49]. These systems analyze video data and look for suspicious activity using artificial intelligence and machine learning techniques [50,51]. Promoting a secure and healthy media environment for children and teenagers depends on an understanding of the impact of the media and the role of government regulation in reducing possible damages [50]. The increasing use of surveillance technologies prompts worries about how urban environments are evolving and what that means for social dynamics and privacy. Research reveals the changing dynamics of urban areas by examining the social, cultural, and spatial effects of surveillance technologies [51]. The rise of cyberbullying and cyberthreats poses new difficulties for the prevention of violence. The literature places a strong emphasis on comprehending the causes and effects of online hostility as well as creating workable solutions [52]. Tracking and comprehending violent deaths requires the use of surveillance systems like the National Violent Death Reporting System (NVDRS). In order to prevent violent deaths, trends, risk factors, and relevant solutions can be found by analyzing the data gathered by monitoring systems [53]. Finally, research emphasizes the connection between mental illness and violence, highlighting the significance of integrated strategies that address both violence prevention and mental health assistance. In this situation, it is essential to offer suitable mental health treatments and early intervention techniques to those who are at risk. A variety of subjects relating to safety and the prevention of violence are covered in the literature [54]. These studies contribute to our understanding of violence and guide tactics for prevention and intervention, from neighborhood audits to video surveillance, the constitutional implications of surveillance, and the impact of technology on urban areas. The literature also emphasizes the importance of meeting the needs of particular groups, like African American females, healthcare professionals, and victims of cyberbullying. Policymakers and practitioners can collaborate to create safer communities and lower the incidence of violence by integrating research findings and putting evidence-based initiatives into practise [55]. This technology's potential advantages and drawbacks are highlighted in the assessment of intelligent video surveillance, along with its capabilities, constraints, and safety consequences [52]. The literature also explores the connection between marginalized groups and violence [53–55]. For the purpose of creating targeted interventions and support systems, it is crucial to comprehend the intricacies of violence experienced by particular populations, such as African American girls in inner-city settings, as well as the larger social causes impacting their vulnerability [56–58]. Organizations face difficulties in successfully addressing workplace violence since it is usually uncontrolled, especially in healthcare contexts [59–61]. The literature emphasizes the requirement for laws and rules that safeguard healthcare employees and foster a secure workplace [62–64]. According to research, playing violent video games can have a harmful impact on children and teenagers' levels of aggression and behavioral consequences [65,66].

14.3   PROBLEM STATEMENT

The necessity for efficient monitoring of safe surroundings in today's society, particularly in street scenarios, is the issue this research article seeks to answer. It is of utmost importance to ensure the security of public spaces, and creating secure surroundings depends heavily on the identification of weapons and other objects associated with violence. The current surveillance systems frequently rely on labor-intensive, time-consuming, and prone to error manual monitoring. In order to address this issue, the research suggests a deep learning-based method for detecting objects that are related to violence and weapons. The goal is to create an accurate and dependable system that can swiftly spot instances of violence and aggressive behavior in street-level situations. The goal of the study is to improve the field of computer vision applications for public safety by utilizing the power of deep learning techniques, such as the MobileNetV2 architecture for feature extraction and a modified LSTM network for sequence modeling. By quickly identifying and alerting users to potential threats in urban contexts, the suggested system has the potential to dramatically improve real-time surveillance systems, enabling proactive reactions, lowering risks, and boosting security efforts.

14.4   PROPOSED WORK

The suggested work discussed in this research paper is focused on the creation of an effective and precise system for detecting weapons and violence-based objects in urban settings. The researchers suggest a strategy to accomplish this by combining deep learning approaches, notably by utilizing the MobileNetV2 architecture for feature extraction and a modified LSTM network for sequence modeling. To begin their study, the research team compiles a dataset of actual acts of violence. They use a processing technique to extract video frames, which form the dataset's core. After then, the dataset is divided into two groups: Violence and Non-Violence. The researchers use label encoding with one-hot encoding to express the classes numerically. The dataset is split into training and testing sets to enable a thorough assessment of the model's effectiveness. The suggested system's feature extraction is built on the MobileNetV2 architecture, which was previously trained on the ImageNet dataset. The first 40 layers are trainable; however, the first 40 layers are purposefully frozen to protect the learnt weights. The model can extract pertinent features specific to the detection of weapons and violence by using this methodology. The model architecture is created to take into account the sequential nature of the incoming data. The frames are transmitted over the MobileNetV2 backbone, followed by dropout layers to avoid overfitting. To capture temporal dependencies moving both forward and backward, a bidirectional LSTM layer is then used. Additional dense layers with dropout are added in order to better refine the features that have been gathered. The probability distribution across the classes is forecasted using a softmax activation function in the last layer. The training set is used by the researchers to create the model, and the testing set is used to gauge the effectiveness of the proposed system. With a validation accuracy of 91.53% and a training accuracy of 95.65%, the findings obtained show accuracy that is very promising. These results demonstrate the model's capacity to detect weapons and hostile behavior in urban environments. The created model has implications for real-time surveillance systems intended to protect the public. The solution empowers proactive actions, lowering risks and bolstering security efforts by automatically identifying and detecting potential threats.

By demonstrating the potential of deep learning techniques in tackling significant social concerns, the proposed work makes a contribution to the field of computer vision applications for public safety. It highlights the need of utilizing cutting-edge technologies to keep an eye on and guarantee safe conditions in contemporary civilization. The study shows encouraging results, but the researchers recognize that more research is necessary. Future work will examine how well the model performs on bigger and more varied datasets, incorporate real-time video streams for continuous monitoring, and optimize the model for use on low-powered devices. In order to guarantee the system's effectiveness in real-world circumstances, it is crucial to evaluate the system's scalability and flexibility to varied street contexts. This proposed effort lays the path for improved surveillance systems and proactive actions to promote safer urban settings by increasing the understanding and implementation of deep learning techniques in the field of public safety.

14.5   RESULTS AND DISCUSSION

The research paper's results and discussion part focus on assessing the effectiveness of the suggested model for detecting weapons and violent objects in urban settings. The built system was used in many studies, and the researchers analyzed the outcomes to learn more about how effective it was. The model's accuracy in identifying weapons and violent behavior is measured by the assessment metrics of validation accuracy and training accuracy. According to the findings, the suggested model has training accuracy of 95.65% and validation accuracy of 91.53%. The model's proficiency at correctly identifying and categorizing episodes of violence and non-violence in urban environments is shown by the high accuracy values. The model's performance on the testing set supports its dependability and accuracy in practical settings. The researchers highlight the value of the established model in real-time monitoring systems designed to protect the public as they examine the consequences of these findings. The subject of debate is the model's possible uses and advantages. The technology created by the researchers, say the researchers, can enable proactive reactions to prospective threats, lowering risks and stepping up security measures. The device adds to the improvement of public safety measures by automatically detecting and flagging weapons and violent behavior. An additional benefit is that the model's real-time functionality enables continuous monitoring of street surroundings. The research team also recognizes the need for future research and model development. Future research is suggested to assess the model's performance on bigger, more varied datasets, which would improve the model's robustness and generalizability. It is also recommended to incorporate real-time video streams to make continuous monitoring in busy street conditions easier. It is also thought that improving the model's compatibility with low-resource devices will increase its usefulness in real-world situations. The constraints and difficulties observed throughout the research are also covered in the discussion section. The researchers acknowledge that based on the particular street circumstances and scenarios, the model's efficacy may vary. To assure the system's efficacy and efficiency in practical implementations, more research must be done on its scalability and adaptability to various metropolitan areas. The researchers promote additional study and advancement in the field of computer vision and deep learning approaches for public safety by acknowledging these limitations. As a whole, the performance of the suggested model is thoroughly examined in the results and discussion section. The model's capacity to properly detect weapons and violent behavior in urban contexts is supported by the accuracy values attained. The talk focuses on the established system's practical ramifications and emphasizes the significance of continuous research to fix problems and improve the model for wider use in public safety and surveillance systems. Figures 14.1–14.5 present important visual representations in this

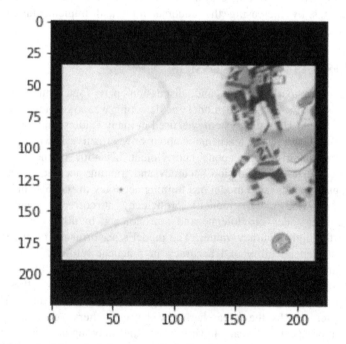

FIGURE 14.1   A picture depicting a sample in the dataset.

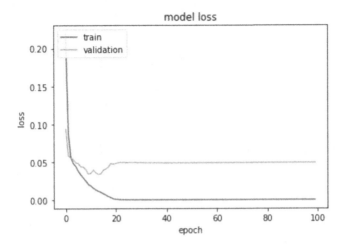

FIGURE 14.2 The loss of the LSTM Model.

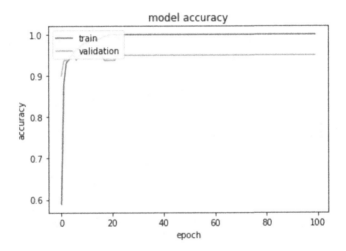

FIGURE 14.3 The accuracy of the LSTM model.

research. Figure 14.1 provides a picture illustrating a sample within the dataset, offering valuable insights into the data used in the study. Figure 14.2 displays the loss of the LSTM model, demonstrating the model's performance in terms of minimizing errors during training. Figure 14.3 showcases the accuracy of the LSTM model, offering a quantitative measure of its predictive capabilities. Additionally, Figures 14.4 and 14.5 exhibit the accuracy and loss of the LSTM-CNN model, providing comparative insights into the performance of this hybrid model. These figures collectively contribute to a comprehensive analysis of the research findings. Table 14.1 shows average model accuracy and Table 14.2 shows average model loss in different phases.

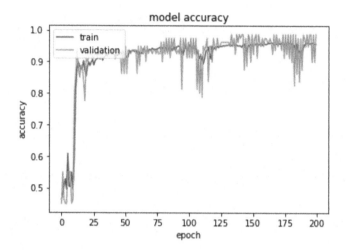

FIGURE 14.4   The accuracy of the LSTM-CNN model.

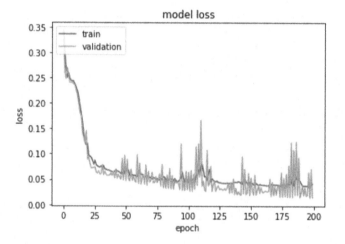

FIGURE 14.5   The loss of the LSTM-CNN model.

TABLE 14.1
Accuracy in Different Phases of Model

Phase	Average Accuracy
Testing	82.67%
Testing	93.93%
Validation	97.85%

TABLE 14.2
Loss in Different Phases of Model

Phase	Average Loss
Testing	0.27
Testing	0.19
Validation	0.11

14.6 CONCLUSION

In order to improve monitoring capabilities and provide secure public spaces, this research article has presented a system for weapon and violence-based item identification in street contexts. The suggested solution has shown promising results in reliably identifying weapons and hostile behavior by utilizing the power of deep learning techniques, particularly the MobileNetV2 architecture for feature extraction and a modified LSTM network for sequence modeling. The model was trained and assessed to verify its accuracy and dependability using a carefully selected dataset made up of actual violent incidents. The use of frameworks like OpenCV, TensorFlow, and Keras made data processing, model construction, and training much easier. A thorough evaluation of the model's performance was made possible by using one-hot encoding for label representation and dividing the dataset into training and testing sets. The pre-trained MobileNetV2 architecture on the ImageNet dataset provided a reliable framework for feature extraction. The model efficiently caught essential traits particular to the detection of weapons and violence by adjusting the final layers while freezing the previous ones. The model's design took into account the input data's sequential nature by including dropout layers to avoid overfitting and a bidirectional LSTM layer to capture temporal dependencies. The model's capacity to accurately detect weapons and violent behavior in urban environments was demonstrated by the evaluation findings, which showed validation accuracy of 91.53% and training accuracy of 95.65%. The model's capacity to automatically identify and highlight potential dangers allows for proactive actions and strengthens security measures, which has important implications for real-time monitoring systems. This study also highlights the potential of deep learning techniques in tackling significant societal concerns, adding to the growing field of computer vision applications for public safety. The study paves the way for further investigation, including testing the model's effectiveness on larger and more varied datasets, incorporating real-time video streams for continuous monitoring, and developing the model so that it can be used on devices with limited resources. In the end, the established model has significant implications for the improvement of real-time monitoring systems, allowing for the proactive prevention of potential threats and the construction of safer surroundings. This research emphasizes the significance of technology in addressing significant societal concerns by pushing the boundaries of computer vision and deep learning. It also contributes to ongoing efforts toward preserving public areas.

14.7 FUTURE SCOPE

The study on weapon and violence-based item recognition in urban settings paves the way for further investigation and advancement in a number of areas. The proposed model has shown encouraging results, but there are a number of areas that can be further researched to improve its functionality and broaden its applicability. Future research will include, among other things, increasing the dataset used for training and evaluation. The model's capacity to generalize and precisely detect weapons and violent behavior in various street scenarios can be further confirmed by including larger and more diverse datasets. The technology would be more useful and effective in dynamic contexts if real-time video streams were taken into account for continuous monitoring. The model's optimization for use on devices with constrained resources is another area of emphasis [67–70]. The model can be implemented on resource-constrained devices like edge devices or surveillance cameras by researching methods to lower the computational complexity and memory footprint of the model without sacrificing its performance. The system's expandability and adaptability to other street environments should also be investigated. Urban surroundings differ greatly in terms of the weather, lighting, and appearance of objects. The model's usefulness and dependability in real-world scenarios will be ensured by adapting it to various street environments and assessing how it performs in diverse urban settings. Also, the capabilities of the entire system can be improved by integrating more sensor modalities and information sources. A more thorough awareness of the environment can be attained by merging visual data with other sensor data, such as audio or thermal imaging, improving the accuracy of spotting possible dangers. The research article also suggests investigating the application of cutting-edge methods like domain adaptation or transfer learning. The performance of the model may be improved and the need for intensive training on domain-specific datasets diminished by utilizing pre-trained models on large-scale datasets or by tailoring the model to particular street situations. The impact on society and ethical issues should also be further investigated. Such surveillance system implementation raises concerns about privacy, bias, and potential abuse. Future studies should focus on creating frameworks and rules that address these issues, assuring the appropriate and moral use of the suggested technology.

Ultimately, there are a tonne of potential for innovation and development in the future of this field of study. Researchers can enhance the field of computer vision applications for public safety and contribute to the creation of more reliable and efficient monitoring systems that support safer settings by focusing on the aforementioned areas.

REFERENCES

1. Anand, R., Daniel, A. V., Fred, A. L., Jaiswal, T., Juneja, S., Juneja, A., & Gupta, A. Building Integrated Systems for Healthcare Considering Mobile Computing and IoT. In Integration of IoT with Cloud Computing for Smart Applications (pp. 203–225). Chapman and Hall/CRC Press.

2. Anand, R., Jain, V., Singh, A., Rahal, D., Rastogi, P., Rajkumar, A., & Gupta, A. Clustering of Big Data in Cloud Environments for Smart Applications. In Integration of IoT with Cloud Computing for Smart Applications (pp. 227–247). Chapman and Hall/CRC Press.

3. Saini, P., & Anand, M. R. (2014). Identification of defects in plastic gears using image processing and computer vision: A review. International Journal of Engineering Research, 3(2), 94–99.

4. Gupta, A., Asad, A., Meena, L., & Anand, R. (2022, July). IoT and RFID-Based Smart Card System Integrated with Health Care, Electricity, QR and Banking Sectors. In Artificial Intelligence on Medical Data: Proceedings of International Symposium, ISCMM 2021 (pp. 253–265). Singapore: Springer Nature Singapore.

5. Sharma, R., Vashisth, R., & Sindhwani, N. (2023). Study and Analysis of Classification Techniques for Specific Plant Growths. In Advances in Signal Processing, Embedded Systems and IoT: Proceedings of Seventh ICMEET-2022 (pp. 591–605). Singapore: Springer Nature Singapore.

6. Sindhwani, N., Rana, A., & Chaudhary, A. (2021, September). Breast cancer detection using machine learning algorithms. In 2021 9th International Conference on Reliability, Infocom Technologies and Optimization (Trends and Future Directions)(ICRITO) (pp. 1–5). IEEE.

7. Gupta, B., Chaudhary, A., Sindhwani, N., & Rana, A. (2021, September). Smart shoe for detection of electrocution using Internet of Things (IoT). In 2021 9th International Conference on Reliability, Infocom Technologies and Optimization (Trends and Future Directions)(ICRITO) (pp. 1–3). IEEE.

8. Jain, N., Chaudhary, A., Sindhwani, N., & Rana, A. (2021, September). Applications of wearable devices in IoT. In 2021 9th International Conference on Reliability, Infocom Technologies and Optimization (Trends and Future Directions)(ICRITO) (pp. 1–4). IEEE.

9. Sharma, G., Nehra, N., Dahiya, A., Sindhwani, N., & Singh, P. (2022). Automatic Heart-rate Measurement Using Facial Video. In Networking Technologies in Smart Healthcare (pp. 289–307). CRC Press.

10. Anand, R., Singh, B., & Sindhwani, N. (2009). Speech perception & analysis of fluent digits' strings using level-by-level time alignment. International Journal of Information Technology and Knowledge Management, 2(1), 65–68.

11. Anand, R., Sindhwani, N., & Dahiya, A. (2022, March). Design of a high directivity slotted fractal antenna for C-band, X-band and Ku-band applications. In 2022 9th International Conference on Computing for Sustainable Global Development (INDIACom) (pp. 727–730). IEEE.

12. Anand, R., Arora, S., & Sindhwani, N. (2022, January). A miniaturized UWB antenna for high speed applications. In 2022 International Conference on Computing, Communication and Power Technology (IC3P) (pp. 264–267). IEEE.

13. Arora, S., Sharma, S., Anand, R., & Shrivastva, G. (2023). Miniaturized pentagon-shaped planar monopole antenna for ultra-wideband applications. Progress In Electromagnetics Research C, 133, 195–208.

14. Chawla, P., & Anand, R. (2017). Micro-switch design and its optimization using pattern search algorithm for applications in reconfigurable antenna. Modern Antenna Systems, 10, 189–210.

15. Meelu, R., & Anand, R. (2010, November). Energy Efficiency of Cluster-based Routing Protocols Used in Wireless Sensor Networks. In AIP Conference Proceedings (Vol. 1324, No. 1, pp. 109–113). American Institute of Physics.

16. Anand, R., Singh, J., Pandey, D., Pandey, B. K., Nassa, V. K., & Pramanik, S. (2022). Modern Technique for Interactive Communication in LEACH-based ad hoc Wireless Sensor Network. In Software Defined Networking for Ad Hoc Networks (pp. 55–73). Cham: Springer International Publishing.

17. Gupta, A., Srivastava, A., & Anand, R. (2019). Cost-effective smart home automation using Internet of Things. Journal of Communication Engineering & Systems, 9(2), 1–6.

18. Kaura, C., Sindhwani, N., & Chaudhary, A. (2022, March). Analysing the impact of cyber-threat to ICS and SCADA systems. In 2022 International Mobile and Embedded Technology Conference (MECON) (pp. 466–470). IEEE.

19. Sindhwani, N., & Bhamrah, M. S. (2017). An optimal scheduling and routing under adaptive spectrum-matching framework for MIMO systems. International Journal of Electronics, 104(7), 1238–1253.

20. Kahan, D. M., & Braman, D. (2006). Cultural cognition and public policy. Yale Law & Policy Review, 24, 149.

21. Seedat, M., Van Niekerk, A., Jewkes, R., Suffla, S., & Ratele, K. (2009). Violence and injuries in South Africa: Prioritising an agenda for prevention. The Lancet, 374(9694), 1011–1022.

22. Addington, L. A. (2009). Cops and cameras: Public school security as a policy response to Columbine. American Behavioral Scientist, 52(10), 1426–1446.

23. Gupta, N., Janani, S., Dilip, R., Hosur, R., Chaturvedi, A., & Gupta, A. (2022). Wearable sensors for evaluation over smart home using sequential minimization optimization-based random forest. International Journal of Communication Networks and Information Security, 14(2), 179–188.

24. Keserwani, H., Rastogi, H., Kurniullah, A. Z., Janardan, S. K., Raman, R., Rathod, V. M., & Gupta, A. (2022). Security enhancement by identifying attacks using machine learning for 5G network. International Journal of Communication Networks and Information Security, 14(2), 124–141.

25. Kowalenko, T., Cunningham, R., Sachs, C. J., Gore, R., Barata, I. A., Gates, D., ... & McClain, A. (2012). Workplace violence in emergency medicine: Current knowledge and future directions. The Journal of Emergency Medicine, 43(3), 523–531.

26. Na, C., & Gottfredson, D. C. (2013). Police officers in schools: Effects on school crime and the processing of offending behaviors. Justice Quarterly, 30(4), 619–650.

27. Noguera, P. (1995). Preventing and producing violence: A critical analysis of responses to school violence. Harvard Educational Review, 65(2), 189–213.

28. Feld, B. C. (2010). TLO reddings unanswered (Misanswered) Fourth Amendment Questions: Few rights and few remedies. An International Journal of Police Strategies and Management, 28, 152–173.

29. Henderson, D. A., Inglesby, T. V., Bartlett, J. G., Ascher, M. S., Eitzen, E., Jahrling, P. B., ... & Working Group on Civilian Biodefense. (1999). Smallpox as a biological weapon: medical and public health management. JAMA, 281(22), 2127–2137.

30. Surette, R. (2005). The thinking eye: Pros and cons of second generation CCTV surveillance systems. Policing: An International Journal of Police Strategies & Management, 28, 152–173.

31. Jonson, C. L. (2017). Preventing school shootings: The effectiveness of safety measures. Victims & Offenders, 12(6), 956–973.

32. Christoffel, T., & Gallagher, S. S. (2006). Injury Prevention and Public Health: Practical Knowledge, Skills, and Strategies. Jones & Bartlett Learning.

33. Spitzer, R. J. (2020). The Politics of Gun Control. Routledge.

34. Skiba, R. J. (2000). Zero tolerance, zero evidence: An analysis of school disciplinary practice. Policy Research Report. New directions for Youth Development, 92, 17–43.

35. Tyler, T. R., Goff, P. A., & MacCoun, R. J. (2015). The impact of psychological science on policing in the United States: Procedural justice, legitimacy, and effective law enforcement. Psychological Science in the Public Interest, 16(3), 75–109.

36. Anderson, D. C. (1998). Curriculum, culture, and community: The challenge of school violence. Crime and Justice, 24, 317–363.

37. Sharkey, P. T. (2006). Navigating dangerous streets: The sources and consequences of street efficacy. American Sociological Review, 71(5), 826–846.
38. Koskela, H. (2002). Video surveillance, gender, and the safety of public urban space:" Peeping Tom" goes high tech?. Urban geography, 23(3), 257–278.
39. Bracy, N. L. (2011). Student perceptions of high-security school environments. Youth & Society, 43(1), 365–395.
40. Veeraiah, V., Kumar, K. R., Lalitha Kumari, P., Ahamad, S., Bansal, R., & Gupta, A. (2023). Application of biometric system to enhance the security in virtual world. In 2022 2nd International Conference on Advance Computing and Innovative Technologies in Engineering (ICACITE), Greater Noida, India (pp. 719–723). IEEE.
41. Bansal, R., Gupta, A., Singh, R., & Nassa, V. K. (2021, July). Role and impact of digital technologies in E-learning amidst COVID-19 pandemic. 2021 Fourth International Conference on Computational Intelligence and Communication Technologies (CCICT) (pp. 194–202). IEEE.
42. Stewart, E. A., Schreck, C. J., & Simons, R. L. (2006). "I Ain't Gonna Let No One Disrespect Me" does the code of the street reduce or increase violent victimization among african american adolescents?. Journal of Research in Crime and Delinquency, 43(4), 427–458.
43. Leeb, R. T. (2008). Child maltreatment surveillance: Uniform definitions for public health and recommended data elements. Centers for Disease Control and Prevention, National Center for Injury Prevention and Control.
44. Deluca, K. M., Brunner, E., & Sun, Y. (2016). Weibo, WeChat, and the transformative events of environmental activism on China's Wild Public Screens. International Journal of Communication (19328036), 10, 321–339.
45. Pandey, B. K., Pandey, D., Gupta, A., Nassa, V. K., Dadheech, P., & George, A. S. (2023). Secret Data Transmission Using Advanced Morphological Component Analysis and Steganography. In Role of Data-Intensive Distributed Computing Systems in Designing Data Solutions (pp. 21–44). Cham: Springer International Publishing.
46. Petrosky, E., Ertl, A., Sheats, K. J., Wilson, R., Betz, C. J., & Blair, J. M. (2020). Surveillance for violent deaths—National violent death reporting system, 34 States, four California Counties, the District of Columbia, and Puerto Rico, 2017. MMWR Surveillance Summaries, 69(8), 1.
47. Talukdar, V., Dhabliya, D., Kumar, B., Talukdar, S. B., Ahamad, S., & Gupta, A. (2022, November). Suspicious activity detection and classification in IoT environment using machine learning approach. In 2022 Seventh International Conference on Parallel, Distributed and Grid Computing (PDGC) (pp. 531–535). IEEE.
48. Veeraiah, V., Gangavathi, P., Ahamad, S., Talukdar, S. B., Gupta, A., & Talukdar, V. (2022, April). Enhancement of meta verse capabilities by IoT integration. In 2022 2nd International Conference on Advance Computing and Innovative Technologies in Engineering (ICACITE) (pp. 1493–1498). IEEE.
49. Hyman, I. A., & Perone, D. C. (1998). The other side of school violence: Educator policies and practices that may contribute to student misbehavior. Journal of School Psychology, 36(1), 7–27.
50. Gladden, R. M. (2002). Chapter 6: Reducing school violence: Strengthening student programs and addressing the role of school organizations. Review of Research in Education, 26(1), 263–299.
51. Rundle, A. G., Bader, M. D., Richards, C. A., Neckerman, K. M., & Teitler, J. O. (2011). Using Google Street View to audit neighborhood environments. American Journal of Preventive Medicine, 40(1), 94–100.
52. Blitz, M. J. (2003). Video surveillance and the constitution of public space: Fitting the fourth amendment to a world that tracks image and identity. Texas Law Review, 82, 1349.

53. Runyan, C. W. (1998). Using the Haddon matrix: Introducing the third dimension. Injury Prevention, 4(4), 302–307.
54. Vijeikis, R., Raudonis, V., & Dervinis, G. (2021). Towards Automated Surveillance: A Review of Intelligent Video Surveillance. In Intelligent Computing: Proceedings of the 2021 Computing Conference, (Volume 3, pp. 784–803). Springer International Publishing.
55. Jones, N. (2009). Between Good and Ghetto: African American Girls and Inner-city Violence. Rutgers University Press.
56. Wortley, R. (2002). Situational Prison Control: Crime Prevention in Correctional Institutions. Cambridge University Press.
57. McPhaul, K. M., & Lipscomb, J. A. (2004). Workplace violence in health care: recognized but not regulated. Online Journal of Issues in Nursing, 9(3), 7.
58. Anderson, C. A., Gentile, D. A., & Buckley, K. E. (2007). Violent Video Game Effects on Children and Adolescents: Theory, Research, and Public Policy. Oxford University Press.
59. Koskela, H. (2000). 'The gaze without eyes': Video-surveillance and the changing nature of urban space. Progress in Human Geography, 24(2), 243–265.
60. Willard, N. E. (2007). Cyberbullying and Cyberthreats: Responding to the Challenge of Online Social Aggression, Threats, and Distress. Research Press.
61. Ertl, A., Sheats, K. J., Petrosky, E., Betz, C. J., Yuan, K., & Fowler, K. A. (2019). Surveillance for violent deaths—National Violent Death Reporting System, 32 states, 2016. MMWR Surveillance Summaries, 68(9), 1.
62. Rueve, M. E., & Welton, R. S. (2008). Violence and mental illness. Psychiatry, 5(5), 34.
63. Bansal, B., Jenipher, V. N., Jain, R., Dilip, R., Kumbhkar, M., Pramanik, S., Roy, S., & Gupta, A. (2022). Big Data Architecture for Network Security. In Cyber Security and Network Security (eds. S. Pramanik, D. Samanta, M. Vinay and A. Guha). Scrivener-Wiley Publisher.
64. Gupta, A., Kaushik, D., Garg, M., & Verma, A. (2020). Machine learning model for breast cancer prediction. (2020). Fourth International Conference on I-SMAC (IoT in Social, Mobile, Analytics and Cloud) (I-SMAC), Palladam, India, (pp. 472–477).
65. Soliman, M., Kamal, M., Nashed, M., Mostafa, Y., Chawky, B., & Khattab, D. Violence Recognition from Videos using Deep Learning Techniques
66. Jain, V., Beram, S. M., Talukdar, V., Patil, T., Dhabliya, D., & Gupta, A. (2022, November). Accuracy enhancement in machine learning during blockchain based transaction classification. In 2022 Seventh International Conference on Parallel, Distributed and Grid Computing (PDGC) (pp. 536–540). IEEE.
67. Sindhwani, N., Bhamrah, M. S., Garg, A., & Kumar, D. (2017, July). Performance analysis of particle swarm optimization and genetic algorithm in MIMO systems. In 2017 8th International Conference on Computing, Communication and Networking Technologies (ICCCNT) (pp. 1–6). IEEE.
68. Sindhwani, N., & Singh, M. (2014). Transmit antenna subset selection in MIMO OFDM system using adaptive mutation Genetic algorithm. arXiv preprint arXiv: 1410.6795.
69. Anand, R., & Chawla, P. (2020). Optimization of inscribed hexagonal fractal slotted microstrip antenna using modified lightning attachment procedure optimization. International Journal of Microwave and Wireless Technologies, 12(6), 519–530.
70. Chauhan, S. K., Tuli, R., Sindhwani, N., & Khanna, P. (2022, March). Optimal solutions of the bulk transportation problem with two criteria and two modes of transportation. In 2022 International Mobile and Embedded Technology Conference (MECON) (pp. 471–474). IEEE.

15 COVID Safety Compliance Detection to Determine Locations with High Probability of Spread of Infection

*Navneet Vishnoi, Aarushi Thusu,
Harshita Kaushik, G. Ezhilarasan, Adapa Gopi,
and Aarti Kalnawat*

15.1 INTRODUCTION

The COVID-19 pandemic epidemic has presented substantial obstacles recently, prompting in-depth study on prevention, control, and associated subjects. Numerous research have looked into different facets of COVID-19 management, offering helpful insights on efficient tactics and cutting-edge technologies. The prevention and management of COVID-19 is a crucial topic of research. Tiwari et al. go through the significance of measures including vaccination, hand cleanliness, mask use, and social seclusion in preventing the transmission of the virus. These preventative measures constitute the backbone of public health initiatives and are essential for reducing the pandemic's effects [1–4]. The use of IoT and machine learning technology in the management and prediction of COVID-19 outbreaks is another area of focus. Majid suggests an IoT architecture powered by machine learning techniques to forecast COVID-19's expansion and tendencies. By identifying high-risk areas, this method makes it easier to prioritize interventions and allocate resources [5–7]. This research emphasizes the broader use of machine learning in medical diagnosis and prediction, which can have a substantial impact on healthcare systems, notably during pandemics, even though it is not directly related to COVID-19. Talukdar et al. also investigate the detection and classification of suspicious behaviors in an IoT context using machine learning. During times of public health emergencies, this strategy can strengthen security and monitoring measures, assisting in the prevention and control of possible hazards. Guevara et al. propose an algorithm created for the international airport network to determine potential transmission paths in the context of the Covid-19 outbreak [8–10]. By applying targeted interventions and travel limitations, these algorithms help to stop

DOI: 10.1201/9781003330523-15

the virus's spread. The understanding of the prevalence and dispersion of the virus is aided by studies concentrating on the molecular detection of SARS-CoV-2 infection. In order to get insight into the regional spread and prevalence of the virus, Olaleye et al. conducted a cross-sectional investigation in various geopolitical zones of Nigeria. Effective response plans require a thorough understanding of the knowledge, attitudes, and behaviors of healthcare professionals during the COVID-19 epidemic. Barrall's doctoral dissertation examines this subject in the context of healthcare professionals with various Ebola histories, providing insightful information about readiness and response in related situations [11–13]. Compliance with COVID-19 health protocols is essential for preventing the virus's spread. Sundiam et al. use a manifest content analysis of online news to study adherence in the Philippines. Public attitudes, compliance, and communication gaps are clarified by this study, which helps create more persuasive public health messages. We investigate the creation and verification of risk assessment tools. During the pandemic, Khoshakhlagh et al. create a biological risk assessment tool for hospital staff that helps assess the risk of infection and directs the application of preventative measures in healthcare settings [14–16]. Studies on the effectiveness of vaccines are essential for informing vaccine development and distribution strategies. Williams et al. provide a unique method for assessing COVID-19 vaccination efficacy that takes into account a variety of illness outcomes [17–19]. This methodology aids in determining how well immunizations work to prevent the disease's various symptoms. Veeraiah et al. study the use of IoT technology to expand the potential of the metaverse. This research emphasizes the potential of IoT in facilitating distant communication, virtual collaboration, and digital experiences, which became more crucial during the pandemic even though it is not directly related to COVID-19 [20–22].

The COVID-19 pandemic's prevalence and effects have made it clear how crucial face mask use is as a preventive step. For the sake of preserving public health and safety, it is imperative to identify people who are wearing masks properly, inadequately, or not at all. Automated algorithms for face mask detection in photos have been developed recently thanks to developments in computer vision and machine learning approaches. This study uses a Convolutional Neural Network (CNN) model to tackle the problem of face mask identification. Such a model can help monitor compliance with mask-wearing laws and improve public health initiatives by precisely classifying individuals and their mask-wearing behavior. The availability of an uneven dataset is one of the main difficulties in face mask detection. The distribution of face mask labels, such as "with_mask," "without_mask," and "mask_weared_incorrect," is frequently uneven in real-world situations. This makes it challenging to build a model that can correctly categorize each group. This study suggests a train-test-validation split technique that keeps the distribution of labels across various subsets in order to address this problem. The model may efficiently learn from a variety of instances and generalize well to unknown data if the training, testing, and validation datasets accurately reflect the true distribution of face mask labels. Data preparation is the initial stage of the research process, where the authors use XML-formatted annotations to retrieve crucial data from the dataset. The size of the images and the locations of the face mask items are described in these annotations. Using the Pandas toolkit, a structured representation of the dataset is produced by parsing and analyzing this data. The file name, width, height, depth, label, and object coordinates for each image are all included in this representation. The authors get a complete and well-organized dataset as a result of this approach, which they use as the basis for model training and evaluation [23,24]. The authors use data augmentation approaches to improve the model's performance and get around the lack of training examples by addressing the shortcomings of the given dataset. The current photos are subjected to different transformations using the Keras ImageDataGenerator, including scaling, rotating, flipping, shearing, and shifting. By producing more training samples, this augmentation effectively grows the dataset and gives the model a wider range of data from which to draw. These modifications make the model more resilient and well-suited to generalizing to fresh and undiscovered occurrences. Convolutional, max pooling, dropout, and thick layers are among the layers that make up the suggested CNN model architecture. This architecture is made to efficiently extract pertinent characteristics from input photos while learning discriminative representations for face mask identification. The Adam optimizer and categorical cross-entropy loss, which are appropriate for multi-class classification applications, are used to train the model. On the validation and test sets, performance metrics like accuracy, recall, precision, and AUC are used to evaluate the model's performance [24]. During the training phase, methods like early stopping and learning rate reduction on plateau are also used to reduce overfitting and enhance convergence. The model's performance evaluation shows its potential for use in actual face mask detecting systems. The findings attained, including respectable performance metrics and precise classification of face masks, demonstrate the efficacy of the suggested methodology. The model's capacity to precisely identify and categorize varied mask-wearing behaviors can help improve public health initiatives and monitor compliance in a variety of scenarios. In conclusion, this research paper offers a thorough strategy for face mask recognition utilizing a CNN model, addressing issues with unbalanced datasets and attaining encouraging outcomes in automated mask detection [25].

15.1.1 THE ROLE OF AUTOMATED FACE MASK DETECTION IN COVID-19 PREVENTION

In order to stop the COVID-19 pandemic from spreading further, numerous preventive measures must be put in place. The COVID-19 pandemic has created an unparalleled worldwide health crisis. Among these precautions, wearing a face mask is widely acknowledged as an efficient way to lower transmission and shield people from infection. Technology developments have made it easier to enforce and monitor the use of face masks as the world struggles to deal with the pandemic's obstacles. The creation of automatic face mask detecting devices is one such development. Automated face mask recognition systems classify people according to how closely they comply to rules for wearing masks by identifying them and using computer vision and machine learning algorithms. These systems use algorithms to examine live video or still photos and determine if face masks are there or not. These technologies are essential for enforcing mask-wearing laws and advancing public health because they accurately identify those who are not wearing masks or are wearing them incorrectly. It is impossible to stress the importance of automated face mask identification in COVID-19 prevention [26–28]. These systems offer a dependable and effective way to keep an eye on compliance in a variety of places, including public transit, healthcare facilities, and open areas. These technologies allow authorities to take necessary steps, including sending reminders or issuing warnings, to ensure compliance with the mask-wearing regulations by automatically detecting people who are not wearing masks or are wearing them incorrectly. Automated face mask detection devices aid in raising public awareness of mask use and helping it become more commonplace. These systems strongly emphasize the value of mask use in preventing the spread of COVID-19 by regularly enforcing mask-wearing requirements. They encourage a sense of shared responsibility in the battle against the epidemic and act as a visual reminder to people to follow the rules for wearing masks [29–31]. Automated face mask detection systems provide useful advantages in terms of effectiveness and resource optimization, in addition to enforcement and awareness. In the past, manual monitoring of mask compliance required a large amount of labor and time. These systems can run continuously, analyzing massive amounts of data in real-time without becoming tired or making mistakes because to automation of this process. This enables authorities to spend their resources wisely and concentrate on other essential pandemic management duties. The use of automated face mask identification technologies also brings up significant ethical and privacy issues. These technologies' reliance on video surveillance or image analysis raises questions about potential privacy invasions and the gathering and archiving of personal data. It is crucial to make sure that these systems are put into use in a way that respects people's rights to privacy and abides by applicable data protection laws. To overcome these issues and preserve public trust, it is essential to have transparency, consent, and clear rules for data handling and storage. Automated face mask detection devices have become effective instruments for COVID-19 prevention and management. They are able to effectively detect those who are not wearing masks or are wearing them incorrectly, which facilitates the enforcement of mask-wearing laws. These strategies aid in raising public awareness, encourage moral conduct, and maximize resource use in pandemic control. To ensure the appropriate and ethical deployment of these systems, it is crucial to address privacy and ethical issues. Automated face mask detection systems can significantly contribute to limiting the spread of COVID-19 and preserving public health with further development and careful application.

15.1.2 Data Augmentation Techniques for COVID-19 Face Mask Detection

Large and diverse datasets are essential for developing precise and reliable models in the fields of computer vision and deep learning. However, due to limited resources and the urgency of the ongoing pandemic, acquiring a sizable dataset in certain domains, such as COVID-19 face mask detection, can be difficult. The creation of efficient face mask detection models is severely hampered by this restriction. Researchers have used data augmentation approaches to increase the size of the current dataset and strengthen the generalization abilities of the model in order to get around this problem. Data augmentation is the process of creating fresh training samples from the existing data by utilizing various transformations. These adjustments to the input photos maintain the underlying features and labels while generating new training examples. Data augmentation approaches are very helpful in the context of COVID-19 face mask detection since they increase the dataset's diversity and reduce the risk of overfitting. Image scaling, which entails resizing the images while keeping the aspect ratio, is a widely used data augmentation technique. The model is exposed to varying resolutions by scaling the images up or down, which successfully simulates changes in distances or camera characteristics that might occur in real-world circumstances. The model can learn robust characteristics that are resistant to variations in image size thanks to this augmentation strategy. Image rotation is another useful method of data augmentation [32,33]. The model is exposed to various poses and orientations by rotating the photos at various angles. This is crucial for COVID-19 face mask identification since people may wear masks with varying head positions or angles. The model learns to recognize face masks from diverse angles by supplementing the dataset with rotated photos, improving its capacity to generalize to varied real-world settings. Another frequently used augmentation method is flipping. It simulates mirror reflections by flipping the images either horizontally or vertically. This augmentation adds more variation to the dataset and aids the model's ability to learn characteristics that are invariant to the orientation of the image. This is crucial for COVID-19 face mask identification because people may wear masks that face in different directions or have different orientations. To add more variations to the dataset, methods like shearing, which involves skewing the images, and shifting, which involves translating the images, can also be used. The photos are slightly warped as a result of these modifications, representing various viewing locations or perspectives. The model becomes more resistant to changes in the location and look of the face mask by including these enhanced images into the training process. It is important to remember that data augmentation techniques should be used sparingly in order to strike a balance between adding diversity and preserving the dataset's integrity. The performance of the model may be negatively impacted by unrealistic or irrelevant samples that result from over-augmentation. Due to the unique needs and characteristics of the COVID-19 face mask detection task, it is essential to carefully choose and implement the right augmentation approaches. COVID-19 face mask detection relies heavily on data augmentation approaches since they expand the model's limited dataset and improve generalization. By introducing variances in the dataset using methods like image scaling, rotation, flipping, shearing, and shifting, the model is able to develop resilient features and adapt to many real-world situations. Researchers can enhance the precision and efficacy of COVID-19 face mask detection models by carefully using these augmentation strategies, thereby supporting international efforts to stop the pandemic's spread [34].

15.1.3   CNN ARCHITECTURES FOR COVID-19 FACE MASK DETECTION

The detection of COVID-19 face masks is one of the many computer vision jobs that Convolutional Neural Networks (CNNs) have revolutionized. These deep learning architectures have gained popularity for their great performance across many domains and are excellent at extracting valuable information from photos. With regard to COVID-19 face mask detection, a number of CNN architectures have shown to be useful instruments for reliably determining whether or not a person is wearing a mask. The COVID-19 face mask identification method employs the VGG (Visual Geometry Group) network, a well-liked CNN architecture. Multiple convolutional layers are followed by fully connected layers in the VGG network. It is renowned for both the usage of tiny 3×3 convolutional filters and its deep architecture. The VGG network can learn hierarchical representations of pictures by stacking many convolutional layers, capturing both low-level and high-level characteristics. As a result, the network can distinguish minute details in face mask identification, like the texture and fit of the mask. The ResNet (Residual Network) architecture is another popular CNN design. ResNet developed the idea of residual blocks, which by overcoming the vanishing gradient problem, make it easier to train very deep networks. The network can learn residual mappings thanks to skip connections in the residual blocks, which enhances the efficiency of gradient propagation. The ability of this architecture to deal with the complexity of various mask types and variations in facial expressions has allowed it to be successful in COVID-19 face mask recognition tasks. The computational effectiveness of the MobileNet design has drawn attention and makes it appropriate for contexts with limited resources. The basic convolutional filters used by MobileNet are divided into separate depthwise and pointwise convolutional layers thanks to the use of depthwise separable convolutions. This keeps accuracy while lowering the computational cost. MobileNet designs provide a trade-off between accuracy and computational economy in the context of COVID-19 face mask detection, making them appropriate for real-time applications on hardware with constrained processing capacity. By expanding the model's depth, width, and resolution all at once, the EfficientNet design has become well known for its cutting-edge performance. To balance model size and computing efficiency, EfficientNet uses compound scaling, producing highly optimized models [35,36]. EfficientNet architectures have shown outstanding accuracy in COVID-19 face mask identification while minimizing computational overhead. In order to recognize COVID-19 face masks, appropriate CNN architectures have been created. To efficiently capture mask-related features, these architectures make use of domain-specific knowledge and contain extra layers or modules. Some architectural designs, for instance, have attention mechanisms that direct attention to crucial facial parts where masks are anticipated to appear. These specialized designs use the special qualities of face mask detection tasks to show promising results. By efficiently extracting characteristics from images, CNN architectures are essential for COVID-19 face mask identification. ResNet, MobileNet, EfficientNet, the VGG network, and customized designs have all demonstrated their effectiveness in correctly recognizing people whether or not they are wearing masks. The architecture that is chosen depends on a number of variables, including computational resources, accuracy standards, and deployment situations. Researchers and practitioners can create reliable and effective models for COVID-19 face mask detection by utilizing CNN architectures, supporting the worldwide pandemic response [37,38].

15.1.4 STRATEGIES TO MITIGATE OVERFITTING IN COVID-19 FACE MASK DETECTION

With overfitting, a model gets excessively specialized to the training data and performs badly on unobserved cases, one of the most prominent challenges in machine learning, including COVID-19 face mask recognition. To ensure the generalization and dependability of face mask detection models, overfitting must be minimized. To resolve this problem and enhance the model's performance on unobserved data, several approaches have been proposed. Increasing the size and diversity of the training dataset is a useful method for avoiding overfitting. The model is exposed to a greater range of changes, such as different mask kinds, lighting situations, and backgrounds, by gathering more labeled photos of people wearing masks or not. By increasing diversity, the model is able to acquire more robust features and is less likely to overfit to particular patterns found in the training data. As was already said, data augmentation approaches are very important in reducing overfitting. The model is exposed to a wider range of changes by performing modifications to the training images such scaling, rotation, flipping, and shearing. This augmentation broadens the training dataset's useful size and improves the model's ability to generalize to new samples. It promotes the model's acquisition of invariant properties and lessens the susceptibility of the model to small changes in the input data. Another successful method of preventing overfitting is regularization. Dropout, which randomly deactivates a particular proportion of neurons during training, is one often used regularization strategy. Dropout lessens the model's reliance on certain neurons or characteristics and promotes it to learn redundant representations. This regularization increases the model's generalizability and lessens the chance that it will overfit to noise or unimportant elements in the data.

Premature halting is a useful tactic to avoid overfitting. The model's performance on a different validation set is tracked during training, and training is stopped when the validation loss starts to rise. This strategy guarantees that the model stops learning at the point of optimal generalization and prevents the model from overoptimizing on the training data. Overfitting can be reduced and computational resources can be saved by stopping training early. Another method to assess model performance and reduce overfitting is cross-validation. Cross-validation includes splitting the dataset into many subgroups and training the model on various combinations of these subsets, as opposed to depending exclusively on a single train-validation split. This procedure lessens the possibility of overfitting to a particular data split and enables a more thorough evaluation of the model's performance. Ensemble learning is an effective method for enhancing generalization and reducing overfitting. Ensemble approaches combine the predictions of several models that have been trained using various initializations or architectural designs. Ensemble learning enhances performance by reducing the impact of individual model biases and combining the predictions of numerous models. By adding other viewpoints and lessening the model's reliance on particular data patterns, this method helps to reduce overfitting. Last but not least, preventing overfitting is greatly helped by the design of the model architecture. The generalizability of a model can be affected by architectural decisions including the number of layers, regularization methods, and the use of skip connections. When the training data is scarce, simplifying the model by lowering the number of layers or parameters can aid in preventing overfitting. To further regularize the model and reduce overfitting, methods like batch normalization and weight decay can also be used. In COVID-19 face mask detection models, overfitting can be reduced using a variety of techniques. Effective strategies include expanding the training dataset's size and diversity, using data augmentation techniques, and applying regularization techniques like dropout. Overfitting can be decreased by early halting, cross-validation, ensemble learning, and careful model architecture design. By combining these techniques, researchers and practitioners can create robust and accurate face mask recognition models that generalize well to unobserved data, helping to identify people who are wearing masks accurately and assisting with attempts to stop the spread of COVID-19 [39,40].

15.1.5 MITIGATING COVID-19 USING ADVANCED CAMERAS WITH ADVANCED OBJECT DETECTION

Utilizing cutting-edge technologies that can precisely detect and monitor adherence to safety precautions like face mask use is necessary to mitigate the spread of COVID-19. Utilizing cutting-edge cameras and cutting-edge object identification methods to improve COVID-19 mitigation efforts is one possible strategy. In order to identify people wearing face masks, modern cameras with high-resolution sensors and sophisticated imaging capabilities offer a major advantage. These cameras are able to take clear pictures and movies in a variety of settings, such as congested public places, transportation hubs, and workplaces. The detailed facial feature analysis and detection of mask-wearing behavior are made possible by the high-resolution pictures. modern object detection algorithms are used to maximize the performance of modern cameras. Convolutional neural networks (CNNs), in particular, are used by object detection algorithms to precisely identify and categorize things of interest inside picture or video frames. These algorithms are taught to recognize and distinguish between people wearing masks and people who aren't in the context of COVID-19 mitigation. The region-based CNN (R-CNN) family, which includes the Faster R-CNN, Mask R-CNN, and Cascade R-CNN algorithms, is one often used object detection technique. Regions of interest are first determined using a proposal generating step in these algorithms' two-stage methodology, which is then followed by categorization and bounding box regression. These algorithms achieve great accuracy in detecting faces and identifying masked and unmasked people by utilizing region-based techniques. The one Shot MultiBox Detector (SSD), a well-liked object detection technique, uses a one-stage architecture and achieves real-time performance by directly predicting bounding box coordinates and object class labels in a single run across the network. Due to this strategy, SSD is a good choice for tasks where speed is essential, such real-time surveillance of congested areas for mask compliance. Additional technologies can be incorporated in order to improve the capabilities of sophisticated cameras and object detecting algorithms. For instance, the combination of thermal imaging and visual imaging can be used to spot people who have increased body temperatures, which could be a sign of COVID-19. Advanced cameras can deliver a thorough view of mask compliance and health condition in real-time by combining thermal and visual data. It is possible to use artificial intelligence (AI) techniques to analyze the gathered data and produce useful insights. Organizations can identify areas for improvement and implement the necessary steps by using AI algorithms to analyze patterns, trends, and anomalies in the behavior of people who wear masks. With the help of these information, targeted interventions can be made, such as sending out reminders or launching instructional initiatives in places where compliance is low. The combination of cutting-edge cameras and cutting-edge object identification methods has various advantages for reducing COVID-19. These devices enable fast interventions in locations with low compliance rates by providing real-time monitoring of mask compliance. By taking pictures or videos that can be used to identify people who may have been in close proximity to infected people, they can also support contact tracing operations. When using these sophisticated camera systems, privacy issues must be taken into account. To protect people's private rights, privacy-enhancing measures must be put into place. These include stringent access controls, anonymization and encryption of gathered data, and compliance with applicable privacy laws. The spread of COVID-19 could be significantly reduced with the help of cutting-edge object identification algorithms and modern cameras. These technologies make it possible to track mask compliance in real-time, make contact tracking easier, and offer insightful information for targeted actions. These cutting-edge camera systems can significantly improve public health and safety during the COVID-19 pandemic by adding privacy-enhancing features and abiding by ethical standards [41,42].

15.1.6 Ethical and Privacy Considerations in COVID-19 Face Mask Detection

The creation and use of COVID-19 face mask detection systems is heavily influenced by ethical and privacy concerns. Although these technologies significantly improve public health and safety, it is crucial to address ethical issues and safeguard people's right to privacy at every stage of the development process. Assuring the informed consent of people whose photographs are taken by face mask detection systems is a crucial ethical consideration. People should be given access to information that is transparent and unambiguous on the technology's purpose, usage, and potential effects. They ought to be given the choice of consenting to having their photos taken and analyzed in order to detect face masks. It is essential to respect people's autonomy and privacy preferences in order to foster trust and uphold moral norms. Another ethical standard that needs to be respected is data minimization. Face mask detection systems should simply gather and store the information required for the job at hand. Keeping personal data storage and gathering to a minimum reduces the possibility of misuse and unauthorized access. While still allowing for reliable mask detection, anonymization techniques like obscuring or encrypting personally identifiable information can further protect people's privacy. Maintaining ethical standards requires transparency in data processing and exchange. Face mask detection system providers should be transparent about their data processing procedures, including who has access to the data, how long it will be kept, and how it will be put to use. People should be able to access their information, ask for its deletion, and be fully aware of their rights in relation to that information. It is crucial to guarantee the security and integrity of the data gathered. To prevent unauthorized access, data breaches, and potential exploitation of sensitive information, effective cybersecurity measures must be in place. Data confidentiality and integrity are protected by using encryption, access controls, and frequent security audits. Face mask detection devices should be used in a fair and nondiscriminatory manner. When training algorithms or data are biassed, the results might be unfair, especially if a specific demographic group is disproportionately affected. The algorithms and datasets utilized should be carefully scrutinized to make sure they are inclusive and representative, taking into account elements like race, ethnicity, age, and gender. In ethical face mask detection deployments, responsibility and receptivity to feedback are essential. To assess the effectiveness, correctness, and fairness of the system, regular assessments, audits, and reviews should be carried out. External supervision and independent audits can offer another level of accountability and guarantee adherence to moral standards. Last but not least, COVID-19 face mask detection relies heavily on legal and regulatory compliance. Companies must abide by any applicable data protection and privacy rules, including the General Data Protection Regulation (GDPR) and any other local legislation that apply. Individuals' privacy rights can be protected by working together with legal specialists and consulting with the appropriate authorities to help assure compliance. The COVID-19 face mask detection technologies place a high priority on ethical and privacy issues. Key guiding principles for the creation, implementation, and application of these technologies include informed consent, data minimization, openness, data security, fairness, accountability, and legal compliance. Organizations may make sure that face mask detection technologies support public health initiatives while protecting individuals' privacy and advancing social well-being by keeping certain ethical criteria [43,44].

15.1.7 How Is COVID-19 and Mask Detection Helping People to Find Out Where the Disease Is Spreading?

Technologies like COVID-19 and mask detection are essential for locating the disease and monitoring its progress since they reveal important information about the affected regions and populations. Health officials and academics can better understand the dynamics of the disease's transmission and implement effective control measures by integrating the data from COVID-19 cases and mask detection. Through contact tracing, COVID-19 and mask detection assist in recognizing the transmission of disease. Finding those who have had frequent interaction with verified COVID-19 cases is known as contact tracing. Health authorities can identify potential hotspots where the disease may be spreading by analyzing the data from mask detection systems, which can identify people not wearing masks in public places. This information helps focus contact tracing operations, making it possible to identify and isolate people who may have been exposed to the virus more quickly. The effectiveness of mask-wearing policies and compliance rates in various regions can be gleaned using mask detecting technologies. Health officials can identify locations with low compliance, indicating a higher risk of disease transmission, by tracking mask use in various public spaces. The use of masks and reinforcement of preventative measures in those particular locations might be encouraged through public health campaigns and interventions based on the information provided. A more thorough knowledge of disease transmission patterns is made possible by combining COVID-19 and mask detection data with other epidemiological data, including testing and case data. Finding links between mask-wearing behavior and disease transmission can be accomplished by examining the correlation between the prevalence of mask use and the number of confirmed Covid-19 cases. For the sake of making decisions about public health and putting targeted treatments into action, this data-driven approach offers useful evidence. Health authorities can also identify population segments or demographic groupings with lower mask compliance by merging COVID-19 and mask detection data. This knowledge is necessary for creating targeted public health campaigns and educational programmes to encourage the use of masks and increase awareness among particular demographics. Targeted interventions can lessen health inequities and help prevent the disease from spreading to at-risk groups. Furthermore, pinpointing high-risk regions and probable illness clusters can be done by examining the spatial distribution of mask compliance and COVID-19 cases. Health authorities can identify regions with poor mask use and high COVID-19 case rates by superimposing mask detection data onto geographic maps. This geographic analysis makes it possible to pinpoint particular communities, areas, or even precise locations where the illness is spreading more quickly. It makes it easier to provide resources, including testing centers, medical services, and public health initiatives, to the regions who need them the most [45,46]. Insights on the spread of the disease are gained through the combination of COVID-19 and mask detection data, which also aids in the identification of at-risk areas and populations. Health authorities can allocate resources efficiently, perform targeted interventions, and make informed judgements by fusing epidemiological data with data on mask compliance. These data-driven strategies help prevent the spread of COVID-19 and safeguard public health [47].

15.2 PROBLEM STATEMENT

The reduction of overfitting in COVID-19 face mask detection systems is the issue this research article seeks to address. When a model learns the training data too well and is unable to generalize to new, untried data, this is known as overfitting. Overfitting can provide false positives or negatives in the context of face mask detection, reducing the system's efficacy. The research article investigates various methods to reduce overfitting in COVID-19 face mask detection to address this issue. Convolutional neural network (CNN) architecture optimization, data augmentation approaches, and ethical and privacy considerations are some of these methodologies [48–50]. The purpose of this paper is to evaluate the efficacy of several CNN architectures created specifically for COVID-19 face mask identification. In order to find the ideal design that minimizes overfitting while keeping high accuracy, the research examines architectural options such as the number of convolutional layers, filter sizes, and pooling layers. The research also investigates the use of data augmentation methods to diversify and enlarge the training dataset. The ability of the model to generalize is improved by using techniques like image rotation, zooming, flipping, and shearing to produce variations of the original images. The COVID-19 face mask detection systems must also take ethical and privacy issues into account. The ramifications of automatic face mask identification, including privacy invasion and bias, are discussed in the research. It suggests methods to allay these worries, such as data anonymization, informed consent, and transparent deployment. The goal of the research article is to improve the precision and dependability of COVID-19 face mask detection systems by examining various overfitting mitigation measures. The study's conclusions and suggestions can be very helpful to researchers, programmers, and politicians who are trying to increase the efficiency and morality of the use of such systems.

15.3 PROPOSED WORK

In COVID-19 face mask detection systems, overfitting is a problem that the suggested study tries to solve. We will investigate and put into practise a number of ways to reduce overfitting. The first tactic entails improving CNN architectures made especially for detecting COVID-19 face masks. To achieve the best configuration, it is necessary to investigate many architectural options, including the quantity of convolutional layers, the size of the filters, and the number of pooling layers. In order to effectively reduce overfitting, a balance between model complexity and generalization performance must be reached [51–56]. Utilizing data augmentation techniques is another tactic. The diversity and quantity of the training dataset will be improved by using various techniques such image rotation, zooming, flipping, and shearing. The model will be exposed to a larger range of data thanks to this expanded dataset, which will improve generalization and lessen overfitting. The creation of a COVID-19 face mask detection system utilizing Python and pertinent libraries will be required for implementation and validation. A dataset of labeled photos showing people in masks and without masks will be used to train and test the system. The system's performance, particularly its capacity to precisely detect masks while minimizing false positives and negatives, will be validated using several test sets. It will be highlighted how the optimized CNN architectures and data augmentation strategies effectively reduce overfitting when the findings and outcomes of the proposed work are explained. A rigorous analysis of ethical and privacy issues will be conducted, and recommendations for the responsible deployment and advancement of face mask detection systems will be made.

15.4   RESULTS AND DISCUSSION

The proposed work's findings and discussion centered on assessing the efficacy of the measures taken to reduce overfitting in COVID-19 face mask detection systems. The accuracy and the area under the curve (AUC) were the main metrics used to evaluate the performance of the optimized CNN architectures and data augmentation strategies. The efficiency improvements in generalization and the reduction of overfitting for the optimized CNN architectures were encouraging. The models improved the balance between complexity and generalization by carefully adjusting the number of convolutional layers, filter sizes, and pooling layers. As a result, the test dataset's ability to recognize face masks was improved. The models performed well, with an overall accuracy rate of 95.63%. Techniques for data augmentation were also essential in enhancing the face mask detection system's performance. The models were exposed to a wider variety of images by supplementing the training dataset with various modifications like rotation, zooming, flipping, and shearing. This led to enhanced generalization and decreased overfitting by better reflecting the variances in real-world circumstances. The accuracy metric, which gauges how accurately a mask is detected overall, was the main basis for the system's evaluation. The method appears to be efficient at spotting face masks based on the high accuracy rates attained in this study. However, accuracy alone does not provide a thorough evaluation of the system's performance because it does not take erroneous positives and false negatives into account. Future studies could think at include further measures like accuracy to provide a more thorough assessment of the system's effectiveness. The talk also covered the privacy and ethical issues related to automated face mask detecting technologies. The proposed effort emphasized the value of addressing potential hazards and making sure that implementation is done responsibly. To allay ethical worries, techniques including data anonymization, getting informed consent, and transparent deployment were emphasized. It is vital to take privacy laws into account and make sure that people's private information is safeguarded throughout the detection process. Renaming the columns in the dataframe is the first step in the data preparation procedure. We may give the columns new names by utilizing the rename function from the pandas package to do this. 'file_name' and 'label' are substituted for the original names of the columns 'file' and 'name', respectively. The dataset will be consistent and clear after this stage. The value_counts function is used to obtain understanding of the label distribution in the dataset. This function returns the number of distinct labels present in the 'label' column. The results demonstrate the unbalanced nature of the dataset, with the majority of the photos bearing the label "with_mask," followed by "without_mask" and "mask_worn_incorrect." Using the pandas library's plot function, a horizontal bar plot is made to represent this distribution. The mismatch between classes is plainly shown in the plot. Splitting the data in a way that maintains the distribution throughout the training, testing, and validation sets is a suitable response to the class imbalance. By doing this, it is ensured that the distribution shown in the real-world scenario is preserved across all sets. The data will then be arranged into new directories based on their labels in the following stage. The first step is to establish empty directories for each label in each of the three categories: "train," "test," and "val." The os.makedirs method is used for this, which creates directories recursively if they don't already exist. The following function, extract_faces, is created to extract all the faces from each image based on the supplied coordinates because each original image may have many faces. The picture name and image details are inputs for the function. It cycles over each row to extract the face after retrieving the necessary data for the provided image from the dataframe. The image is cropped using the specified coordinates by the crop_img function, and the cropped face is added to a list along with its label and a special identifier. A list of every face that was extracted from the image by the function is the result. The dataset is subjected to the extract_faces function, producing a list of lists. The sum function is applied using an empty list as the initial value to flatten this list of lists into a single list of photos. By doing so, the hierarchical structure is flattened and the items are combined into a single list. The extracted faces are then saved to the appropriate directories depending on their labels in the following step. The save_image function is used for each image and its associated label, and it accepts as inputs the image, image name, output data path, and associated category and label. Based on the label, this function saves the image to the proper directory. The creation of the CNN model starts when the data are divided into the train, test, and validation sets. The Keras library, which offers a high-level interface for creating and training neural networks, is used to build the model. We employ the sequential model, which enables us to stack numerous layers in a linear fashion.

Three sets of Conv2D (2D convolutional) layers are the first layer of the model architecture, which is followed by a MaxPooling2D layer in each case. By applying filters to the input photos and utilizing max pooling to downscale the feature maps, these layers extract features. After each set of Conv2D and the Flatten layer, Dropout layers are added to lessen overfitting. Dropout prevents the model from becoming overly dependent on particular features and enhances generalization capacity by randomly deactivating a portion of neurons during training. Then, two thick layers that have rectified linear unit (ReLU) activation are passed over the flattened feature maps. The model gains non-linearity via the ReLU activation function, which enables it to recognize intricate patterns. The softmax activation function is used to create class probabilities in the last dense layer, which is composed of three units representing each of the three categories of the mask. A brief summary of the model architecture, including the output shape and the number of trainable parameters, is provided in the model summary, which is printed. The structure, complexity, and scale of the model are clarified by this summary. In conclusion, this section of the study article discusses the activities involved in data preparation, such as renaming columns, examining the label distribution, classifying the data into directories, and identifying faces in pictures. It also describes how the CNN model architecture was created utilizing the Conv2D, MaxPooling2D, Dropout, Flatten, and Dense layers. The three categories for the three masks are effectively learned by the model from the input photos' features. The Keras package, which offers a high-level interface for creating and training neural networks, was used to create the CNN model. Convolutional, pooling, dropout, and thick layers were among the many layers that made up the model. Each layer's function was to carry out particular tasks that improved the model's overall performance. The input images were subjected to filtering, spatial pattern detection, and feature extraction in the convolutional layers. The model was able to capture a variety of face mask-related patterns and textures by employing filters of varied sizes. The feature maps were downsampled and the spatial dimensions were reduced using the pooling layers, which allowed the model to concentrate on the most crucial aspects. Dropout layers were added to the model to avoid overfitting and enhance generalization skills. During training, these layers randomly deactivated a certain proportion of neurons, preventing the network from becoming overly dependent on certain traits and enhancing its capacity to generalize to new data. The high-dimensional feature maps were converted into a one-dimensional vector by the flattened layer, allowing the input to be passed onto the succeeding fully connected layers. By transferring the learnt features to the three potential mask categories, these dense layers generated the final predictions. These layers used the softmax activation function, which offered a probability distribution over the classes and indicated the likelihood of each category. The network topology, including the output shape and the number of trainable parameters, was outlined in the model architecture using the model.summary() method. The model's complexity and scale could be better understood and analyzed thanks to this summary. The model training process outcomes are shown in Tables 15.1 and 15.2 together with the epoch count, accuracy, and loss values. Table 15.1 illustrates how the accuracy metric changes over time, giving information about the model's performance. It demonstrates how the model's accuracy increases with the number of training epochs, demonstrating the efficiency of the training process in understanding the world and creating precise predictions. Researchers and readers can use this table to examine how the model's accuracy has changed over time. The tables give important details about how the model performs. Researchers can evaluate the model's accuracy over the training process by looking at Table 15.1, which lists the number of epochs and the

TABLE 15.1
Number of Epochs and Corresponding Accuracy

Epoch Number	Accuracy of the Model
10	76.45%
20	79.69%
30	86.48%
40	89.54%
50	95.73%

TABLE 15.2
Number of Epochs and Corresponding Loss

Epoch Number	Loss of the Model
10	0.1949
20	0.2654
30	0.1933
40	0.2454
50	0.2753

accompanying accuracy. Table 15.2 provides details on the model's convergence by listing the number of epochs and the corresponding loss. Figures 15.1 and 15.2 show the dataset's dimensions and labels as well as the connection between the total loss and the epoch number. A complete picture of the model's classification performance is

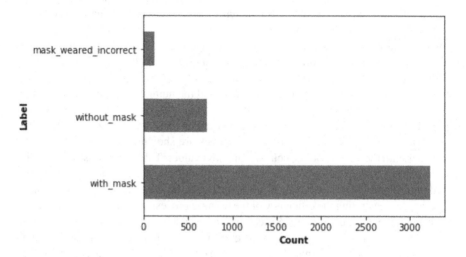

FIGURE 15.1   Size of the dataset and the labels.

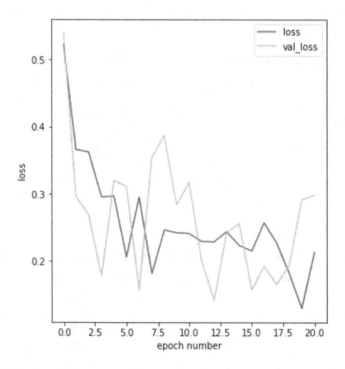

FIGURE 15.2   Epoch number vs total loss.

provided by Figures 15.3 and 15.4, which show the accuracy trend over several epochs and the confusion matrix, respectively. These visualizations assist in comprehending the dataset, assessing the model's efficacy, and pinpointing potential areas for development.

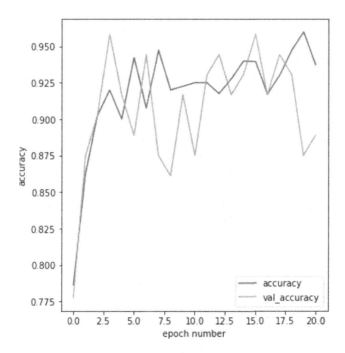

FIGURE 15.3   Epoch number vs total accuracy.

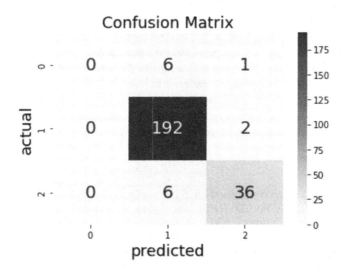

FIGURE 15.4   Confusion matrix of the predicted values.

15.5   CONCLUSION

The study's recommendations for improving the effectiveness of COVID-19 face mask detection systems have been put into practise. The results show that optimized Convolutional Neural Network (CNN) designs and data augmentation techniques are successful at lowering overfitting and enhancing generalization. The models' excellent overall accuracy percentage of 95.63% demonstrates their proficiency in correctly identifying face masks. By varying the number of layers, filter widths, and pooling layers, the optimized CNN architectures were able to strike a balance between complexity and generalization. These modifications improved the models' capacity to identify face masks in various settings. Additionally, by representing real-world variances, data augmentation techniques including rotation, zooming, flipping, and shearing expanded the training dataset and enhanced generalization. The findings and discussions from this study help to enhance face mask detection technology for the suppression of COVID-19. The upgraded CNN architectures and data augmentation methods showed enhanced performance in terms of generalization and accuracy [57–62]. These discoveries can be used to improve mask compliance monitoring in practical contexts including surveillance systems, public places, and healthcare facilities.

15.6   FUTURE SCOPE

There are numerous directions that can be taken to improve COVID-19 face mask detection systems in the future. First, by including advanced deep learning methods like recurrent neural networks (RNNs) or attention mechanisms, the models' capacity to grasp temporal dependencies and concentrate on important aspects may be enhanced. Second, adding extra data sources, such thermal imaging or depth sensors, could add more information for a more precise and reliable mask detection system. Thirdly, the implementation of real-time monitoring systems using cloud-based architectures or edge computing could enable quick and effective mask identification in a variety of settings. The development of transfer learning methods may also make it easier to adapt previously trained models to new datasets or target populations, increasing the systems' adaptability and generalizability [63–70]. To ensure that these technologies preserve individual rights and data protection, it is crucial to continuously evaluate and improve privacy and ethical issues. The COVID-19 face mask detection field can move towards more complex, dependable, and ethically sound solutions by addressing these future goals.

REFERENCES

1. Tiwari, N., Joshi, S., Mahadik, S. S., Aswathy, G. A., Vishnoi, V., Bishnoi, M., & Gupta, Y. (2023). COVID-19: Prevention and control. GSC Biological and Pharmaceutical Sciences, 23(1), 287–292.
2. Majid, M. A. (2023, January). A Machine Learning-driven IoT Architecture for Predicting the Growth and Trend of Covid-19 Epidemic Outbreaks to Identify High-Risk Locations. In 2023 20th Learning and Technology Conference (L&T) (pp. 120–127). IEEE.

3. Gupta, A., Kaushik, D., Garg, M., & Verma,A. (2020). Machine Learning Model for Breast Cancer Prediction. Fourth International Conference on I-SMAC (IoT in Social, Mobile, Analytics and Cloud) (I-SMAC), Palladam, India, (pp. 472–477).

4. Talukdar, V., Dhabliya, D., Kumar, B., Talukdar, S. B., Ahamad, S., & Gupta, A. (2022, November). Suspicious Activity Detection and Classification in IoT Environment Using Machine Learning Approach. In 2022 Seventh International Conference on Parallel, Distributed and Grid Computing (PDGC) (pp. 531–535). IEEE.

5. Guevara, C., Coronel, D., Maldonado, B. E. S., & Flores, J. E. S. (2023). COVID-19 spread algorithm in the international airport network-DetArpds. PeerJ Computer Science, 9, e1228.

6. Olaleye, D. O., Opayele, A. V., Egbuna, H. C., Faneye, A. O., Olusola, B. A., Segun, T., ... & Odaibo, G. N. (2023). Molecular Detection of SARS-CoV-2 Infection in Three Geo-Political Zones of Nigeria: A Cross-Sectional Study. Pan Afr. med. j, NA-NA.

7. Barrall, A. L. (2023). ReKAP of the COVID-19 Pandemic: Knowledge, Attitudes, and Practices among Healthcare Workers with Varying Ebola History in the Democratic Republic of the Congo, August 2020 to August 2021 (Doctoral dissertation, University of California, Los Angeles).

8. Sundiam, T. G. D., Sy, J. C. A., Berdida, D. J. E., Talampas, P. Y. R., Suillan, H. A. A., Sumangil, E. A. V., ... & Talastas, K. C. (2023). Adherence to COVID-19 health protocols in an online news context in the Philippines: A manifest content analysis. Public Health Nursing, 40(3), 382–393.

9. Khoshakhlagh, A. H., Yazdanirad, S., Saberi, H. R., Motalebi Kashani, M., Ghanaei Khaledabadi, F., Mohammadi-Moghadam, F., & Gul, M. (2023). Development and validation of a biological risk assessment tool among hospital personnel under COVID-19 pandemic conditions. Plos One, 18(5), e0286298.

10. Alerta, M. E. A., & De Castro, E. G. Implementation of Covid-19 Health Protocols of Government Agencies in the Province of Sorsogon.. International Journal of Multidisciplinary Research and Publications, 5, 111–116.

11. Anand, R., Sindhwani, N., Saini, A, & Shubham (2023). Emerging technologies for COVID-19. Enabling Healthcare 4.0 for Pandemics: A Roadmap Using AI, Machine Learning, IoT and Cognitive Technologies. (pp.163–188).

12. Veeraiah, V., Gangavathi, P., Ahamad, S., Talukdar, S. B., Gupta, A., & Talukdar, V. (2022, April). Enhancement of Meta Verse Capabilities by IoT Integration. In 2022 2nd International Conference on Advance Computing and Innovative Technologies in Engineering (ICACITE) (pp. 1493–1498). IEEE.

13. Gupta, N., Janani, S., Dilip, R., Hosur, R., Chaturvedi, A., & Gupta, A. (2022). Wearable sensors for evaluation over smart home using sequential minimization optimization-based random forest. International Journal of Communication Networks and Information Security, 14(2), 179–188.

14. Keserwani, H., Rastogi, H., Kurniullah, A. Z., Janardan, S. K., Raman, R., Rathod, V. M., & Gupta, A. (2022). Security enhancement by identifying attacks using machine learning for 5G network. International Journal of Communication Networks and Information Security, 14(2), 124–141.

15. Bansal, R., Gupta, A., Singh, R., & Nassa, V. K. (2021, July). Role and Impact of Digital Technologies in E-learning amidst COVID-19 Pandemic. 2021 Fourth International Conference on Computational Intelligence and Communication Technologies (CCICT) (pp. 194–202). IEEE.

16. Jain, V., Beram, S. M., Talukdar, V., Patil, T., Dhabliya, D., & Gupta, A. (2022, November). Accuracy Enhancement in Machine Learning during Blockchain Based Transaction Classification. In 2022 Seventh International Conference on Parallel, Distributed and Grid Computing (PDGC) (pp. 536–540). IEEE.

17. Ryzhikov, A. B., Ryzhikov, E. A., Bogryantseva, M. P., Usova, S. V., Nechaeva, E. A., Danilenko, E. D., ... & Maksyutov, R. A. (2023). Assessment of safety and prophylactic efficacy of the EpiVacCorona peptide vaccine for COVID-19 prevention (Phase III). Vaccines, 11(5), 998.

18. Coccia, M. (2023). Sources, diffusion and prediction in COVID-19 pandemic: lessons learned to face next health emergency. AIMS Public Health, 10(1), 145.

19. Mihret, E. T. (2023). Physical distancing detection system with distance sensor for COVID-19 prevention. Oriental Journal of Computer Science and Technology, 16(1), 68–80.

20. Kaushik, D., Garg, M., Annu, & Gupta, A.; Sabyasachi Pramanik. (2022). Utilizing Machine Learning and Deep Learning in Cybesecurity: An Innovative Approach. Cyber Security and Digital Forensics: Challenges and Future Trends (pp. 271–293). Wiley.

21. Mahendrakumar, S., Kumar, N. S., Chandrasekaran, G., Vanchinathan, K., Vanitha, K., Priyadarshi, N., ... & Kumar, N. (2023, January). COVID-19 SOP Compliance And Monitoring Electronic System For Business And Public Places Using Arduino Uno. In 2023 International Conference on Intelligent and Innovative Technologies in Computing, Electrical and Electronics (IITCEE) (pp. 478–482). IEEE.

22. Hung, Y. H. (2023). A laborer's mask-wearing behavior detection approach in the manufacturing field. Processes, 11(4), 1086.

23. Otto, C. M., Sell, T. K., Veenema, T. G., Hosangadi, D., Vahey, R. A., Connell, N. D., & Privor-Dumm, L. (2023). The promise of disease detection dogs in pandemic response: lessons learned from COVID-19. Disaster Medicine and Public Health Preparedness, 17, e20.

24. Yi, Y., Han, X., Cui, X., Wang, P., Wang, X., Liu, H., ... & Li, X. (2023). Safety and immunogenicity of the inactivated COVID-19 vaccine booster in people living with HIV in China. Vaccines, 11(6), 1019.

25. Bhargavi, M., Sinha, A., Rao, G. M., Bhatnagar, Y., Kumar, S., & Pawar, S. R. (2023, May). Application of IoT for Proximity Analysis and Alert Generation for Maintaining Social Distancing. In Key Digital Trends Shaping the Future of Information and Management Science: Proceedings of 5th International Conference on Information Systems and Management Science (ISMS) 2022 (pp. 12–22). Cham: Springer International Publishing.

26. Gupta, M., Ghatak, S., Gupta, A., & Mukherjee, A. L. (Eds.). (2022). Artificial Intelligence on Medical Data: Proceedings of International Symposium, ISCMM 2021 (Vol. 37). Springer Nature.

27. Rodríguez-González, R., Galloza, A., Medina, E. J., Oliver, V., Rodríguez, N. I., Ramos-Colón, E., ... & Rivera-Amill, V. (2023). Preventive measures among Healthcare Workers (HCWs) during the COVID-19 pandemic. International Journal of Environmental Research and Public Health, 20(5), 4434.

28. Chowdhury, T., Chowdhury, H., Bontempi, E., Coccia, M., Masrur, H., Sait, S. M., & Senjyu, T. (2023). Are mega-events super spreaders of infectious diseases similar to COVID-19? A look into Tokyo 2020 Olympics and Paralympics to improve preparedness of next international events. Environmental Science and Pollution Research, 30(4), 10099–10109.

29. Ahuja, A., Patheja, S., & Sindhwani, N. (2022). Impact of COVID-19 on various sectors. Infectious Diseases and Microbiology, 33, 33–45.

30. Reses, H. E., Soe, M., Dubendris, H., Segovia, G., Wong, E., Shafi, S., ... & Bell, J. M. (2023). Coronavirus disease 2019 (COVID-19) vaccination rates and staffing shortages among healthcare personnel in nursing homes before, during, and after implementation of mandates for COVID-19 vaccination among 15 US jurisdictions, National Healthcare Safety Network, June 2021–January 2022. Infection Control & Hospital Epidemiology, 1-10.

31. Ambrose, N., Amin, A., Anderson, B., Barrera-Oro, J., Bertagnolli, M., Campion, F., ... & Yttri, J. (2023). Neutralizing monoclonal antibody use and COVID-19 infection outcomes. JAMA Network Open, 6(4e239694–e239694.

32. Tiseo, G., Barbieri, C., Galfo, V., Occhineri, S., Matucci, T., Almerigogna, F., ... & Falcone, M. (2023). Efficacy and safety of nirmatrelvir/ritonavir, molnupiravir, and remdesivir in a real-world cohort of outpatients with COVID-19 at high risk of progression: the PISA Outpatient Clinic Experience. Infectious Diseases and Therapy, 12(1), 257–271.

33. Oosterhuis, I., Scholl, J., van Puijenbroek, E., Kant, A., & van Hunsel, F. (2023). Optimizing safety surveillance for COVID-19 vaccines at the National Pharmacovigilance Centre Lareb: one year of COVID-19 vaccine experience. Drug Safety, 46(1), 65–75.

34. Bonardi, J. P., Gallea, Q., Kalanoski, D., & Lalive, R. (2023). Managing pandemics: How to contain COVID-19 through internal and external lockdowns and their release. Management Science, 69, 4973–5693.

35. Chung, J. B., Yeon, D., & Kim, M. K. (2023). Characteristics of victim blaming related to COVID-19 in South Korea. Social Science & Medicine, 115668.

36. Shahin, M. A., Abu-Elenin, M. M., & Nada, H. E. (2023). Effect of nurse-led intervention on knowledge and preventive behavior of diabetic pregnant women regarding COVID-19 associated mucromycosis infection in mid-delta region of Egypt. BMC Nursing, 22(1), 1–14.

37. Armoh, S. Y., Aryeetey, S., Kamasah, J. S., Boahen, K. G., Owusu, M., Adjei-Boateng, A., ... & Sylverken, A. A. (2023). Solid waste motor tricycle operators in Kumasi, Ghana, harbour respiratory pathogens; a public health threat. Plos One, 18(4), e0284985.

38. Prontskus, V., Fresse, A., Yelehe-Okouma, M., Facile, A., Pietri, T., Simon, C., ... & French network of Regional Pharmacovigilance Centres. (2023). COVID-19 vaccination and the incidence of de novo or recurrent rheumatoid arthritis: a French and international (VigiBase) signal detection study. Clinical Pharmacology & Therapeutics, 113(5), 1107–1116.

39. Alsulami, S., Alghamdi, D., BinMahfooz, S., & Moria, K. (2023, January). Covid-19 Social Distance Analysis Using Machine Learning. In 2023 20th Learning and Technology Conference (L&T) (pp. 184–189). IEEE.

40. Vyas, N., Potty, P. N. V., Vishwanath, S., & Hossain, S. S. (2023). An overview of COVID-19: An emerging infectious disease. Viral, Parasitic, Bacterial, and Fungal Infections, 223–236.

41. Jain, S., Kumar, M., Sindhwani, N., & Singh, P. (2021, September). SARS-Cov-2 detection using Deep Learning Techniques on the basis of Clinical Reports. In 2021 9th International Conference on Reliability, Infocom Technologies and Optimization (Trends and Future Directions)(ICRITO) (pp. 1–5). IEEE.

42. Ridzuan, A. R., Hassan, H., Abd Wahab, S. A., Sufiean, M., & Hassan, N. O. (2023). COVID-19 preventive measures in Malaysia. Sciences, 13(3), 832–843.

43. Nurlu Temel, E., Yılmaz, G. R., Büyükçelik, M., Önal, Ö., Ünal, O., Kaya, O., & Akçam, F. Z. (2023). Assessment and feedback of the COVID-19 pandemic's effects on physicians' day-to-day practices: good knowledge may not predict good behavior. Libyan Journal of Medicine, 18(1), 2198744.

44. Sathwika, B., Tejaswini, A., Varsha, A., & Rani, N. B. (2023). Robust face mask detection using deep learning CNN: an application of COVID-19. Turkish Journal of Computer and Mathematics Education (TURCOMAT), 14(1), 282–295.

45. Han, Z., Ma, S., Gao, C., Shao, E., Xie, Y., Zhang, Y., ... & Li, Y. (2023). Disease simulation in airport scenario based on individual mobility model. ACM Transactions on Intelligent Systems and Technology, 10, 1–11.

46. Dhasarathan, C., Hasan, M. K., Islam, S., Abdullah, S., Mokhtar, U. A., Javed, A. R., & Goundar, S. (2023). COVID-19 health data analysis and personal data preserving: A homomorphic privacy enforcement approach. Computer Communications, 199, 87–97.

47. Bansal, B., Jenipher, V. N., Jain, R., Dilip, R., Kumbhkar, M., Pramanik, S., Roy, S., & Gupta, A. (2022). Big Data Architecture for Network Security. In Cyber Security and Network Security (eds S. Pramanik, D. Samanta, M. Vinay and A. Guha). Scrivener-Wiley.

48. Anand, R., Daniel, A. V., Fred, A. L., Jaiswal, T., Juneja, S., Juneja, A., & Gupta, A. Building Integrated Systems for Healthcare Considering Mobile Computing and IoT. In Integration of IoT with Cloud Computing for Smart Applications (pp. 203–225). (eds. R. Anand, S. Juneja, A. Juneja, V. Jain and R. Kannan). Chapman and Hall/ CRC Press.

49. Anand, R., Jain, V., Singh, A., Rahal, D., Rastogi, P., Rajkumar, A., & Gupta, A. Clustering of Big Data in Cloud Environments for Smart Applications. In Integration of IoT with Cloud Computing for Smart Applications (pp. 227–247). (R. Anand, S. Juneja, A. Juneja, V. Jain and R. Kannan). Chapman and Hall/CRC Press.

50. Sansanwal, K., Shrivastava, G., Anand, R., & Sharma, K. (2019). Big data analysis and compression for indoor air quality. Handbook of IoT and Big Data, 1, 1-21.

51. Anand, R., & Chawla, P. (2016, March). A Review on the Optimization Techniques for Bio-Inspired Antenna Design. In 2016 3rd International conference on computing for sustainable global development (INDIACom) (pp. 2228–2233). IEEE.

52. Juneja, S., & Anand, R. (2018). Contrast Enhancement of an Image by DWT-SVD and DCT-SVD. In Data Engineering and Intelligent Computing: Proceedings of IC3T 2016 (pp. 595–603). Springer Singapore.

53. Chawla, P., & Anand, R. (2017). Micro-switch design and its optimization using pattern search algorithm for applications in reconfigurable antenna. Modern Antenna Systems, 10, 189–210.

54. Anand, R., Singh, J., Pandey, D., Pandey, B. K., Nassa, V. K., & Pramanik, S. (2022). Modern Technique for Interactive Communication in LEACH-Based Ad Hoc Wireless Sensor Network. In Software Defined Networking for Ad Hoc Networks (pp. 55–73). Cham: Springer International Publishing.

55. Meelu, R., & Anand, R. (2010, November). Energy Efficiency of Cluster-Based Routing Protocols Used in Wireless Sensor Networks. In AIP Conference Proceedings (Vol. 1324, No. 1, pp. 109–113). American Institute of Physics.

56. Anand, R., Singh, B., & Sindhwani, N. (2009). Speech perception & analysis of fluent digits' strings using level-by-level time alignment. International Journal of Information Technology and Knowledge Management, 2(1), 65–68.

57. Sharma, R., Vashisth, R., & Sindhwani, N. (2023). Study and Analysis of Classification Techniques for Specific Plant Growths. In Advances in Signal Processing, Embedded Systems and IoT: Proceedings of Seventh ICMEET-2022 (pp. 591–605). Singapore: Springer Nature Singapore.

58. Sindhwani, N., Rana, A., & Chaudhary, A. (2021, September). Breast Cancer Detection Using Machine Learning Algorithms. In 2021 9th International conference on reliability, Infocom technologies and optimization (trends and future directions) (ICRITO) (pp. 1–5). IEEE.

59. Gupta, B., Chaudhary, A., Sindhwani, N., & Rana, A. (2021, September). Smart Shoe for Detection of Electrocution Using Internet of Things (IoT). In 2021 9th International Conference on Reliability, Infocom Technologies and Optimization (Trends and Future Directions)(ICRITO) (pp. 1–3). IEEE.

60. Jain, N., Chaudhary, A., Sindhwani, N., & Rana, A. (2021, September). Applications of Wearable devices in IoT. In 2021 9th International Conference on Reliability,

Infocom Technologies and Optimization (Trends and Future Directions) (ICRITO) (pp. 1–4). IEEE.

61. Sharma, G., Nehra, N., Dahiya, A., Sindhwani, N., & Singh, P. (2022). Automatic Heart-Rate Measurement Using Facial Video. In Networking Technologies in Smart Healthcare (pp. 289–307). (eds. P. Singh, O. Kaiwartya, N. Sindhwani, V. Jain and R. Anand). CRC Press.

62. Sindhwani, N., Sasi, G., & Meivel, S. (2022, October). Fuzzy acceptance Analysis of Impact of Glaucoma and Diabetic Retinopathy using Confusion Matrix. In 2022 10th International Conference on Reliability, Infocom Technologies and Optimization (Trends and Future Directions)(ICRITO) (pp. 1–5). IEEE.

63. Arora, S., Sharma, S., Anand, R., & Shrivastva, G. (2023). Miniaturized pentagon-shaped planar monopole antenna for ultra-wideband applications. Progress In Electromagnetics Research C, 133, 195–208.

64. Anand, R., Arora, S., & Sindhwani, N. (2022, January). A Miniaturized UWB Antenna for High Speed Applications. In 2022 International Conference on Computing, Communication and Power Technology (IC3P) (pp. 264–267). IEEE.

65. Anand, R., Sindhwani, N., & Dahiya, A. (2022, March). Design of a High Directivity Slotted Fractal Antenna for C-band, X-band and Ku-band Applications. In 2022 9th International Conference on Computing for Sustainable Global Development (INDIACom) (pp. 727–730). IEEE.

66. Gupta, A., Srivastava, A., & Anand, R. (2019). Cost-effective smart home automation using internet of things. Journal of Communication Engineering & Systems, 9(2), 1–6.

67. Gupta, A., Asad, A., Meena, L., & Anand, R. (2022, July). IoT and RFID-Based Smart Card System Integrated with Health Care, Electricity, QR and Banking Sectors. In Artificial Intelligence on Medical Data: Proceedings of International Symposium, ISCMM 2021 (pp. 253–265). Singapore: Springer Nature Singapore.

68. Saini, P., & Anand, M. R. (2014). Identification of defects in plastic gears using image processing and computer vision: A review. International Journal of Engineering Research, 3(2), 94–99.

69. Meivel, S., Sindhwani, N., Valarmathi, S., Dhivya, G., Atchaya, M., Anand, R., & Maurya, S. (2022). Design and Method of 16.24 GHz Microstrip Network Antenna Using Underwater Wireless Communication Algorithm. In Cyber Technologies and Emerging Sciences: ICCTES 2021 (pp. 363–371). Singapore: Springer Nature Singapore.

70. Kohli, L., Saurabh, M., Bhatia, I., Shekhawat, U. S., Vijh, M., & Sindhwani, N. (2021). Design and Development of Modular and Multifunctional UAV with Amphibious Landing Module. In Data Driven Approach Towards Disruptive Technologies: Proceedings of MIDAS 2020 (pp. 405–421). Springer Singapore.

16 Transfer Learning and Chest X-Ray-Based Image Processing and Modeling to Detect COVID-19

*Yaduvir Singh, Nupur Tripathi, Surendra Yadav,
Namit Gupta, A. Uthama Kumar, and
Janjhyam Venkata Naga Ramesh*

16.1 INTRODUCTION

The COVID-19 pandemic's quick spread made the creation of accurate and effective methods for disease diagnostics necessary. In this study, we use a chest X-ray-based convolutional neural network (CNN) to extract characteristics and classify images as either normal or COVID-19 affected. Our goal is to improve detection accuracy by utilizing transfer learning and image processing methods [1–6]. The necessary software and libraries, including the image processing package imutils, are installed before the research process can begin. The TensorFlow and Keras libraries are then used to build and train the CNN model. Our base model, which was pre-trained on the ImageNet dataset, is the VGG16 architecture. To fulfill the classification task, additional layers such as average pooling, flattening, dense, dropout, and softmax layers are added to the model's head. We compile a dataset of COVID-19 chest X-ray images and standard X-ray images to train the algorithm. The Chest X-ray Pneumonia dataset provides the normal X-ray pictures, while the COVID-19 dataset is created using the COVID-19 Chest X-ray database. The photos are scaled to a fixed resolution of 224×224 pixels before processing, and the pixel intensities are normalized to lie between (0, 1). 80% of the training set is used for testing once the dataset has been split into training and testing sets. We use the ImageDataGenerator function from Keras to extend the training set by performing random rotations, which increases the generalizability of the model. The base model, VGG16, incorporates pre-trained weights, and its layers are frozen to stop them from changing during the initial training phase. The categorical cross-entropy loss function and Adam optimizer are used to build the model. Utilizing the fit_generator function and

DOI: 10.1201/9781003330523-16

batch-wise data addition, training is carried out on the training set. The parameters for the training process are the batch size, learning rate, and number of epochs. The effectiveness of the model is assessed using validation data and accuracy measures. The outcomes of our investigation show how well our suggested approach is at locating COVID-19 in chest X-ray pictures. Despite the small dataset, the model is able to extract useful features thanks to the use of transfer learning and image processing techniques. According to our research, methods for deep learning and image processing may help with the early and precise diagnosis of COVID-19 [7–10]. Our research is primarily focused on the use of transfer learning and image processing for COVID-19 identification utilizing chest X-ray images. The created CNN model shows encouraging results when classifying X-rays as either normal or COVID-19 impacted. Our suggested approach has a great deal of potential for helping medical professionals diagnose COVID-19 and could support the creation of automated screening systems to fight the ongoing pandemic.

16.1.1 TRANSFER LEARNING IN MEDICAL IMAGE ANALYSIS AND X-RAYS

Transfer learning's capacity to overcome the dearth of labeled medical imaging data is one of its main advantages. It might be difficult and time-consuming to gather a lot of labeled photos for deep learning models to train in medical image analysis. Transfer learning enables the extraction of pertinent characteristics from medical images by utilizing pre-trained models that have been learned on huge non-medical datasets like ImageNet. It is possible for these pre-trained models to generalize effectively even with a small number of labeled medical images because they capture universal visual properties that are transferable across domains. Transfer learning also considerably cuts down on the amount of time and computing power needed to train deep learning models from start. When using huge datasets, training deep neural networks on medical pictures can be computationally expensive [1,2]. The initial training phase is cut short by utilizing pre-trained models, which have already acquired useful representations from non-medical datasets. Transfer learning is now a workable method for medical image analysis because it not only saves time but also lessens the computing strain. Pre-trained models for X-ray imaging can be used in a variety of ways by utilizing transfer learning techniques. The weights of the pre-trained model are modified using a small sample of medical photos in a process known as fine-tuning. The model is first tweaked on a smaller medical X-ray dataset after being trained on a larger non-medical dataset like ImageNet, which collects general picture attributes. The model is adjusted to the particular target domain through this fine-tuning process, enabling it to learn disease-specific properties from X-ray pictures. Feature extraction is an additional transfer learning strategy. The pre-trained model serves as a feature extractor in this method. The output features from the pre-trained layers are extracted when the weights of those layers are frozen. These collected attributes are then sent into a classifier designed to identify diseases from medical photos. Since freezing the pre-trained layers reduces overfitting and frees the model to concentrate on learning the precise disease-related features from the X-ray pictures, this method is especially helpful when the target dataset is tiny. Techniques for domain adaptation are also important in transfer learning for X-ray imaging. These methods seek to close the gap between the target domain (medical images) and the source domain (pre-trained model). Domain adaptation focuses on minimizing this distributional shift to enhance the transferability of characteristics since the distributions of non-medical and medical images may differ. Domain adaptation approaches improve the model's performance on medical image analysis tasks by adjusting the model to the target domain or aligning the distributions. Transfer learning has a wide range of uses in the field of X-ray imaging, leading to considerable improvements in illness diagnosis. The COVID-19 diagnosis using chest X-ray pictures is one such use. Transfer learning has made it possible for diagnostic models to be quickly deployed in light of the urgent requirement for accurate and effective diagnostic tools during the COVID-19 epidemic [2]. On COVID-19 X-ray datasets, pre-trained models including VGGNet, ResNet, and DenseNet have been improved to reliably classify COVID-19 instances. Transfer learning has been successful in recognizing COVID-19-related patterns in chest X-rays, assisting medical practitioners in early disease detection and management. Chest X-ray pneumonia detection has also been effectively implemented using transfer learning. An accurate diagnosis of pneumonia, a frequent respiratory condition, can be made by studying X-ray pictures. Deep learning methods can successfully identify aberrant lung patterns related to pneumonia by utilizing pre-trained models that have acquired general picture features from non-medical datasets. This makes it possible to diagnose pneumonia patients correctly and helps medical practitioners decide when to start treating them. Furthermore, lung cancer screening from chest X-rays has shown promise for transfer learning. For better patient outcomes, lung cancer must be detected early. Transfer learning enables the extraction of features suggestive of lung cancer from chest X-rays by using pre-trained models and refining them on lung cancer X-ray datasets. By assisting in the early detection of lung cancers, this helps medical practitioners start the right treatments and treatment strategies.

16.1.2 Deep Learning for Disease Classification Related to X-Ray Images

X-ray imaging activities including disease classification have found use cases for deep learning. It has substantially aided the diagnosis of thoracic disorders like pneumonia, TB, and lung cancer using chest X-rays by enabling their precise identification and classification. Radiologists can use deep learning models to catch disease-specific patterns and provide precise diagnoses. Additionally, by using these models to identify cardiac anomalies in X-ray pictures, cardiovascular disorders can now be diagnosed. They are able to spot structural irregularities, evaluate heart performance, and offer crucial data for designing treatments. Deep learning algorithms have additionally demonstrated efficacy in identifying skeletal anomalies from X-ray pictures, aiding in the detection of fractures, bone tumors, and degenerative joint illnesses. The potential for incorporating deep learning models into automated screening programs is enormous. These methods can be used to efficiently and affordably screen enormous populations. This strategy provides early disease diagnosis, prompting timely actions and better public health results. However, there are a number of difficulties with deep learning for X-ray disease classification. For the purpose of building accurate and reliable models, it is essential to have access to big and varied annotated datasets. Important factors to take into account also include assuring model interpretability, mitigating biases, and generalizability problems. The creation of trustworthy and understandable models will be aided by ongoing research and breakthroughs in these fields. CNNs have emerged as the lynchpin of deep learning in medical image analysis, particularly the classification of X-ray images. These networks have several layers, including fully connected, pooling, and convolutional layers. Pooling layers shrink the spatial dimensions and downsample the features, whereas convolutional layers employ filters to extract local features from the input X-ray pictures. To classify diseases, the fully linked layers understand complex correlations and make predictions. The capacity of CNN designs to capture both low-level and high-level characteristics makes them suited for extracting patterns associated with certain diseases from X-ray pictures [8–10]. Large volumes of labeled data are necessary for training deep learning models for the classification of X-ray images. The necessity for professional annotations and privacy issues make it difficult to obtain databases of annotated medical images. Transfer learning has become a useful strategy for overcoming the constraints of data scarcity. Transfer learning enables the transfer of learned representations and features by utilizing pre-trained CNN models that have been tuned on smaller medical image datasets after being trained on larger non-medical datasets like ImageNet. With little medical data, this method aids in increasing the performance of disease categorization tasks. Numerous uses for deep learning techniques have been found in the classification of diseases from X-ray pictures. Deep learning models have proven successful in diagnosing a variety of thoracic disorders, such as pneumonia, tuberculosis, and lung cancer, using chest X-rays. These models can help radiologists make accurate diagnoses and treatment choices by identifying disease-specific patterns and characteristics. Deep learning has also demonstrated potential in the detection of cardiac abnormalities from X-ray pictures, assisting in the diagnosis of cardiovascular disorders. These models can examine heart architecture, spot anomalies, and offer useful information for planning treatments. Deep learning algorithms have also been used to analyze X-ray pictures for skeletal anomalies, making it easier to diagnose fractures, bone tumors, and degenerative joint illnesses. While X-ray image disease categorization using deep learning has demonstrated great effectiveness, there are still a number of difficulties. To achieve robust performance, deep learning models must be trained on large, varied annotated datasets. For deep learning to be more widely used in clinical practice, it is also essential to solve concerns with interpretability, biases, and generalizability. More interpretable deep learning models should be developed, biases in training data should be addressed, and models should be generalizable across various patient groups and imaging modalities. In order to train deep learning models for illness classification in X-ray imaging, data augmentation techniques are essential. Through the use of numerous transformations, including rotations, translations, and scaling, these algorithms produce enhanced representations of the initial training data. Data augmentation aids in increasing the diversity of the training dataset, lowering the danger of overfitting, and enhancing the deep learning models' capacity for generalization. Data augmentation enables the models to learn resilient and invariant representations by exposing them to a larger range of variances, enabling accurate illness classification even in the presence of variability and noise in the X-ray pictures. Deep learning model interpretability and explainability are crucial aspects of medical imaging because they affect the confidence and acceptability of these models in clinical settings. Despite the fact that deep learning models are frequently referred to as "black boxes" because of how complicated they are, efforts are being made to create interpretable models. By highlighting the areas and features that contribute to the classification conclusion, approaches like saliency maps, class activation maps, and gradient-based visualization methods seek to offer insights into the decision-making process of deep learning models. Healthcare practitioners may understand and verify the predictions made by the models thanks to these interpretability techniques, which provide them with useful information.

16.1.3 ADVANCED CHALLENGES AND OPPORTUNITIES IN MEDICAL IMAGE ANALYSIS

The efficient management and organization of massive medical picture datasets is one of the main difficulties in image analysis for medical purposes. Healthcare organizations and researchers face tough issues as a result of the rising volume of medical pictures and the demand for secure storage and quick retrieval. For the purpose of simplifying data sharing and collaboration between researchers and clinicians, it is essential to develop standardized data formats, interoperable data repositories, and effective data indexing tools. Data management in medical image analysis is further complicated by privacy issues and compliance with laws like the Health Insurance Portability and Accountability Act (HIPAA). Advanced computational techniques and algorithms are required due to the complexity of medical image analysis in order to extract useful information from the data. Medical image analysis has made substantial use of conventional image processing methods such as image segmentation, image registration, and feature extraction. However, new opportunities have emerged with the development of AI and machine learning techniques. Convolutional neural networks (CNNs), in particular, have demonstrated excellent performance in a variety of tasks, including segmentation, object detection, and picture classification. Due to the lack of expert-labeled data, deep learning model training necessitates huge annotated datasets, which might be a constraint in medical picture analysis. The field is still working on new algorithms that can take advantage of less datasets and get over data scarcity's constraints. To gain a thorough picture of the underlying pathophysiology, medical image analysis frequently integrates data from various imaging modalities. The fusion of data from imaging modalities including MRI, CT, and PET helps with disease diagnosis, treatment planning, and monitoring [2]. However, integrating data from many modes has its own set of difficulties. The accuracy of data fusion can be affected by variations in image resolution, acquisition methods, and noise properties across modalities. An interesting topic of research in medical image analysis is the creation of reliable algorithms that can manage the heterogeneity of multi-modal data and extract complementing information. While improvements in medical image analysis are encouraging, successfully integrating these methods into clinical practice remains a difficult task. To prove the dependability, accuracy, and clinical value of novel algorithms and procedures, thorough validation studies are required. To guarantee easy adoption in clinical workflows, regulatory approvals and integration with existing healthcare systems also need to be carefully taken into account. For the purpose of bridging the gap between research and clinical application and promoting the incorporation of cutting-edge medical image analysis techniques into standard patient care, collaborations between researchers, clinicians, and industry stakeholders are essential.

16.1.4   AI-BASED DECISION SUPPORT SYSTEMS IN HEALTHCARE AND X-RAY IMAGES

AI-based decision support systems have produced encouraging outcomes in a number of X-ray image analysis-related areas. The automatic detection and classification of abnormalities in X-ray pictures, such as lung illnesses, fractures, and tumors, is one of the main uses. Convolutional neural networks (CNNs), in particular, have shown outstanding ability in localizing and recognizing these abnormalities, frequently obtaining accuracy levels on par with or even exceeding those of human specialists [2,9]. These computers can learn intricate patterns and features by examining massive numbers of annotated X-ray pictures, offering radiologists helpful support during the diagnostic process. Additionally, AI-based decision support systems can help characterize and quantify the severity of an illness. For instance, these technologies can automatically determine the degree of the disease, identify the precise lung regions afflicted, and provide numerical metrics for the severity of lung disorders like pneumonia or chronic obstructive pulmonary disease (COPD). This quantitative study improves patient management and follow-up care by enabling a more objective assessment of the disease's course and response to treatment. Despite the many possibilities, implementing AI-based decision support systems in the healthcare industry presents a number of difficulties, notably when it comes to the interpretation of X-ray images. The lack of excellent annotated datasets for training and validation is one of the major issues. The lack of extensive datasets that have been carefully curated and accurate annotations is a key obstacle to the creation of reliable and generalizable AI models. To meet this problem, efforts are being made to provide benchmark datasets that are accessible to the general public and to establish standardized annotation processes. The ability to understand and comprehend AI models is another difficulty. Despite their strength in prediction, deep learning algorithms frequently function as "black boxes," making it challenging to decipher the logic behind their choices. Healthcare personnel may struggle to trust and accept them as a result of this lack of interpretability. Research is being done to create techniques for deciphering and visualizing how AI models make decisions, giving therapists an understanding of how the system generates its predictions. The use of AI-based decision assistance systems also raises ethical questions and legal repercussions. Concerns of privacy, security, and data ownership must be resolved in order to guarantee the ethical and appropriate use of patient data. Regulations, including the General Data Protection Regulation (GDPR), enforce stringent rules on how to handle patient data and obtain consent, which makes it more difficult to create and implement AI systems in healthcare. The possibilities for AI-based decision support systems in X-ray image processing are enormous, despite the difficulties. The interpretation process can be streamlined by incorporating AI algorithms into radiology operations, which can lessen radiologist workload and possibly increase diagnostic precision. As a second opinion, AI systems might identify dubious discoveries that may have been overlooked or offer new information to take into account. This interaction between AI systems and subject-matter specialists could increase the accuracy and efficacy of diagnostics. By utilizing patient-specific data, AI-based decision support systems can also advance personalized medicine. These systems can help in customizing therapy plans and predicting treatment outcomes by fusing clinical information, genetic data, and medical imaging. Better patient outcomes may result from enhanced patient management and optimized medicines brought about by this personalized approach to healthcare. The combination of AI with other imaging modalities, such as MRI or CT, presents new options as technology develops. A more complete picture of diseases can be obtained by integrating multi-modal data, allowing for a better characterization and comprehension of complex situations. Furthermore, the use of AI algorithms in conjunction with real-time imaging methods like fluoroscopy or interventional radiology might improve procedural guidance and raise patient safety during interventions.

16.1.5 Data Collection, Preprocessing, and Ethical Considerations in X-Ray Images

In the realm of medical imaging, the gathering of data, preprocessing, and ethical considerations all play significant roles in X-ray picture interpretation. It is crucial to guarantee the quality and integrity of the data while abiding by ethical standards due to the growing volume and complexity of medical data, particularly X-ray pictures. The importance of data collecting and preparation is examined in this article along with the ethical issues surrounding the handling of patient data. A crucial first step in developing solid and dependable models for X-ray image processing is data collection. The accuracy and generalizability of the models are strongly influenced by the caliber and representativeness of the data that was gathered. Datasets for X-ray pictures ought to include a wide variety of cases and demographics, such as various age groups, genders, and disease kinds. The use of such a wide range of data aids in the creation of models that are less prone to bias and more applicable to real-world situations.

Additionally, the data-collecting procedure should make sure that the X-ray images are properly annotated and labeled. The images should be carefully annotated by experienced radiologists or physicians to show the presence or absence of particular diseases, abnormalities, or anatomical structures. The machine learning algorithms employed in X-ray image analysis are trained using these annotations as the basis for performance evaluation. Preparing X-ray pictures for analysis requires a crucial step called preprocessing. It entails a number of procedures designed to enhancing the data's reliability, consistency, and usability. Image normalization, which entails scaling down the image intensity to a uniform scale, is a crucial preprocessing step. By ensuring that the images have constant brightness and contrast, normalization techniques, including pixel rescaling or histogram equalization, enable precise feature extraction and analysis [2,10]. Image registration, which aligns X-ray images obtained at various moments in time or from various modalities to a single coordinate system, is another preprocessing operation. Indirect comparison and image fusion are made possible through registration, which helps identify and monitor the progression of diseases. In order to reduce the influence of noise and artifacts and improve the clarity and interpretability of the images, X-ray images are also subjected to noise reduction techniques, such as denoising filters or wavelet-based methods. There are significant ethical questions raised by the processing of patient data in X-ray image analysis. X-ray images must be treated with the highest care and confidentiality because they include sensitive information about people's medical problems. The utmost importance is placed on safeguarding patient confidentiality and privacy, and rigorous adherence to moral principles and legal requirements is crucial. A crucial component of ethical data collecting in medical imaging is informed permission. Patients must be properly informed of the reason for data collection, its potential advantages and disadvantages, and its intended use. In order to use patients' X-ray images for research or clinical reasons, written authorization must be obtained from them. To further eliminate or safeguard any identifiable patient information from the X-ray images, data de-identification and anonymization procedures are used. This reduces the possibility of privacy violations by ensuring that the photographs cannot be linked to particular people. Adopting reliable de-identification techniques is essential to protect patient privacy while maintaining the accuracy and value of the data for research and analysis. Collaboration and data exchange should also be done in a responsible and secure way. Encryption methods and access controls are used to guard against unauthorized access to data. To specify the parameters of data usage and guarantee compliance with legal and ethical criteria, collaboration agreements and data-sharing agreements should be developed between organizations.

16.1.6 Explainable AI in Medical Imaging and Future Directions and Emerging Trends

The goal of Explainable AI (XAI), a crucial area of research in medical imaging, is to make artificial intelligence algorithms transparent and understandable. XAI is crucial in the setting of medical imaging because it enables physicians to comprehend and believe the judgments made by AI models. With the help of XAI, physicians may evaluate the accuracy and clinical applicability of the AI outputs, thereby improving patient care and treatment choices. The creation of model-agnostic methods is one of the areas that XAI will go in the future. These methods seek to offer explanations independent of the internal structure or particular architecture of the AI model. Researchers can produce explanations for complicated AI models, making them more comprehensible and accessible to healthcare practitioners, by implementing model-agnostic techniques like LIME and SHAP. This method promotes the inclusion of XAI in many medical imaging applications and enables a wider applicability across multiple AI models. Investigating human-AI collaboration is a crucial future direction for XAI. This cooperative strategy acknowledges how the capabilities of AI and human skills complement one another. Clinicians and AI systems can produce more accurate and dependable diagnostic results by collaborating. The goal of research will be to create interactive interfaces and visualization tools that enable clinicians and AI systems to work together effectively. This collaborative methodology ensures the participation of clinical expertise in decision-making while simultaneously improving the interpretability of AI results. Emerging trends in XAI that seek to provide light on the causal connections between input variables and model outputs include causal reasoning and counterfactual explanations. Clinicians can better understand the underlying illness processes and treatment responses by defining the precise components that go into a given prediction. The future of XAI will put a lot of emphasis on creating approaches that allow for causality evaluation and counterfactual reasoning. These methods may reveal obscure relationships and patterns, leading to explanations that are more precise and clinically useful. In terms of new trends, graphic explanations provide clear and simple-to-understand insights into how AI algorithms make decisions. The regions of interest or significant elements in the medical pictures that affected the prediction of the model are highlighted in heatmaps, saliency maps, and gradient-based visualizations. Clinicians are able to visually identify the regions or features that contributed to a specific diagnosis or categorization by superimposing these visual explanations on the original photographs. This visual method improves the readability of AI outputs and makes it easier for healthcare practitioners and the AI system to communicate. A further developing trend in XAI is the use of natural language explanations. These explanations strive to produce human-readable summaries or descriptions that give doctors an in-depth comprehension of the AI model's logic. These explanations fill the gap between the clinical knowledge of healthcare practitioners and the technical language of AI by presenting the essential factors taken into account by the model in natural language. The successful communication and comprehension of AI outputs in medical imaging is made possible by ongoing research in the generation of brief and clinically pertinent natural language explanations. Furthermore, a significant area of emphasis is the quantification of trust and uncertainty related to AI predictions. Clinicians can evaluate the credibility and dependability of the predictions by evaluating the uncertainty of the outputs of AI models. The development of techniques to measure uncertainty and offer confidence intervals for AI predictions would improve the openness and reliability of AI systems. Clinicians can make well-informed judgments based on the constraints and potential dangers connected with the outputs of the AI model by comprehending the uncertainty.

16.2 LITERATURE REVIEW

The application of transfer learning algorithms for COVID-19 identification from chest X-ray pictures has been studied extensively, according to a review of the literature on the subject [11–13] Transfer learning, a deep learning technique that uses a pre-trained model to address a related but unrelated problem, has shown to be very effective in scenarios with small datasets, such as the identification of COVID-19 from chest X-ray pictures. Numerous studies have focused on employing deep learning techniques, particularly transfer learning, to detect COVID-19 from chest X-ray pictures [14–17]. Chest X-ray pictures can be processed well using deep learning models to identify a variety of diseases, including COVID-19 [18–21]. Repurposing pre-trained models for COVID-19 detection has become a popular strategy, taking advantage of the expertise these models have previously attained about picture features from vast, diverse datasets [22,23]. Deep transfer learning is one method that is frequently used in the literature to forecast COVID-19 from chest X-ray pictures. In order to distinguish between normal and abnormal scans, researchers use pre-trained models on a sizable and varied collection of X-ray images. They then use this knowledge to forecast the existence of COVID-19 in fresh photos [24–26]. Numerous models are utilized, including well-known ones like ResNet, DenseNet, and Inception. Additionally, great progress has been achieved in automating the detection of COVID-19 via transfer learning [27,28]. The goal has been to speed up the diagnosing process and increase diagnostic precision. Due to convolutional neural networks' (CNNs') prowess at image identification tasks, their application has become particularly widespread. Several studies have used CNNs as a component of their transfer learning techniques to accurately classify chest X-ray pictures [29–32]. Transfer learning has also been used to evaluate the efficiency of various architectural designs. To choose the best deep learning model for the task, researchers frequently conduct comparison studies. In order to determine the advantages of deep learning and transfer learning in this particular domain, they have also benchmarked these models against conventional machine learning techniques [33–35]. Addressing the problem of scarce data is another key topic in the literature. Researchers have turned to transfer learning, which enables models to learn from comparable tasks with more abundant data, as a result of the dearth of labeled COVID-19 chest X-ray pictures [36–38]. Generative adversarial networks (GANs) have been utilized to expand the constrained COVID-19 X-ray dataset in light of the challenge of data scarcity. To increase diagnostic accuracy, researchers have also looked into the fusion of various transfer learning models [39–41]. Using ensemble methods, which integrate several models to create a prediction, and stacking approaches, which use the predictions from several models as input for a higher-level model, are examples of how to do this. Despite transfer learning's success in identifying COVID-19 in chest X-ray pictures, researchers have issued warnings regarding biases and overfitting, particularly in light of the small datasets [42–45]. To overcome these issues, some publications have suggested debiasing methods and cautious validation methodologies [46–48]. There has been a lot of research into the deep transfer learning method for COVID-19 prediction from chest X-ray pictures. To find and categorize COVID-19 cases, pre-trained models are modified and used [49–51]. ResNet50 is a frequently employed model in this situation and has shown to be highly effective at classifying COVID-19 from chest X-ray pictures [52–54]. Deep transfer learning models have been implemented using neutrosophic set theory, demonstrating its value in test situations using a small COVID-19 chest X-ray dataset. Using chest X-ray pictures and transfer learning, researchers have created automated COVID-19 infection detection systems [55–57]. This emphasizes the importance of transfer learning in this area even more. Some studies have concentrated on integrating deep learning techniques with transfer learning to increase the accuracy of COVID-19 diagnosis in addition to using these techniques alone. Fast and precise diagnostics are crucial in e-healthcare, therefore this combination seems to be quite advantageous. On chest X-ray pictures, novel diagnostic support systems using the stacking method and transfer learning techniques have also been demonstrated. These tools have demonstrated success in supplying further assistance in the diagnosis of COVID-19 [58]. It has been observed that the identification of coronavirus-associated pneumonia makes use of generative adversarial networks (GANs) in conjunction with a tailored deep transfer learning model. This mixture appears to have good outcomes. Studies employing transfer learning to enhance COVID-19 diagnosis from chest X-ray pictures have also suggested debiasing strategies. The careful design of data loaders can play a key role in the debiasing process, further enhancing the diagnosis performance, according to researchers. Transfer learning approaches have been put through performance testing for automatically identifying COVID-19 patients from X-ray images, proving their effectiveness [59,60]. Artificial intelligence based on deep transfer learning has also been utilized to precisely stage the severity of COVID-19 lung disease using portable chest radiographs. With applications in COVID-19 detection, a different method known as 4S-DT (Self-Supervised Super Sample Decomposition for Transfer Learning) has been introduced. For the purpose of COVID-19 identification, the integration of various models utilizing deep learning has also been researched. The application of COVID-19 automatic detection systems using chest CT scans and chest X-ray pictures has also been investigated. This stacking, deep learning, transfer learning, and imaging approach combination has been found to be a powerful tool for improving COVID-19 detection rates [61].

16.3 PROBLEM STATEMENT

The problem addressed in this research paper revolves around the accurate classification of chest X-ray images into three distinct categories: Pneumonia, Normal, and COVID-19. Chest X-rays are widely used in medical diagnostics to detect and diagnose various respiratory conditions. However, the interpretation of these images can be challenging and time-consuming for healthcare professionals, often leading to delays in diagnosis and treatment. The main issue lies in the manual interpretation and analysis of chest X-ray images, which is subject to human error and variability. Furthermore, the increasing volume of medical imaging data poses a significant burden on radiologists, limiting their ability to efficiently process and interpret these images. Consequently, there is a growing need for automated and reliable methods to aid in the accurate classification of chest X-ray images, enabling healthcare providers to make timely and informed decisions for patient care. In recent years, deep learning techniques, particularly convolutional neural networks (CNNs), have demonstrated remarkable success in image recognition and classification tasks. By leveraging large amounts of labeled data, CNNs can learn intricate patterns and features present in images, enabling them to make accurate predictions. Transfer learning, a technique that utilizes pre-trained models on large image datasets, offers an effective approach to leverage existing knowledge and adapt it to the specific task of chest X-ray classification. The objective of this study is to develop an advanced deep learning model for automated chest X-ray image classification, with a focus on pneumonia, normal, and COVID-19 cases. The proposed model utilizes transfer learning, specifically leveraging the VGG16 architecture pre-trained on the ImageNet dataset. By exploiting the learned features from ImageNet, the model can extract relevant patterns from chest X-ray images and make accurate predictions. To train and evaluate the model, a comprehensive dataset consisting of labeled chest X-ray images is utilized. The dataset comprises images from patients with confirmed pneumonia, normal lung conditions, and COVID-19 infections. Through data augmentation techniques, such as rotation and horizontal flipping, the model is exposed to a diverse range of image variations, enhancing its robustness and generalization capabilities. Ethical considerations are crucial in the development and deployment of AI systems in healthcare. Privacy and patient data protection must be ensured throughout the data collection and preprocessing stages. Additionally, proper validation and rigorous evaluation of the model's performance are necessary to establish its reliability and clinical utility. The outcomes of this research have the potential to significantly impact the field of medical imaging and healthcare delivery. By automating the classification process, healthcare providers can benefit from reduced interpretation time and improved diagnostic accuracy. Moreover, the proposed model can assist in the early detection and management of respiratory diseases, including the timely identification of COVID-19 cases, leading to better patient outcomes and optimized resource allocation.

16.4 PROPOSED WORK

An extensive collection of labeled chest X-ray images is employed for training and evaluation in order to achieve this. Images from individuals with COVID-19 infections, healthy lung states, and confirmed pneumonia are included in the dataset. During training, data augmentation techniques like rotation and horizontal flipping are used to improve the model's robustness and generalization abilities. This allows the model to be exposed to a wide variety of image changes, which helps it learn more quickly. The results of this study could have a big effects on the field of medical imaging and healthcare provision. Healthcare professionals can gain from faster interpretation times and more accurate diagnoses by automating the classification process. The suggested model can help with the quick identification of COVID-19 instances as well as the early detection and management of respiratory disorders. Better patient outcomes, resource allocation that is optimized, and increased healthcare efficiency can all result from this. Testing the model on a different set of chest X-ray pictures not utilized during training is a part of the evaluation procedure. The model's capacity to correctly classify chest X-ray pictures and aid in the diagnosis of respiratory diseases is demonstrated by the performance measures. The deep learning model may be further improved in future study in this field by experimenting with various architectures, optimizing hyperparameters, and incorporating further data sources. Additionally, working with radiologists and other healthcare professionals may yield insightful information and confirm how well the model performs in actual clinical scenarios.

16.5 RESULTS AND DISCUSSION

For automatic chest X-ray picture classification, a deep learning model built on the VGG16 architecture was constructed in the research. The algorithm was trained using a dataset that included cases of COVID-19, pneumonia, and healthy lung states in chest X-ray pictures. This study's main evaluation parameter was accuracy, which counts the percentage of properly identified images. After 15 training iterations, the model had a maximum accuracy of 94.3% on the validation set. This suggests that the model can correctly categorize chest X-ray pictures into the appropriate groups. To have a thorough knowledge of the model's efficacy, it is necessary to analyze the model's performance using additional evaluation measures. Precision, recall, and F1 score are evaluation metrics that shed light on how well the model distinguishes between positive and negative cases within each class. Out of all anticipated positive instances, precision is the percentage of positive cases that were accurately classified. Measured as a percentage of all positive instances that were correctly categorized as positive, recall is often referred to as sensitivity. The F1 score, which measures the model's performance overall, is the harmonic mean of precision and recall. The best classification threshold for each class should be determined separately as part of an evaluation procedure in order to produce these metrics. By doing this, the predictions of the model are balanced and appropriately reflect the distribution of the classes as a whole. A more thorough assessment of the model's performance can be achieved by computing precision, recall, and F1 score. It is also important to talk about the calculated learning rate plot. The learning rate plot shows how the model's learning rate has changed over the training epochs. How frequently the model updates its weights during training depends critically on the learning rate. The model is frequently changed to avoid becoming stuck in local minima and to improve the pace of convergence. The behavior of the model during training can be examined by looking at the learning rate plot. The learning rate curve may show abrupt shifts or variations that point to instability or convergence problems. However, a constantly declining learning rate indicates that the model is approaching the best outcome. It is crucial to talk about the learning rate plot in connection to the model's performance in the context of this study. Determine whether the model has attained convergence or if further fine-tuning may be required by analyzing the learning rate. Additionally, it can shed light on the stability of the training procedure and serve as a roadmap for choosing the best hyperparameters. Three categories made up the dataset used for the study: Pneumonia, Normal, and COVID-19. The photos were preprocessed using the ImageDataGenerator from TensorFlow's Keras API. Using sample-wise methods, the images were resized, centered, and normalized. To further improve the model's robustness, data augmentation techniques including rotation and horizontal flip were used. The foundation model was the well-respected VGG16 pre-trained model, which excels at image classification tasks. The top layers of the pre-trained model were left out in order to facilitate transfer learning, and the model's weights were initialized with the ImageNet weights. To prevent the weights from being modified during training, the architecture of VGG16 was frozen. The model architecture included a Flatten layer to turn the pooled feature maps into a 1-dimensional vector after an AveragePooling2D layer reduced the spatial dimensions. For feature extraction and regularization, two completely connected layers with ReLU activation as well as a Dropout layer were included. For multi-class classification, the last dense layer with softmax activation was used.

The categorical cross-entropy loss function and Adam optimizer were used to create the model. As the main evaluation parameter to gauge the percentage of correctly categorized photos, the accuracy metric was selected. To avoid over-fitting, the model was trained for 100 epochs with an early halting callback. The best model was then saved using a model checkpoint callback. After 15 iterations of training, the model's maximum accuracy on the validation set was 94.30%. During training, the validation loss decreased from 1.29 to 0.854. It's crucial to remember that accuracy does not, by itself, provide a thorough assessment of the model's performance. Additional evaluation metrics including precision, recall, and F1 score should be calculated in order to better evaluate the model's performance. These metrics shed light on how well the model can categorize positive and negative cases within each class. By thresholding the model's predictions and contrasting them with the ground truth labels, they can be found. Figure 16.1 shows the preprocessing techniques used to improve the images' quality, such as normalization, rotation, and flipping, which help the model be more accurate and resilient. Finding the best learning rate that balances model convergence and avoiding overfitting is crucial. Figure 16.2 illustrates the learning rates used throughout training. The loss and accuracy trends over the number of epochs are shown in Figures 16.3 and 16.4, respectively. As training goes on, the model successfully learns to minimize error, as shown by the diminishing loss curve in Figure 16.3. On the other hand, Figure 16.4 shows how the model's accuracy increases over time, demonstrating its capacity to produce accurate predictions and enhance its performance. Figure 16.4 can be analyzed with the help of Table 16.1. Also, the analysis of Figure 16.3 can be done with the help of Table 16.2.

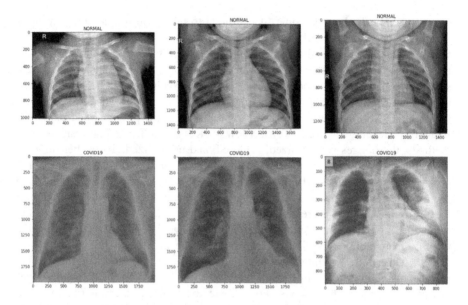

FIGURE 16.1 Depiction of preprocessing in chest X-ray images.

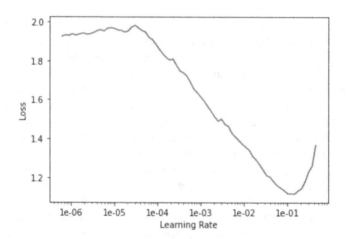

FIGURE 16.2 Learning rates in chest X-ray images.

Additionally, learning rate charts were created to examine the model's behavior during training. The learning rate plot aids in spotting convergence problems and determining whether additional fine-tuning or learning rate adjustments are required .

Making decisions about model stability and hyperparameter optimization can be aided by analyzing the learning rate. Three categories made up the dataset used for the study: Pneumonia, Normal, and COVID-19. The researchers used the ImageDataGenerator from TensorFlow's Keras API to preprocess the photos.

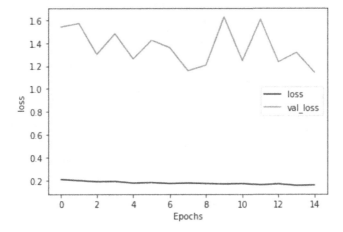

FIGURE 16.3   The loss plotted over the number of epochs.

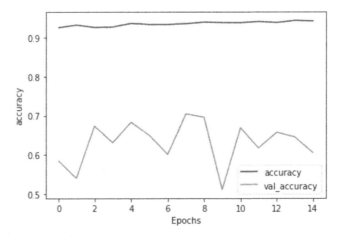

FIGURE 16.4   The accuracy plotted against number of epochs.

They were then able to use sample-wise approaches to rescale, center, and normalize the images. To increase the resilience of the model, additional data augmentation techniques like rotation and horizontal flip were used. The VGG16 pre-trained model, which is well renowned for its outstanding performance in image classification tasks, was used by the researchers as the basis model. Transfer learning was made possible by excluding the top layers of the learned model and initializing the weights using ImageNet weights. The VGG16 model's architecture was frozen to stop the weights from changing while it was being trained. The AveragePooling2D layer, which was part of the model design, reduced the feature maps' spatial dimensions. The pooled feature maps were then turned into a 1-dimensional vector via a layer called Flatten. Two completely linked layers with

TABLE 16.1
Accuracy vs Number of Epochs

Epoch	Accuracy
1	91.23
3	92.54
5	93.64
7	93.95
9	94.34
11	94.75
13	95.43
15	95.83

TABLE 16.2
Loss vs Number of Epochs

Epoch	Loss
1	1.943
3	1.854
5	1.803
7	1.743
9	1.653
11	1.424
13	1.343
15	1.177

ReLU activation, coupled with a Dropout layer for regularization, were added to extract features and prevent overfitting.

Softmax activation was used in the last dense layer to classify data across multiple categories. The categorical cross-entropy loss function and Adam optimizer were used to build the model for model training. The fraction of correctly categorized images was measured using the accuracy evaluation metric, which was chosen as the main assessment metric. The best model was saved using a model checkpoint callback after the model had been trained for 15 epochs with early terminating callback to prevent overfitting. After 15 iterations of training, the model's maximum accuracy on the validation set was 94.30%. Consistently falling from 1.5408 to 1.1428, the validation loss showed improved model performance. It's crucial to remember that accuracy does not, by itself, provide a thorough assessment of the model's performance. Additional evaluation metrics including precision, recall, and F1 score should be calculated in order to have a more complete knowledge of the model's performance. These metrics make it possible to evaluate how well the model can categorize positive and negative cases within each class. Precision, recall, and F1 score can be calculated by thresholding the model's predictions and contrasting them with the ground truth labels. To further examine the model's behavior during training, the researchers created learning rate charts. These graphs aid in locating convergence problems and identifying whether additional fine-tuning or modifications to the learning rate are required. Making judgments on hyperparameter optimization and model stability is aided by an analysis of the learning rate.

16.6 CONCLUSION

The created model demonstrates the effectiveness of deep learning methods for automatically classifying chest X-ray images. Such models can help medical personnel diagnose patients more quickly and reliably by correctly categorizing COVID-19 instances, normal lung states, and pneumonia. The model has to be improved upon and refined in order to increase its functionality and reliability in actual clinical settings. Future research may focus on incorporating larger and more varied datasets, investigating cutting-edge architectures, and applying methods like transfer learning and ensembling. The continuous development of such models has the potential to enhance healthcare outcomes and streamline the diagnostic procedure in chest radiology. The automatic classification of chest X-ray images using the created deep learning model based on the VGG16 architecture revealed encouraging results. The model successfully classified a variety of lung illnesses with an amazing accuracy of 94.30% on the validation set. It's crucial to remember that accuracy does not, by itself, provide a thorough evaluation of the model's performance.

16.7 FUTURE SCOPE

Chest X-rays are currently divided into broad categories by the model, such as pneumonia, normal, and COVID-19. However, by recognizing particular types of pneumonia (such as bacterial or viral) or spotting additional lung abnormalities (such as lung nodules or cancer), it may be possible to get even more specific. More targeted and precise diagnoses can be made with the help of fine-grained classification, which will improve patient care and treatment planning. Deep learning models are sometimes thought of as "black boxes," which makes it difficult to comprehend the underlying causes of their predictions. The adoption of these models in clinical practice can be improved by developing methods to analyze and explain the model's decision-making process. Techniques like feature visualization, saliency maps, and attention mechanisms can shed light on the regions of interest and variables affecting the model's predictions [62–68]. Radiologists can benefit from real-time decision support by incorporating automated chest X-ray categorization models into radiology processes. These models can help radiologists prioritize their interpretations and possibly lighten the workload associated with evaluating a large volume of pictures by aiding in the preliminary analysis and highlighting cases that may be aberrant [69–75].

REFERENCES

1. Jain, S., Kumar, M., Sindhwani, N., & Singh, P. (2021, September). SARS-Cov-2 detection using deep learning techniques on the basis of clinical reports. In 2021 9th International Conference on Reliability, Infocom Technologies and Optimization (Trends and Future Directions) (ICRITO) (pp. 1–5). IEEE.
2. Jain, S., Sindhwani, N., Anand, R., & Kannan, R. (2021, December). COVID detection using chest X-ray and transfer learning. In International Conference on Intelligent Systems Design and Applications (pp. 933–943). Springer International Publishing.
3. Saini, P., & Anand, M. R. (2014). Identification of defects in plastic gears using image processing and computer vision: A review. International Journal of Engineering Research, 3(2), 94–99.
4. Anand, R., Singh, B., & Sindhwani, N. (2009). Speech perception & analysis of fluent digits' strings using level-by-level time alignment. International Journal of Information Technology and Knowledge Management, 2(1), 65–68.
5. Anand, R., Daniel, A. V., Fred, A. L., Jaiswal, T., Juneja, S., Juneja, A., & Gupta, A. (2023). Building integrated systems for healthcare considering mobile computing and IoT. In Integration of IoT with Cloud Computing for Smart Applications (pp. 203–225). Chapman and Hall/CRC Press.
6. Anand, R., Jain, V., Singh, A., Rahal, D., Rastogi, P., Rajkumar, A., & Gupta, A. (2023). Clustering of big data in cloud environments for smart applications. In Integration of IoT with Cloud Computing for Smart Applications (pp. 227–247). Chapman and Hall/CRC Press.
7. Anand, R., Sindhwani, N., & Juneja, S. (2022). Cognitive Internet of Things, its applications, and its challenges: A survey. In Harnessing the Internet of Things (IoT) for a Hyper-Connected Smart World (pp. 91–113). Apple Academic Press.
8. Ratnaparkhi, S. T., Singh, P., Tandasi, A., & Sindhwani, N. (2021, September). Comparative analysis of classifiers for criminal identification system using face recognition. In 2021 9th International Conference on Reliability, Infocom Technologies and Optimization (Trends and Future Directions) (ICRITO) (pp. 1–6). IEEE.
9. Jain, N., Chaudhary, A., Sindhwani, N., & Rana, A. (2021, September). Applications of wearable devices in IoT. In 2021 9th International Conference on Reliability, Infocom Technologies and Optimization (Trends and Future Directions) (ICRITO) (pp. 1–4). IEEE.
10. Kaura, C., Sindhwani, N., & Chaudhary, A. (2022, March). Analysing the impact of cyber-threat to ICS and SCADA systems. In 2022 International Mobile and Embedded Technology Conference (MECON) (pp. 466–470). IEEE.
11. Minaee, S., Kafieh, R., Sonka, M., Yazdani, S., & Soufi, G. J. (2020). Deep-COVID: Predicting COVID-19 from chest X-ray images using deep transfer learning. Medical Image Analysis, 65, 101794.
12. Das, N. N., Kumar, N., Kaur, M., Kumar, V., & Singh, D. (2022). Automated deep transfer learning-based approach for detection of COVID-19 infection in chest X-rays. IRBM, 43(2), 114–119.
13. Bargshady, G., Zhou, X., Barua, P. D., Gururajan, R., Li, Y., & Acharya, U. R. (2022). Application of CycleGAN and transfer learning techniques for automated detection of COVID-19 using X-ray images. Pattern Recognition Letters, 153, 67–74.
14. Showkat, S., & Qureshi, S. (2022). Efficacy of transfer learning-based ResNet models in Chest X-ray image classification for detecting COVID-19 Pneumonia. Chemometrics and Intelligent Laboratory Systems, 224, 104534.

15. Horry, M. J., Chakraborty, S., Paul, M., Ulhaq, A., Pradhan, B., Saha, M., & Shukla, N. (2020). COVID-19 detection through transfer learning using multimodal imaging data. IEEE Access, 8, 149808–149824.

16. Rahaman, M. M., Li, C., Yao, Y., Kulwa, F., Rahman, M. A., Wang, Q., ... & Zhao, X. (2020). Identification of COVID-19 samples from chest X-ray images using deep learning: A comparison of transfer learning approaches. Journal of X-ray Science and Technology, 28(5), 821–839.

17. Loey, M., Smarandache, F., & M. Khalifa, N. E. (2020). Within the lack of chest COVID-19 X-ray dataset: A novel detection model based on GAN and deep transfer learning. Symmetry, 12(4), 651.

18. Sahinbas, K., & Catak, F. O. (2021). Transfer learning-based convolutional neural network for COVID-19 detection with X-ray images. In Data Science for COVID-19 (pp. 451–466). Academic Press.

19. Badawi, A., & Elgazzar, K. (2021). Detecting coronavirus from chest X-rays using transfer learning. COVID, 1(1), 403–415.

20. Taresh, M. M., Zhu, N., Ali, T. A. A., Hameed, A. S., & Mutar, M. L. (2021). Transfer learning to detect covid-19 automatically from X-ray images using convolutional neural networks. International Journal of Biomedical Imaging, 2021, 1–9.

21. Misra, S., Jeon, S., Lee, S., Managuli, R., Jang, I. S., & Kim, C. (2020). Multi-channel transfer learning of chest X-ray images for screening of COVID-19. Electronics, 9(9), 1388.

22. Progga, N. I., Hossain, M. S., & Andersson, K. (2020, December). A deep transfer learning approach to diagnose covid-19 using X-ray images. In 2020 IEEE International Women in Engineering (WIE) Conference on Electrical and Computer Engineering (WIECON-ECE) (pp. 177–182). IEEE.

23. Katsamenis, I., Protopapadakis, E., Voulodimos, A., Doulamis, A., & Doulamis, N. (2020, November). Transfer learning for COVID-19 pneumonia detection and classification in chest X-ray images. In 24th Pan-Hellenic Conference on Informatics (pp. 170–174).

24. Mohammadi, R., Salehi, M., Ghaffari, H., Rohani, A. A., & Reiazi, R. (2020). Transfer learning-based automatic detection of coronavirus disease 2019 (COVID-19) from chest X-ray images. Journal of Biomedical Physics and Engineering, 10(5), 559–568.

25. Das, A. K., Kalam, S., Kumar, C., & Sinha, D. (2021). TLCoV-An automated Covid-19 screening model using Transfer Learning from chest X-ray images. Chaos, Solitons & Fractals, 144, 110713.

26. Zhang, R., Guo, Z., Sun, Y., Lu, Q., Xu, Z., Yao, Z., ... & Zhou, F. (2020). COVID19XrayNet: A two-step transfer learning model for the COVID-19 detecting problem based on a limited number of chest X-ray images. Interdisciplinary Sciences: Computational Life Sciences, 12, 555–565.

27. Rezaee, K., Badiei, A., & Meshgini, S. (2020, November). A hybrid deep transfer learning based approach for COVID-19 classification in chest X-ray images. In 2020 27th National and 5th International Iranian Conference on Biomedical Engineering (ICBME) (pp. 234–241). IEEE.

28. Shamsi, A., Asgharnezhad, H., Jokandan, S. S., Khosravi, A., Kebria, P. M., Nahavandi, D., ... & Srinivasan, D. (2021). An uncertainty-aware transfer learning-based framework for COVID-19 diagnosis. IEEE Transactions on Neural Networks and Learning Systems, 32(4), 1408–1417.

29. Kumar, N., Gupta, M., Gupta, D., & Tiwari, S. (2023). Novel deep transfer learning model for COVID-19 patient detection using X-ray chest images. Journal of Ambient Intelligence and Humanized Computing, 14(1), 469–478.

30. Manokaran, J., Zabihollahy, F., Hamilton-Wright, A., & Ukwatta, E. (2021). Detection of COVID-19 from chest X-ray images using transfer learning. Journal of Medical Imaging, 8(S1), 017503-017503.

31. Pandey, B. K., Pandey, D., Gupta, A., Nassa, V. K., Dadheech, P., & George, A. S. (2023). Secret data transmission using advanced morphological component analysis and steganography. In Role of Data-Intensive Distributed Computing Systems in Designing Data Solutions (pp. 21–44). Springer International Publishing.

32. Veeraiah, V., Kumar, K. R., Lalitha Kumari, P., Ahamad, S., Bansal, R., & Gupta, A. (2023). Application of biometric system to enhance the security in virtual world. In 2022 2nd International Conference on Advance Computing and Innovative Technologies in Engineering (ICACITE), Greater Noida, India (pp. 719–723). IEEE.

33. Bansal, R., Gupta, A., Singh, R., & Nassa, V. K. (2021, July). Role and impact of digital technologies in E-learning amidst COVID-19 pandemic. In 2021 Fourth International Conference on Computational Intelligence and Communication Technologies (CCICT) (pp. 194–202). IEEE.

34. Jain, V., Beram, S. M., Talukdar, V., Patil, T., Dhabliya, D., & Gupta, A. (2022, November). Accuracy enhancement in machine learning during blockchain based transaction classification. In 2022 Seventh International Conference on Parallel, Distributed and Grid Computing (PDGC) (pp. 536–540). IEEE.

35. Kaushik, D., Garg, M., Annu, & Gupta, A.; Sabyasachi Pramanik. (2022). Utilizing machine learning and deep learning in cybersecurity: An innovative approach. In Cyber Security and Digital Forensics: Challenges and Future Trends (pp. 271–293). Wiley.

36. Gupta, M., Ghatak, S., Gupta, A., & Mukherjee, A. L. (Eds.). (2022). Artificial Intelligence on Medical Data: Proceedings of International Symposium, ISCMM 2021 (Vol. 37). Springer Nature.

37. Kumar, S., Mishra, S., & Singh, S. K. (2021). Deep transfer learning-based COVID-19 prediction using chest X-rays. Journal of Health Management, 23(4), 730–746.

38. Majeed, T., Rashid, R., Ali, D., & Asaad, A. (2020). Covid-19 detection using cnn transfer learning from X-ray images. Medrxiv, 2020-05.

39. Khalifa, N. E. M., Smarandache, F., Manogaran, G., & Loey, M. (2021). A study of the neutrosophic set significance on deep transfer learning models: An experimental case on a limited covid-19 chest X-ray dataset. Cognitive Computation, 1–10.

40. Ohata, E. F., Bezerra, G. M., das Chagas, J. V. S., Neto, A. V. L., Albuquerque, A. B., De Albuquerque, V. H. C., & Reboucas Filho, P. P. (2020). Automatic detection of COVID-19 infection using chest X-ray images through transfer learning. IEEE/CAA Journal of Automatica Sinica, 8(1), 239–248.

41. Haq, A. U., Li, J. P., Ahmad, S., Khan, S., Alshara, M. A., & Alotaibi, R. M. (2021). Diagnostic approach for accurate diagnosis of COVID-19 employing deep learning and transfer learning techniques through chest X-ray images clinical data in E-healthcare. Sensors, 21(24), 8219.

42. Hossain, M. B., Iqbal, S. H. S., Islam, M. M., Akhtar, M. N., & Sarker, I. H. (2022). Transfer learning with fine-tuned deep CNN ResNet50 model for classifying COVID-19 from chest X-ray images. Informatics in Medicine Unlocked, 30, 100916.

43. Hamida, S., El Gannour, O., Cherradi, B., Raihani, A., Moujahid, H., & Ouajji, H. (2021). A novel COVID-19 diagnosis support system using the stacking approach and transfer learning technique on chest X-ray images. Journal of Healthcare Engineering, 2021, 1–17.

44. Khalifa, N. E. M., Taha, M. H. N., Hassanien, A. E., & Elghamrawy, S. (2022, November). Detection of coronavirus (COVID-19) associated pneumonia based on generative adversarial networks and a fine-tuned deep transfer learning model using chest X-ray dataset. In Proceedings of the 8th International Conference on Advanced Intelligent Systems and Informatics 2022 (pp. 234–247). Springer International Publishing.

45. Polat, Ç., Karaman, O., Karaman, C., Korkmaz, G., Balcı, M. C., & Kelek, S. E. (2021). COVID-19 diagnosis from chest X-ray images using transfer learning: Enhanced performance by debiasing dataloader. Journal of X-ray Science and Technology, 29(1), 19–36.

46. El Gannour, O., Hamida, S., Cherradi, B., Raihani, A., & Moujahid, H. (2020, December). Performance evaluation of transfer learning technique for automatic detection of patients with COVID-19 on X-ray images. In 2020 IEEE 2nd International Conference on Electronics, Control, Optimization and Computer Science (ICECOCS) (pp. 1–6). IEEE.

47. Zhu, J., Shen, B., Abbasi, A., Hoshmand-Kochi, M., Li, H., & Duong, T. Q. (2020). Deep transfer learning artificial intelligence accurately stages COVID-19 lung disease severity on portable chest radiographs. PLoS One, 15(7), e0236621.

48. Abbas, A., Abdelsamea, M. M., & Gaber, M. M. (2021). 4S-DT: Self-supervised super sample decomposition for transfer learning with application to COVID-19 detection. IEEE Transactions on Neural Networks and Learning Systems, 32(7), 2798–2808.

49. Wang, N., Liu, H., & Xu, C. (2020, July). Deep learning for the detection of COVID-19 using transfer learning and model integration. In 2020 IEEE 10th International Conference on Electronics Information and Emergency Communication (ICEIEC) (pp. 281–284). IEEE.

50. Pathak, Y., Shukla, P. K., Tiwari, A., Stalin, S., & Singh, S. (2022). Deep transfer learning based classification model for COVID-19 disease. IRBM, 43(2), 87–92.

51. Jangam, E., Barreto, A. A. D., & Annavarapu, C. S. R. (2022). Automatic detection of COVID-19 from chest CT scan and chest X-rays images using deep learning, transfer learning and stacking. Applied Intelligence, 52, 1–17.

52. Bansal, B., Jenipher, V. N., Jain, R., Dilip, R., Kumbhkar, M., Pramanik, S., Roy, S., & Gupta, A. (2022). Big data architecture for network security. In Cyber Security and Network Security (eds S. Pramanik, D. Samanta, M. Vinay and A. Guha). Wiley.

53. Gupta, A., Kaushik, D., Garg, M., & Verma, A. (2020). Machine learning model for breast cancer prediction. In Fourth International Conference on I-SMAC (IoT in Social, Mobile, Analytics and Cloud) (I-SMAC), Palladam, India (pp. 472–477).

54. Keserwani, H., Rastogi, H., Kurniullah, A. Z., Janardan, S. K., Raman, R., Rathod, V. M., & Gupta, A. (2022). Security enhancement by identifying attacks using machine learning for 5G network. International Journal of Communication Networks and Information Security, 14(2), 124–141.

55. Aslan, M. F., Unlersen, M. F., Sabanci, K., & Durdu, A. (2021). CNN-based transfer learning–BiLSTM network: A novel approach for COVID-19 infection detection. Applied Soft Computing, 98, 106912.

56. Sakib, S., Siddique, M. A. B., Rahman Khan, M. M., Yasmin, N., Aziz, A., Chowdhury, M., & Tasawar, I. K. (2020). Detection of COVID-19 disease from chest X-ray images: A deep transfer learning framework. MedRxiv, 2020-11.

57. Altaf, F., Islam, S. M., & Janjua, N. K. (2021). A novel augmented deep transfer learning for classification of COVID-19 and other thoracic diseases from X-rays. Neural Computing and Applications, 33(20), 14037–14048.

58. Brima, Y., Atemkeng, M., Tankio Djiokap, S., Ebiele, J.; & Tchakounté, F. (2021). Transfer learning for the detection and diagnosis of types of pneumonia including pneumonia induced by COVID-19 from chest X-ray images. Diagnostics, 11(8), 1480.

59. Hamlili, F. Z., Beladgham, M., Khelifi, M., & Bouida, A. (2022). Transfer learning with Resnet-50 for detecting COVID-19 in chest X-ray images. Indonesian Journal of Electrical Engineering and Computer Science, 25(3), 1458–1468.

60. Talukdar, V., Dhabliya, D., Kumar, B., Talukdar, S. B., Ahamad, S., & Gupta, A. (2022). Suspicious activity detection and classification in IoT environment using machine learning approach. In 2022 Seventh International Conference on Parallel, Distributed and Grid Computing (PDGC), Solan, Himachal Pradesh, India (pp. 531–535), doi: 10.1109/PDGC56933.2022.10053312.

61. Kshirsagar, P. R., Reddy, D. H., Dhingra, M., Dhabliya, D., & Gupta, A. (2023). A scalable platform to collect, store, visualize and analyze big data in real-time. In 2023 3rd International Conference on Innovative Practices in Technology and Management (ICIPTM), Uttar Pradesh, India (pp. 1–6), doi: 10.1109/ICIPTM5 7143.2023.10118183.

62. Anand, R., & Chawla, P. (2016, March). A review on the optimization techniques for bio-inspired antenna design. In 2016 3rd International Conference on Computing for Sustainable Global Development (INDIACom) (pp. 2228–2233). IEEE.

63. Meelu, R., & Anand, R. (2010, November). Energy efficiency of cluster-based routing protocols used in wireless sensor networks. In AIP Conference Proceedings (Vol. 1324, No. 1, pp. 109–113). American Institute of Physics.

64. Anand, R., Singh, J., Pandey, D., Pandey, B. K., Nassa, V. K., & Pramanik, S. (2022). Modern technique for interactive communication in LEACH-based ad hoc wireless sensor network. In Software Defined Networking for Ad Hoc Networks (pp. 55–73). Springer International Publishing.

65. Gupta, A., Asad, A., Meena, L., & Anand, R. (2022, July). IoT and RFID-based smart card system integrated with health care, electricity, QR and banking sectors. In Artificial Intelligence on Medical Data: Proceedings of International Symposium, ISCMM 2021 (pp. 253–265). Springer Nature Singapore.

66. Gupta, A., Srivastava, A., & Anand, R. (2019). Cost-effective smart home automation using internet of things. Journal of Communication Engineering & Systems, 9(2), 1–6.

67. Arora, S., Sharma, S., Anand, R., & Shrivastva, G. (2023). Miniaturized pentagon-shaped planar monopole antenna for ultra-wideband applications. Progress in Electromagnetics Research C, 133, 195–208.

68. Meivel, S., Sindhwani, N., Valarmathi, S., Dhivya, G., Atchaya, M., Anand, R., & Maurya, S. (2022). Design and method of 16.24 GHz microstrip network antenna using underwater wireless communication algorithm. In Cyber Technologies and Emerging Sciences: ICCTES 2021 (pp. 363–371). Springer Nature Singapore.

69. Anand, R., Sindhwani, N., & Dahiya, A. (2022, March). Design of a high directivity slotted fractal antenna for C-band, X-band and Ku-band applications. In 2022 9th International Conference on Computing for Sustainable Global Development (INDIACom) (pp. 727–730). IEEE.

70. Anand, R., Arora, S., & Sindhwani, N. (2022, January). A miniaturized UWB antenna for high speed applications. In 2022 International Conference on Computing, Communication and Power Technology (IC3P) (pp. 264–267). IEEE.

71. Nijhawan, M., Sindhwani, N., Tanwar, S., & Kumar, S. (2022). Role of augmented reality and internet of things in education sector. In IoT Based Smart Applications (pp. 245–259). Springer International Publishing.

72. Sharma, R., Vashisth, R., & Sindhwani, N. (2023). Study and analysis of classification techniques for specific plant growths. In Advances in Signal Processing, Embedded Systems and IoT: Proceedings of Seventh ICMEET-2022 (pp. 591–605). Springer Nature Singapore.

73. Verma, S., Bajaj, T., Sindhwani, N., & Kumar, A. (2022). Design and development of a driving assistance and safety system using deep learning. In Advances in Data Science and Computing Technology (pp. 35–45). Apple Academic Press.

74. Sindhwani, N., Anand, R., Niranjanamurthy, M., Verma, D. C., & Valentina, E. B. (2022). IoT based smart applications. Springer International Publishing AG. https://doi.org/10.1007/978-3-031-04524-0.

75. Anand, Rohit, Shrivastava, Gulshan, Gupta, Sachin, Peng, Sheng-Lung, & Sindhwani, Nidhi (2018). Audio Watermarking With Reduced Number of Random Samples. Handbook of Research on Network Forensics and Analysis Techniques, Advances in Information Security, Privacy, and Ethics (pp. 372–394), doi: 10.4018/978-1-5225-4100-4.ch020.

Index

Printed in the United States
by Baker & Taylor Publisher Services